EXAM CRA

The CISA Cram Sheet

This Cram Sheet contains distilled information in key areas of knowledge pertinent to the CISA exam. Review this information as the last thing you do before you enter the testing center, paying special attention to those areas in which you feel that you need the most review.

IS AUDIT PROCESS

1. The traditional role of an IS auditor in a control self-assessment (CSA) should be that of a facilitator.

2. Using a statistical sample to inventory the tape library is an example of a substantive test.

3. Audit responsibility enhancement is an objective of a control self-assessment (CSA) program.

4. If proper identification and authentication are not performed during access control, no accountability can exist for any action performed.

5. IS auditors are *most* likely to perform compliance tests of internal controls if, after their initial evaluation of the controls, they conclude that control risks are within the acceptable limits. Think of it this way: If any reliance is placed on internal controls, that reliance must be validated through compliance testing. High control risk results in little reliance on internal controls, which results in additional *substantive* testing.

6. In planning an audit, the *most* critical step is identifying the areas of high risk.

7. Prior audit reports are considered of lesser value to an IS auditor attempting to gain an understanding of an organization's IT process than evidence directly collected.

8. When evaluating the collective effect of preventative, detective, or corrective controls within a process, an IS auditor should be aware of the point at which controls are exercised as data flows through the system.

9. The primary purpose of audit trails is to establish accountability and responsibility for processed transactions.

10. When implementing continuous monitoring systems, an IS auditor's first step is to identify high-risk areas within the organization.

11. Auditing resources are allocated to the areas of highest concern, as a benefit of a risk-based approach to audit planning.

12. Inherent risk is associated with authorized program exits (trap doors).

13. After an IS auditor has identified threats and potential impacts, the auditor should identify and evaluate the existing controls.

14. Generalized audit software can be used to search for address field duplications.

15. The use of statistical sampling procedures helps minimize detection risk.

16. Lack of reporting of a successful attack on the network is a great concern to an IS auditor.

17. Detection risk results when an IS auditor uses an inadequate test procedure and concludes that material errors do not exist when errors actually exist.

18. An integrated test facility is considered a useful audit tool because it compares processing output with independently calculated data.

MANAGEMENT, PLANNING, AND ORGANIZATION OF IS

19. A bottom-up approach to the development of organizational policies is often driven by risk assessment.

20. An IS auditor's primary responsibility is to advise senior management of the risk involved in not implementing proper segregation of duties, such as having the security administrator perform an operations function.

21. Data and systems owners are accountable for maintaining appropriate security measures over information assets.

22. Business unit management is responsible for implementing cost-effective controls in an automated system.

23. Proper segregation of duties prohibits a system analyst from performing quality-assurance functions.

24. The primary reason an IS auditor reviews an organization chart is to better understand the responsibilities and authority of individuals.

and the costs associated with recovery. Although DRP results in an increase of pre- and post-incident operational costs, the extra costs are more than offset by reduced recovery and business impact costs.

86. Mitigating the risk and impact of a disaster or business interruption usually takes priority over transferring risk to a third party such as an insurer.

87. A cold site is often an acceptable solution for preparing for recovery of noncritical systems and data.

88. Offsite data storage should be kept synchronized when preparing for recovery of time-sensitive data such as that resulting from transaction processing.

89. Any changes in systems assets, such as replacement of hardware, should be immediately recorded within the assets inventory of a business continuity plan.

90. Shadow file processing can be implemented as a recovery mechanism for extremely time-sensitive transaction processing.

BUSINESS APPLICATION SYSTEM DEVELOPMENT, ACQUISITION, IMPLEMENTATION, AND MAINTENANCE

91. Obtaining user approval of program changes is very effective for controlling application changes and maintenance.

92. A clause for requiring source code escrow in an application vendor agreement is important to ensure that the source code remains available even if the application vendor goes out of business.

93. Library control software restricts source code to read-only access.

94. Decision trees use questionnaires to lead the user through a series of choices to reach a conclusion.

95. Regression testing is used in program development and change management to determine whether new changes have introduced any errors in the remaining unchanged code.

96. Source code escrow protects an application purchaser's ability to fix or change an application in case the application vendor goes out of business.

97. Determining time and resource requirements for an application-development project is often the most difficult part of initial efforts in application development.

98. The project sponsor is ultimately responsible for providing requirement specifications to the software-development team.

99. A primary high-level goal for an auditor who is reviewing a system-development project is to ensure that business objectives are achieved. This objective guides all other systems-development objectives.

100. Regression testing should use data from previous tests to obtain accurate conclusions regarding the effects of changes or corrections to a program, and ensure that those changes and corrections have not introduced new errors.

101. Whenever an application is modified, the entire program, including any interface systems with other applications or systems, should be tested to determine the full impact of the change.

102. An IS auditor should carefully review the functional requirements in a systems-development project to ensure that the project is designed to meet business objectives.

103. The quality of the metadata produced from a data warehouse is the most important consideration in the warehouse's design.

104. Procedures to prevent scope creep are baselined in the Design Phase of the Systems-Development Life Cycle (SDLC) model.

105. Function point analysis (FPA) provides an estimate of the size of an information system based on the number and complexity of a system's inputs, outputs, and files.

106. Application controls should be considered as early as possible in the systems-development process, even in the development of the project's functional specifications.

107. User management assumes ownership of a systems-development project and the resulting system.

108. Rapid Application Development (RAD) is used to develop strategically important systems faster, reduce development costs, and still maintain high quality.

BUSINESS PROCESS EVALUATION AND RISK MANAGEMENT

109. Run-to-run totals can verify data through various stages of application processing.

110. Input/output controls should be implemented for both the sending and the receiving application in an integrated systems environment.

111. The board of directors and executive officers are ultimately accountable for the functionality, reliability, and security within IT governance.

112. Authentication techniques for sending and receiving data between EDI systems is crucial to prevent unauthorized transactions.

113. Data-mining techniques can be used to help identify and investigate unauthorized transactions.

114. After identifying potential security vulnerabilities, the IS auditor should perform a business impact analysis of the threats that would exploit the vulnerabilities.

115. Network environments often add to the complexity of program-to-program communication, making application systems implementation and maintenance more difficult.

55. A long asymmetric encryption key (public-key encryption) increases encryption overhead and cost.

56. Creating user accounts that automatically expire by a predetermined date is an effective control for granting temporary access to vendors and external support personnel.

57. Worms are malicious programs that can run independently and can propagate without the aid of a carrier program such as email.

58. Outbound traffic filtering can help prevent an organization's systems from participating in a distributed denial-of-service (DDoS) attack.

59. Identifying network applications such as mail, web, or FTP servers to be externally accessed is an initial step in creating a proper firewall policy.

60. Improperly configured routers and router access lists are a common vulnerability for denial-of-service attacks.

61. With public-key encryption, or asymmetric encryption, data is encrypted by the sender using the recipient's public key, and the data is then decrypted using the recipient's private key.

62. Trojan horse programs are a common form of Internet attack.

63. The SSL protocol provides confidentiality through symmetric encryption such as Data Encryption Standard, or DES.

64. Network performance-monitoring tools are used to measure and ensure proper network capacity management and availability of services.

65. Information systems security policies are used as the framework for developing logical access controls.

66. Intrusion-detection systems (IDS) are used to gather evidence of network attacks.

67. Time stamps are an effective control for detecting duplicate transactions such as payments made or received.

68. Traffic analysis is a passive attack method used by intruders to determine potential network vulnerabilities.

69. File encryption is a good control for protecting confidential data that resides on a PC.

70. Although many methods of fire suppression exist, dry-pipe sprinklers are considered to be the most environmentally friendly.

71. Logical access controls should be reviewed to ensure that access is granted on a least-privilege basis per the organization's data owners.

72. A callback system is a remote access control in which the user initially connects to the network systems via dial-up access, only to have the initial connection terminated by the server, which then subsequently dials back the user at a predetermined number stored in the server's configuration database.

73. End-user involvement is critical during the business impact assessment phase of business continuity planning.

74. Redundancy provides both integrity and availability. Organizations should use offsite storage facilities to maintain redundancy of current and critical information within backup files.

75. Of the three major types of BCP tests (paper, walk-through, and preparedness), only the preparedness test uses actual resources to simulate a system crash and validate the plan's effectiveness.

76. The primary purpose of business continuity planning and disaster-recovery planning is to mitigate, or reduce, the risk and impact of a business interruption or disaster. Total elimination of risk is impossible.

77. Disaster recovery for systems typically focuses on making alternative processes and resources available for transaction processing.

78. If a database is restored from information backed up before the last system image, the system should be restarted before the last transaction because the final transaction must be reprocessed.

79. Of the three major types of BCP tests (paper, walk-through, and preparedness), a walk-through test requires only that representatives from each operational meet to review the plan.

80. An offsite processing facility should *not* be easily identifiable externally because easy identification would create an additional vulnerability for sabotage.

81. Criticality of assets is often influenced by the business criticality of the data to be protected and by the scope of the impact upon the organization as a whole. For example, the loss of a network backbone creates a much greater impact on the organization as a whole than the loss of data on a typical user's workstation.

82. Although the primary business objective of BCP and DRP is to mitigate the risk and impact of a business interruption, the dominating objective remains the protection of human life.

83. Of the three major types of offsite processing facilities (hot, warm, and cold), a cold site is characterized by at least providing for electricity and HVAC. A warm site improves upon this by providing for redundant equipment and software that can be made operational within a short time.

84. Minimizing single points of failure or vulnerabilities of a common disaster are mitigated by geographically dispersing resources.

85. With the objective of mitigating the risk and impact of a major business interruption, a disaster-recovery plan should endeavor to reduce the length of recovery time necessary

25. If an IS auditor observes that project-approval procedures do not exist, the IS auditor should recommend to management that formal approval procedures be adopted and documented.

26. Ensuring that security and control policies support business and IT objectives is a primary objective of an IT security policies audit.

27. The board of directors is ultimately accountable for developing an IS security policy.

28. When auditing third-party service providers, an auditor should be concerned with ownership of programs and files, a statement of due care and confidentiality, and the capability for continued service of the service provider in the event of a disaster.

29. Proper segregation of duties normally prohibits a LAN administrator from also having programming responsibilities.

30. When performing an IS strategy audit, an IS auditor should review both short-term (one-year) and long-term (three- to five-year) IS strategies, interview appropriate corporate management personnel, and ensure that the external environment has been considered. The auditor should *not* focus on procedures in an audit of IS strategy.

31. Above all else, an IS strategy must support the business objectives of the organization.

32. IS assessment methods enable IS management to determine whether the activities of the organization differ from the planned or expected levels.

33. Batch control reconciliations is a compensatory control for mitigating risk of inadequate segregation of duties.

34. An audit client's business plan should be reviewed before an organization's IT strategic plan is reviewed.

35. Key verification is one of the best controls for ensuring that data is entered correctly.

36. Allowing application programmers to directly patch or change code in production programs increases risk of fraud.

TECHNICAL INFRASTRUCTURE AND OPERATIONAL PRACTICES

37. A mesh network topology provides a point-to-point link between every network host. If each host is configured to route and forward communication, this topology provides the greatest redundancy of routes and the greatest network fault tolerance.

38. Layering perimeter network protection by configuring the firewall as a screened host in a screened subnet behind the bastion host provides a higher level of protection from external attack than a firewall alone.

39. An IS auditor usually places more reliance on evidence directly collected, such as through personal observation.

40. The directory system of a database-management system describes the location of data and the access method.

41. The transport layer of the TCP/IP protocol suite provides for connection-oriented protocols, to ensure reliable communication.

42. Improper file access becomes a greater risk when implementing a database system.

43. Electronic data interface (EDI) supports intervendor communication while decreasing the time necessary for review because it is usually configured to readily identify errors requiring follow-up.

44. To properly protect against unauthorized disclosure of sensitive data, hard disks should be demagnetized prior to disposal or release.

45. An IS auditor can expect to find system errors to be detailed in the console log.

46. When reviewing print systems spooling, an IS auditor is most concerned with the potential for unauthorized printing of report copies.

47. Atomicity enforces data integrity by ensuring that a transaction is either completed in its entirety or not at all. Atomicity is part of the ACID test reference for transaction processing.

48. Functioning as a protocol-conversion gateway for wireless WTLS to Internet SSL, the WAP gateway is a component that warrants critical concern and review for the IS auditor when auditing and testing controls that enforce message confidentiality. During protocol conversion, WTLS is decrypted and then re-encrypted with SSL. Therefore, the traffic is in plain text for a brief moment at the WAP gateway.

49. When trying to determine the existence of unauthorized access to data by a user or program, the IS auditor often reviews the system logs.

50. Proper segregation of duties prevents a computer operator (user) from performing security administration duties.

51. A graphical map of the network topology is essential for the IS auditor to obtain a clear understanding of network management.

52. Modems (modulation/demodulation) convert analog transmissions to digital, and digital transmissions to analog, and are required for analog transmissions to enter a digital network.

53. If users have direct access to a database at the system level, risk of unauthorized and untraceable changes to the database increases.

54. Neural networks are effective in detecting fraud because they have the capability to consider a large number of variables when trying to resolve a problem.

EXAM CRAM™ 2

CISA

Allen Keele

Keith Mortier

CISA Exam Cram

International Standard Book Number: 0-7897-3272-6

Library of Congress Catalog Card Number: 2004116161

Printed in the United States of America

Fourth Printing: May 2008

12 11 10 09 08   9 8 7 6 5 4

Trademarks

Warning and Disclaimer

Bulk Sales

Que Publishing offers excellent discounts on this book when ordered in quantity for bulk purchases or special sales. For more information, please contact

U.S. Corporate and Government Sales

1-800-382-3419

corpsales@pearsontechgroup.com

For sales outside the U.S., please contact

International Sales

international@pearsoned.com

Publisher
Paul Boger

Executive Editor
Jeff Riley

Acquisitions Editor
Carol Ackerman

Development Editor
Sean Dixon

Managing Editor
Charlotte Clapp

Project Editor
Andy Beaster

Copy Editor
Krista Hansing

Indexer
Erika Millen

Proofreader
Juli Cook

Technical Editor
Donald Glass

Publishing Coordinator
Pamalee Nelsen

Multimedia Developer
Dan Scherf

Interior Designer
Gary Adair

Cover Designer
Anne Jones

Page Layout
Juli Cook

CERTIFICATION

Que Certification • 800 East 96th Street • Indianapolis, Indiana 46240

A Note from Series Editor Ed Tittel

You know better than to trust your certification preparation to just anybody. That's why you, and more than 2 million others, have purchased an Exam Cram book. As Series Editor for the new and improved Exam Cram 2 Series, I have worked with the staff at Que Certification to ensure you won't be disappointed. That's why we've taken the world's best-selling certification product—a two-time finalist for "Best Study Guide" in CertCities' reader polls—and made it even better.

As a two-time finalist for the "Favorite Study Guide Author" award as selected by CertCities readers, I know the value of good books. You'll be impressed with Que Certification's stringent review process, which ensures the books are high quality, relevant, and technically accurate. Rest assured that several industry experts have reviewed this material, helping us deliver an excellent solution to your exam preparation needs.

Exam Cram 2 books also feature a preview edition of PrepLogic's powerful, full-featured test engine, which is trusted by certification students throughout the world.

As a 20-year-plus veteran of the computing industry and the original creator and editor of the Exam Cram Series, I've brought my IT experience to bear on these books. During my tenure at Novell from 1989 to 1994, I worked with and around its excellent education and certification department. At Novell, I witnessed the growth and development of the first really big, successful IT certification program—one that was to shape the industry forever afterward. This experience helped push my writing and teaching activities heavily in the certification direction. Since then, I've worked on nearly 100 certification related books, and I write about certification topics for numerous Web sites and for *Certification* magazine.

In 1996, while studying for various MCP exams, I became frustrated with the huge, unwieldy study guides that were the only preparation tools available. As an experienced IT professional and former instructor, I wanted "nothing but the facts" necessary to prepare for the exams. From this impetus, Exam Cram emerged: short, focused books that explain exam topics, detail exam skills and activities, and get IT professionals ready to take and pass their exams.

In 1997 when Exam Cram debuted, it quickly became the best-selling computer book series since "*...For Dummies,*" and the best-selling certification book series ever. By maintaining an intense focus on subject matter, tracking errata and updates quickly, and following the certification market closely, Exam Cram established the dominant position in cert prep books.

You will not be disappointed in your decision to purchase this book. If you are, please contact me at etittel@jump.net. All suggestions, ideas, input, or constructive criticism are welcome!

Acknowledgements

I would like to thank Ron Keele, my brother, for his incredible contribution to this product. He *single-handedly* created the entire code source and compilation for this program, including the very complex and robust exam engine and Microsoft MSI installation. His incredible free-lance, part-time, late-night dedication to this project has allowed us to put forth a product that we are extremely proud of, and did so within a 75 day period. Ron is available for contract programming engagements, and can be contacted at RonK@certifiedtechtrainers.com.

I'd like to thank Keith Mortier for his dogged determination as a co-author to make this book the best that it can be. I also thank Carol Ackerman, Acquisitions Editor for Que Publishing, for her wonderful project management and patience. I've worked with other publishers in the past, and Carol is a gem! And finally, I thank the various editing staff, including Sean Dixon, Andy Beaster, and Krista Hansing, for their wonderful efforts to make this book a polished and accurate piece exam prep guide.

—Allen Keele

About the Authors

As president and chief executive officer of Certified Information Security, **Allen Keele** has more than 15 years of experience in information security and risk management, including 5 years of conducting professional advanced IT lectures and seminars across the United States and throughout the United Kingdom and Caribbean. His lectures have attracted students from leading organizations that include the United States Marine Corps., Deloitte & Touche, Ernst & Young, Lloyds, Thomson Financial, Microsoft Corporation, Blue Cross–Blue Shield, Boston University, PriceWaterhouseCoopers, Fujitsu, and many others.

➤ In 2004, Mr. Keele spoke many times on behalf of the Institute for Internal Auditors (IIA) and for the Information Systems Audit and Control Association (ISACA).

➤ Mr. Keele was a featured speaker for ISACA at its North American conference, CACS, in May 2004.

➤ Mr. Keele also was featured as the keynote speaker for Ernst & Young's InfoSec 2003 in Barbados, for the 14th Annual Caribbean Central Bankers Conference in June 2003, and for an engagement with Clemson University in April 2003.

Considered an expert in several diverse technologies, Mr. Keele currently holds more than 24 professional and technical accreditations, including these:

➤ Certified Information Security Manager and Systems Auditor (**CISM/CISA**), by ISACA

➤Certified Information Systems Security Professional (**CISSP**), by (ISC)

➤ CompTIA **Security+**

➤ Security Certified Network Professional (**SCNP**), by Security Certified Program

➤ Check Point Certified Security Expert Plus and Instructor (**CCSE+/CCSI**)

- Cisco Certified Network Professional, Network Associate, and Design Associate (**CCNP/CCNA/CCDA**)

- Nokia Certified Security Administrator and VPN Gateway Administrator (**NSA/NVGA**)

- Microsoft Certified Systems Engineer for NT 4.0 and Windows 2000 (**MCSE**)

- Citrix Certified Enterprise Administrator and Instructor (**CCEA/CCI**)

- IBM Professional Server Expert (**PSE**)

Mr. Keele is also a published author with four texts currently available: *Check Point Next Generation Security Administration* (ISBN B0000692A2, Syngress Media, 2002), *CCSA Check Point Certified Security Administrator Study Guide (Exam 156-210)* (ISBN 0072194200, Syngress Media, 2002), *Configuring Citrix MetaFrame for Windows 2000 Terminal Services* (ISBN 1928994180, Syngress, 2000), and *CCA Citrix Certified Administrator: MetaFrame 1.8, Exam 218* (ISBN 0072124393, Syngress Media, 2000).

Allen also occasionally authors articles for well-respected online journals such as *Tech Republic*. He holds a Bachelor of Business Administration degree in risk management from the University of Georgia, has attended Universität Mannheim, and is conversationally fluent in German.

As president of LMI Solutions, **Keith Mortier** has more than 15 years of experience in information technology, security, and risk management and serves clients in multiple industries. His hands-on experience includes strategic technology planning, risk management, information security auditing, and enterprise architecture development across many industries, including corporations, government, and associations.

Mr. Mortier holds a Bachelor of Science in computer information systems and is an active member of the Information Systems Audit and Control Association. Mr. Mortier holds the Certified Information Systems Security Professionals (CISSP) and the Certified Information Systems Auditor (CISA) designations.

About the Technical Editor

As a security professional and IT auditor, **Donald R. Glass** CISSP, CISA, CCNA MCSE^2, CNE^2, has helped Fortune 500 companies manage their information technology risks in order to increase their business. He's the current President of the ISACA South Florida Chapter, and one of the chapter's most renowned CISA review course instructors. Author of several information security and IT audit articles, Donald is recognized as a leader in the information security and IT audit field. Among the companies Donald has worked with are PricewaterhouseCoopers, Grant Thornton LLP and Enterprise Risk Management. You can contact him at donald@donaldglass.com.

Contents at a Glance

Table of Contents

We Want to Hear from You!

As the reader of this book, *you* are our most important critic and commentator. We value your opinion and want to know what we're doing right, what we could do better, what areas you'd like to see us publish in, and any other words of wisdom you're willing to pass our way.

As an executive editor for Que Publishing, I welcome your comments. You can email or write me directly to let me know what you did or didn't like about this book—as well as what we can do to make our books better.

Please note that I cannot help you with technical problems related to the topic of this book. We do have a User Services group, however, where I will forward specific technical questions related to the book.

When you write, please be sure to include this book's title and author as well as your name, email address, and phone number. I will carefully review your comments and share them with the author and editors who worked on the book.

Email: feedback@quepublishing.com

Mail: Jeff Riley
            Executive Editor
            Que Publishing
            800 East 96th Street
            Indianapolis, IN 46240 USA

For more information about this book or another Que Certification title, visit our website at www.examcram2.com. Type the ISBN (excluding hyphens) or the title of a book in the Search field to find the page you're looking for.

Introduction

Welcome to *Information Systems Audit and Controls Association's Certified Information Systems Auditor (CISA) Exam Cram 2!* Whether this is your first or your fifteenth *Exam Cram 2* series book, you will find information here that will help ensure your success as you pursue knowledge, experience, and certification. This introduction explains ISACA certification programs in general and talks about how the *Exam Cram 2* series can help you prepare for the CISA exam. This chapter discusses the basics of ISACA certification exams, including a description of the testing environment and a discussion of test-taking strategies. Chapters 1 through 7 are designed to remind you of everything you need to know to take—and pass—the CISA certification exam. The two sample tests at the end of the book should give you a reasonably accurate assessment of your knowledge—and, yes, we've provided the answers and their explanations to the tests. Read the book and understand the material, and you'll stand a very good chance of passing the test.

Exam Cram 2 books help you understand and appreciate the subjects and materials you need to pass ISACA certification exams. *Exam Cram 2* books are aimed strictly at test preparation and review. They do not teach you everything you need to know about a topic. Instead, we present and dissect the questions and problems we've found that you're likely to encounter on a test. We've worked to bring together as much information as possible about ISACA certification exams.

Nevertheless, to completely prepare yourself for any ISACA test, we recommend that you begin by taking the Self-Assessment that is included in this book, immediately following this introduction. The Self-Assessment will help you evaluate your knowledge base against the requirements for an ISACA Certified Information Systems Auditor under both ideal and real circumstances.

Based on what you learn from the Self-Assessment, you might decide to begin your studies with some classroom training, some practice with systems auditing, or some background reading. On the other hand, you might decide to read one of the many study guides available from ISACA or third-party vendors on certain topics, including the award-winning certification preparation series from Que Publishing. We also recommend that you supplement your study program with visits to www.examcram2.com to receive additional practice questions, get advice, and track the CISA program.

About the CISA Exam and Content Areas

The Information Systems Audit and Control Association (ISACA) developed the Certified Information Systems Auditor (CISA) program in 1978 to accomplish these goals:

➤ Develop and maintain a testing instrument that could be used to evaluate an individual's competency in conducting information systems audits

➤ Provide a mechanism for motivating information systems auditors to maintain their competencies and monitoring the success of the maintenance programs

➤ Aid top management in developing a sound information systems audit function by providing criteria for personnel selection and development

The CISA program is designed to assess and certify individuals in the IS audit, control, or security profession who demonstrate exceptional skill, judgment and proficiency in IS audit, control, and security practices.

More than 35,000 professionals have earned the CISA certification since inception, and the certification is widely respected as a premier information security and information systems auditing accreditation. The certification continues to grow in acceptance and employer desirability; more than 15,000 candidates are expected to register for the 2005 exam (15% growth from 2004).

The CISA exam is offered only once per year, in early June; the exam for 2005 is offered on June 11. You may register as early as February 2, 2005, and the registration deadline is March 30, 2005. You should note that this exam is not computerized and is not provided through conventional testing centers such as Prometric or Vue. You may register online at www.isaca.org or take the exam at any ISACA chapter location. The current published exam registration fee is $385 for members and $505 for nonmembers. The best place to learn more about the CISA certification and the CISA exam is www.isaca.org.

The Information Systems Audit and Control Association states that the tasks and knowledge required of today's and tomorrow's information systems audit professional serve as the blueprint for the CISA examination. These areas are defined through a Practice Analysis that is conducted at regular intervals and consists of both process and content components in a CISA's job function. Accordingly, exams consist of tasks that are routinely performed by a CISA and the required knowledge to perform these tasks.

How valuable is the CISA certification to employers and individuals? Sometimes the best measure of a certification's value is reflected by how certification holders feel about the certification after having achieved it. In 2001, ISACA surveyed its membership to obtain feedback from CISA certified professionals as to whether obtaining the certification had advanced their careers. Seventy-one percent of members holding the CISA certification affirmed the value of the certification toward career advancement, and 75% of all members, certified and noncertified alike, felt that the CISA certification would be valuable for career advancement in the future.

Another measure of a certification's value can be found by assessing the desirability of the certification to employers. How many employers desire the certification as an employment prerequisite? Looking to popular job boards on the Internet such as Monster.com, TotalJobs.com, and Workthing.com, we can see that the quantity and quality of jobs requiring CISA certification are growing every month.

What is driving the employer demand for the CISA certification? Companies are under growing pressure to improve, document, and test their methods for managing information. As the late Dr. W. E. Deming (1900–1993) was able to prove, the quest for quality of processes and product is achieved through careful measurement of what exists, thorough analysis of defects, and effective remediation and correction. The quest for quality is just that: a quest. This means that quality improvement is an ongoing process that requires continuous reassessment. Assessing the capability of information systems to support business goals while maintaining information confidentiality, integrity, and reliability is exactly what a Certified Information Systems Auditor (CISA) does well.

It is easy enough to create and implement a technology for processing information, which is what the majority of individuals within the information technology (IT) industry are tasked with. However, using IT to facilitate communication and information management is only half the story. Today we need to make sure that IT not only does what it is supposed to do, but also that it will not do what it is not supposed to do. For example, we have created systems to facilitate online commerce and transaction processing. Will those same systems ensure that no transactional errors occur? Will those systems resist accidental or purposeful and malicious modification of data? Do the systems protect the information confidentiality well enough to comply with new privacy laws and standards? We cannot know the answers to these questions unless we have professionally reviewed, measured, and tested the systems. Again, this is what a CISA does.

Although many organizations strive to ensure quality of processes and manufacturing according to ISO standards such as the ISO 9000 series, for competitive reasons, other organizations are forced to invest in quality assurance to comply with the law. Either way, most organizations are spending increasing amounts of money to improve corporate governance. We draw from this example to show the importance of improving IT governance in today's corporate and governmental environment.

In the United States, the healthcare industry is painfully aware of the effects the Health Insurance Portability and Accountability Act (HIPAA) has had on how it does business and manages information. How does an affected healthcare entity prove systems compliance with HIPAA? Why, an audit must be performed! Who directs or assists such a specialized systems audit? Finding someone certified to perform professional systems audits might be a good start. A CISA perhaps?

Likewise, other U.S. legislation, such as the Gramm-Leach-Bliley Act of 1999 (affecting financial institutions) and the Sarbanes-Oxley Act of 2002 (affecting all organizations that are publicly traded on the New York Stock Exchange), are forcing companies to change they way they do business and manage information. Other countries around the world have instituted similar laws or are in the process of creating similar laws. Just look at the United Kingdom's Combined Code, more commonly known as the Turnbull report, and you will see what we mean. Proving compliance with any legislation requires testing and documentation. Testing and documentation of systems controls is what a CISA systems auditor does. The simple fact is that there are new and compelling reasons for companies and government agencies to increase and improve systems auditing, and they need CISA professionals to help them.

The CISA examination is quite broad in scope. The following is a brief description of each topic area. As we move through the chapters, we cover each area in greater detail and provide a map for navigating the CISA exam.

➤ **Area 1**—Management, planning, and organization of IS comprise 11% of the exam. Evaluate strategy, policies, standards, procedures, and related practices for the management, planning, and organization of IS.

➤ **Area 2**—Technical infrastructure and operational practices comprise 13% of the exam. Evaluate the effectiveness and efficiency of the organization's implementation and ongoing management of technical and operational infrastructure to ensure that they adequately support the organization's business objectives.

➤ **Area 3**—Protection of information assets comprises 25% of the exam. Evaluate IT infrastructure security to ensure that it satisfies the organization's business requirements for safeguarding information assets against unauthorized use, disclosure, modification, damage, and loss.

➤ **Area 4**—Disaster recovery and business continuity comprise 10% of the exam. Evaluate the process for developing and maintaining documented, communicated, and tested plans for the continuity of business operations and IS processing in the event of a disruption.

➤**Area 5**—Business application system development, acquisition, implementation, and maintenance comprise 16% of the exam. Evaluate the methodology and processes by which the business application system development, acquisition, implementation, and maintenance are undertaken to ensure that they meet the organization's business objectives.

➤ **Area 6**—Business process evaluation and risk management comprise 15% of the exam. Evaluate business systems and processes to ensure that risks are managed in accordance with the organization's business objectives.

➤ **Area 7**—The IS audit process comprises 10% of the exam. Conduct IS audits in accordance with generally accepted IS audit standards and guidelines to ensure that the organization's information technology and business systems are adequately controlled, monitored, and assessed.

Reference: www.isca.org

How to Prepare for the Exam

The CISA exam is somewhat difficult to prepare for because it is very broad in scope and asks indirect questions requiring strong cognitive skills. The exam is also unusual in its format. The exam is not computerized and is presented as 200 multiple-choice questions in a paper exam booklet. You are required to provide your answers on a familiar "fill-in-the-bubble" answer sheet.

This is not an exam that you can adequately prepare for by simply rote-memorizing terms and definitions. You need to be able to analyze a scenario and answer by combining various knowledge points from various topic areas. Successfully completing this exam requires a great deal of thought and analysis to properly choose the "best" solution from several "viable" solutions. Having successfully passed the CISA, CISSP, Security+, SCNP, CCSE,

CCSI, CCNP, CCNA, MCSE, CCEA, and a multitude of other technical and professional certifications, Allen Keele is able to provide valuable exam-taking tips in the audiovisual presentation of the computer-based training available on the accompanying CD-ROM within this book.

Additional Exam-Preparation Resources

Because the scope of the CISA certification is so broad, you could spend months, or even years, reading the myriad of books recommended by ISACA. Unfortunately, there is not much available for the individual seeking a concise distillation of the exam topics only—hence the need for this book! However, other resources are available via additional books and instructor-led training.

➤ **Information Systems Audit and Controls Association (ISACA)**— ISACA sells exam-preparation materials on its website, and we recommend that you seriously consider augmenting your studies with these two:

  ➤ *CISA Review Manual*—Note that this book is purposed as a *review* manual. As such, many of my students have found it difficult to prepare for the CISA exam with this book because it tends to focus on strictly review points rather than teaching the supporting concepts. It has been my experience that much of the exam relates to the content of ISACA's *CISA Review Manual*, but you should be forewarned that it does not seem to provide 100% of the content necessary to pass the exam. We personally found it impossible to do well on ISACA's practice exams after having thoroughly read this book. In spite of this, we recommend it as a supplemental resource. This book is available for purchase at www.isaca.org.

  ➤ *CISA Review Questions, Answers, and Explanations CD-ROM (650 Questions) Edition*. This is an excellent resource, if you can afford it. Although you should not expect to see a great deal of direct overlap with your real exam, the practice questions provided in this resource nicely fortify your ability to achieve success on exam day. We found the questions to relate much more closely to the actual exam than the content from the *CISA Review Manual*. The questions might not teach you necessary concepts as well as other mediums, but this is an excellent resource for final exam preparation. This resource is available for purchase at www.isaca.org.

➤ **Instructor-led training**—Instructor-led training for CISA exam preparation is somewhat scarce. As a matter of fact, comprehensive training for information systems and controls auditing is scarce as well. Some ISACA chapters provide review sessions in the months just before the exam. These sessions can vary in price and are not controlled for content quality or consistency by ISACA itself. Whereas ISACA provides template material to present from, the chapters have complete discretion regarding what is actually delivered and how it is delivered. Typically, the sessions are provided by chapter members on a volunteer basis in their spare time. As you can see, it is difficult to really be sure of what to expect in terms of the quality of content and presentation style. Session locations and registration information is available at www.isaca.org.

A few professional training organizations are starting to offer specialized training for systems auditing and assurance. One of the authors of this book, Allen Keele, is the lead content developer and lecturer for IT auditing and assurance courses provided by Certified Tech Trainers. As such, he has developed a very specialized custom curriculum focused on the core essentials of IT auditing and IT governance best practices. Certified Tech Trainers provides these courses at various locations throughout the world. These courses are far more than simple exam-preparation reviews and are priced accordingly. However, if you are looking for a complete course on IS auditing so that you can learn about CISA exam topics, as well as many other critical IS auditing topics not covered on the exam or in this book, you might want to take a look at CTT's course offerings and decide whether instructor-led training is a viable and attractive alternative for you. Session locations and registration information are available at www.certifiedtechtrainers.com.

What This Book Will Do

This book is designed to be read as a pointer to the areas of knowledge you will be tested on. In other words, you might want to read the book one time just to get insight into how comprehensive your knowledge of this topic is. The book is also designed to be read shortly before you go for the actual test and to give you a distillation of the field of systems auditing in as few pages as possible. We think you can use this book to get a sense of the underlying context of any topic in the chapters—or to skim-read for Exam Alerts, bulleted points, summaries, and topic headings.

We have drawn on material from ISACA's own listing of knowledge requirements, from other preparation guides, and from the exams themselves. We have also drawn from a battery of third-party test-preparation tools and technical websites, as well as from our own experience with application development and the exam. Our aim is to walk you through the knowledge you will need—looking over your shoulder, so to speak—and point out those things that are important for the exam (Exam Alerts, practice questions, and so on). Much of the explanation of concepts has been derived from Certified Tech Trainer's professional instructor-led training for IT Auditing and Assurance, Information Security Essentials and Best Practices, Business Continuity and Disaster Recovery Management, and Business Continuity: *Incident Response*. By reading this book, you will not only gain from the experience of real-world professional information systems auditors, but you will also enjoy the benefit of costly professional content development.

The CISA exam makes a basic assumption that you already have a strong background in information systems auditing and controls. On the other hand, because the systems auditing requirements and practices constantly evolve, no one can be a complete expert. We have tried to demystify the jargon, acronyms, terms, and concepts. In addition, wherever we think you are likely to blur past an important concept, we have defined the assumptions and premises behind that concept.

Contacting the Authors

We have tried to create a real-world tool that you can use to prepare for and pass the CISA certification exam. We are interested in any feedback you would care to share about the book, especially if you have ideas about how we can improve it for future test-takers. We will consider everything you say carefully and will respond to all reasonable suggestions and comments. You can reach Allen Keele via email at allenk@certifiedtechtrainers.com, and you can reach Keith Mortier via email at kmortier@lmisol.com.

Let us know if you found this book to be helpful in your preparation efforts. We would also like to know how you felt about your chances of passing the exam *before* you read the book and then *after* you read the book. Of course, we would love to hear that you passed the exam—and even if you just want to share your triumph, we would be happy to hear from you.

Thanks for choosing us as your personal trainers, and enjoy the book. We would wish you luck on the exam, but we know that if you read through all the chapters and have some real-world information systems and controls auditing experience, you will not need luck—you will pass the test on the strength of real knowledge!

What This Book Will Not Do

This book will *not* teach you everything you need to know about auditing systems and controls, or even about an auditing standard or procedure. Nor is this book an introduction to computer technology. This book reviews what you need to know before you take the test, with its fundamental purpose dedicated to reviewing the information needed on the ISACA CISA certification exam.

This book uses a variety of teaching and memorization techniques to analyze the exam-related topics and to provide you with everything you will need to know to pass the test. Again, it is *not* a comprehensive introduction to information systems and controls auditing.

About the Book

If you are preparing for the CISA exam for the first time, you should know that we have structured the topics in this book to correspond directly to the CISA exam objective content areas as published by ISACA. The topic areas for the exam often overlap in required understanding and can sometimes seem somewhat redundant. Topic areas can often intertwine, to make elimination of redundancy unavoidable. Try not to let redundancy bother you; instead, let it reinforce the concept interdependencies you need to understand to pass the CISA exam.

We suggest that you read this book from front to back. You will not be wasting your time because nothing we have written is a guess about an unknown exam. We have had to explain certain underlying information on such a regular basis that we have included those explanations here.

After you have read the book, you can brush up on a certain area by using the index or the table of contents to go straight to the topics and questions you want to re-examine. We have tried to use the headings and subheadings to provide outline information about each given topic. After you have been certified, we think you will find this book useful as a tightly focused reference and an essential foundation of information systems and controls auditing.

Each *Exam Cram 2* chapter follows a regular structure, along with graphical cues about especially important or useful material. The structure of a typical chapter is as follows:

➤ **Opening hotlists**—Each chapter begins with lists of the terms you will need to understand and the concepts you will need to master before you can be fully conversant in the chapter's subject matter. We follow the hotlists with a few introductory paragraphs, setting the stage for the rest of the chapter.

➤ **Topical coverage**—After the opening hotlists, each chapter covers the topics related to the chapter's subject.

➤ **Exam Alerts**—Throughout the text, we highlight material most likely to appear on the exam by using a special Exam Alert that looks like this:

> This is what an Exam Alert looks like. An Exam Alert stresses concepts, terms, or best practices that will most likely appear in one or more certification exam questions. For that reason, we think any information presented in an Exam Alert is worthy of unusual attentiveness on your part.

Even if material is not flagged as an Exam Alert, *all* the content in this book is associated in some way with test-related material. What appears in the chapter content is critical knowledge.

➤ **Notes**—This book is an overall examination of information systems and controls auditing. As such, we dip into many aspects of systems auditing. Where a body of knowledge is deeper than the scope of the book, we use notes to indicate areas of concern.

> Cramming for an exam will get you through a test, but it will not make you a competent information systems auditing professional. Although you can memorize just the facts you need to become certified, your daily work in the field will rapidly put you in water over your head if you do not know the underlying principles of systems auditing and IT governance.

➤ **Tips**—We provide tips that will help you to build a better foundation of knowledge or to focus your attention on an important concept that reappears later in the book. Tips provide a helpful way to remind you of the context surrounding a particular area of a topic under discussion.

> An IS auditor's primary responsibility is to advise senior management of the risk involved in not implementing proper segregation of duties, such as having the security administrator perform an operations function.

➤ **Practice questions**—This section presents a short list of test questions related to the specific chapter topic. Following each question is an explanation of both correct and incorrect answers. The practice questions highlight the areas we found to be most important on the exam.

The bulk of the book follows this chapter structure, but we would like to point out a few other elements:

➤ **Glossary**—This is an extensive glossary of important terms used in this book.

➤ **The Cram Sheet**—This appears as a tear-away sheet inside the front cover of this *Exam Cram 2* book. It is a valuable tool that represents a collection of the most difficult-to-remember facts and numbers we think you should memorize before taking the test. Remember, you can dump this information out of your head onto a piece of paper as soon as you enter the testing room. These are usually facts that we have found require brute-force memorization. You need to remember this information only long enough to write it down when you walk into the test room. Be advised that you will be asked to surrender all personal belongings other than pencils before you enter the exam room itself.

You might want to look at the Cram Sheet in your car or in the lobby of the testing center just before you walk into the testing center. The Cram Sheet is divided under headings, so you can review the appropriate parts just before each test.

➤ **The CD**—The CD also contains the Certified Tech Trainers exam-simulation software. The included software provides an additional 200 practice questions in electronic format. CTT's practice questions even include audiovisual mentored feedback for each question, to reteach you the information you need to correctly answer the question, or possibly just to teach you professional exam-taking shortcuts for answering difficult questions. In addition to more practice questions with audio/video mentored feedback, the CD contains a short audiovisual presentation by one of this book's authors, Allen Keele. The presentation gives you a good orientation to "set the scene" for this book, the CISA certification, and the information systems auditing and security environment.

Self-Assessment

I've included a Self-Assessment in this *Exam Cram* to help you evaluate your readiness to tackle Certified Information Systems Auditor (CISA) for ISACA certification. Before you tackle this Self-Assessment, however, I'll talk about the concerns you might face when pursuing a CISA certification and what an ideal candidate might look like.

Certified Information Systems Auditors in the Real World

In the next section, I describe an ideal CISA candidate, knowing full well that only a few actual candidates meet this ideal. In fact, my description of that ideal candidate might seem downright scary. But take heart; although the requirements to obtain a CISA certification may seem formidable, they are by no means impossible to meet. However, you should be keenly aware that it does take time, requires some expense, and calls for a substantial effort.

You can get all the real-world motivation you need from knowing that many others have gone before you. You can follow in their footsteps. If you're willing to tackle the process seriously and do what it takes to gain the necessary experience and knowledge, you can take—and pass—the certification exam. In fact, the *Exam Crams* and the companion *Exam Preps* are designed to make it as easy as possible for you to prepare for these exams, but prepare you must!

The Ideal ISACA Certified Information Systems Auditor Candidate

Just to give you some idea of what an ideal Certified Information Systems Auditor candidate is like, here are some relevant statistics about the background and experience such an individual should have. ISACA requires the following for CISA certification (these details are listed on ISACA's website at www.isaca.org):

➤ Successful completion of the CISA examination

➤ Information systems auditing, control, or security experience

➤ Adherence to ISACA's Code of Professional Ethics

➤ Adherence to the continuing professional education program

➤ Compliance with the information systems auditing standards

Taking a closer look at the experience requirements, ISACA explains that a CISA candidate should have the following:

➤ A minimum of five years of professional IS auditing, control, or security work experience.

➤ Substitution and waivers of such experience may be obtained as follows:

> ➤ A maximum of one year of information systems experience **OR** one year of financial or operational auditing experience can be substituted for one year of information systems auditing, control, or security experience.

> ➤ 60 to 120 completed college semester credit hours (the equivalent of an Associate's or Bachelor's degree) can be substituted for one or two years, respectively, of information systems auditing, control, or security experience.

> ➤ Two years as a full-time university instructor in a related field (such as computer science, accounting, or information systems auditing) can be substituted for one year of information systems auditing, control or security experience.

Experience must have been gained within the 10-year period preceding the application for certification or within 5 years from the date of initially passing the examination. Application for certification must be submitted within five years from the passing date of the CISA exam. All experience will be verified independently with employers.

I believe that well under half of all certification candidates meet these requirements. In fact, most probably meet less than half of these requirements (that is, at least when they begin the certification process). However, because all those who have their certifications already survived this ordeal, you can survive it, too—especially if you heed what this Self-Assessment can tell you about what you already know and what you need to learn.

Put Yourself to the Test

The following series of questions and observations is designed to help you figure out how much work you'll face in pursuing CISA certification and what kinds of resources you can consult on your quest. Be absolutely honest in your answers, or you'll end up wasting money on an exam you're not ready to take. There are no right or wrong answers—only steps along the path to certification. Only you can decide where you really belong in the broad spectrum of aspiring candidates.

Two things should be clear from the outset, however:

➤ Even a modest background in computer science will be helpful.

➤ Hands-on experience with testing, documenting, and advising on internal systems controls is an essential ingredient for certification success.

Educational Background

1. Have you ever taken any computer-related classes? (Yes or No)

   If yes, proceed to question 2; if no, proceed to question 4.

2. Have you taken any classes on formal systems audit concepts and practices? (Yes or No)

   If yes, you will probably be able to handle the questions relating to the "best" way to respond to systems auditing key issues. If you're rusty, brush up on the formal frameworks, standards, and procedures for systems auditing, and maybe even attend a short CISA preparation review seminar before taking the exam. Such courses are offered by ISACA chapters themselves or can be found at professional information security and systems auditing training centers such as Certified Tech Trainers (www.certifiedtechtrainers.com). If the answer is no, consider some professional training in this area. I strongly recommend a good high-level systems auditing class, such as "IT Auditing and Assurance," provided by Certified Tech Trainers. If this title doesn't appeal to you, ISACA has recommendations for other resources (www.isaca.org).

3. Have you taken any networking concepts or technologies classes? (Yes or No)

   If yes, you will probably be able to handle the networking terminology, concepts, and technologies (but brace yourself for frequent departures from normal usage). If you're rusty, brush up on basic networking concepts and terminology. If your answer is no, you might want to check out some titles on the Transport Communication Protocol/Internet Protocol (TCP/IP).

4. Have you done any reading on systems auditing frameworks and standards? (Yes or No)

   If yes, review the requirements from questions 2 and 3. If you meet them, move to the next section, "Hands-On Experience." If you answered no, consult the recommended reading for both topics. This kind of strong background will be of great help in preparing for the CISA exam.

5. Are you knowledgeable and experienced in risk-management concepts and practices? Fully 60% of a systems auditor's job is ensuring that the organization being audited has handled risk appropriately. If you answered yes to this question, your intuition for "best auditing practices" will be much keener and more accurate. If you answered no to this question, you should consider attending a professional instructor-led class on systems auditing. Books do not seem to be well suited to transferring risk management perspective gained from experience.

Hands-On Experience

Another important key to success on all ISACA tests is hands-on experience. If I leave you with only one realization after taking this Self-Assessment, it should be that there's no substitute for time spent performing systems auditing according to frameworks and standards, on which you'll be tested repeatedly and in depth.

You can obtain the exam objectives, practice questions, and get other information about ISACA exams from the ISACA Certification page on the Web at www.isaca.org.

If you have the funds or your employer will pay your way, consider taking a class led by a professional systems-auditing instructor. Systems auditing intertwines widely disparate concepts, and the class will only be as good as the wide scope of knowledge and experience of the instructor leading it.

Testing Your Exam Readiness

Whether you attend a formal class on a specific topic to get ready for an exam or use written materials to study on your own, some preparation for the ISACA certification exams is essential. At up to $505 a try, pass or fail, you want to do everything you can to pass on your first try. Not only can failed attempts be very expensive to your pocketbook, but remember that ISACA provides testing only once per year. If you fail an attempt, you will need to wait an entire year to try again. This delay can often mean much more than the cost of the repeated exam. It can mean that you are not able to obtain or maintain a career in systems auditing! That's where studying comes in.

We have included in this book several practice exam questions for each chapter and two sample tests, so if you don't score well on the chapter questions, you can study more and then tackle the sample tests at the end of chapter.

For any given subject, consider taking a class if you've tackled self-study materials, taken the practice test, and failed anyway. If you can afford the privilege, the opportunity to interact with an instructor and fellow students can make all the difference in the world. For information about systems auditing classes, visit the Certification Program page at www.isaca.org, or at www.certifiedtechtrainers.com.

   6. Have you taken a practice exam on your chosen test subject? (Yes or No)

     If yes—and you scored 90% or better, you're probably ready to tackle the real thing. If your score isn't above that crucial threshold, keep at it until you break that barrier. If you answered no, go back and study the book some more, and repeat the practice tests. Keep at it until you can comfortably break the passing threshold.

There is no better way to assess your test readiness than to take a good-quality practice exam and pass with a score of 90% or better. When I'm preparing, I shoot for 95+%, just to leave room for the "weirdness factor" that sometimes shows up on ISACA exams.

One last note: I hope it makes sense to stress the importance of hands-on experience in the context of the exams. As you review the material for the exams, you'll realize that hands-on experience with systems auditing key concepts and best practices is invaluable.

Onward, Through the Fog!

After you've assessed your readiness, undertaken the right background studies, obtained the hands-on experience that will help you understand the products and technologies at work, and reviewed the many sources of information to help you prepare for a test, you'll be ready to take a round of practice tests. When your scores come back positive enough to get you through the exam, you're ready to go after the real thing. If you follow our assessment regimen, you'll not only know what you need to study, but you'll also know when you're ready to take the CISA exam this June. Good luck!

The Information Systems (IS) Audit Process

Key concepts you will need to understand:

- ✓ ISACA IS Auditing Standards and Guidelines and Code of Professional Ethics
- ✓ IS auditing practices and techniques
- ✓ Techniques to gather information and preserve evidence
- ✓ Control objectives and controls related to IS
- ✓ Types of risk: IS, business, and audit risk

- ✓ How to determine an organization's use of system platforms, IT infrastructure and applications
- ✓ Risk-analysis methods, principles, and criteria
- ✓ Audit planning and management techniques
- ✓ How to communicate the audit results
- ✓ Personnel-management techniques

Techniques you will need to master:

- ✓ Develop and implement a risk-based IS audit strategy and objectives, in compliance with generally accepted standards, to ensure that the organization's information technology and business processes are adequately controlled, monitored, and assessed, and are aligned with the organization's business objectives
- ✓ Plan specific audits to ensure that the IS audit strategy and objectives are achieved
- ✓ Obtain sufficient, reliable, relevant, and useful evidence to achieve the audit objectives

- ✓ Analyze information gathered to identify reportable conditions and reach conclusions
- ✓ Review the work performed to provide reasonable assurance that objectives have been achieved
- ✓ Communicate audit results to key stakeholders
- ✓ Facilitate the implementation of risk-management and control practices within the organization

Conducting IS Audits in Accordance with Generally Accepted IS Audit Standards and Guidelines

To understand the material required for the exam, you must first understand what an auditor is and is not. An IS auditor is responsible for assessing the strength and effectiveness of controls that are designed to protect information systems, and to ensure that audit engagements are planned, designed, and reviewed based on the assessed level of risk that irregular and illegal acts might occur. These acts could be material to the subject matter of the IS auditor's report. The IS auditor is not qualified to determine whether an irregular, illegal, or erroneous act has occurred, but has the responsibility to report suspected acts to the appropriate parties. Determining whether information systems safeguard assets and maintaining data integrity are the primary objectives of an IS audit function.

ISACA IS Auditing Standards and Guidelines and Code of Professional Ethics

To ensure the audit is comprehensive, you will use guidelines to assist you in applying IS Auditing Standards. These standards define the mandatory requirements for IS auditing and reporting, as well as provide a minimum level of performance for auditors. The Information Systems Auditing Association (ISACA) provides the auditing community with guidance in the form of auditing guidelines, standards, and polices specific to information systems (IS) auditing. One of the goals of the ISACA is to advance globally applicable standards to meet its vision. The development and dissemination of the IS Auditing Standards is a cornerstone of the ISACA professional contribution to the audit community. The ISACA framework for the IS Auditing Standards provides multiple levels of guidance for conducting IT audits.

There are 8 categories and 12 overall IS auditing standards. IS Auditing Standards are brief mandatory requirements for certification holders' reports on the audit and its findings. IS Auditing Guidelines and Procedures give detailed guidance on how to follow those standards. The IS Auditing Guidelines provide a framework an IS auditor normally follows, with the understanding that in some situations the auditor will not follow that guidance. In this case, it is the IS auditor's responsibility to justify the way in which the work is done. The Procedures examples show the steps performed by an IS auditor and are more informative than IS Auditing Guidelines. Table 1.1. provides ISACA's definition of standards, guidelines, and procedures.

Table 1.1 IS Auditing Procedures	
Standards	Define mandatory requirements for IS auditing and reporting. Standards inform IS auditors of the minimum level of acceptable performance required to meet the professional responsibilities set out in the ISACA Code of Professional Ethics for IS auditors. Standards inform management and other interested parties of the profession's expectations concerning the work of practitioners Holders of the Certified Information Systems Auditor (CISA) designation of requirements. Failure to comply with these standards can result in an investigation into the CISA-holder's conduct by the ISACA Board of Directors or appropriate ISACA committee and, ultimately, in disciplinary action.
Guidelines	Provide guidance in applying IS Auditing Standards. The IS auditor should consider them in determining how to achieve implementation of the standards, use professional judgment in their application, and be prepared to justify any departure. The objective of the IS Auditing Guidelines is to provide further information on how to comply with the IS Auditing Standards.
Procedures	Provide examples of procedures an IS auditor might follow in an audit engagement. The procedure documents provide information on how to meet the standards when performing IS auditing work, but they do not set requirements. The objective of the IS Auditing Procedures is to provide further information on how to comply with the IS Auditing Standards.

Auditing Standards Explained

The examples are constructed to follow the IS Auditing Standards and the IS Auditing Guidelines, and provide information on following the IS Auditing Standards. To some extent, they also establish best practices for procedures to be followed.

Codification

The eight standards categories are the first three digits in a document number. IS Auditing Standards begin with 0; Standards for IS Control

Professionals begin with 5. The standards numbers are the second three numbers in the document. The third set of three digits in a document number is the number of the guideline. Procedures are listed separately and numbered consecutively by issue date.

For example, document 060.020.040 is a guideline. It provides guidance in the sixth standard category, Performance of Audit Work. The guidance applies to the second standard in that category, Evidence. It is the fourth guideline listed under Evidence. Procedures are numbered consecutively as they are issued, beginning with 1.

Use

It is suggested that during the annual audit program, as well as during individual reviews throughout the year, the IS auditor should review the standards to ensure compliance with them. The IS auditor can refer to the ISACA standards in the report, stating that the review was conducted in compliance with the laws of the country, applicable audit regulations, and ISACA standards. Table 1.2 is the ISACA framework for the IS auditor. This framework is broken down into multiple levels of guidance.

Table 1.2	ISACA Auditing Standards	
010	Audit Charter	
010.010	Responsibility, Authority, and Accountability	The responsibility, authority, and accountability of the information systems audit function are to be appropriately documented in an audit charter or engagement letter.
020	Independence	
020.010	Professional Independence	In all matters related to auditing, the information systems auditor is to be independent of the auditee in attitude and appearance.
020.020	Organizational Relationship	The information systems audit function is to be sufficiently independent of the area being audited, to permit objective completion of the audit.
030	Professional Ethics and Standards	
030.010	Code of Professional Ethics	The information systems auditor is to adhere to the Code of Professional Ethics of the Information Systems Audit and Control Association.

(continued)

Table 1.2	ISACA Auditing Standards *(continued)*	
030.020	Due Professional Care	Due professional care and observance of applicable professional auditing standards are to be exercised in all aspects of the information systems auditor's work.
040	Competence	
040.010	Skills and Knowledge	The information systems auditor is to be technically competent, with the skills and knowledge necessary to perform the auditor's work.
040.020	Continuing Professional Education	The information systems auditor is to maintain technical competence through appropriate continuing professional education.
050	Planning	
050.010	Audit Planning	The information systems auditor is to plan the information systems audit work to address the audit objectives and to comply with applicable professional auditing standards.
060	Performance of Audit Work	
060.010	Supervision	Information systems audit staff are to be appropriately supervised to provide assurance that audit objectives are accomplished and applicable professional auditing standards are met.
060.020	Evidence	During the course of the audit, the information systems auditor is to obtain sufficient, reliable, relevant, and useful evidence to achieve the audit objectives effectively. The audit findings and conclusions are to be supported by appropriate analysis and interpretation of this evidence.
070	Reporting	
070.010	Report Content and Form	The information systems auditor is to provide a report, in an appropriate form, to intended recipients upon the completion of audit work. The audit report is to state the scope, objectives, period of coverage, and nature and extent of the

(continued)

Table 1.2	ISACA Auditing Standards *(continued)*	
		audit work performed. The report is to identify the organization, the intended recipients, and any restrictions on circulation. The report is to state the findings, conclusions, and recommendations, and any reservations or qualifications that the auditor has with respect to the audit.
080	Follow-Up Activities	
080.010	Follow-Up	The information systems auditor is to request and evaluate appropriate information on previous relevant findings, conclusions, and recommendations to determine whether appropriate actions have been implemented in a timely manner.

The primary purpose of an audit charter is to describe the authority and responsibilities of the audit department.

The ISACA Code of Professional Ethics

As an auditor, you will have access to a variety of information, including intellectual property, internal controls, legal contracts, internal procedures, and both business and IT strategies. ISACA has set forth a Code of Professional Ethics to guide the professional and personal conduct of members of the association and its certification holders.

Members and ISACA certification holders shall…

➤ Support the implementation of and encourage compliance with appropriate standards, procedures, and controls for information systems.

➤ Perform their duties with objectivity, due diligence, and professional care, in accordance with professional standards and best practices.

➤ Serve in the interest of stakeholders in a lawful and honest manner, while maintaining high standards of conduct and character, and not engage in acts discreditable to the profession.

➤ Maintain the privacy and confidentiality of information obtained in the course of their duties unless disclosure is required by legal authority.

Such information shall not be used for personal benefit or released to inappropriate parties.

➤ Maintain competency in their respective fields and agree to undertake only those activities that they can reasonably expect to complete with professional competence.

➤ Inform appropriate parties of the results of work performed, revealing all significant facts known to them.

➤ Support the professional education of stakeholders in enhancing their understanding of information systems security and control.

Failure to comply with this Code of Professional Ethics can result in an investigation into a member's or certification holder's conduct and, ultimately, in disciplinary measures.

As an auditor, it is important that you pay particular attention to maintaining the privacy and confidentiality of information obtained in the course of your duties and informing the appropriate parties of the results of work performed, revealing all significant facts known to you.

Although management is ultimately responsible for preventing and detecting irregular or illegal acts, you must plan the IT audit engagement based on the assessed level of risk that these acts might occur and design audit procedures that can identify these acts. The auditor then should create a report of the findings of the audit revealing all significant facts known to him or her.

As previously stated, auditors are not qualified to determine whether an irregular, illegal, or erroneous act has occurred. If during the course of the audit the auditor suspects that these acts have occurred, the auditor must report this to one or more of the following parties:

➤ The IS auditors' immediate supervisor and possibly the corporate governance bodies, such as the board of directors or audit committee

➤ Appropriate personnel within the organization, such as a manager who is at least one level above those who are suspected to have engaged in such acts

➤ Corporate governance bodies, if top management is suspected

➤ Legal counsel of other appropriate external experts

NOTE   For more information on ISACA's auditing standards, guidelines, and code of professional ethics, visit www.isaca.org.

As we know, privacy is an issue at the forefront in today's society. A majority of organizations have developed privacy polices that outline how they collect, store, protect, and use private information, along with controls designed to protect private information. As an auditor, you will assess the strength and effectiveness of controls designed to protect personally identifiable information in organizations. This will help ensure that management develops, implements, and operates sound internal controls aimed at protecting the private information that it collects and stores during the normal course of business.

So far, we have provided you with auditors' responsibilities, the ISACA code of ethics, and definitions for guidelines, standards, and procedures for IS auditing. At this point, you might be asking yourself, "What am I getting myself into?" and "What is IS auditing really?"

Whether you are a financial auditor, are a network or security systems engineer, or are new to IS auditing, rest assured that we will guide you through the auditing process and assist you in understanding how the IS audit process and its components fit together. We start at the top by providing you with IS audit planning and management techniques.

As you read through the remainder of this chapter and the following chapters, keep in mind that we start from the auditor's perspective in planning the IS audit and add the components as we go along. Be sure to use all the resources available to you to completely understand the topic before moving forward. You have the CBT and the questions at the end of each chapter to keep you focused and on track. To help solidify the process and components in your mind as you read, apply the things you are learning to your own organization; try to envision the planning, documentation, and people you would communicate with (at both the management and operational levels); imagine what type of information you could expect to receive/review; and consider how you would communicate your results at all levels in the organization.

Keep in mind that the work you perform can directly assist in the successful assessment and mitigation of risk and overall security of the organization you are auditing. If performed successfully, it will be a factor in ensuring the success of the organization, management, employees, and continued service to customers. Good luck and have fun!

Ensuring That the Organization's Information Technology and Business Systems Are Adequately Controlled, Monitored, and Assessed

The organization's management is responsible for preventing and detecting illegal or irregular acts. Although the IS auditor is not qualified to determine whether an irregular, illegal, or erroneous act has occurred, auditors are responsible for assessing the level of risk that irregular and illegal acts might occur. This is accomplished by designing audit procedures that consider the assessed risk level for irregular and illegal acts. The IS auditor then should review the results of audit procedures for indications of such acts. If the IS auditor suspects that these acts have occurred, the auditor must report the finding immediately to the immediate supervisor and possibly corporate governance bodies, such as the board of directors or audit committee. In addition, the IS auditor is responsible for ensuring that management develop, implement, and operate sound internal controls aimed at the protection of private information. The IS auditor should assess the strength and effectiveness of controls designed to protect personally identifiable information within the organization.

ISACA's COBIT Framework

Other resources available through ISACA are the COBIT resources. COBIT is intended for use by business and IT management as well as IS auditors. Therefore, its use ensures business objectives and the communication of best practices and recommendations are based on a commonly understood and well-respected standard reference. These resources can be used as a source of best-practice guidance. Each of the following is organized by an IT management process, as defined in the COBIT Framework. The COBIT framework provides good practices for the management of IT processes in a manageable and logical structure, meeting the multiple needs of enterprise management by bridging the gaps between business risks, technical issues, control needs, and performance measurement requirements. Auditors will review IS for formal risk-management strategies for systems development and implementation projects, as well as acquisition, development, change management, and implementation of IT applications.

COBIT management guidelines are composed of maturity models, critical success factors, key goal indicators, and key performance indicators.

COBIT control objectives provide the critical insight needed to delineate a clear policy and good practice for IT controls and incorporate 318 specific, detailed control objectives throughout the 34 high-level control objectives.

The COBIT framework provides 11 processes in the management and deployment of IT systems:

➤ Develop a strategic plan

➤ Articulate the information architecture

➤ Find an optimal fit between the IT and the organization's strategy

➤ Design the IT function to match the organization's needs

➤ Maximize the return of the IT investment

➤ Communicate IT policies to the user community

➤ Manage the IT workforce

➤ Comply with external regulations, laws, and contracts

➤ Conduct IT risk assessments

➤ Maintain a high-quality systems-development process

➤ Incorporate sound project-management techniques

NOTE COBIT, issued by the IT Governance Institute and now in its third edition, is increasingly internationally accepted as good practice for control over information, IT, and related risks. Its guidance enables an enterprise to implement effective, pervasive, and intrinsic governance over the IT throughout the enterprise.

Control Self-Assessment

The control self-assessment (CSA) is a formal, documented, collaborative process in which management or work teams are directly involved in judging and monitoring the effectiveness of controls. The CSA does not replace an audit, but its main objective is to enhance audit responsibility. A primary benefit derived from an organization that employs control self-assessment (CSA) techniques is that it can identify high-risk areas that might need a detailed review later.

The CSA is generally accompanied by workshops in which the IS auditor leads and guides the clients in assessing their environment. This enables auditors to serve as assessment facilitators and shifts some of the control-monitoring responsibilities to the functional areas.

The traditional role of an IS auditor in a control self-assessment (CSA) should be that of a facilitator.

Risk-Based IS Audit Strategy and Objectives

One of the significant challenges facing auditors today is *what* to audit. The tighter integration of information systems and business processes, and the continued complexity of these systems, combined with limited resources and the ever-increasing pace of business, make auditing everything an impossible task. One of the techniques that management and auditors can use to allocate limited audit resources is a risk-based audit approach. The risk-based audit approach helps ensure that appropriate levels of protection are applied to information assets.

A benefit of the risk-based approach to audit planning is that auditing resources are allocated to the areas of highest concern (risk).

Many types of risk are associated with business and auditing. These risks are identified during the planning stage of the audit and are used as the foundation for control review. *Risk assessment* is the process of reviewing the threats and vulnerabilities, their effects on the assets being audited, and the projected loss frequency and severity. The organization can then use the risk assessment to determine how to remediate risk to the lowest possible level. Keep in mind that risk can never be reduced to zero and that there are a finite amount of resources to mitigate risk. *Risk mitigation* consists of reducing risk to a tolerable level by implementing controls that reduce the risk; the remaining risk is called *residual risk*. Residual risk can be mitigated by transference to a third party. A variety of risks are associated with business and the process of auditing:

➤ **Business risk**—The risk that a business will not achieve its stated business goals or objectives. Business risk can be affected by both internal and external factors.

➤ **Security risk**—The risk that unauthorized access to data will adversely affect the integrity of that data. Poor data integrity can lead to poor decision making and contribute to business risk.

➤ **Continuity risk**—This is the risk associated with systems availability and its capability to utilize backups to recover.

➤ **Audit risk**—The risk that the information of financial reports might contain material errors or that the IS auditor might not detect an error that has occurred. This term is also used to describe the level of risk an auditor is prepared to accept during an audit engagement. A *material error* is an error that should be considered significant to any party concerned with the item in question.

➤ **Inherent risk**—The risk that a material error could occur, assuming that there are no related internal controls to prevent or detect the error. Inherent risk is the susceptibility of an area or process to an error that could be material. An example is when an authorized program has exits (trap doors) because they provide flexibility for inserting code to modify or add functionality.

➤ **Control risk**—The risk that a material error exists that would not be prevented or detected on a timely basis by the system of internal controls.

➤ **Detection risk**—Detection risk results when an IS auditor uses an inadequate test procedure and concludes that material errors do not exist, when, in fact, they do.

An auditor should create and follow a specific predefined set of processes to set control objectives, gather evidence, review the evidence, and produce a findings conclusion and recommendations. The following steps help define your responsibilities as an auditor:

1. Plan the IT audit engagement based on an assessed level of risk that irregular and illegal acts might occur, and that such acts could be material to the subject matter of the IS auditor's report.

2. Design audit procedures that consider the assessed risk level for irregular and illegal acts.

3. Review the results of the audit procedures for indications of irregular and illegal acts.

4. Assume that acts are not isolated.

5. Determine how the act slipped though the internal control system.

6. Broaden audit procedures to consider the possibility of more acts of this nature.

7. Conduct additional audit procedures.

8. Evaluate the results of the expanded audit procedures.

9. Consult with legal counsel and possibly corporate governance bodies to estimate the potential impact of the irregular and illegal acts, taken as a whole, on the subject matter of the engagement, audit report, and organization.

10. Report all facts and circumstances of the irregular and illegal acts (whether suspected or confirmed) if the acts have a material effect on the subject matter of the engagement or organization.

11. Distribute the report to the appropriate internal parties, such as managers who are at least one level above those who are suspected or confirmed to have committed the acts, or corporate governance.

Aligning Controls with the Organization's Business Objectives

IT governance provides structure to functions and processes within the IT organization. Because of the critical dependency of business on its information systems, the governance structure must ensure that the IT organizational strategy is aligned with the business strategy. The implementation of the IT strategy will help ensure that IT processes contain the necessary controls to reduce risk to the organization and its business objectives. IT resources should be used responsibly, and IT risks should be managed appropriately.

Steering Committee

The organization should have an IT steering committee to ensure that the IS department's strategy directly aligns with the organization's corporate mission and objectives and efficient use of IT resources. The IT steering committee is a formal organization usually composed of senior managers representing the business areas, with duties outlined in a charter. The charter outlines what authority and responsibilities are assigned to the committee and is a strong indicator that senior management supports the steering committee. One of the functions of the IT steering committee is to keep detailed minutes of the meeting, to document both procedural functions of the committee and its decisions. The committee is responsible for ensuring that the organization's leadership (board of directors and senior management) is informed in a timely manner via the minutes and additional reporting, if required.

Although the committee is responsible for reviewing issues such as new and ongoing projects, major equipment acquisitions, and the review and approval of budgets, it does not usually get involved in the day-to-day operations of the IS department. The IT steering committee uses project plans, work breakdown structures, and policy/procedures to review the alignment of the IT department with the organizational mission. Generally, the IT steering committees will meet one to two times per month in a formal meeting at which the head of the IT department and project managers present their progress on major projects, propose new projects and policies, or refine procedures.

The lack of a formal chartered IT steering committee could be an indication that the IT department is not correctly aligned with the organization's strategy. In the absence of an IT steering committee, the auditor might find that projects do not support the mission of the organization; that they are not on time or on budget, usually because of the lack of external controls; and that policies are outdated or not communicated or followed consistently throughout the organization. The auditor might also find situations in which an IT steering committee is present, but, because of the lack of a formal charter or direction from senior managers of the organization, members are unclear about their duties or level of authority. The IT steering committee meetings should focus on alignment and should refrain from becoming involved in the operational details of the IS department. In both of these situations, the IT steering committee is not ensuring the efficient use of data-processing resources, examining costs associated with projects, or setting priorities for the IT department.

Strategic Planning

Organizations should have processes for the development and review of *strategic plans*. Strategic plans ensure that the organization meets its goals and objectives, and, if properly reviewed, reflect the current direction of the organization and associated business units, including the IS department. The strategic-planning process should involve senior management, to ensure that the plan addresses the established goals and objectives, and a review process that enables the organization to update or change the strategic plan in the event of goal or objective changes. Strategic plans should incorporate both long-term (three to five years) and short-term (one to two years) strategic objectives of the organization, and are the responsibility of senior management. When auditing the IS strategic-planning process and implementation, the auditor should review overall goals and business plans but should not focus on procedures. Reviewing management's long-term strategic plans helps the IS auditor gain an understanding of an organization's goals and objectives.

The IS policies, procedures, standards, and guidelines are all implemented to support the overall strategic plan. Policies and procedures reflect the actual operational implementation of the strategic plan and should have a formal process for creation, communication, and review. Although most organizations have policies in place, they are often "shelf ware," meaning that they are created once, generally communicated to new employees, and then put on the shelf. The danger with this implementation is that there is the lack of ongoing review of policies and procedures to ensure that they align with the strategic plan. This leads to instances in which employees are not aware of policies and procedures as they apply to the day-to-day work. A review of the strategic plan, policies, procedures, and observations will identify whether there is correct alignment within the organization. Additional review of and questions of who has ownership of the strategic planning and policy creation/implementation and how often plans are reviewed or updated will indicate the presence or absence of a formal process.

Organizational Structure

IT departments should have a clearly defined structure that outlines authority and responsibility, and defines the hierarchal structure. This structure is usually defined in an organization chart, which helps the IS auditor determine whether there is proper segregation of functions. In addition, each employee should have a job description that provides a detailed outline of job function and the tasks associated with that function. Per ISACA, segregation of duties avoids the possibility that a single person could be responsible for diverse and critical functions in such a way that those errors or misappropriations could occur and not be detected in a timely manner and in the normal course of business processes.

The structure of the IT department and its responsibilities could change slightly based on the goals of the organization, but Figure 1.1 shows ISACA's outline of an organizational structure and descriptions of the functions.

To maintain proper control of IT projects, including the acquisition, design, implementation, and maintenance of the IT infrastructure, the IT department should implement the following disciplines:

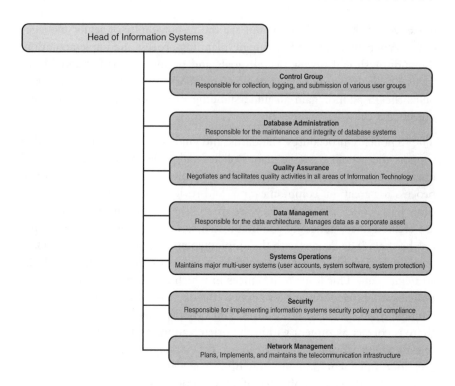

Figure 1.1 The outline of an organizational structure.

➤ **Personnel management**—This is done in accordance with organizational policies and procedures for hiring, promotion, retention, and termination of employees and personnel. Proper implementation ensures that employees are qualified to perform their jobs and are promoted and retained to consistently improve the quality of the IT operations.

➤ **IT project management**—All new and existing projects should include project plans that outline the resources required for the project, milestones, return on investment, and regular milestone reviews. The combination of the IT steering committee reviews and independent audits ensures that projects stay on time and on budget and that they meet the strategic objectives of the organization.

➤ **IT change management**—Change management is a formal documented process for introducing technology changes into the environment. Proper change control ensures that changes are documented, approved, and implemented with minimum disruption to the production environment and provide maximum benefits to the organization.

➤ **Financial management**—The process of budget development includes forecasting, monitoring, and analyzing financial information as it applies to resources. This management process ensures the adequate allocation of funds, proper distribution of funds within the different IT functions (operations, security, and so on), and any gaps that exist between IT investments and the benefits provided by those investments.

We discuss these disciplines in further detail throughout the book, but it is important to note that they might fall within a single group or be used across operational groups to efficiently manage IT resources.

IT Department Head

The department is headed by an information technology manager/director, or in larger organizations, by a chief information officer. The head of the IT department is responsible for the overall operation of the IT department, including budget authority, hiring, training and retaining of qualified people, and alignment of IT as a service organization, to ensure that the organization can meet strategic objectives and operational goals.

Security Department

The security department is enabled through senior management's understanding of risk and application of the resources to mitigate risk. The security department's functions are guided through policies and procedures, and should remain separate from IT functions. The security administrator should report directly to the head of the security department or, in some cases, to the board of directors. This person is responsible for ensuring that users are complying with security policy and that the policy is adequate to prevent unauthorized access to company assets (including intellectual property, data, programs, and systems).

Quality Assurance

Quality-assurance personnel usually perform two functions. First they ensure that all personnel are following quality processes. As an example the QA personnel ensure that the IT department adheres to standards and procedures for IP addressing conventions. Second, quality-control personnel are responsible for testing and review, to verify that software is free of defects and meets user expectations. All functional and operational testing is performed as part of the SDLC and must be complete before systems go into production.

Applications

The applications function is divided into two categories: Systems programmers are responsible for maintaining operating systems and systems software. Application programmers are responsible for developing new systems and maintaining applications that are in production.

In keeping with proper segregation of duties, managers must ensure that application programmers use a code library (test-only) while creating and updating code, and that they do not have access to production programs. The test-only programs should be reviewed and put into production by a separate group. Systems programmers should have access to entire systems, and management should use compensating controls such as access and change logs to monitor and ensure that they have access to only the system libraries for which they are responsible. The use of a compensating control reduces the risk associated with a control that is not adequate. Another example of compensating controls is a risk associated with unauthorized viewing of sensitive data. Although access controls are in place, there is a possibility that unauthorized users might still review sensitive data. To compensate for limitations of access controls, additional controls can be added:

➤ Extensive risk analysis on the systems containing sensitive data

➤ Increased supervisory review of access logs and application-level audit reports

Systems analysts are involved during the initial phase of the systems-development life cycle and ensure that the needs of users are incorporated into the system or application requirements and high-level design documents.

Data Management

The database administrator (DBA) is responsible for defining data structures and for maintaining those structures in the organization's database systems. The DBA acts as a data custodian by ensuring that database design, structure, relationships, and maintenance support the needs of the organization and its users, and for maintaining the quality and security of data. The DBA generally has access to all of the organization's data, both test and production. Although it is not practical to prohibit access to the data, management should implement compensating controls to monitor DBA activities. These controls can include using access logs, logging structural changes to databases, and applying detective controls over the use of database tools.

Technical Support

Technical support personnel fall into three categories. The first and most common are the help desk technicians. The help desk is responsible for assisting end users with problems or issues with desktops or workstations, and personnel frequently participate in configuring and deploying new equipment, operating systems, and applications. Network administrators are responsible for the network infrastructure, which includes routers, switches, and firewalls. They are also responsible for the performance of the network, as well as redundancy, proper network segmentation, and backups of critical systems. In smaller organizations, network administrators might be responsible for security administration of the systems, including firewall configuration, access control, and authorization activities. Systems administrators are responsible for maintaining the systems that provide services to the organization. These can include file/print sharing, email, and virus prevention and detection. The administrator can add or remove users (set up user accounts), grant access to resources, install system-wide software, and allocate storage.

Operations

The operations group is responsible for computer operations and usually includes computer operators, librarians, and data entry operators. A majority of the organization's information, or input/output, is maintained by the operations group and can include data input, report generation, data output via magnetic media, and operations activities scheduling.

Segregation of Duties

Segregation of duties is an important means by which fraudulent or malicious acts can be discouraged or prevented.

A common example of improper segregation of duties is allowing a single person within operations or the help desk to have the responsibility of ordering hardware/software, receiving and managing asset or inventory control. This type of structure could allow a single person to order and receive IT equipment without adding it to the asset-control system and, therefore, creates the opportunity for theft of equipment. In small organizations in which proper segregation of duties is not possible, the IT department must set up compensating controls. In this instance, the IT department could institute a daily/weekly review of all orders by a manager, to ensure that equipment is being added to the asset-control system.

The structure of the organization must consider segregation of incompatible duties, keeping in mind that segregation between operations and programming, as an example, might not be possible in smaller environments. The use of compensating controls, such as audit trails, might be acceptable to mitigate the risk that exists because of improper segregation of duties. IT functions such as systems development, computer operations, and security should be segregated.

The primary purpose of audit trails is to establish accountability and responsibility for processed transactions.

IS Auditing Practices and Techniques

An auditor can perform a variety of audit types. Our primary topic is IT auditing, but it is important to understand the procedures associated with each type of audit:

> ➤ **Financial audit**—A financial audit often involves detailed, substantive testing. This kind of audit relates to information integrity and reliability; its purpose is to assess the correctness of the organization's financial statements.

> ➤ **Operation audit**—An operation audit is designed to evaluate the internal control structure in a given process or area. IS audits of application controls or logical security systems are examples of operation audits.

> ➤ **Integrated audit**—An integrated audit combines the testing of controls and substantive testing for the completeness, validity, and integrity of the information. An SAS 94 audit is an example of an integrated audit.

> ➤ **Administrative audit**—This audit assesses issues related to the efficiency of operation productivity within an organization.

> ➤ **Information systems audit**—This process collects and evaluates evidence to determine whether information systems and related resources adequately safeguard assets, maintain data and system integrity, provide relevant and reliable information, achieve organizational goals effectively, consume resources efficiently, and have in effect internal controls that provide reasonable assurance that business, operation, and control objectives will be met.

➤ **Compliance audit**—Compliance auditing involves an integrated series of activities focused on investigating and confirming whether products or services comply with internal policy or external guidelines or laws. Sarbanes-Oxley and the Health Insurance Portability Act are examples of external laws that require compliance.

Per ISACA, a CISA candidate will not be asked about specific laws or regulations but may be questioned about how one would audit for compliance with laws and regulations. The examination tests knowledge of only accepted global practices.

Audit Planning and Management Techniques

The IS auditor should follow an IT audit life cycle in the planning, assessment, and execution of the audit. The audit life cycle should include the following steps:

1. Plan

2. Assess risk

3. Prepare and plan an audit program

4. Conduct a preliminary review of the audit area/subject

5. Evaluate the audit area/subject

6. Gather evidence

7. Conduct compliance testing

8. Conduct substantive testing

9. Form conclusions

10. Deliver audit opinion (communicate results)

11. Follow up

Per ISACA, proper planning is the necessary first step in performing effective audits. The IS auditor's first task should be to gather background information, such as business sector, applied benchmarks, specific trends, and regulatory and legal requirements. This enables the auditor to better understand what to audit. After gathering initial information, the auditor should identify the audit subject and audit objectives, define the scope, establish the information systems and functions involved, and identify the needed resources.

In preparation for the audit, the auditor should either use an existing audit methodology or create one. The *audit methodology* is a set of documented audit procedures to ensure that the auditor achieves the planned audit objectives. Establishment of the audit methodology encompasses all phases of the audit and creates a repeatable, consistent approach to audits in the organization. The methodology should be documented and approved by the audit management and should be communicated to the audit staff.

Table 1.3 lists the phases of a typical audit.

Table 1.3 Phases of an Audit	
Audit Subject	**Identification of the Audit Area(s)**
Audit objective	Identify the reason for the audit. For example, an objective might be that access to intellectual property is properly controlled.
Audit scope	Identify the systems or functions of the organization included in the review.
Preaudit planning	Identify the skill sets and resources required.
	Identify the information sources—policies, procedures, project plans, logs, and so on.
	Identify the locations or facilities included in the audit.
Audit procedures and steps for gathering data	Identify and select the process to verify and test controls. Identify the individuals to interview.
	Identify and obtain policies, standards, and procedures.
	Develop audit procedures to verify and test controls.
Procedures for evaluating the test or review results	Identify a process for review and evaluation of auditing results.
Procedures for communication with management	Develop procedures for the communication of the audit report. Develop procedures for communication during the audit process.
Audit report preparation	Identify follow-up.
	Identify procedures to evaluate/test operational efficiency and effectiveness.
	Identify procedures to test controls.
	Review and evaluate the soundness of documents, policies, and procedures.

Using the audit methodology, the auditing department can create boundaries for the audit, ensure consistent processes, and identify specific steps to be performed during the audit. The combined effect is that the auditing function has a trail of what entities were audited, who was interviewed, what material was collected, and how controls were verified. This ensures that the audit report is complete without exceeding the audit boundaries, and provides confidence that the procedures that were followed met the objectives of the audit.

A risk-based audit approach helps management effectively utilize limited auditing resources by identifying areas of high risk in the organization. This method helps prioritize audits, and information gathered from risk analysis facilitates more effective corporate governance by ensuring that audit activities are directed to high business risk areas, maximizing the effectiveness of audit activities.

In a risk-based approach to auditing, the IS auditor gains an understanding of the client's environment and information systems, and determines which areas are high-risk, or material. These areas then become the focus of the audit. The alternative to the risk-based approach is for the auditing department to evaluate the organization's entire environment and operating system. This is often referred to as the "old model" of auditing. In planning an audit, the *most* critical step is to identify the areas of high risk. The IS auditor should use the following risk-based approach to creating an audit plan:

1. Gather information and plan.

    A. Knowledge of business and industry

    B. Audit results from earlier years

    C. Recent financial information

    D. Regulatory statutes

    E. Inherent risk assessments

2. Determine internal controls and obtain an understanding of how they function.

    A. Control environment

    B. Control procedures

    C. Detection risk assessment

    D. Control risk assessment

    E. Equate total risk

3. Perform compliance tests.

4. Perform substantive tests.

5. Conclude the audit.

The ISACA IS auditing guideline on planning the IS audit states, "An assessment of risk should be made to provide reasonable assurance that material items will be adequately covered during the audit work. This assessment should identify areas with relatively high risk of existence of material problems."

Information Systems Audits

During an information systems audit, the IS auditor should review the internal control environment of information systems and the use of these systems. The IS audits usually evaluate processing controls, system input/output backup and recovery plans, and security. Four main types of audits are used in reviewing information systems:

➤ **Attestation**—The auditor provides assurance on something for which the client is responsible. This type of audit is considered a compliance audit and can ensure internal or external compliance.

➤ **Finding and recommendation**—This is a consulting or advisory engagement in which the auditor performs a less structured type of engagement, such as a systems-implementation engagement.

➤ **SAS 94**—This type of audit is referred to as an integrated audit. Typically, this is part of a regular financial audit, in which the auditor must evaluate controls around a client's information system and the entries that are processed through that system.

Attestation

The objective of a true attestation audit is to render an opinion on whether the reader of the statement or report can be reasonably sure that the information contained in the report is correct. An attestation audit can include reports on descriptions of systems of internal controls and compliance with statutory, contractual, or regulatory requirements.

Types of attestation audits include the following:

➤ Data analytic reviews

➤ Commission agreement reviews

➤ WebTrust engagements

➤ Systrust engagements

➤ Financial projections

➤ Compliance reviews

An example of attestation standards is the WebTrust audit standards introduced by the American Institute of Certified Public Accountants (AICPA) and the Canadian Institute of Chartered Accountants (CICA). The AICPA/CICA WebTrust provides a set of standards for reviewing e-commerce websites to ensure security, online privacy, availability, confidentiality, and process integrity. Auditors examine both the company and the e-commerce website with regard to business practices, transaction integrity, and information protection. If the site passes inspection per the AICPA statements on standards for attestation engagements, the auditor should create an independent accounts report for submission to the AICPA. The AICPA then issues a WebTrust seal to the website. This seal represents a third-party, AICPA, attestation that the website meets the AICPA/CICA standards.

Other types of attestation audits include compliance audits. In these audits, the auditor verifies that the organization's business practices have sufficient controls to meet contractual or regulatory standards. Regulatory standards might include HIPAA, Sarbanes-Oxley, GLBA, or others.

These types of auditing engagements require that the auditor clearly understand the business functions, have a high degree of technical proficiency, and be able to conduct security and integrity tests to verify that the systems meet the standards.

Findings and Recommendations

Findings and recommendations do not produce an opinion; they provide a summary of the work performed in connection with the engagement. These consulting or advisory types of engagements can include review of the following:

➤ System implementations

➤ Enterprise resource planning

➤ System security reviews

➤ Database application reviews

➤ Internal audit services

The IS auditor defines the audit objectives and, through the examination of sufficient, competent, and relevant information, testing, and other evaluations, develops the audit report. The IS auditor must understand the business functions, clearly define the audit objectives, and have the technical proficiency to conduct the required review and testing.

SAS 70

The Statement on Auditing Standards (SAS) 70, "Service Organizations," is a recognized auditing standard developed by AICPA. The SAS 70 audit or service auditor's examination is widely recognized and indicates that an organization has been through an in-depth audit of its control activities, including controls over IT and related processes. The opinions offered in an SAS 70 report can be created only by a Certified Public Accountant (CPA). Two types of SAS 70 audits exist, appropriately named Type I and Type II. In a Type I report, the IS auditor expresses an opinion on whether the organization's description of its controls is aligned with the controls that are actually in place and whether the controls achieve the specified control objectives. In a Type II report, the IS auditor expresses an opinion on the items in Type I and whether the controls that were tested were operating effectively to provide reasonable assurance that the control objectives were achieved.

The SAS 70 report is an independent third-party review of the organization's controls and states that the controls meet the control objectives. This report helps the organization build trust with customers and third-party partners. The specialization of IT services and outsourcing of some or part of those services means an increased reliance on partners; a service organization might have to entertain audit requests from partners or customers as a condition of providing services. The SAS 70 audit ensures that the service organization will not have to perform multiple audits at the request of potential partners and customers, and that all potential partners and customers will have access to the same information about the organization's business practices and controls.

SAS 94

The Statement on Auditing Standards (SAS) 94, "The Effect of Information Technology on the Auditor's Consideration of Internal Control in a Financial Statement Audit," amends SAS 55 and provides guidance to auditors on the impact of IT on internal controls. The SAS 94 audit complies with the SAS 55 requirement to obtain an understanding of the five internal control components: the control environment, risk assessment, control activities, information and communication monitoring, and how IT impacts the overall audit strategy. For this reason, the SAS 94 is considered an integrated audit. In other words, the IS auditor must ensure that the information provided by IT systems is accurate and complete, and also must understand what procedures (whether manual or automated) were used in preparing the financial statements. The SAS 94 standard acknowledges that IT systems and their associated controls can be so significant that the quality of the audit evidence depends on those controls and that the IT process for managing and creating financial statements has a major influence on the audit.

The IS auditor should examine IT system controls and determine whether the controls prevent unauthorized access to menus, programs, and data:

➤ Destruction or improper changes

➤ Unauthorized, nonexistent, or inaccurate transactions

➤ Errors or fraud

The IS auditor needs a high degree of technical proficiency to integrate an SAS 94 audit. During the audit planning, the IS auditor should identify the types of misstatements that could occur and should consider the factors that affect the risk of material misstatement. In addition, the auditor should identify controls that are likely to prevent or detect material misstatement in specific assertions and should test those controls. In addition, the auditor must understand both the business practices and the manual and automated processes used in creating the financial statements.

 | The CISA Exam might not ask specifically about audit types (SAS 70 and SAS 94), but it is important to understand the difference between audit types. Additional information can be found on the American Institute of Certified Public Accountants website, www.aicpa.org.

Attribute Sampling

Attribute sampling deals with the rate of occurrence or frequency of items that have a certain attribute. The attribute either is there or is not. The policy/procedure either exists or does not. Attribute sampling is the primary sampling method used for compliance testing.

When the IS auditor uses attribute sampling, the results are expressed as a sample frequency or error rate. An example of expressing an error rate is review system logs in which one event, such as a daily backup, is not logged 1 day in 100. This would represent a 1% sample error rate. There may be 1,000 logs to review, so the IS auditor must choose a sample (100 logs) of the total population (1,000 logs); the error rate of the sample population is most likely to be the same error rate for the entire population because the sample population should be representative of the entire population.

Variable Sampling

Variable sampling deals with variations in some unit of measure. As an example, system logs should have time stamps for the start and end of backups on a given day. Those times might vary, depending on the type of backup or the amount of data backed up.

When the IS auditor uses variable sampling, a random sample can produce results that can be expressed as a percentage. Going back to the example of the backups when using variable sampling, the auditor would choose a sample (100 logs) of the total population (1,000 logs), sampling only the same type of backups (daily), and would sample the start and end times of the backup. The results of the random sample might show that on 10 out of the 100 days reviewed, the backups took 50% less time. This percentage of the sample population is most likely to be the same percentage of the entire population.

As the IS auditor gathers samples from the environment, it is important to ensure that the sample population is representative of the total population. The sampling confidence coefficient is a percentage expression of the probability that the characteristics of the sample are considered a true representation of the population. If the organization has stronger controls, there will be less reliance on sampling, which will allow for a smaller accepted sample size (confidence coefficient). If the strength of controls is not known, the auditor must choose a larger sample size to provide a greater confidence coefficient. The confidence coefficient is expressed in percentages; a 95% confidence coefficient is considered a high degree of confidence. If incorrect assumptions are made about a population that the sample is selected from, this introduces sampling risk. Sampling risk is calculated using this formula:

Sampling risk = 1 − Confidence coefficient

 If an auditor knows that internal controls are strong, the auditor risks less detection error, resulting in a decrease in reliance on sampling. Therefore, smaller samples can be used even though the confidence coefficient is lowered for the sampling process.

So what have we learned from these particular samples? In the case of error sampling, there are days when the backups either are not logged or do not run for some reason, introducing risk into the environment by either not being able to recover from a data error (backup not running) or not being able to ensure that the backups are actually running (not logging). When reviewing the results of variable sampling, we find that daily backups that should require approximately the same amounts of time for backup do not.

Assuming that there have not been significant changes in the amount of data being backed up, the results of variable sampling might indicate errors in the backup program. The cause of these errors could include the exclusion of data that should be backed up or start and end times not logged correctly 10% of the time.

Substantive Tests

Substantive testing substantiates the integrity of actual processing, sometimes called *transaction integrity*. This type of testing provides an appropriate assurance of detecting the possibility of material errors. Neither attribute nor variable sampling is a perfect fit for substantive testing because attribute sampling measures frequencies/percentages, not value, and variable sampling measures averages. The IS auditor can use one or both sampling methods combined with observation and interviews as a part of substantive testing.

Compliance Tests

Compliance testing tests controls in the environment, to ensure that they are being applied in a manner that complies with the organization's policies and procedures. Using the examples discussed in sampling, the auditor tests to see that backups are backing up all data and logging in accordance with back-up policies and business continuity planning. The IT auditor used both types of testing (attribute and variable) to meet the compliance testing objective.

A distinction that can be made between compliance testing and substantive testing is that compliance testing tests controls, whereas substantive testing tests details.

IS auditors are *most* likely to perform compliance tests of internal controls if, after their initial evaluation of the controls, they conclude that control risks are within the acceptable limits.

Another example of compliance testing involves obtaining a list of current users with access to the network or applications and verifying that those listed are current employees.

Audit Conclusions

After reviewing documentation, performing testing, and completing interviews and observations, the auditor is ready to form conclusions. This process involves identifying information that is material to the audit scope and issues that represent substantial control weaknesses. Per ISACA Guideline 50, *materiality* in an IT audit is determined in a qualitative manner as it relates to controls around the information system. A control is deemed material if its absence prevents control objectives from being met; the auditor determines materiality for an information system or operation that processes financial transactions by assessing the value of the assets controlled by the system or the volume of transactions processed through the system. As a part of the report conclusions, the auditor must draft a management letter; any material misstatements in the financial statements should be reported to management immediately. Management then evaluates responses to the findings, states corrective actions to be taken, and determines the timing for implementing these anticipated corrective actions.

Per ISACA Guidelines 70, the audit opinion should include the following:

➤ Name of the organization

➤ Title, signature, and data

➤ Statement of audit objectives and whether these were met

➤ Scope of the audit

➤ Any scope limitations

➤ Intended audience

➤ Standards used to perform the audit

➤ Detailed explanation of findings

➤ Conclusion, including reservations or qualifications

➤ Suggestions for corrective action or improvement

➤ Significant subsequent events

Obtaining Evidence

In the normal course of an audit, the auditor should obtain specific documentation relating to the audit area. This information should be sufficient, reliable, relevant, and useful to achieve the audit objectives; it can include earlier audits, business plans, financial information, policies and procedures, results of test procedures, interviews, and observations. Gathering background information pertinent to the new audit is the first task an IS auditor should complete when performing an audit in an unfamiliar area. The information obtained is collectively known as *evidence*. The audit methodology and audit plan state the process and specific objectives of the audit. Sometimes there might be insufficient evidence or evidence that was gathered outside the scope of the audit and that, therefore, would not have relevance in the audit report.

Earlier audit reports are considered of lesser value to an IS auditor attempting to gain an understanding of an organization's IT process than evidence directly collected.

In the event of insufficient evidence, the auditor might not be able to meet the objectives of the audit. In other words, the evidence gathered would be insufficient to determine whether the controls were at the appropriate level. Although all the evidence obtained will help the auditor reach the audit conclusion, not all evidence has the same level of reliability. The reliability of evidence is based on the following criteria:

➤ **Independence of the provider of the evidence**—Evidence gained from outside the organization being audited is generally more reliable than evidence gained internally, as long as that evidence is gained from a reliable source. As a general rule, outside entities do not have a vested interest in the outcome of the audit.

As an example, a confirmation letter received from an outside source is usually considered more reliable than evidence provided by the client being audited.

➤ **Qualification of the individual providing the information/ evidence**—Regardless of whether the individual providing the evidence is inside or outside the organization, the qualification of the individual determines the reliability of the evidence. This is also true of the auditor: If the auditor does not have a thorough grasp of the area being audited or the results of testing in that area, he or she might not collect the evidence required or might misunderstand the results of the test.

➤ **Objectivity of the evidence**—A variety of types of evidence is collected, and the objectivity of the evidence makes it more reliable. If tests are performed against account balances or a specific security control, this is more objective than interviews with personnel on account balances or the effectiveness or relevance of the security control.

➤ **Timing of evidence**—Some evidence might not be available because of internal procedures properly eliminating evidence or fairly high rates of change regarding the evidence. The timing of evidence collection might not coincide with the audit plan and timeline.

During the audit, evidence should be collected from a variety of sources to meet the audit objectives. Regardless of the type of evidence collected, the auditor should stay focused on the objectives, not the nature of the evidence. Some of the evidence-gathering techniques include review of IS organization structures, to look for proper segregation of duties, and review of IS policies, procedures, and standards. These policies and standards can include IS development documents, test plans and reports, program change logs and histories, user and operations manuals, security policies, and QA reports. In addition, the auditor should interview the appropriate personnel and observe processes and employee performance. The combination of this information should provide a clear view of the function being audited at a variety of levels and ensure that there is correlation and consistency among the actual operations, controls, and written policy/procedures.

 The purpose and scope of the audit determines the extent to which data will be collected during an IS audit.

Organization's Use of System Platforms, IT Infrastructure, and Applications

For the auditor to understand the IT organization, he or she must gather information at various levels within the IT organization. A strong understanding of the organizational structure, policies, procedures, and standards enables the auditor to meet the outlined objectives.

The auditor should review the organizational structure to ensure segregation of duties and to identify personnel authority and responsibility. Firsthand evidence such as observation and interviews usually provides the best evidence of the segregation of duties in an IS department.

Further review of individual job descriptions provides specific levels of authority and tasks that specific individual should perform. A review of the policies provides a high-level overview of the guidance provided to all personnel within the functional area, as well as any controls that are applied. IS auditors are *most* likely to perform compliance tests of internal controls if, after their initial evaluation of the controls, they conclude that control risks are within the acceptable limits. The procedures and standards are a further definition of policies and one of the ways to ensure consistent application of policies within the IT organization. Figure 1.2 shows the top-down integration of strategic plans, policies, and procedures.

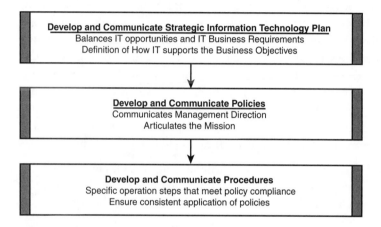

Develop and Communicate Strategic Information Technology Plan
Balances IT opportunities and IT Business Requirements
Definition of How IT supports the Business Objectives

Develop and Communicate Policies
Communicates Management Direction
Articulates the Mission

Develop and Communicate Procedures
Specific operation steps that meet policy compliance
Ensure consistent application of policies

Figure 1.2   Policy diagram.

Techniques to Gather Information and Preserve Evidence

A clear understanding of the organizational structure, functions, and strategy is important in gathering information. The auditor uses a variety of techniques to gather and correlate information, and the auditor is responsible for assessing both the quantity (*sufficient*) and the quality (*competent*) of the evidence gathered. Competent evidence is both valid and relevant to the audit objectives. Audit judgment is used to determine when the sufficiency is accomplished. The auditor should be aware of the different types of evidence gathered and the rules of evidence because both the audit findings and the conclusions are supported by this evidence.

The auditor should review information pertaining to the organizational structure, to ensure adequate segregation of duties. This is a key control in the IS environment. The auditor should understand both general and specific controls, to be able to evaluate the overall effectiveness of these controls. The organizational structure and job descriptions provide specific information on the daily roles and responsibilities for the IS organization.

Organizations invest heavily in developing, acquiring, and maintaining critical systems that support critical functions. Extreme care should be exercised in managing IT applications in order to minimize risk and maximize return on investment. Software business risk is the likelihood that the new system will not meet the applications user's business needs, requirements, or expectations, and is often caused by a lack of discipline in managing the software-development process. Lack of discipline from poor management can result in scope creep, introducing the risk of the project exceeding the time and cost estimates originally provided for the project. The auditor should review policies and procedures to ensure that the objectives of the strategic plan are being met. The auditor should review standards and look for a minimum level of information systems documentation. The systems development life cycle (SDLC) defines how the organization acquires, develops, changes, and implements IT infrastructure and applications. This documentation addresses how the IS organization functions and can include the following:

➤ **Phase 1: Feasibility study**—The feasibility study enables management to identify and quantify the cost savings of a new system, and estimate the payback schedule for costs incurred in implementing the system.

➤ **Phase 2: Requirements definition**—The requirements definition maps the major requirements to the solution. It involves management and end users to make sure the new system will support the business needs. Users specify automated and nonautomated resource needs and how they want to have them addressed in the new system. A requirements definition should ensure that the requirements are complete, consistent, unambiguous, verifiable, modifiable, testable, and traceable. A review of the requirements definition allows the auditor to determine whether adequate security requirements have been defined for the new system.

➤ **Phase 3: System design**—The requirements gathered in Phase 2 assist in establishing a baseline of system and subsystem specifications that describe the parts of the system, how they interact, and how the system will be implemented using the chosen hardware, software, and network facilities. The design phase is normally involved in the translation of the user requirements in IT terms; this will be the foundation needed for the development of the system.

➤ **Phase 4: Development**—In the system-development phase, the programming and testing take place. The testing verifies and validates what has been developed. The responsibilities primarily rest with the programmers and system analysts who are building the system.

The programmers should use program-coding standards, which are essential to simply and clearly read and understand code without requiring specification review. Programmers should design the code with more cohesion (dedication to a single function) and less coupling (interaction with other functions), resulting in less troubleshooting and software maintenance. Online programming facilities increase programming productivity, lower development cost, reduce response time, and expand programming resources available, but they can increase risk of inappropriate access and version control. This risk can lead to reduced integrity of programming and processing, and valid changes can be overwritten by invalid changes.

Different types and levels of testing exist for new applications. Bottom-up testing tests programs or modules while progressing toward testing the entire system. Bottom-up testing allows for a modular approach to testing and can be started before the entire system is complete; it detects errors in critical modules early. Top-down testing tests major functions or processes early in the development, and detects interface errors sooner.

Testing at different levels and with separate testing elements ensures that the system meets the performance requirements (performance testing), that it can be recovered (recovery testing), and that it meets the security requirements (security testing). Basic testing elements include these:

> ➤ **Whitebox testing**—Logical paths through the software are tested using test cases that exercise specific sets of conditions and loops.

> ➤ **Blackbox testing**—This testing examines an aspect of the system with regard to the internal logical structure of the software.

> ➤ **Function/validation testing**—This tests the functionality of the system against the detailed requirements.

> ➤ **Regression testing**—A portion of the test scenarios is rerun, to ensure that changes or corrections have not introduced new errors.

> ➤ **Parallel testing**—Test data is fed into both the new and old systems, and the results are compared.

➤ **Phase 5: Implementation**—Implementation is the final phase in the system development lifecycle. This phase puts the new system into operation. It includes final user acceptance testing and can include certification and accreditation processes. The tasks in this phase measure to ensure that the system meets the intended objectives and establishes appropriate levels of internal control.

The auditor should look for evidence of a structured approach to applications management with defined life-cycle phases and progression points. Advantages to the auditor of such an approach include the following:

➤ The IS auditor's influence is increased when there are formal procedures and guidelines identifying each phase in the application life cycle and the extent of auditor involvement.

➤ The IS auditor can review all relevant areas and phases of the systems-development project and can report independently to management on the adherence to planned objectives and company procedures.

If controls are lacking as a result of the organizational structure or of the software methods used, or if the processes are disorderly (informal), the IS auditor must advise the project management team and senior management of the deficiencies. It might also be necessary to notify those involved in the development and acquisition activities of appropriate controls or processes.

 IS auditors involved actively in the design and implementation of the application system risk having their independence impaired.

Control Objectives and Controls Related to IS (Such as Preventative and Detective)

The combination of organizational structure, policies and procedures, and best practices that are implemented to reduce risk is called *internal controls*. Internal controls are used by the organization to provide a reasonable assurance that the business objectives will be met and risk will be prevented, detected, or corrected. Preventative control objectives detect problems before they arise, monitor both operations and inputs, and prevent errors, omissions, or malicious acts from occurring. Using an access-control system (think user/password combination) is an example of a preventative control. Detective controls are used to detect and report the occurrence of an error, omission, or malicious act. Using audit trails is an example of a detective control. Corrective controls minimize the impact of threat, identify the cause of a problem, and modify the system to minimize future occurrences of the problem. Using a rollback facility in a database environment is an example of a corrective control. When evaluating the collective effect of preventative, detective, or corrective controls within a process, an IS auditor should be aware of the point at which controls are exercised as data flows through the system.

Internal controls operate at all levels of the organization and should be continuously monitored to ensure their effectiveness. The auditor should be primarily concerned with the overall strength of the control or combination of controls to ensure that it meets its stated objective. Control procedures can be manual or automated and generally fall into three categories:

➤ **Internal accounting controls**—Primarily used in accounting operations. They apply to safeguarding the assets and reliability of financial data and records.

➤ **Operational controls**—Used in day-to-day operations to ensure that the operation is meeting business objectives.

➤ **Administrative controls**—Used to ensure compliance with management policy.

As an example, access controls are implemented to ensure confidentiality, integrity, and availability of information systems and their associated data. Confidentiality is the assurance that the information will not be disclosed to unauthorized individuals, programs, or processes. Integrity ensures that the data is not altered in an unauthorized way. Availability ensures timely access to information by authorized users, programs, or processes. Table 1.4 identifies specific controls, how they are implemented, and their classification (preventative, detective, corrective).

Table 1.4	Controls					
Area	**Transaction Type**	**Control Objective**	**Control Activity**	**Audit Procedure**	**Class**	**Method**
Information systems operations	Safeguard IT systems	Network access is restricted to authorized users and restricts unauthorized activity	Examine access policy. Users must fill out a system authorization form and be granted access by IS management.	Gather and review samples of the system operations form. Compare the form to identify users who have current access and current employees of the organization.	Preventative	Manual

(continued)

Table 1.4	Controls *(continued)*					
Area	Transaction Type	Control Objective	Control Activity	Audit Procedure	Class	Method
			IS management verifies users with access to a department listing provided by department managers, to ensure that access is appropriate and accurate.	Review previously completed access verification audit results, and determine that appropriate IS management approval was obtained and that exceptions were properly resolved.	Detective	Manual
			Audit logging is enabled for both successful and unsuccessful access, and access to the logs is restricted to IS management.	Compare access logs against a list of current employees and users, and determine whether there are patterns of unsuccessful access (password guessing) or successful access during inappropriate hours or from unauthorized systems or networks.	Corrective	Manual

Internal control objectives define the desired purpose or desired outcome associated with the implementation of the control. Table 1.5 outlines control objectives, their associated activities, and the audit procedures.

Table 1.5 Example of a Control Matrix

Control Objectives	Control Activities	Audit Procedures
1. Independent Management Reviews		
Management should perform periodic independent reviews (including internal and external audits) of IT operations, to ensure that policies and procedures have been implemented and are working effectively.	Management establishes a schedule for periodic independent reviews of the IT operations. Management establishes formal follow-up procedures, to ensure that identified deficiencies are addressed in a timely manner.	a. Evaluate IT's policies and procedures, internal review schedules, and so on, to determine whether they provide periodic independent reviews of the IT operations and follow up on identified deficiencies.
2. Organization		
Duties and responsibilities should be adequately segregated so that no one person can perpetrate and conceal material errors or misstatements.	Management ensures that duties and responsibilities are segregated within the information systems department, to avoid perpetration and concealment of errors.	a. Evaluate the organization structure to determine whether the information technology (IT) department reports at a high enough level to allow it to act independently. This procedure does not evaluate the existence of the control activity described in the same row. A more appropriate audit procedure is to review the organizational structure, review the job descriptions within the IT department, and evaluate whether duties are adequately segregated.
3. Software Acquisition, Development, and Modification		
System and application software should be consistent with management objectives, should operate within specifications, should be tested before implementation, and should not be susceptible to unauthorized modification.	Management establishes and maintains a standard development methodology that contains the following control elements: • Written requirements/ specifications reviewed and approved by application users and management • Participation of appropriate user and management personnel throughout all phases of	b. If the preliminary risk assessment indicates that further audit effort is necessary, examine at least one recent major software acquisition, development, or modernization project to determine the following: (1.) Whether written requirements and specifications were reviewed and approved by applicable users and management (2.) Whether appropriate IT user and management personnel participated throughout all phases of the software acquisition, development, or modification

(continued)

Table 1.5 Example of a Control Matrix *(continued)*		
Control Objectives	**Control Activities**	**Audit Procedures**
	software acquisition, development, and modification • Documentation for all software programs, including purchased software and modifications to existing software • Validation, verification, and testing by management and information systems personnel, to determine that software operates in conformity with design specifications and meets user requirements • Final written approval from management, users, and information systems personnel before implementation	(3.) Whether all software programs, including purchased software and modifications to existing software, are documented (4.) Whether validation, verification, and testing was performed by management, users, and IT personnel, to determine that the software operates in conformity with design specifications and meets user requirements (5.) Whether final written approval from management, users, and IT personnel was obtained before implementation

The first step in aligning IT with an organization's corporate goals is having and working on an appropriate level of planning. The IT department should have long-range (three- to five-year) and short-range (one-year) plans. These plans should provide specific solutions that ensure the growth and profitability of the organization, as well as identify both internal and external opportunities and controls that meet the organizational objectives.

Establishing a sound IT management methodology through sound project management and IT organizational policies ensures that organizational goals are fulfilled and business risks are reduced. IT managers must define roles and articulate the value of the IT function. The roles and responsibilities must have clearly defined job descriptions and authority levels, and must incorporate proper segregation of duties.

A high-level steering committee should be formed to ensure that the IS department closely supports the corporate mission and objectives:

➤ The committee should include various senior managers representing all organizational business areas.

➤ Duties and responsibilities should be defined in a formal charter.

➤ The committee should not become involved in routine operations.

➤ The committee should monitor major projects and the status of IS project plans and budgets; establish priorities; approve policies, standards, and procedures; and monitor overall IS performance.

➤ The committee should act as a liaison between the IS department and user departments.

➤ Formal minutes of the IS steering committee meetings should be maintained to document the committee's activities and decisions, and to inform the board of directors of IS activities.

IS structures reflect the requirements of the organization. Figure 1.3 outlines a common structure to provide you with a definition of roles, responsibilities, and job types.

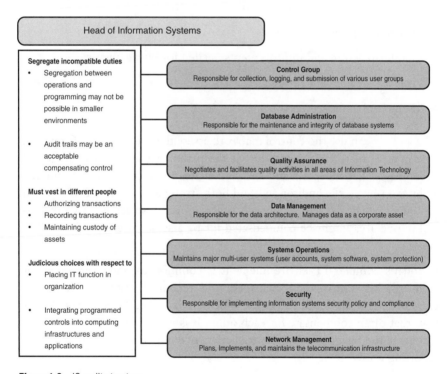

Figure 1.3   IS audit structure.

Reviewing the Audit

An important step before developing the audit conclusions is to evaluate the evidence gathered for strengths and weaknesses. The auditor must make judgments based primarily on experience. This review process is critical to the outcome of the findings and recommendations. ISACA's standard for IS auditing 030.020, Professional Care guides the auditor while performing the audit, along with the determination of strengths and weaknesses of the evidence.

The IS auditor might need a high degree of specialized technical proficiency and might need to provide consulting or advisory services with regard to the findings and recommendations. Auditors do not produce an opinion; they simply provide a summary of the work performed in connection with the engagement. The IS auditor might provide the following services:

➤ Systems implementation reviews

➤ Enterprise resource-planning implementations

➤ Security reviews (Enterprise, SAP, Oracle, Peoplesoft)

➤ Database application reviews

➤ IT infrastructure and improvements needed for engagements

➤ Project-management reviews

➤ IT internal audit services

The auditor can use the control matrix to assess the proper level of controls. The control matrix is created during the planning stages of the audit and encompasses known errors and known controls to detect errors. During the audit and review, the auditor will find both strong and weak controls, which should all be considered when evaluating the overall structure. A weak control in one area might be compensated for by a stronger control in another area.

In today's complex IT environment, it is common to find overlapping or compensating controls. IT managers and technical resources frequently employ defense-in-depth strategies, which are based on layered sets of controls that often compensate for each other. It is important for the auditor to recognize the relationship and overall effect of compensating controls before reporting a weakness.

Part of the review pertains to the materiality of the evidence. The question of materiality is based on the auditor's judgment but should be also based on the determination of what information would be pertinent to the different levels of management that the audit findings and recommendations will be communicated to.

As an example, an access-control weakness on a standalone computer at a remote site will be material to management at that site but might not be material to management at headquarters.

Communicating Audit Results

The IS auditor is ultimately responsible to senior management and to the audit committee of the board of directors. Before communicating the results to senior management, the IS auditor should discuss the findings with the management staff of the audited entity to gain agreement on the findings and to develop a course of corrective action.

An internal audit department that organizationally reports exclusively to the chief financial officer (CFO) rather than to an audit committee is very likely to have its audit independence questioned.

Because audit reports are the final work product of the audit process, it is imperative that the IS auditor be concerned with the following:

➤ Providing a balanced objective report based on the evidence that is material to the audit

➤ Ensuring that the facts presented in the report are correct

➤ Ensuring that recommendations are feasible and cost-effective

➤ Describing negative issues in conjunction with positive, constructive comments

➤ Focusing on improving processes and controls while reporting on controls already in place

➤ Ensuring independence in the reporting process

The structure and content of the report will vary by organization but will usually have the following parts:

➤ Introduction to the report

   ➤ Statement of audit objectives

   ➤ Statement of scope

   ➤ Period of audit coverage

   ➤ Statement on the nature and extent of the audit

   ➤ Statement of procedures examined during the audit

➤ Auditor's conclusion and opinion

   ➤ Adequacy of controls and procedures examined during the audit

➤ Auditor's reservations or qualifications

   ➤ Statement of whether the controls were adequate or inadequate

   ➤ Support for the conclusion and overall evidence

➤ Detailed audit findings

   ➤ Evidence included or not included in the report, based on materiality

   ➤ A restatement of the guidance provided by upper management

➤ Limitations to the auditor

   ➤ Any limitations of evidence, access, and so on

➤ Statement of the IS audit guidelines followed

The report might vary, depending on the audience to which it is presented and management guidance with regard to the report. The IS auditor might present findings and recommendations to the auditee, senior management, and the board of directors; in each case, the audit would contain not only a different focus, but possibly subsets of information gathered during the audit.

 As an example, if an auditor discovers that the organization's computers contain unauthorized software, the auditor should report the use of the unauthorized software to auditee management and highlight the need to prevent recurrence.

The audit report should provide specific recommendations to management. As a result of the findings and recommendations, management should create an action plan to implement corrective actions. Keep in mind that resource constraints might prevent management from implementing all the audit recommendations; however, the auditor should obtain a commitment with expected dates for corrective action.

An exit interview should be conducted at the conclusion of the audit. This provides the auditor with an opportunity to discuss the scope and the findings and recommendations of the audit. The exit interview also assures the auditor that the facts presented in the report are correct and that the recommendations are realistic (cost-effective), and establishes the implementation dates for corrective action.

Responsibility, authority, and accountability of the IS audit function must be documented and approved by the highest level of management.

Facilitating Risk Management and Control Practices

Risk can be defined as the possibility of something adverse happening. *Risk management* is the process of assessing risk, taking steps to reduce risk to an acceptable level (mitigation), and maintaining that acceptable level of risk. Earlier, this chapter defined the different types of risks, such as business risk and continuity risk. As a part of ongoing IT procedures, a formal risk-management process must be incorporated into the planning, acquisition, development, testing, and deployment of information systems. Organizations can choose to transfer, reject, reduce, or accept risks.

An example of transferring risk occurs when a company or individual purchases insurance. The company might purchase insurance on assets so that, in the event of theft, damage, or destruction, the asset can be replaced or repaired. The insurance might cover most of the asset, or the business might opt to pay a lower annual fee, thereby increasing the deductible on claims. The deductible on the claim would be the organization's residual risk.

IS, Business, and Audit Risk (Such as Threats and Impacts)

An effective risk-management program should enable the organization to realize its business objectives by doing the following:

➤ Better securing IT systems that store, process, or transmit organizational information

➤ Enabling management to make well-informed risk-management decisions to justify expenditures that are part of the IT budget

Risk management encompasses three processes: risk assessment, risk mitigation, and risk transference.

The risk-assessment process includes identifying information resources or assets that are vulnerable and might need protection. Assets are resources, processes, products, or computer infrastructures that an organization has determined must be protected. Identifying these assets includes prioritizing and might involve mission criticality/sensitivity or asset value. Examples of assets include the following:

➤ Hardware/software

➤ Information/data

➤ Services

➤ Organization documents

➤ Personnel

➤ Intellectual capital

➤ Inventory

➤ Cash

➤ Physical assets (buildings, equipment, and so on)

The next step in the process is defining the threats associated with the asset(s) and the probability of the exercise of vulnerabilities. A vulnerability is a weakness in internal controls that could be exploited by a threat to gain unauthorized access to information or disrupt systems. *Threats* are defined as a potential danger (hazard) to information systems; the hazard is something that increases the likelihood of loss. Threats can generally be classified as natural, environmental, or manmade; they have the potential to cause such harm to the asset as destruction, disclosure, modification, or disruption. Some common classes of threats can include these:

➤ Natural threats (fire, flood, earthquake, tornado)

➤ Environmental threats (power, smoke, explosion)

➤ Human threats (internal or external)

➤ (Intentional) Hacker, criminal, terrorist, ex-employee

➤ (Accidental) Errors, accidents, misuse

The result of a threat exercising a vulnerability is called an *impact*; this can result in a loss to the organization's resources. The impact might be quantitative (direct loss of money, opportunity, disruption) or qualitative (breach of legislation, damage to reputation, endangerment of staff, breach of confidence) and represents either a direct or an indirect loss to the organization.

After the resources, threats, vulnerabilities, and priorities have been established, the organization must determine whether the risk is acceptable; if not, the auditor should identify and evaluate the existing controls. This evaluation determines which controls, if any, should be implemented to further reduce risk or minimize the residual risk. These controls can be actions, devices, procedures, or techniques, and can be measured based on design strength or the likelihood of effectiveness. When evaluating the strength of controls, the IS auditor should consider whether the controls are preventative or detective, manual or programmed, and formal or informal (ad-hoc).

After the organization has applied controls to the resource through transfer or reduction, the remaining risk is called *residual* risk. The organization's management can use the presence of residual risk to identify areas that need additional control or less stringent controls (more cost-effective). The organization's acceptance of residual risk takes into account the organizational policy, risk-management plan and measurement, and the cost-effectiveness of implementing controls.

The objective of risk management is to mitigate risk to an acceptable level. Risk is mitigated, or reduced, by implementing cost-effective controls. IT managers, the steering committee, and auditors should implement a risk-management process with the goal of protecting the organization and its capability to perform its business functions, not just the organization's IT assets.

Risk-Analysis Methods, Principles, and Criteria

Senior management must support risk analysis in the organization for it to be successful. Risk analysis is the process of identifying risk in the organization, quantifying the impact of potential threats, and providing cost/benefit justification for the implementation of controls. The organization must establish the purpose of the risk-management program, which might vary by organization but should include specific objectives such as reducing the cost of insurance in the organization or ensuring that background-screening processes are cost-effective. Clearly defining the purpose of the program enables senior managers to evaluate the results of risk management and determine its effectiveness. Generally, the executive director working with the board of directors defines the purpose for the risk-management program. As with all programs in the organization, the risk-management program must have a person or team charged with developing and implementing the program. The risk-management committee and associated team will be utilized at all levels within the organization and will need the help of the operations staff and board members to identify areas of risk and develop suitable mitigation strategies.

Risk analysis can use either a quantitative approach, which attempts to assign real numbers to the cost of threats and the amount of damage, or a qualitative approach, which uses a ranking method to analyze the seriousness of the threat against the sensitivity of the asset.

As an example of a risk-management process, let's take a look at the identification of a critical asset, threats, and vulnerabilities, and the review of implementing controls.

The organization has servers located at one of its satellite offices in San Diego, California. The servers are critical to the organization's business objectives. Although redundant servers and data are available via a redundant facility, the organization wants to ensure that it can resume business operations in San Diego as quickly as possible. The organization has performed a vulnerability assessment of the servers in San Diego. The facility has not been hit by an earthquake, but it wants to identify the likelihood that it will and to identify specific controls to mitigate this risk. As a result of the vulnerability assessment, the organization discovered that a relatively small earthquake (leaving the facility intact) could cause disruption to the servers if the racks topple or are disconnected from the network. For this scenario, we review our summary of the risk equation:

Risk = Threat × Vulnerability × Cost of asset

Threat = Earthquake (5 in the last 15 years large enough to damage the facility or at least move or topple office equipment)

Vulnerability = Annualized rate of occurrence. 15 years ÷ 5 earthquakes = .33 expected earthquakes per year.

Cost of asset = Total hardware (rack + servers) = $35,000 + outage cost per day ($3,000) × 3 days (time to bring up secondary servers) = $9,000 + 35,000 = $42,000

The organization could put in place quite a few controls to mitigate the risk.

It could develop a hot site that contains up-to-date information from the servers in San Diego, at the cost of $125,000 annually. It could implement earthquake-proof controls (earthquake rack-mounting equipment), for a one-time cost of $5,000. The organization could move the servers from San Diego to another satellite office, headquarters, or hosting facility, for a one-time cost of $10,000 and an annual cost of $15,000.

All three solutions would mitigate the risk associated with earthquakes at the San Diego facility, but we will use our equation to identify which is cost-effective:

Threat = (15 ÷ 5) = Vulnerability = .33 × Cost of asset = 42,000 = 13,860

The equation states that the cost of the control should not exceed $13,860 annually, so we can compare this against the cost associated with the hot site ($125,000), the earthquake rack ($12,000), and the server move ($15,000), and readily identify that the earthquake rack-mounting is the most cost-effective control for this threat. Keep in mind that this scenario identifies only one threat and the cost of the control to mitigate that threat. In actuality, the total of all controls for all threats would be compared against the cost of the asset to determine cost-effectiveness.

Risk management is the process that allows IT managers to balance the operational and economic costs of protective measures and achieve gains in mission objectives by protecting the IT systems and data that support their organization's objectives.

Communication Techniques

To ensure that the information systems strategy aligns with the organization's goals, senior IT managers need to effectively communicate with senior management and the business functional areas. In this chapter, we have discussed some of the tools available to IT management and their role in enabling communications throughout the organization. The IT steering committee assists in providing clear guidance to the IT department, to ensure that acquisition and integration activities align with the organizational strategy. In addition, the senior managers of the IT steering committee receive regular status updates on projects in progress, the cost of projects, and issues that impact the critical path of those projects. The change-control board serves as another vehicle of communication to the organization. The change-control board reviews and documents changes at all levels of the IT infrastructure and regularly reviews milestones. In addition, the individual project manager maintains project schedules defining milestones and resources that are being utilized.

IT senior management should use this information to provide both status- and decision-based information for both formal and informal reporting to the organization. IT managers use real-time and historical reporting to show continuous improvement and provide ad-hoc information required by functional business areas to facilitate decision making. The better IT management understands the organization, particularly the individual business functions, the better it can provide timely and effective solutions.

The increased reliance on and integration of IT in business requires IT and senior management to make quicker decisions regarding IT infrastructure. The internal competition among the business functions for IT resources presents challenging and sometimes conflicting priorities. A strong line of communication will help the organization reduce conflict and ensure the efficient use of IT resources.

Personnel-Management Techniques

The term *information systems* is usually interpreted as the hardware/software and processes that provide data and services. An information system also includes the personnel who implement and maintain information systems. The organization should have organizational policies and procedures for hiring, termination, promotion, and retention. The existence of and adherence to these policies and procedures reduces overall risk for the organization and improves the quality of the staff. An organization that effectively communicates and enforces procedures ensures that the staff is as effective and efficient as possible; in turn, this improves the overall effectiveness and efficiency of information systems.

In addition to internal policies and procedures, organizations must develop policies that ensure compliance with external laws and regulations. Some internal policies might include the following:

➤ Employee handbooks

➤ Company visions and ethics statements

➤ Security policies

➤ Descriptions of employee benefits

➤ Vacation and holiday policies

➤ Rules on overtime

➤ Performance evaluation timelines and procedures

➤ Emergency procedures

➤ When disciplinary actions are taken

To protect itself, the organization should implement controls (hiring practices) to ensure that prospective employees have the skill sets and background necessary to perform the duties outlined in the job description. Some of these controls might include education verification, past job performance, and local and federal criminal checks. Upon hiring, the organization might implement confidentiality agreements or noncompete agreements, or bond employees to protect against losses due to theft, neglect, or errors.

As part of employees' introduction into the organization, they should be aware of promotion policies, training, required time reporting, and vacation procedures. In addition, the organization should schedule regular formal communication of company policies and procedures. This communication might take the form of required presentations, periodic reviews of all policies by the employees, or formal training.

Written policies relating to vacation and termination are important in reducing business risk. If employees are required to take regular vacations, it allows others to take over duties in their absence and reduces opportunity for that person to commit improper or illegal acts. It might also be possible to discover fraudulent activity, assuming that there is no collusion between employees. A termination policy ensures that, upon employee separation, the assets of the organization are protected. All keys and access badges must be turned in, and login and password information must be suspended or removed. Termination policies should include procedures for both voluntary and involuntary terminations. Involuntary or immediate terminations are an emotional time for the organizational management as well as the employee, and delineating specific procedures ensures that the employee is properly escorted from the premises, that the employee turns in all material owned by the organization, and that staff and security personnel receive notification regarding the employee's status.

Employees who know specifically what is required from them tend to be happier employees and, therefore, perform better than employees who are unaware of the organization's policies and procedures. As an IS auditor, you must look for the existence of personnel policies, the frequency of communication, and a formal process for change. While observing and questioning employees, you can determine whether the policies are communicated and observed by employees as they are performing within their functional areas.

Practice Questions

1. If an organization chooses to implement a control self-assessment program, the auditor should participate primarily as a:
   - ❏ A. Monitor
   - ❏ B. Facilitator
   - ❏ C. Project leader
   - ❏ D. The auditor should not participate in the organization's CSA program because doing so would create a potential conflict of interest.

   Answer: B. The traditional role of an IS auditor in a control self-assessment (CSA) should be that of a facilitator.

2. Which of the following elements must be present to properly log activities and achieve accountability for actions performed by a user?
   - ❏ A. Identification and authorization only
   - ❏ B. Authentication and authorization only
   - ❏ C. Identification and authentication only
   - ❏ D. Authorization only

   Answer: C. If proper identification and authentication are not performed during access control, no accountability can exist for any action performed.

3. When initially planning a risk-based audit, which of the following steps is MOST critical?
   - ❏ A. Evaluating the organization's entire environment as a whole
   - ❏ B. Establishing an audit methodology based on accepted frameworks, such as COBIT or COSO
   - ❏ C. Documenting procedures to ensure that the auditor achieves the planned audit objectives
   - ❏ D. The identification of the areas of high risk for controls failure

   Answer: D. In planning an audit, the MOST critical step is identifying areas of high risk.

4. What is the PRIMARY purpose of audit trails?
   - ❏ A. To better evaluate and correct audit risk resulting from potential errors the auditor might have committed by failing to detect controls failure
   - ❏ B. To establish a chronological chain of events for audit work performed
   - ❏ C. To establish accountability and responsibility for processed transactions
   - ❏ D. To compensate for a lack of proper segregation of duties

   Answer: C. Although secure audit trails and other logging are used as a compensatory control for a lack of proper segregation of duties, the primary purpose of audit trails is to establish accountability and responsibility for processed transactions.

5. Which of the following is the MOST appropriate type of risk to be associated with authorized program exits (trap doors)?

   ❏ A. Inherent
   ❏ B. Audit
   ❏ C. Detection
   ❏ D. Business

   Answer: A. Inherent risk is associated with authorized program exits (trap doors).

6. When performing an audit of an organization's systems, the auditor's first step should be to:

   ❏ A. Develop a strategic audit plan
   ❏ B. Gain an understanding of the focus of the business of the organization
   ❏ C. Perform an initial risk assessment to provide the foundation for a risk-based audit
   ❏ D. Determine and define audit scope and materiality

   Answer: B. The IS auditor's first step is to understand the business focus of the organization. Until the auditor has a good understanding of the organization's business goals, objectives, and operations, the auditor will not be able to competently complete any of the other tasks listed.

7. Which of the following risks results when the auditor uses an insufficient test procedure, resulting in the auditor's ill-informed conclusion that material errors do not exist, when, in fact, they do?

   ❏ A. Business risk
   ❏ B. Detection risk
   ❏ C. Audit risk
   ❏ D. Inherent risk

   Answer: B. Detection risk results when an IS auditor uses an inadequate test procedure and concludes that material errors do not exist when, in fact, they do.

8. Which of the following is considered the MOST significant advantage of implementing a continuous auditing approach?

   ❏ A. It can improve system security when used in time-sharing environments that process a large number of transactions.
   ❏ B. It can provide more actionable audit results because of the increased input from management and staff.
   ❏ C. It can identify high-risk areas that might need a detailed review later.
   ❏ D. It can significantly reduce the amount of resources necessary for performing the audit because time constraints are more relaxed.

   Answer: A. The PRIMARY advantage of a continuous audit approach is that it can improve system security when used in time-sharing environments that process a large number of transactions.

9. When an IS auditor finds evidence of minor weaknesses in controls, such as use of weak passwords, or poor monitoring of reports, which of the following courses of action is MOST appropriate for the auditor?

   - ❑   A.   Take corrective action by informing affected users and management of the controls vulnerabilities
   - ❑   B.   Realize that such minor weaknesses of controls are usually not material to the audit
   - ❑   C.   Immediately report such weaknesses to IT management
   - ❑   D.   Take no corrective action whatsoever, and simply record the observations and associated risk arising from the collective weaknesses into the audit report

   Answer: D. While preparing the audit report, the IS auditor should record the observations and the risk arising from the collective weaknesses.

10. Which of the following is considered to present the GREATEST challenge to using test data for validating processing?

   - ❑   A.   Potential corruption of actual live data
   - ❑   B.   Creation of test data that covers all possible valid and invalid conditions
   - ❑   C.   Test results being compared to expected results from live processing
   - ❑   D.   Data isolation issues associated with high-speed transaction processing

   Answer: B. Creating test data that covers all possible valid and invalid conditions is often the greatest challenge in using test data.

2

Management, Planning, and Organization of IS

Key concepts you will need to understand:

- ✓ Components of IS strategies, policies, standards, and procedures
- ✓ Processes for the development, deployment, and maintenance of IS strategies, policies, standards, and procedures
- ✓ IS project-management strategies and policies
- ✓ IT governance, risk management, and control frameworks
- ✓ IS problem- and change-management strategies and policies
- ✓ IS quality-management strategies and policies
- ✓ IS information security-management strategies and policies
- ✓ IS business continuity–management strategies and policies

- ✓ Contracting strategies, processes, and contract-management practices
- ✓ Roles and responsibilities of IS functions (for example, segregation of duties)
- ✓ Principles of IS organizational structure and design
- ✓ IS management practices, key performance indicators, and performance-measurement techniques
- ✓ Relevant legislative and regulatory issues (for example, privacy and intellectual property)
- ✓ Generally accepted international IS standards and guidelines

Techniques you will need to master:

- ✓ Evaluate the IS strategy and the process for its development, deployment, and maintenance to ensure that it supports the organization's business objectives
- ✓ Evaluate the IS policies, standards, and procedures, and the processes for their development, deployment and maintenance, to ensure that they support the IS strategy
- ✓ Evaluate IS management practices to ensure compliance with IS policies, standards, and procedures

- ✓ Evaluate IS organization and structure to ensure appropriate and adequate support of the organization's business requirements in a controlled manner
- ✓ Evaluate the selection and management of third-party services to ensure that they support the IS strategy

Strategy, Policies, Standards, and Procedures

The primary goal of auditing information systems is to determine whether IT processes support business requirements in the most effective and secure manner. As a starting point, the IS auditor should review the following:

➤ **Organization business plan**—Establish an understanding of the organization's mission and objectives.

➤ **IT strategic plan**—Establish both the short-term (one-year) and long-term (three- to five-year) plans.

➤ **Organizational charts**—Establish the responsibility and authority of individuals.

➤ **Job descriptions**—Establish responsibility and accountability for employee actions.

➤ **Policies/procedures**—Define strategic objectives in operational activities.

 Reviewing an audit client's business plan should be performed before reviewing an organization's IT strategic plan.

Strategic Planning

The goal of strategic planning is to ensure that the organization's long-term (three- to five-year) and short-term (one-year) strategies are defined in writing and that there is a regular review process. The strategic plans make sure that the organization meets its goals and objectives and, if there is a proper review cycle, reflect the current direction of the organization and its business units. Although the strategic objectives are the responsibility of senior management, the planning process should include the senior managers, managers of the business units, and IT managers. An organization's implementation of IT will be less likely to succeed if senior management is not committed to strategic planning. IT management then can align the IS strategy with the business strategy.

This sounds like a simple process, but a number of companies create both the business and IS strategy but do not have a process for regular review and update. Above all else, the IS strategy must support the business objectives of the organization. When performing an IS strategy audit, an IS auditor should review both short-term (one-year) and long-term (three- to five-year) IS strategies, interview appropriate corporate management personnel, and ensure that the external environment has been considered. The auditor should not focus on actual procedures during an audit of IS strategy.

Policies and procedures define the actual operational implementation of the strategic plan and, like the strategic plan, should have a formal process for creation, communication, and review. As stated earlier, policies and procedures are subject to change more often than the strategic plan as they guide operational activities. An IS auditor not only reviews the policies and procedures, but through interview and observation, the auditor also determines whether the procedures are being followed, aligns them with the strategic plan, and guides current operational activities. In addition to creating a formal process for review and update, the auditor should be able to identify specific ownership for these activities and how often they are performed. Undefined creation, review, and communication or ownership are indicators of the absence of a formal process.

 Involving senior management in the development of a strategic plan is critical to planning success.

IS Steering Committee

The IS steering committee ensures that the IT department's strategy and implementation of the strategy directly align with the business strategy as well as the corporate mission and objectives. The steering committee is composed of senior managers who assist in the selection, approval, prioritization, and ongoing review of major IT projects, planning, and budgets. The IS auditor looks for the existence of a formalized committee with a charter, procedures, and defined responsibilities. The IT steering committee maintains detailed meeting minutes as a part of its ongoing reporting to senior management. This reporting ensures that the board of directors and senior management are informed of major IT projects and the status of ongoing projects in a timely manner.

The term "major IT projects" is an important distinction to the IS auditor, evidence that the IT steering committee is getting involved in the day-to-day operations of the IT department. This is an indicator that the committee might not be following the charter or is unclear in its responsibilities. If the committee is providing guidance on day-to-day operations, it will have difficulty determining whether the projects and budgets are aligned with the business objectives, and its reporting to senior management will reflect operational issues instead of overall strategy. This type of review will not ensure alignment or the efficient and effective use of IT resources.

The absence of a formal, chartered IT steering committee could indicate that IT projects are not aligned with the organization's strategy. With a lack of external controls (the IT steering committee), some projects might not support the mission of the organization, or projects might not come in on time or within budget.

 A primary purpose of the IS steering committee is to ensure efficient use of data-processing resources.

The Components of IS Strategies, Policies, Standards, and Procedures

As an IS auditor, you can learn a significant amount about an organization by reviewing the strategic plan and organizational and lower-level policies. These documents can provide background on the business objectives and mission, as well as the line or operational policies supporting that mission. If you review strategy and policies before doing observation and conducting interviews, you might identify areas in which potential gaps exist, help define whether the organization has a clear process for policy development, and determine whether the organization is using a top-down or bottom-up approach to policy development.

Policy Development

Organizations follow different approaches in policy development. The top-down approach aligns organization-wide policies with the business strategy; department- and office-level policy then is created in accordance with strategy and organizational policy. The top-down approach works to ensure that all policies are aligned with the organizational strategy, but it generally requires more time to develop and implement and might not address immediate operation priorities of the organization.

Other organizations create policy using the bottom-up approach. They identify immediate areas of concern, compliance, or risk, and develop policy for those areas by performing a risk assessment. Although this approach is more time- and cost-effective, it creates the risk that policies might not align with organizational policies and strategy.

A bottom-up approach to the development of organizational policies is often driven by a risk assessment.

A variety of policy types exist, and it is important that the organization and the auditor understand the distinction between policy types and their enforcement:

➤ **Regulatory**—These policies are written to ensure that the organization is following standards set by a specific industry and are regulated by law. These types of policies are frequently used in financial institutions, healthcare facilities, public utilities, and the federal government.

➤ **Advisory**—These policies strongly recommend certain types of behaviors, actions, or activities for the organization. These types of policies outline possible consequences for noncompliance and are enforced internally within the organization.

➤ **Informative**—These policies are generally not enforceable and are considered "teaching" policies. These types of policies are used in most organizations.

In addition to different policy types, different subsets of the organization need to develop and comply with lower-level policies. Human resources policies at the policy level are those that most of us are familiar with; these policies pertain to training, travel, hiring, promotion, and termination. These policies are implemented organization-wide, regardless of function or authority level, and they guide the actions of employees. The policies should have a process for review as well as communication within the organization, and should address both the long- and short-term objectives of the organization. There are a variety of methods for communicating policy; these might take the form of awareness training, employee manuals, company newsletters, or legal banners. It is important that clear responsibilities are defined and programs are put in place to ensure that employees are aware of and understand the organization's policies.

IT Policy

Although senior managers are responsible for the development, review, and communication of policy, a significant portion of policies pertains to information systems acquisition (hardware/software), compliance, security, network and operations, continuity of operations, and financial/accounting policies.

Table 2.1 lists some definitions of policy types that are used by organizations and that pertain to IT functions.

Table 2.1 Areas of Policy Development	
Planning policies	Responsibility: Who is involved with planning?
	Timing: When does planning take place?
	Process: How should planning be conducted?
	Deliverables: What planning documents are produced?
	Priorities: What are the most and least critical planning issues?
Organizational policies	Structure: What is the organizational form of the IT function?
	Information architecture: Is the infrastructure aligned with the organization's mission?
	Communication: Do all affected parties know the IT strategy and policies?
	Compliance: Are all external regulations and laws being addressed?
	Risk assessment: Are IT risks identified, measured, and controlled?
Hardware policy	Acquisition: How is hardware acquired from outside vendors?
	Standards: What are the hardware compatibility standards?
	Performance: How are computing capabilities tested?
	Configuration: Where should client/servers, personal computers, and similar technology be used?
	Service providers: Should third-party service bureaus be used, and when?
Network policy	Acquisition: How is network technology acquired from outside vendors?

(continued)

Table 2.1	Areas of Policy Development *(continued)*
	Standards: What are the network compatibility standards (LAN, Internet, intranet, and so on)?
	Performance: How much bandwidth is needed, and is the network fast enough?
	Configuration: What are the logical and physical configuration standards (server, firewalls, routers, and so on)?
	Adaptability: Does the network have the capability to support emerging business models?
Security policies	Testing/evaluation: How is security tested or evaluated?
	Access: Who can have access to what information and applications?
	Monitoring: Who monitors security, and how?
	Firewalls: Are firewalls effectively configured and utilized?
	Violations: What happens if an employee or external entity violates security?
Operations policy	Structure: How is the operations function structured?
	Responsibilities: Who is responsible for transaction processing?
	Input: How does data enter into the information system?
	Processing: What processing modes are used?
	Error handling: Who should correct erroneous input/processing items?
Contingency policy	Backup: What are the backup procedures?
	Recovery: What is the recovery process, and how is it tested?
	Disasters: Who is in charge, and what is the plan?
	Alternate sites: What types of sites are available for off-site processing?
Financial and accounting policies	Project management: Are IT projects prioritized, managed, and monitored?
	Revenue generation: Should services be sold inside or outside the organization?
	Technology investments: Are the investment returns being properly evaluated?
	Funding priorities: Where and how should resources be allocated most effectively?
	Budgets: Are budgets aligned with funding levels and priorities, and aligned with strategy?

Policies are high-level documents that align with the business strategy (both long and short term) and represent the corporate philosophy. The organization's management is responsible for the formulation, documentation, communication, and control of policies. The development of these policies and their implementation show an organization's commitment (due care and diligence) to the use, operation, and security of information systems.

IS auditors should look for both policies and procedures that apply to all phases of the system development life cycle (SDLC) and ensure that they align with the organization's strategy. The SDLC encompasses the planning, analysis, design, implementation, integration/testing, acceptance, maintenance, and security of information systems. The SDLC is a formal model that represents the phased implementation of information systems. The definition of detailed tasks might change by organization, but Figure 2.1 outlines the high-level tasks of an SDLC.

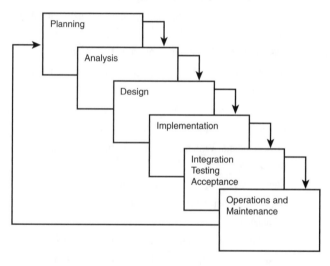

Figure 2.1   SDLC diagram.

Procedures

Procedures are detailed documents that incorporate the intent of the parent policy and that document administrative and operational processes. In some cases, procedures provide step-by-step details for performing a function and writing in a clear and concise manner to allow easy understanding and implementation.

The procedures outline how to perform various business processes within the IT environment and the controls associated with them. The change in business process should drive policy and procedure changes, but this is not always the case. In today's fast-moving business environment, it is not uncommon for business processes to frequently change because of procedures, compliance, or the influence of new technologies in the organization. An IS auditor must pay particular attention to the process for review and implementation of procedures because they are the most fluid documents in the organization. In addition, the auditor might find through direct observation or interviews that the defined procedures are not being followed. This is an indication that there is no defined process for review and update of the procedures, or that the people working in the operational environments are not properly trained on the procedures associated with their function.

The lack of procedures or adherence to procedures could be indicators of a larger issue: Necessary controls in the environment are being bypassed by ad-hoc procedures. In this case, the procedure, or lack thereof, makes it difficult for the auditor to identify controls and ensure that the process is efficient and secure.

When determining the effectiveness of IS policies communication, an auditor typically reviews interviews with user and IS personnel, information-processing facilities operations and procedures manuals, and user department systems and procedures manuals.

Evaluating IS Management Practices to Ensure Compliance with IS Policies, Standards, and Procedures

As stated earlier, reviewing the business strategy, the IT strategy, and associated policies and procedures before conducting interviews and observations should provide the auditor with a clear view of the organization's objectives and mission and any potential gaps in policy or procedures. As a part of the interview and observation process, the auditor should observe personnel in the performance of their duties and assist in identifying the following:

➤ **Organizational functions**—Ensure the individual who is assigned and authorized to perform a particular function is the person who is actually doing the job. This process allows the auditor to ensure that the organizational chart and job descriptions reflect the individuals actually performing the function.

➤ **Process/procedures (actual vs. documented)**—Direct monitoring of process/procedures as they take place, and perform walk-through and gather evidence of compliance or any deviations.

All procedures should incorporate controls over the business process. As a part of the planning phase, the IS auditor should identify control objectives associated with each business process and ensure that the procedure is followed and that controls meet the control objectives. IT control objectives enable the IS auditor to more clearly understand the desired result or purpose of implementing specific control procedures. The IS auditor should check to see that the procedures are understood and executed correctly, determine whether control objectives are fulfilled, and should determine whether a review process is in place for change control. When auditing this area of IT, the auditor should look for areas of concern that could indicate potential problems. This can include the following:

➤ No review process in place for strategy, policies, or procedures

➤ Deviations from existing policy or procedures

➤ Reliance on key personnel for procedures instead of those documented

➤ The lack of documented procedures or outdated procedures

➤ Policies or procedures that are not in compliance with laws

➤ Undefined processes relating to hardware/software acquisition and implementation

➤ Undefined processes for managing projects (personnel, milestones, budget)

During the IT audit process, the auditor should ensure that a process exists for strategy, policy and procedure development, communication, and review. This review process can be part of a change-control process (CCP). The CCP is implemented in organizations as a way to provide a formal review and change-management process for systems and associated documentation. The change-control board (CCB) similar to the IT steering committee, is a formal process, that is chartered by senior management. The CCB should accept requests for changes to systems and documentation, and should review and approve or deny recommended changes. The CCB also might be charged with the periodic review of strategy, policies, and procedures as part of its charter.

As an example of an ad-hoc procedure that is not aligned with a documented procedure, we can review the following example.

Imagine that the IS auditor is reviewing the back-up procedures for the organization's servers. The documented procedure states that the backups are performed by the backup operator who is responsible for configuring the backups, labeling the tapes, managing off-site storage, and performing log review. The procedure further states that a backup job is scheduled to run every evening to back up the organization's servers. The backup software should be configured to connect to the server, back up the data, verify that the data was backed up, log any anomalies, and move to the next server. While monitoring the process, the auditor finds that the data is being backed up and logged, and the backup software then connects the next server.

While questioning the backup operator, the IS auditor inquires about why the data backed up on the tape is not verified and then logged. The backup operator states that the procedure was created when the company had only five servers, which could be backed up and verified in about eight hours. With the addition of 10 servers, the backup procedure cannot back up and verify all the servers in the environment in the eight-hour backup window. The backup operator asked for additional equipment after the servers were installed but has not received it. The backup operator therefore changed the actual procedure to back up the servers without verifying, to ensure that all 15 servers could be backed up during the eight-hour backup window.

This scenario identifies a few areas of concern:

➤ The planning/acquisition process might not be working correctly because the new servers did not include capacity planning for backup software, hardware, and tapes.

➤ There might not be a process for reviewing procedures to ensure that they are aligned with the strategy and actual processes in the environment.

➤ Removing the verification procedure in the process could lead to the inability to recover from a disaster or data loss.

➤ The backup operator might not have the proper level of training to perform the function because he might not understand the potential risk of disabling the verification function.

In this case, the difference between the actual documented procedure and the ad-hoc procedure on the surface appears small, but it can have far-reaching effects. This type of scenario could be an indicator of risk in the environment.

Evaluating the Process for Strategy Development, Deployment, and Maintenance

The IT department should have a clear process for developing IS strategy. This process should include the development, communication, and implementation of the strategy. If this process does not exist, the auditor will find indicators throughout the review of strategy, policy/procedures, and observations. The lack of an IS strategy or a strategy that is outdated or not communicated indicates that IT might not be aligned with the business strategy and that a change in business strategy might not be reflected in the IT department's policy. An IS auditor should recognize key development risk indicators, including these:

➤ Development projects that are not aligned with the strategic plan

➤ Feasibility studies that do not consider the following areas:

　➤ Technical feasibility

　➤ Financial feasibility

　➤ Cultural feasibility

➤ Senior management and users who are not involved

➤ Business process analyses that are not performed

The IT strategy should align with the business strategy, ensure efficient use of IT resources, and serve as the basis for IT policy and procedures. Although the development of IT strategy is an IT function, it should include stakeholders in the organization, as well as senior management. The participation of stakeholders (such as senior managers of business functions) helps ensure that the strategy meets the goals of the organization and business functions, and helps keep the strategy aligned when the business strategy changes. When performing an audit of IS strategic planning, it is unlikely that the IS auditor would assess specific security procedures. During an IS strategy review, overall goals and business plans would be reviewed to determine whether the organization's plans are consistent with its goals.

Principles of IS Organizational Structure and Design

The organizational structure and design of the information systems department should ensure efficient and effective use of IT resources. These resources should have clearly defined duties and the associated policies and procedures. The IT organization needs to ensure proper segregation of duties to reduce the risk of errors or misappropriations associated with the information systems or data.

Evaluating IS Organization and Structure

Both the organization and the IT department should create and maintain an organizational chart. This chart reflects a clearly defined structure and provides a clear definition of the IT department's hierarchy, authority, and responsibility. The organizational chart, combined with job descriptions, provides the auditor with a clear definition of individual responsibilities and the reporting structure. A review of these documents helps the IS auditor ensure that there is proper segregation of duties based on job function and detailed tasks associated with the function. Per ISACA, segregation of duties avoids the possibility that a single person could be responsible for diverse and critical functions in such a way that errors or misappropriations could occur and not be detected in a timely manner during the normal course of business processes. During the development of the department's hierarchy, IT management should consider the following:

➤ Segregation of incompatible duties

  ➤ Segregation between operations and programming might not be possible in smaller environments.

  ➤ Audit trails might be an acceptable compensating control.

➤ Vesting in different people

  ➤ Authorizing transactions

  ➤ Recording transactions

  ➤ Maintaining custody of assets

➤ Accomplishing judicious choices with respect to…

  ➤ Placing the IT function in the organization

➤ Integrating programmed controls into computing infrastructures and applications (with IS auditors possibly included in the project team as control advocates and experts)

As stated in Chapter 1, "The Information Systems (IS) Audit Process," each function within the organization should have a clear definition of the duties to perform that function. While performing operational tasks, certain functions act as controls across the IT organization and must be segregated accordingly. A clear example is the role of the security function within the IT organization. This function is responsible for the implementation and maintenance of security controls, to ensure the confidentiality, integrity, and availability of systems and information. As such, security personnel should not be involved in the day-to-day operational administration of information systems. To illustrate this point, consider the following scenario:

Generally, systems administrators are responsible for the operational maintenance of systems and, in most cases, are responsible for the creation, maintenance, and termination of user accounts for the systems. In a properly segregated environment, administrators would create user accounts and the associated profile information but would not assign access rights to systems or data. After the user account and profile information was created, the security administrator, with approval from the application owner(s), would enable access to the systems and data that the users required to perform their jobs.

Although the assignment of access rights is performed by the security administrator, the authorization of access to data is provided by application/data owners. This ensures an adequate segregation of duties between IS and end users. This segregation of duties ensures that no one function or individual can create user accounts and provide access to systems and data. As an example of the improper segregation of duties, consider the ramifications if either the systems administrator or the security administrator could both create accounts and assign access rights. A single person would then have the ability to create a fictitious user account and provide access to payroll information, private employee information, or the organization's intellectual property.

 An IS auditor's primary responsibility is to advise senior management of the risk involved in not implementing proper segregation of duties, such as having the security administrator perform an operations function.

In smaller environments, it is often difficult to completely segregate incompatible duties. In these cases, the organization must use compensating controls such as audit trails and specific levels of approval before a task can be completed. IT functions such as systems development, computer operations, and security should be segregated by either function or the use of compensating controls. Keep in mind that functions within organizations can be combined. As an example, a quality-control administrator could be responsible for change control and problem management. Combining these duties does not create a situation in which errors or misappropriations could occur.

Table 2.2 shows example IT functions that should not be combined.

Table 2.2 Proper Segregation of Duties			
	Systems Development	Computer Operations	Security Administration	Explanation
Systems development	X	X		Applications development staff has access to systems, business applications, and other key software, and should not be allowed to process end-user information or maintain custody of corporate data and business applications (computer operations).
Computer operations	X			Computer operations staff are responsible for entering data, processing information, and disseminating output, and should not be involved in systems development or security administration because they might be able to bypass controls associated with data transactions.
Security administration	X	X		Security administrators are responsible for safeguarding resources, including ensuring that business software and applications are secure, and ensuring the safety of corporate information, communication, networks, and physical facilities.

X = Functions should not be combined

Designing the ultimate structure of the IT function is often determined by cultural, political, and economic forces inherent in the organization. The design process should consider internal controls to reduce errors, misappropriation, or fraud. As an example, IT management should separate systems development, computer operations, and computer security. If these functions cannot be separated, compensating controls should be put in place. The IS auditor should ensure that systems developers and computer operators are segregated and that the IT function forms a separate security specialization, to maintain custody of software applications and corporate data.

Evaluating Use of Third-Party Services

Outsourcing is a contractual arrangement between the organization and a third party for information systems and associated development, processing, or hosting. This contract relinquishes control over part or all of the information processing to an external party. Organizations often use third-party resources as a way to offset IT costs within the organization or if a particular skill set is required that does not exist in the organization.

A variety of reasons exist for outsourcing. Organizations must ensure that IT processing resources achieve the same level of confidentiality, availability, and integrity that they would have if they were located within the organization. The organization's management might decide to outsource functions to focus on core competencies, as a cost-savings measure, or to gain flexibility to the organization. Many organizations choose to outsource data processing to obtain necessary IT expertise from outside sources. This expertise might range from software to data entry monitoring or internal quality assurance processes, to reduce data errors. In data entry, key verification is one of the best controls for ensuring that data is entered correctly. The key verification processes ensure that after data has been keyed once (or recognized), it is keyed again by a second independent operator. As each keystroke is made, the system flags any differences, and these can be immediately verified and corrected. These types of processes might be best provided by a third party instead of being developed in-house.

These services can be provided by a third party:

➤ Data entry

➤ Application hosting

➤ Design and development of systems or applications

➤ Conversion of legacy system

➤ Help desk support

➤ Payroll processing

➤ Check processing

➤ Electronic bill payment

➤ Credit card operations

It is important to remember that third-party providers (service organizations) face the same threats to information security and controls that all organizations do. The service provider must manage security and risk well.

Some of the criteria for outsourcing, for example, is if the applications development backlog is greater than three years, if more than 50% of the programming costs is spent on system maintenance, or if duplicate information systems functions exist at two or more sites. In these instances, outsourcing the function can help consolidate duplicate functions or reduce development costs and increase delivery time. Organizations should be concerned with both the security (confidentiality and integrity) of their systems and their availability; they should use legally binding contracts to ensure that third-party service providers perform as expected. The contracts should articulate the roles and responsibilities of each party, services to be performed, service-level agreements, contract duration, services costs, dispute resolution, and dissolution agreements.

The contractual agreement generally includes a *service-level agreement* (*SLA*). The SLA outlines the level of service (uptime, downtime, and response time) for the outsourced information systems. The SLA usually outlines a guaranteed level of service, and this is used as a management tool to control the information resources maintained by the service provider. Outsourcing is a long-term strategy, and service-level providers face the same risks as organizations. The organization must ensure that proper contractual agreements provide the necessary level of assurance that the information systems will meet the expectations of the organization.

An IS auditor should always review availability reports when auditing service-level agreements (SLA) for minimum uptime compliance.

Organizations can reduce the risk of outsourcing by doing the following:

➤ Having clearly defined, measurable shared goals and rewards

➤ Utilizing multiple vendors for redundancy

➤ Developing performance metrics

➤ Requiring external auditing of service providers' facilities, practices, and systems

Organizations might request that third parties provide the results of a recent audit report or implement an SAS 70 audit. A Type I or Type II audit assures the organization of the existence and effectiveness of internal controls relative to the service provided. An SAS 70 Type I audit is a "walkthrough" that describes the service provider's internal controls but does not perform detailed testing of these controls. A Type II provides detailed testing of the controls around the service provided.

The auditor's report generally contains a report of the independent auditors, a description of the relevant policies and procedures, control objectives, and results of the service auditor's tests or the operating effectiveness of the control objectives and any other client control considerations. IS auditors should look for third-party assurance of the service provider's design, implementation, and management of controls. These reports often adhere to auditing standards by a reputable organization, such as SAS 70 (AICPA; United States), Section 5900 of the Handbook of Auditing (CICA; Canada), or FIT 1/94 (FIT; United Kingdom). If the third party does not have or will not allow a third-party audit, the organization should look elsewhere for services.

A typical service auditor report should contain the following information:

➤ Report of independent auditors

➤ Description of relevant policies and procedures (provided by client organizational management)

➤ Control objectives specified by the client organization's management, along with the results of the service auditor's tests of the operation effectiveness of the control objectives

➤ Client control considerations

Per ISACA, the auditor should be aware of the following risks associated with outsourcing:

➤ Contract protection—A contract that adequately protects the company

➤ Audit rights—The right to audit vendor operations

➤ Continuity of operations—Continued service in the event of a disaster

➤ Integrity, confidentiality, and availability of organization-owned data

➤ Personnel—Lack of loyalty toward customers, or disgruntled customers/employees, over the outsource agreement

➤ Access control/security administration (vendor controlled)

➤ Violation reporting and follow-up (vendor controlled)

➤ Change control and testing (vendor controlled)

➤ Network controls (vendor controlled)

➤ Performance management (vendor controlled)

Most risk in outsourcing to third-party providers is the disruption of services through either natural or artificial occurrences, such as natural disasters or security breaches. When auditing a potential third-party service provider, an IS auditor often requests proof of each provider's business continuity plan (BCP). Table 2.3 lists some examples of this risk and mitigation.

Table 2.3 Example of Risk-Mitigation Strategy	
Risk	**Risk Mitigation**
Business disruption because a service provider fails to perform as expected	Legally binding contracts should exist between the company and service providers, articulating the roles and responsibilities of each party, services to be performed, service-level agreements, contract duration, service costs, dispute resolutions, dissolutions arrangements, and so on.
	Both the client and service organizations' IT functions must agree on a backup and recovery plan. The plan should be periodically tested.
Security breach	The client organization's IT function must work with the service provider to ensure the security and confidentiality of company information.

When auditing third-party service providers, the IS auditor should be concerned with ownership of program and files, a statement of due care and confidentiality, and the capability of continued service of the provider in the event of a disaster. These should be clearly stated in the contract between the third-party provider and the organization. The contract should have a regular review process to ensure that the third-party provider's contractual obligations are aligned with the IT strategies, procedures, and organizational goals.

As an example, an outsourcing contract for IT facilities should clearly define ownership of intellectual property.

Careful monitoring of the performance of an outsourced service is critical to ensure that services are delivered to the company as required.

Examining IS Management and Practices

The development of an IT strategic plan leads to the development of corporate or department objectives and serves as the primary guideline for allocating resources. The strategic plan keeps the organization headed in a profitable direction, and long-term planning minimizes the risk that organizational resources will not support the company's overall objectives. IT management is responsible for establishing sound project management and organizational policies. The combination of the IT strategic plan, sound project management, and organizational policies reduces business risks. The lack of these controls might lead to IT management that is crisis-oriented or firefighting.

IS auditors should look for evidence of a prescribed, documented IT planning process. The existence of an ongoing process indicates that the company is constantly and diligently seeking an optimal "fit" between the information technology infrastructure and the organization's goals. Establishing a sound IT management methodology through sound project management, IT organizational hierarchy, and policies ensures that organizational goals are better fulfilled and that business risks are reduced.

IS Project-Management Strategies and Policies

The core principles of project management include the development of a detailed plan, the reporting of project activity against the plan, and the adjustment of the plan to enable corrective action. All project plans should be assigned to a project manager who is experienced in the area of implementation, who has skills associated with managing projects, and who has a good working relationship with the staff in planning and executing the project.

The following list outlines the five basic phases of the project life cycle. Although the scope and details of particular projects will differ, the phases remain the same:

➤ **Phase I: Plan the project**—This phase includes setting the time, cost, and scope of the project. In a software project, the planning team and project manager determine the relative physical size of the software to be developed; this can be used as a guide for allocating and budgeting resources. The team can use function point analysis to measure the size of an information system based on the number and complexity of inputs and files that a user sees and interacts with.

The project team identifies the resources required, including internal/external personnel, cost, and additional facilities or equipment, and identifies the particular outcome(s) of the project. The team then determines the work breakdown structure, which is the core of the project plan, and identifies specific tasks, the resources assigned to those tasks, and project milestones and dependencies.

➤ **Phase II: Schedule the project**—This phase of the project breaks the project into logically grouped activities and creates a timetable for each activity. The team should create Gantt charts to show timelines, milestones, and dependencies. When this is complete, the team should perform critical path analysis on the project plan. The critical path analysis shows areas of risk due to resource constraints, project timelines, or priority against existing projects.

➤ **Phase III: Monitor continuously**—The project teams should monitor the progress of the project against the baseline using planning benchmarks, milestones, and deliverables. It is important that deviations from the plan be addressed throughout the project, to ensure that the cost, time, and use of valuable resources do not exceed the expected value of the project in meeting the business objectives.

➤ **Phase IV: Controlling the project**—The old adage that "No good plan survives contact with the enemy" is particularly applicable at this point in the project. The project will encounter a variety of constraints and changes throughout the project life cycle. The team might find that business processes have changed, that valuable resources are not available (both people and budget), or that the expected outcomes of particular tasks were not realized. To overcome these types of changes, the teams must be flexible and continually must adjust the plan to keep the project moving. These adjustments might decrease the scope of the project, extend or shorten timelines, or bring on additional resources. The skills of the project manager and the planning team, and adequate communication of the resources on the project are key to successfully overcoming obstacles during this phase.

➤ **Phase V: Closing the project**—This phase includes user acceptance of the products and services, as well as written acceptance of all expected outcomes. The project manager should evaluate the project personnel and reassign remaining project resources. The project history should be chronicled and used to determine whether the original return on investment will be realized as the product goes into production.

As stated earlier, major projects should be submitted to and prioritized by the IS steering committee, to ensure that the project aligns with the business strategy and that resources are available for successful completion of the project. A project manager should be assigned and must have operational control of the project and all resources assigned to the project. These resources might come from within the IT department, from business units, or from external sources. The IS auditor might be included on the project team as a subject matter expert on controls or to provide independent objective review of the project.

A variety of factors can negatively impact a project, its timeline, or its cost. IS auditors also can look for some indicators when reviewing the project-planning process or individual projects.

Project-planning risk indicators include these:

➤ Management does not use a formal project-management methodology.

➤ Project leaders are not adequately experienced in planning or managing projects.

➤ Projects do not have senior-level executive support.

➤ Projects are taking longer to develop than planned.

➤ Projects are costing more than budgeted.

Project risk indicators include these:

➤ Project leaders have insufficient domain expertise.

➤ Project teams are unqualified to handle project size or complexity.

➤ Project team members are dissatisfied.

➤ Projects do not include input from all affected parties.

➤ Project recipients are dissatisfied with project outcomes.

➤ Projects have a high staff turnover rate.

➤ Projects are frequently aborted or suspended.

These are some of the possible risks during project planning and implementation. In reading the following scenario, you can see the actual outcome of risks that are not mitigated.

The IT department's help desk is receiving an increasing number of trouble tickets regarding slow response time on an application server. The server OS is Windows NT. After a cursory review, the system administrators determine that the application server response time would improve drastically if it was upgraded to Windows 2000 server. The remainder of the IT architecture, including the servers that provide user login (authentication services) are currently running Windows NT. The entire server infrastructure is scheduled for a planned upgrade later in the year, but the systems administrators are confident that this upgrade will not affect the applications running on the problem server or the rest of the infrastructure. When the upgrade is completed, the administrators receive a higher number of trouble tickets due to login problems, intermittent outages of the applications on the upgraded server, and network connectivity issues.

Table 2.4 illustrates both the risks involved with performing this upgrade and the lack of planning.

Table 2.4 System Upgrade Risks			
System Component	Problem	Planning Solution	Risk Type
Hardware	The network connectivity problem is related to an incompatible network card and drivers.	A proper plan would have included interoperability testing as well as capacity testing; the incompatible card and drivers would have been discovered before being put into production.	Business risk: The critical applications needed to operate the business are not operating properly. Continuity risk: Lack of proper planning results in downtime for systems and applications. There was no plan to "roll back" the upgrade. Information risks: The information in the applications can be adversely affected

(continued)

Table 2.4 System Upgrade Risks *(continued)*			
System Component	**Problem**	**Planning Solution**	**Risk Type**
			because users cannot enter and update data.
Operating system	The Windows 2000 operating systems does not provide login (authentication) services to users in the old Windows NT infrastructure.	Proper planning and testing would have ensured that the correct resources were tested and reviewed authentication systems to ensure that they were compatible.	Business risk: Critical applications needed to operate the business are not operating properly. Continuity risk: Lack of proper planning results in downtime for systems and applications. There was no plan to "roll back" the upgrade.
Application	The application availability is intermittent.	Proper planning and testing would have ensured that the old applications were compatible with the new Windows 2000 operating system.	Business risk: Critical applications needed to operate the business are not operating properly. Continuity risk: Lack of proper planning results in downtime for systems and applications. There was no plan to "roll back" the upgrade.
Interoperability	Network connectivity is intermittent.	Proper planning and testing would have ensured that the communications protocols with Windows 2000 were compatible with the network infrastructure.	Business risk: Critical applications needed to operate the business are not operating properly. Continuity risk: Lack of proper planning results in downtime for systems and applications. There was no plan to "roll back" the upgrade.

A good project-planning process and regular review reduce overall risks to the business, information, and system. During the project-planning phase, the project-management team and IT management should determine the risk as it applies to expected outcomes and determine ways to mitigate the risk.

 If an IS auditor observes that project approval procedures do not exist, the IS auditor should recommend to management that formal approval procedures be adopted and documented.

IT Governance, Risk Management, and Control Frameworks

Organizations continue to increase their dependency on information systems and invest heavily in the acquisition, development, and maintenance of those systems. These systems support mission-critical business functions and should maximize the organization's return on investment. The combination of a solid governance framework and risk-management process creates a control infrastructure that reduces risk and ensures that IT infrastructure supports the business functions.

IS auditors should look for evidence of a structured approach to the management of systems and applications, and defined life-cycle phases and progression points. The presence of a structured approach provides advantages to the auditor:

➤ The IS auditor's influence is increased when there are formal procedures and guidelines identifying each phase in the business application life cycle and the extent of auditor involvement.

➤ The IS auditor can review all relevant areas and phases of the systems-development project, and can report independently to management on the adherence to planned objectives and company procedures.

The risks associated with improper planning are varied, but the lack of a planning and review process or organization structures are indicators of a lack of controls. The IS auditor must advise the project-management team and senior management of the deficiencies. As stated earlier, the IT department should have proper project-planning procedures that follow a standard system-development life cycle. This project-planning process, combined with change control, ensures proper control over the production IT infrastructure.

In Chapter 1, we defined the different types of risks, such as business risk, continuity risk, and so on. As a part of ongoing IT procedures, a formal risk-management process must be incorporated into the planning, acquisition, development, testing, and deployment of information systems. The IT organization and project managers should use proper risk-management techniques to assess risk, take steps to reduce risk to an acceptable level (mitigation), and maintain that level of risk.

The objectives of an effective risk-management program should enable the organization to realize its business objectives:

➤ Better secure IT systems that store, process, or transmit organizational information

➤ Enable management to make well-informed risk-management decisions to justify expenditures that are part of the IT budget

Proper risk management enables IT managers and senior leadership to balance the operational and economic costs of protective measures and to achieve gains in mission objectives by protecting the IT systems and data that support their organizations' objectives.

IS Problem- and Change- Management Strategies and Policies

To coordinate the planning, design, and implementation of changes that could affect the connected systems or data, such as upgrading hardware or software or adding services, the organization should develop a *change-management* process. The change process is usually facilitated by a chartered *change control board* (*CCB*). A CCB generally is charged with reviewing all changes in the environment and has the authority to accept, deny, postpone, or send back a change request for additional information. The CCB is in place to ensure that the implementation of changes does not disrupt the availability or integrity of data, introduce vulnerabilities, or allocate resources (personnel and money) to projects or changes that do not meet business objectives. The change-management process establishes an open line of communication among all affected parties and allows those parties to provide input that is instrumental in the implementation process as it unfolds.

Change management is an integral part of any production IT infrastructure; it not only approves change in the environment, but it also can schedule changes and monitor milestones of changes that are in progress. The CCB is usually composed of members from the information systems department, as well as senior managers from the business functions. The CCB usually includes an administrator who is responsible for receiving, documenting, and scheduling the review of change requests (CR). The CR should contain all the information necessary to allow the CCB to make an informed decision about the change. A CR typically contains this information:

➤ Originator of the CR

➤ Reason for the change

➤ Work breakdown structure:

> ➤ Project/change milestones
>
> ➤ Resources required (personnel and budget)
>
> ➤ Amount of time the change will take
>
> ➤ A backout plan if the change does not work
>
> ➤ User acceptance testing procedures

➤ Documentation (such as user/system manuals)

➤ Risk assessment:

> ➤ What happens if the change is not made
>
> ➤ Potential effects of the change
>
> ➤ Issues that affect availability, integrity, or confidentiality of systems

The CRs generally are reviewed by *subject matter experts* (*SMEs*) before they are submitted to the CCB and include suggestions or concerns. The SME can be in the business or IT area and can include business managers, users, security personnel, application developers, or network and systems engineers. SMEs provide the board with enough information to make a decision on the request and to understand the impacts in the environment. A formal change-control process is generally applied to systems and application development, but it can apply to network, security, and documentation changes as well.

In a development environment, the CR identifies how the object code will move from development to a test library and how it will test security and control features. The CR also defines how the program will be introduced into the production environment, as well as data conversion, user training, and documentation.

The presence of a formal change-control process ensures that other governance and procedures (project planning, security, and so on) are formally involved in environment changes. In a development environment, it helps to ensure proper segregation of duties because programmers should not be able to make changes to production code and introduce the chance of fraud.

IS Quality-Management Strategies and Policies

Per ISACA, quality assurance usually performs two distinct tasks:

➤ **Quality assurance (QA)**—Helps the IT department ensure that the personnel are following prescribed quality processes. For example, QA helps ensure that programs and documentation adhere to the standards and naming conventions.

➤ **Quality control (QC)**—Is responsible for conducting tests or reviews to verify that software is free from defects and meets user expectations. This can be done at various stages of the development of application systems, but it must be done before the programs are moved into production.

An example of a standard quality-assurance model is the *Software Capability Maturity Model* (*CMM*) developed by Carnegie Melon's Software Engineering Institute. The CMM model provides a framework for improving software life cycle processes and specific metrics to improve the software process. CMM has maturity levels that are designed with continuous process improvement in mind, to increase product and service quality through the implementation of best practices.

> **NOTE**
> ISACA refers to CMM in both its study material and the exam, even though the CMM model was upgraded to CMMI (Capability Maturity Model Integration) in 2000.

Per the CMM model documentation, software process maturity is the extent to which a specific process is explicitly defined, managed, measured, controlled, and effective. The more mature an organization's software process is, the higher the productivity and quality of the software products produced are. As software process maturity increases, the organization institutionalizes its software process via policies, standards, and organizational structures. This institutionalization entails building an infrastructure and a corporate culture that supports the methods, practices, and procedures of the business so that they endure after those who originally defined them have gone. The CMM maturity levels are shown in Figure 2.2.

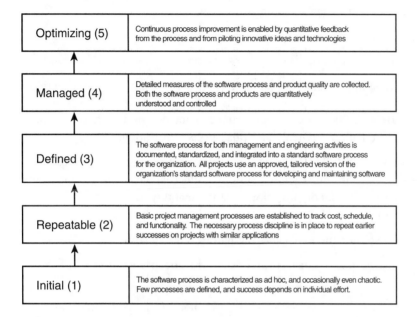

Optimizing (5)	Continuous process improvement is enabled by quantitative feedback from the process and from piloting innovative ideas and technologies
Managed (4)	Detailed measures of the software process and product quality are collected. Both the software process and products are quantitatively understood and controlled
Defined (3)	The software process for both management and engineering activities is documented, standardized, and integrated into a standard software process for the organization. All projects use an approved, tailored version of the organization's standard software process for developing and maintaining software
Repeatable (2)	Basic project management processes are established to track cost, schedule, and functionality. The necessary process discipline is in place to repeat earlier successes on projects with similar applications
Initial (1)	The software process is characterized as ad hoc, and occasionally even chaotic. Few processes are defined, and success depends on individual effort.

Figure 2.2   CMM maturity levels.

IT management can use assessment methods to provide a mechanism to determine whether the activities of the organization have deviated from the planned or expected levels. These methods include IS budgets, capacity and growth planning, industry standards/benchmarking, financial management practices, and goal accomplishment. Quality management is the means by which the IS department processes are controlled, measured, and improved. Management principles focus on areas such as people, change, processes, and security. Industry standards/benchmarking provide a means of determining the level of performance provided by similar information-processing facility environments.

The quality assurance group ensures that the programs and program changes and documentation adhere to established standards.

The *International Organization for Standardization (ISO)* has created the ISO 9000 series, which is implemented by 634,000 organizations in 152 countries. ISO 9000 has become an international reference for quality management requirements in business-to-business dealings. Per ISO, the ISO 9000 family is primarily concerned with "quality management" or what the organization does to fulfill the following:

➤ The customer's quality requirements

➤ Applicable regulatory requirements

➤ Customer satisfaction

➤ Continual improvement of its performance in pursuit of these objectives

ISO 9001/9002/9003 contains guidelines about design, development, production, installation servicing, and final inspection/testing.

Per ISO, ISO 9001:2000, "Quality Management Systems," specifies requirements for a quality-management system. Adherence to these requirements demonstrates that the organization has the capability to consistently provide products that do the following:

➤ Meet customer and applicable regulatory requirements

➤ Enhance customer satisfaction through the effective application of the system

➤ Include processes for continual improvement of the system and the assurance of conformity to customer and applicable regulatory requirements

All requirements of this international standard are generic and are intended to apply to all organizations, regardless of type, size, and product provided.

The 1994 versions of ISO 9001/9002/9003 were combined into a single revised document represented by ISO 9001:2000 (see www.iso.org/iso/en/iso9000-14000/iso9000/faqs.html).

ISO 9126 focuses on the end result of good software processes, such as the quality of the actual software product. ISO 9126 provides definitions of the characteristics and associated quality-evaluation process to be used when specifying the requirements for and evaluating the quality of software products throughout the software life cycle. The following are specific definitions associated with the ISO standards.

➤ ISO/IEC TR 9126-2:2003 provides external metrics for measuring attributes of six external quality characteristics defined in ISO/IEC 9126-1.

➤ Users of ISO/IEC TR 9126-2:2003 can select or modify and apply metrics and measures from ISO/IEC TR 9126-2:2003, or can define application-specific metrics for their individual application domain.

➤ ISO/IEC TR 9126-2:2003 is intended to be used together with ISO/IEC 9126-1.

➤ ISO/IEC TR 9126-2:2003 contains an explanation of how to apply software quality metrics, a basic set of metrics for each subcharacteristic, and an example of how to apply metrics during the software product life cycle. ISO/IEC TR 9126-2:2003 does not assign ranges of values of these metrics to rated levels or to grades of compliance because these values are defined for each software product or a part of the software product, depending on such factors as category of the software, integrity level, and users' needs. Some attributes might have a desirable range of values that does not depend on specific user needs but that depends on generic factors, such as human cognitive factors.

➤ The metrics listed in ISO/IEC TR 9126-2:2003 are not intended to be an exhaustive set. Developers, evaluators, quality managers, and acquirers can select metrics from ISO/IEC TR 9126-2:2003 for defining requirements, evaluating software products, measuring quality aspects, and other purposes.

➤ ISO/IEC TR 9126-3 defines internal metrics.

➤ Internal metrics measure the software itself, external metrics measure the behavior of the computer-based system that includes the software, and quality in use metrics measure the effects of using the software in a specific context of use.

➤ ISO/IEC 9126-4 defines quality in use metrics, for measuring the characteristics or subcharacteristics.

In conjunction with these standards, organizations can perform certification and accreditation activities. These activities are commonly performed within the U.S. federal government and are defined as follows:

➤ **Certification**—This is a major consideration before processing is authorized, but it is not the only consideration. Certification is the technical evaluation that establishes the extent to which a computer system, application, or network design and implementation meet a prespecified set of security requirements.

➤ **Accreditation**—This is the authorization and approval granted to an information system to process in an operational environment. It is made on the basis of a certification by designated technical personnel that the system meets prespecified technical requirements for achieving adequate system security.

Certification activities include testing systems and their controls to ensure that the systems meet the control objectives. When the certification is complete, any deficiencies are noted and forwarded to the appropriate authority for accreditation. During the accreditation process, the approving authority reviews the results of controls testing and determines the level of risk associated with the deficiencies. If the approving authority determines that the risk associated with the deficiencies is acceptable, the system is allowed to process in an operational environment with a plan to correct the deficiencies (remediation). If the level of risk is beyond an acceptable level, the deficiencies must be corrected before the system can go into operation.

The IS auditor must review quality assurance activities to ensure that quality assurance personnel are creating and reviewing prescribed quality processes. The auditor also must make sure that a standard quality-control process is in place for conducting tests or reviews, to verify and ensure that software and systems are free from defects and that they meet user expectations.

NOTE

Quality assurance could be an additional responsibility of the security administrator. Although making the security administrator responsible for application programming, systems programming, or data entry would not provide an adequate segregation of duties, working in quality assurance does *not* constitute improper segregation of duties.

IS Information Security Management Strategies and Policies

The implementation of strong IS security management ensures the protection of information assets (processing resources and data) through effective policy, controls, standardized procedures, and control testing. As stated earlier, security management applies risk-management principles and techniques to assess IT assets, mitigate the risk to these assets, and monitor residual risks. These are the three tenets of information security:

➤ Confidentiality

> ➤ Ability to ensure that the necessary level of secrecy is enforced throughout each junction of data processing, to prevent unauthorized disclosure

➤ Integrity

    ➤ Assurance of accuracy and reliability of data

    ➤ Prevention of unauthorized data modification

    ➤ Prevention of authorized unintentional modification

➤ Availability

    ➤ Reliable and timely access to data and resources for individuals

These tenets are collectively known as the CIA triad. Security management should apply these tenets in the implementation and review of controls within the IT environment. In Chapter 1, you learned about a variety of risk types. Security management implements controls to reduce (mitigate) risk. The following are a list of control categories that reduce risk and help control the IT function:

➤ Security

➤ Input

➤ Processing

➤ Output

➤ Databases

➤ Backup and recovery

Developing and implementing a function dedicated to security in the organization ensures that the risks associated with the business and information systems are mitigated through the use of risk-assessment techniques, policies and procedures, and an overall security strategy. The combination of these security controls ensures that the IT infrastructure is protected against both internal and external threats.

The security function must protect the IT infrastructure through the use of *physical* and *logical* controls. Physical security controls access to facilities, computers, and telecommunications equipment and other assets of the infrastructure. These controls ensure that only authorized users have access to facilities and that policies are in place so that visitors are logged and accompanied by authorized personnel. The physical facility should be configured so that during the normal course of business, visitors such as vending machine suppliers, workmen, and janitorial and repair personnel are monitored and have access only to the areas required to perform their function. Access to the facility can be controlled through the use of security guards, biometric devices (retina scanners, hand geometry, fingerprint scanners), keys and locks, and electronic card readers. All access points to the facility, including doors, windows, and access vents, should contain physical controls to monitor, detect, and control entry. In the case of windows and vents, the organization might deploy cameras, motion detectors, glass-break detectors, and alarms.

A monitoring system should be in place for the facility. This could include cameras, visitor logs, card entry logs, roving guards, and penetration alarms. It is important to remember that having these controls in place should include defining responsibility for regular review and monitoring. As an example, the visitor logs should be regularly reviewed to ensure that visitors are signing in and out of the facility. The logs associated with key cards should be reviewed to ensure that only authorized individuals have access to the facility and to look for anomalies associated with access (authorized individuals coming in during time frames that are not concurrent with their work hours or attempting to access areas of the facility for which they do not have access).

Physical security controls are most often defeated through the use of social engineering, whereby unauthorized persons gain access to the facility by posing as someone they are not (repairman, authorized vendors, and others). Social engineering is the use of physiological tricks on authorized users to gain access to the system. Unauthorized persons might use techniques such as "shoulder surfing," looking over the shoulder of authorized users to identify key codes to access the building, or claiming to have "lost" badges or key cards and persuading an authorized user to help them gain access, or piggybacking behind an authorized user with a valid key card.

The IS auditor should regularly perform penetration tests into the facility. These tests might include breaking into access points through the use of persuasion or brute force, or gaining admission as a visitor and trying to access areas for which they are not authorized. The combination of regular review, monitoring, and testing of physical security controls can identify weaknesses and areas for improvement.

As a rule, logical security controls are more complex to implement and maintain, but they are an integral part of maintaining the confidentiality, availability, and integrity of the IT infrastructure. Logical access controls entail access to the information systems (workstations, servers, telecommunications, and data) of the organization. The most common form for logical access to the information systems is through a terminal or workstation. Logical controls ensure that authorized users have a login (ID) and password, and should apply the control of least privilege: Authorized users should have access to only the applications and data they need to perform their job function.

It is important that the security function in the organization not only implement these controls, but also have regular logging and monitoring of logical access to the systems and data. These policies and procedures should include segregation of duties, logging of access (both successful and unsuccessful), and transaction logs monitoring what systems or applications were accessed by whom and when. Proper segregation of duties ensures that those charged with the review of system and transaction logs do not have the ability to change those logs and that there are clear procedures for reporting any anomalies or incidents found in the logs. A variety of controls are included in logical controls; these are some of the controls that the IS auditor should look for:

➤ Proper segregation of duties with regard to the input and authorization of data

➤ Proper password procedures and complex passwords (the use of alphanumeric characters and symbols, and correct password length)

➤ Regular password changes (30, 60, 90 days)

➤ Proper procedures for new account creation and termination of accounts

➤ Proper systems logging for successful and unsuccessful access attempts

➤ Proper transaction logging for access to applications and data (transaction performed, by whom, and at what time)

➤ Where possible, time periods for which users can log into the system (9 a.m. to 5 p.m.)

➤ Training in place to ensure that users do not provide passwords to unauthorized parties (for example, by phone or with sticky notes at desk)

➤ Clear job descriptions and definitions of application and data access

➤ Regular review of all user accounts, to ensure that only authorized users have access and that access is correct per job function (job description)

➤ Clear process for reporting and investigating incidents and anomalies

In addition to internal user accounts, unauthorized users might gain access to applications and data from outside the organization. Unauthorized users could be existing vendors or suppliers who have access to internal systems, authorized internal users who access from remote locations, or unauthorized users (hackers) gaining access through the Internet. In most cases, organizations will have firewalls in place to protect external access through the Internet. The firewall settings (rules) should be the most restrictive possible and should deny all access except that explicitly required by the external users to perform their function. Firewall logs and access should be regularly reviewed and should have a system in place to notify administrators in the event of unauthorized access. The security function should define incident response and reporting procedures to remove access to critical applications and data in the event of external unauthorized access. These procedures can be as extreme as disconnecting the organization's access to the Internet or can just include removing critical applications for Internet connectivity.

The IS auditor should perform regular review and scanning for known vulnerabilities, as well as attempts to exploit vulnerabilities that are discovered. Penetration testing ensures that the controls in place mitigate the risk in accordance with the system's value or function. The purpose of performing a penetration test is to exploit one or more known vulnerabilities. The combination of regular monitoring, incident reporting, scanning, and penetration testing enables the organization to identify and correct weaknesses within the current security infrastructure.

An information system converts data into information through its collection and processing. The information systems should produce accurate, complete, timely, and reliable information. The organization must control the risks associated with the collection and processing of this data. The integrity of data in the organization is important because all data, with few exceptions, should be considered influential data. Influential data is used throughout the organization for decision making at all levels in the organization. One of the greatest concerns with regard to data is unauthorized access to the data. This might take place at the point of entry into the information system or through unauthorized manipulation or viewing of the data once in the information system. These threats are both internal and external, and they compromise the confidentiality and privacy of data. Organizations today store and use a large amount of data in their information systems, and they often do not have proper controls in place to protect data access or detect such access.

Table 2.5 lists some common examples of risks associated with data integrity.

Table 2.5 Risks Associated with Data Integrity		
Scenario	**Risk Type**	**Control**
Data-entry operators have full access to create, update, and delete data in a customer relationship system. The data-entry operators use a variety of data sources to enter data into the systems (existing paper lists,	Business risk: • Data corruption can occur (with inaccurate data). • Duplicate data Security risk: • Operators can delete data.	Business risk: • Data corruption can occur. Operators should have access to only the functions they need (such as for updates). In applying proper

(continued)

Table 2.5 Risks Associated with Data Integrity *(continued)*		
Scenario	**Risk Type**	**Control**
external customer lists, and emails from the sales staff). There are no controls with regard to duplicate records or restriction of access to certain data or the manipulation of data.	• Operators can view all customers.	segregation of duties, individual transactions might require higher-level approval. • The quality-assurance process should include data validation throughout the entry process. • Processes to validate the completeness, accuracy, and timeliness of data entered (double key entry, verification of data entered against the source, validation through application and database constraints). Security risks: • Operators should have the least amount of privilege necessary to perform their job. • Operators' actions should be logged and reviewed. • Quality assurance measures should be in place to measure operators' accuracy and timeliness. • The systems used for data entry should not have storage devices attached (such as hard drives, floppy drives, USB ports, or external storage).
A construction company uses a system to create pricing as part of its bidding process. The pricing information for materials is provided through electronic data exchange with suppliers, as well as manual data entry by suppliers and internal data entry staff.	Business risk: • Data corruption could occur (with incorrect pricing in bids). • Operators and suppliers have access to internal pricing information.	Business risk: • Operators should have access to only the functions they need (such as for updates). Enforcing a second level of transaction approval ensures proper segregation of duties. • Specific EDI policies, procedures, and standards

(continued)

Table 2.5 Risks Associated with Data Integrity *(continued)*		
Scenario	Risk Type	Control
		should be in place to facilitate the transfer of information. • Quality assurance can be accomplished through validation and error checking throughout the entry process and regular review of database transaction logs. • Processes to validate the completeness, accuracy, and timeliness of data entered include: double key entry, verification of data entered against the source and validation through application and database constraints. • Access control can ensure that only authorized users can view proprietary company information (pricing).

We just identified unauthorized access and the manipulation of data and its effect on data integrity. Another effect on the data integrity is the introduction of errors in the data. These errors might be affected through improper system design, lack of procedures or training, or inadvertent misuse of data.

Proper procedures with regard to system development and testing reduce the introduction of errors in the data. During the system development life cycle, the IT organization should ensure that the requirements for the systems are complete, that the system requirements meet the business requirements of the organization, and that application-development procedures continually test against the requirements. The development of the system should include proper controls at the application level (access, validation, and so on) and the database level (proper data element design, validation, constraints, and error handling). Applications and their associated databases should have regular error-handling routines that ensure that the data entered in the systems meets the business rules as well as external guidelines (compliance). The normal process should include the input of data, a validation process, the creation of a suspense file for transactions that do not meet the validation criteria, and a review of the suspense file by authorized parties before making it part of the production data. This process should include proper segregation of duties, ensuring that those entering data have no part in authorizing, reviewing, or approving data.

The security function in the organization should be involved in all aspects of the system development life cycle, to ensure that proper controls are implemented. The security function should provide specific controls for the confidentiality, availability, and integrity of information systems, to mitigate risk in the organization.

IS Business Continuity Management Strategies and Policies

We discuss *business continuity planning* (*BCP*) and *disaster-recovery planning* (*DRP*) in detail in Chapter 5, "Disaster Recovery and Business Continuity," but it is important to provide definitions and a framework. Although BCP and DRP are commonly interchanged, they are distinctly different. Per ISACA, BCP is a process designed to reduce the organization's business risk from an unexpected disruption of the critical functions or operations (manual or automated) necessary for the survival of the organization. This includes the human and material resources supporting the critical functions and operations, and assurance of the continuity of the minimum level of services necessary for critical operations.

DRP is generally the plan followed by IS to recover an IT processing facility or by business units to recover an operational facility. The IS recovery plan must be consistent with and must support the overall plan of the organization. Disasters are disruptions that cause critical information resources to be inoperative for a period of time, adversely impacting the business operations.

The proper implementation of BCP ensures that critical business functions can withstand a variety of emergencies. The primary responsibility of BCP lies with management; the goal is to minimize the effects of a disaster so that the organization can resume normal operations as soon as possible. BCP is, at best, an annual project and is effective only if it is continuously performed and tested. During BCP, the organization must define what qualifies as a disruptive event or disaster. When we think of disasters, we might think of fires, floods, tornadoes, or terrorist events. In fact, a disaster can include a variety of events that appear smaller in nature but that have a large effect on the organization's continuity. As an example, Wall Street brokers would consider a telecommunications outage a disaster: It restricts their customers' ability to reach them and their ability to perform trading functions. In other businesses, a telecommunications outage would be an annoyance but would not necessarily affect the continuity of the business.

The degree to which a BCP/DRP plan is successful depends on the support and leadership of senior management. Senior management needs to support the plan through development, implementation, and testing, to ensure that the plan will be successful in the event of a disaster. Senior management should establish a BCP policy that includes the commitment of the organization to its stakeholders, shareholders, employees, and partners. This policy should include what aspects of the operation will be included in the BCP/DRP and should define responsibilities throughout the organization.

Per ISACA, an effective BCP has the following components:

➤ Predisaster readiness

➤ Evacuation procedures

➤ Instructions on how to declare a disaster

➤ Identification of the business processes and IT resources to be recovered

➤ Clear identification of the responsibilities in the plan

➤ Clear identification of the person responsible for each function in the plan

➤ Clear identification of contract information

➤ A step-by-step explanation of recovery options

➤ Clear identification of the various resources required for a recovery and continued operation of the organization

➤ Step-by-step application of the constitution phase

Many BCPs fail because of the following:

➤ The BCP is outdated and is not regularly reviewed and tested.

➤ Responsibilities are not clearly defined.

➤ Inadequate testing leads to poorly trained personnel.

➤ The procedures for declaring a disaster are not objective or clearly defined.

➤ The procedures for declaring the end to a disaster are not objective or clearly defined.

The BCP process can be complex and includes all levels of the organization. It is important to remember that this will be an emotional time for all personnel involved; the more detailed the plan and testing are, the better the chance is for success. Senior leadership, security, IT, and managers of business units must be involved in the process to achieve success. The business must identify critical business functions and assign responsibility for all the resources involved with those functions (personnel, procurement, replacement, systems, applications, and data). Senior leadership should involve the marketing or communications department, to define specific communications for each event outlined in the plan and directed communication for the stakeholders (shareholders, employees, and partners). The plan should be part of the change-control process and should be regularly tested and updated to reflect the business requirements. Individual roles and responsibilities should be clearly defined, communicated, and updated.

If the organization follows these rules, it can be reasonably sure that the economic viability of the organization will continue in the event of a disaster.

Contracting Strategies, Processes, and Contract-Management Practices

Contracting is generally used when talking about outsourcing, but this is not always the case. Contracts can be between the organization and the customer or partners. A *contract* is an agreement between or among two or more persons or entities (business, organizations, or government agencies) to do, or to abstain from doing, something in return for an exchange of consideration. If the terms of a contract are breached, the law provides remedies, including recovery of losses or specific performance. A contract is written documentation of a "meeting of the minds" and contains the following five elements:

➤ Offer

➤ Clearly identifies the subject matter of the agreement

➤ Completely describes services, including time, plan, and quality

➤ Identifies goods, including quantity

➤ Consideration

➤ States what the offerer expects in return from the offeree

➤ Acceptance

➤ Identifies the offeree

➤ Is signed and dated by the offeree and the offerer

➤ Legal purpose

  ➤ Must be created for legal purposes under the law (illegal services cannot be consummated via a contract)

  ➤ Must be performable (parties must be able to deliver on their promise)

➤ Capacity

  ➤ Must fit the legal definition for capacity (not under age, under the influence of alcohol or drugs, and so on)

The IS auditor might encounter a variety of contracts. The following paragraphs outline some of the more common contract types.

Employee Contracts

The employment contract is a specific type of agreement and differs slightly from a traditional contract. The offerer (employer) makes a one-sided promise (unilateral), and the offeree (employee) accepts the offer "at-will" based on continued performance. The employee is not bound by the contract because he or she can leave the employer at any time, but the employer is bound to the conditions of the contract and is the only entity that can breach the contract. Employment contracts stipulate titles, responsibilities, performance criteria, and compensation. Employment contracts cannot state the period of time that an employee must work for the employer because this is not enforceable under the law.

Confidentiality Agreement

This is an agreement between employee and employer or, in some cases, partners (with trade secret agreements). The agreement stipulates that the parties agree not to divulge confidential information that they might come in contact with during the course of the agreement. These agreements have specific time periods and should state the information being protected, list the appropriate uses of the information, and identify remedies if the information is divulged.

Trade Secret Agreements

This is an agreement that protects the trade secrets of an organization from disclosure. Such disclosure would negatively affect the economic viability of the company. It is important to note that trade secret agreements are enforceable for an indefinite period of time because when an organization reveals a trade secret, it is no longer protected as intellectual property.

Discovery Agreements

When an employee is specifically hired to develop ideas or innovations, there is a risk to the organization that the employee might claim these as his or her own intellectual property. With a discovery agreement, the employee agrees to transfer ownership of the discovery to the employer.

Noncompete Agreements

This type of agreement is normally put in place when, through the course of work with the employer, the employee learns how the company is successful in relation to its competitors. This might include a business, manufacturing, or sales process. Knowledge of this process would allow the employee to directly compete (either individually or with a competitor). The noncompete agreement must be reasonable with regard to time frame (it cannot be indefinite) and geography, and it cannot unduly restrain an employee from making a living in his or her field.

Contract Audit Objectives

The following bullets outline an excerpt of audit objectives for a contract audit. The objectives might change based on your organization, but we have included some of the more common objectives:

➤ Review the contract and perform the following:

  ➤ Check that the contract has been signed by both parties and according to delegation (the CEO, vice president, and approving authority, for instance).

  ➤ Check the reasonableness of the contract, including terms and conditions, period, rates exchange, and charges.

  ➤ Check that the contract is still valid or binding and legally enforceable (within the period stipulated).

  ➤ Check that all amendments in the contract are authorized by the delegated officials.

➤ Obtain a list of contracts that have expired and review the associated invoices.

> ➤ Establish the expiration date from the contract.

> ➤ Trace an invoice from the transactions listing to transfer batch reports that no payment has been made on these contracts.

> ➤ Review this contract to ensure that it is legally enforceable.

> ➤ Establish where these contracts are kept and who is responsible for the safekeeping of the records.

>> ➤ Access to the records should be restricted to only authorized officials.

>> ➤ Removal of such files should be authorized and approved.

An IS auditor likely will audit a variety of contract vehicles, and it is important to know the differences in what is enforceable (legal) and what is not. The IS auditor must ensure that the contracts have the basic elements outlined and have been executed correctly, and that the contracts have legal review before execution. The organization should assign responsibility for regular review of contract dates and performance measurement, and should ensure that payments are made in accordance with the stipulations of the contract.

Roles and Responsibilities of IS Functions (Including Segregation of Duties)

The combination of a defined organization structure, policies and procedures, and clearly defined job functions ensures that the IT organization can meet the continuing needs of the organization. The IT department continually faces challenges in the form of competing priorities, shifts in business priorities, and operational firefighting. The fast pace of business demands that the IT function be flexible and prepared for changes, as well as stay focused on the long- and short-term goals of the organization. If the IT function is unable to control change introduced into the environment by internal or external factors, IT staff will find themselves disregarding internal controls and will lead themselves and the organization into chaos.

The IT organization has to perform two high-level functions:

> ➤ Support the ongoing operational structure through sound methodologies. This includes support of the network devices, applications, data,

and system users. Policies and procedures (controls) must be followed to reduce overall business and security risk to the organization. Confidentiality, availability, and integrity of systems, applications, and data must be ensured.

➤ Support the development and implementation of new technologies, applications, data, and procedures into the organization. A proven methodology must be provided that aligns IT with the business strategy while mitigating risk in the organization. The introduction of new systems, applications, and data must not put the organization or existing systems at risk.

In most cases, clearly defined procedures and controls ensure that the IT organization can continue its operational mission while introducing new technology. The use of the security function, quality assurance, and the IS auditor assist IT leadership in maintaining and improving these controls.

Senior IT leadership is responsible for ensuring that the IT functions provide value to the organization. One of the top priorities is to ensure that the IT strategy aligns with the organization's strategy; if this strategy is not aligned, IT will move from a position of value within the organization to a cost center with little or no value.

Most IT structures are defined along specific functions such as system development, computer security, computer operations, and user support. During the definition of the structure, management must keep in mind the segregation of incompatible duties. There are four areas of segregation:

➤ Authorization

  ➤ Verifying cash collections and daily balancing reports

  ➤ Approving purchase requisitions or purchase orders

  ➤ Approving time sheets, payroll certifications, leave requests, and cumulative leave records

  ➤ Approving change orders, computer system design, or programming changes

➤ Custody

  ➤ Access to any funds through the collection of funds or processing of payments

  ➤ Access to safes, lock boxes, file cabinets, or other places where money, checks, or other assets are stored

  ➤ Custodian of a petty cash or change fund

➤ Receipt of any goods or services

➤ Maintenance of inventories

➤ Handling or distribution of paychecks and advances, limited purchase checks, or other checks

➤ Record keeping

➤ Preparing cash receipt backups or billings, purchase requisitions, payroll certifications, and leave records

➤ Entering charges or posting payments to an accounts-receivable system

➤ Maintaining inventory records

➤ Reconciliation

➤ Comparing billing documents to billing summaries

➤ Comparing funds collected to accounts-receivable postings

➤ Comparing collections to deposits

➤ Performing surprise counts of funds

➤ Comparing payroll certifications to payroll summaries

Practices Related to the Management of Technical and Operational Infrastructure

Management of the IT infrastructure includes the overall maintenance or systems, user support, problem (incident) management, change management, and quality assurance. The IT department should use industry standards and performance measures to ensure that the IT functions meet the needs of the business through the IT organization's mission, vision, and strategy. The IT organization should establish policies for all phases of the system development life cycle (SDLC), which entails the acquisition, implementation, maintenance, and disposition of information systems. The SDLC should include computer hardware, network devices, communications systems, operating systems, application software, and data. It is important to note that some or all of the IT function might be outsourced to third-party providers, and those similar policies and procedures should exist in addition to the contract and service-level agreements (SLA).

Ensuring security of the information systems and their associated data is another function associated with the SDLC. Maintaining confidentiality, integrity, and availability of information systems ensures the continued economic viability of the organization. The security function is responsible for securing the physical facilities, hardware and software, and data. In addition, IT management must mitigate the risk associated with the disruption of business activities because of system failures or disasters.

Problem Management/Resource Management Procedures

Per the Information Technology Infrastructure Library (ITIL) Service Support Process Model, the goal of effective problem management is to minimize the adverse effect on the organization of incidents and problems caused by errors in the infrastructure, and to proactively prevent the occurrence of incidents, problems, and errors. Incidents or errors can range from hardware or software errors to malicious acts. IT should ensure that all users and administrators are properly trained to use the information systems associated with their function (proactive) and to implement problem-management systems to manage problem tracking, escalation, audit, and intrusion incident response. The IT organization should incorporate policies and procedures relating to problem management, including the recognition, logging, resolution, escalation, tracking, and reporting process. The procedures should define critical applications that require immediate escalation to senior management for priority resolution, as well as methods to ensure that all problems are captured, resolved, and reported.

Help Desk

The help desk is responsible for assisting end users with problems or issues with desktops or workstations, and personnel frequently participate in the configuration and deployment of new equipment, operating systems, and applications. The help-desk calls are usually logged within a help-desk ticketing system. The logging of calls provides information on when the call was received, the type of problem or error, and the resolution time.

Help-desk technicians can provide both remote and onsite support to resolve network, application, and database issues.

Scheduling

The IT function is responsible to users or customers and defines the level of service delivered to customers. Achieving the agreed service level requires the IT organization to manage workflow by planning expected and required capacity and properly planning activities. All work performed in the environment should be scheduled, to ensure that resources are used efficiently and effectively. The workflow of the IT organization should proceed at a steady rate, whether it pertains to normal operations or the introduction of new systems in the environment. The IS auditor should look for internal policies and procedures with regard to project and change management, as well as a clearly defined strategy that meets the needs of the organization over time. If work is either delayed or performed at the last possible minute because of poor planning, the associated controls are usually circumvented. This can lead to unstable and unsecured IT environments and ineffective use of IT resources.

Service-Level Agreements

According to the Foundations of Service Level Management, service-level management is defined as "the disciplined proactive methodology and procedures used to ensure that adequate levels of service are delivered to all IT users in accordance with business priorities and at acceptable cost." Organizations use a service-level agreement (SLA) to establish a common understanding of the nature and level of service required. The SLA should define specific targets for the level of service provided, as well as associated measurements. SLAs can be used in conjunction with third-party agreements or internally in organizations as performance measures. In addition, the service agreement should contain nonperformance clauses that define what happens if the agreed-upon service level is not met. These might include warnings, corrective actions, or financial penalties.

Key Performance Indicators and Performance-Measurement Techniques

It is generally accepted that an organization cannot manage what it cannot measure. Performance measures are used to ensure alignment through the use of performance metrics. Organizations might adopt performance metrics in a variety of areas—marketing, sales, and IT—but the foundation of the metrics remains the same: They ensure progress toward strategic goals over time by using standardized, objective, documented metrics.

As an example, the IT organization might have a commitment to complete all help-desk calls within 24 hours of receipt. Tracking this performance measure would include the regular review of help-desk calls and tickets for entry and closing date, as well as customer surveys to ensure that the issue was successfully resolved. This type of performance measure would be well documented and would include all tasks associated with measurement. For instance, if you measured only the ticket entry and ticket close time for help desk tickets, you might find that all fell within the expected 24 hours. Upon closer inspection, however, you might find that 50% of the time, the issue was not resolved. It is important to note that a performance measure that is not documented or thought out might not produce the expected results.

Exam Prep Questions

1. A bottom-up approach to the development of organizational policies is driven by:

   ❑ A. A review of corporate goals and objectives.

   ❑ B. A structured approach that maps policy objectives to corporate strategy.

   ❑ C. A risk assessment of asset vulnerabilities.

   ❑ D. A business impact analysis of known threats.

   Answer: C. A bottom-up approach to the development of organizational policies is often driven by risk assessment.

2. A primary responsibility of an auditor with regard to improper segregation of duties is to:

   ❑ A. Ensure the enforcement of proper segregation of duties.

   ❑ B. Advise senior management of the risk involved in not implementing proper segregation of duties.

   ❑ C. Participate in the organization's definition of roles and responsibilities, to prevent improper segregation of duties.

   ❑ D. Simply document breaches of proper segregation of duties.

   Answer: B. Remember, it is not an auditor's place to participate in the implementation of controls. As to improper segregation of duties, an IS auditor's primary responsibility is to advise senior management of the risk involved in not implementing proper segregation of duties, such as having the security administrator perform an operations function.

3. Which of the following roles is accountable for the maintenance of appropriate security measures over information assets?

   ❑ A. Data and systems owners, such as the corporate officers

   ❑ B. Data and systems custodians, such as the network administrator and firewall administrator

   ❑ C. Data and systems users, such as the payroll department

   ❑ D. Data and systems managers

   Answer: A. Specific security administration is directed by senior management and implemented by system custodians. Still, ultimate accountability for data and system security lies with senior management.

4. If an IS auditor observes that proper project-approval procedures do not exist, the auditor should:

- ❏ A. Provide detailed procedures that the auditor recommends for implementation.
- ❏ B. Look for evidence of other undocumented approval procedures.
- ❏ C. Recognize that the lack of proper project-approval procedures is a risk indicator for insufficient project-management skills, and recommend project-management training as a compensatory control.
- ❏ D. Recommend to management that proper project-approval procedures be adopted and documented.

Answer: D. If an IS auditor observes that project-approval procedures do not exist, the IS auditor should recommend to management that formal approval procedures be adopted and documented.

5. When auditing third-party service providers, an auditor should be concerned with:

- ❏ A. Ownership of programs and files.
- ❏ B. A statement of due care and confidentiality.
- ❏ C. The capability for continued service in the event of a disaster.
- ❏ D. All of the above.

Answer: D. When auditing third-party service providers, an auditor should be concerned with ownership of the program and files, a statement of due care and confidentiality, and the service provider's capability to provide continued service in the event of a disaster.

6. Proper segregation of duties does not prohibit a LAN administrator from also having programming responsibilities. True or false?

- ❏ A. True
- ❏ B. False

Answer: B. Proper segregation of duties normally prohibits a LAN administrator from also having programming responsibilities because the administrator would have custody of the computing assets, while also having the potential to control transaction authorization and recording.

7. When performing an IS strategy audit, which of the following is LEAST important for the auditor to consider?

- ❏ A. Reviewing short-term plans (one year) and long-term plans (three to five years)
- ❏ B. Reviewing information systems procedures
- ❏ C. Interviewing appropriate corporate management personnel
- ❏ D. Ensure that the external environment has been considered

Answer: B. Information systems procedures are not strategic in nature.

8. Which of the following is MOST important when evaluating an IS strategy?

   ❏ A. Making sure that the IS strategy maximizes efficiency and utilization of current and future IT resources

   ❏ B. Ensuring that information security is considered in all IS initiatives

   ❏ C. Making sure the IS strategy supports corporate goals and objectives

   ❏ D. Ensuring that systems administrators are allowed to provide accurate input on true systems capabilities

   Answer: C. Above all else, an IS strategy must support the business objectives of the organization.

9. Allowing applications programmers to access live production applications for patching and security maintenance breaches proper segregation of duties. True or false?

   ❏ A. True

   ❏ B. False

   Answer: A. Although it is common practice in many organizations, allowing application programmers to change code in production programs increases the risk of fraud.

10. Proper segregation of duties does not prohibit a quality-control administrator from performing change control and problem management. True or false?

   ❏ A. True

   ❏ B. False

   Answer: A. Proper segregation of duties does not prohibit a quality-control administrator from also being responsible for change control and problem management.

Technical Infrastructure and Operational Practices and Infrastructure

Key concepts you will need to understand:

- ✓ Risks and controls related to hardware platforms, system software and utilities, network infrastructure, and IS operational practices
- ✓ Systems performance and monitoring processes, tools, and techniques (for example, network analyzers, system error messages, system utilization reports, load balancing)
- ✓ The process of IT infrastructure acquisition, development, implementation, and maintenance
- ✓ Change control and configuration-management principles for hardware and system software
- ✓ Practices related to the management of technical and operational infrastructure (for example, problem-management/resource-management procedures, help desk, scheduling, service-level agreements)
- ✓ Functionality of systems software and utilities (for example, database-management systems, security packages)
- ✓ Functionality of network components (for example, firewalls, routers, proxy servers, modems, terminal concentrators, hubs, switches)
- ✓ Network architecture (for example, network protocols, remote computing, network topologies, Internet, intranet, extranet, client/server)

Techniques you will need to master:

- ✓ Evaluate the acquisition, installation, and maintenance of hardware to ensure that it efficiently and effectively supports the organization's IS processing and business requirements, and is compatible with the organization's strategies
- ✓ Evaluate the development/acquisition, implementation, and maintenance of systems software and utilities to ensure ongoing support of the organization's IS processing and business requirements, and compatibility with the organization's strategies
- ✓ Evaluate the acquisition, installation, and maintenance of the network infrastructure to ensure
- efficient and effective support of the organization's IS processing and business requirements
- ✓ Evaluate IS operational practices to ensure efficient and effective utilization of the technical resources used to support the organization's IS processing and business requirements
- ✓ Evaluate the use of system performance and monitoring processes, tools, and techniques to ensure that computer systems continue to meet the organization's business objectives

IT Organizational Structure

As an IS auditor, you will need to understand the technical infrastructure of the organization, the IS organizational structure, and the operational practices. IT management is responsible for the acquisition and maintenance of the information architecture. This includes networking devices, servers and operating systems, data storage systems, applications, and the standards and protocols associated with network communication.

IT managers must define the role and articulate the value of the IT function. This includes the IT organizational structure as well as operational practices. The IT management functions are generally divided into two functional areas:

> ➤ **Line management**—Line managers are concerned with the routine operational decisions on a day-to-day basis.

> ➤ **Project management**—Project managers work on specific projects related to the information architecture. Projects are normally a one-time effort with a fixed start, duration, and end that reach a specific deliverable or objective.

The following are line management functions:

> ➤ **Control group**—Responsible for the logging and collection of input for users.

> ➤ **Data management**—Responsible for the data architecture (integrity, validity, and so on).

> ➤ **Database administrator**—Responsible for the maintenance of the organization's database systems

> ➤ **Systems administrator**—Responsible for the maintenance of computer systems and local area networks (LANs). Sets up system accounts, installs system-wide software, and so on.

> ➤ **Network manager/administrator**—Responsible for the planning, implementation, and maintenance of the telecommunications infrastructure.

> ➤ **Quality assurance manager**—Responsible for ensuring the quality of activities performed in all areas of information technology.

The IT functional areas are responsible for the computing infrastructure. This includes computer hardware, network hardware, communications systems, operating systems, and application software and data files. IT management must understand how these elements work together and must establish a control infrastructure (defined functions, policies, procedures, governance) that will reduce risk to the organization during the acquisition, implementation, maintenance, and disposal processes.

A clear understanding of networking and data components enables you to evaluate existing input/output (I/O) controls and monitoring procedures. Organizations should constantly seek to use technology more efficiently and effectively to meet business objectives. This quest will provide a myriad of choices regarding technology and the acquisition, development, implementation, and maintenance of the network as a whole and its individual components.

A clearly defined IT strategic plan combined with acquisition planning, project management, and strong operational practices (policies and procedures) will ensure two things: First, the IT organization will be aligned with the business strategy and objectives. Second, IT resources will be used effectively and efficiently. IT managers consistently balance operational issues and the implementation of new technology. This balancing act creates competing priorities: Operational issues usually fall into the "urgent" category, whereas the implementation of new technology falls into the "important" category. "Urgent" includes application and network issues that negatively impact operational systems. These issues need to be addressed and corrected as quickly as possible to ensure continued operations. "Important" issues include the review, testing, and implementation of new methodologies or technologies to improve the operational environment. If an IT organization allows itself to be driven primarily by urgent issues while putting important issues to the side, it will quickly become a completely reactive environment and will not look forward to properly align technology and business objectives. Adherence to strong operational and planning practices ensures that the IT organization strikes an equal balance between operational issues and future planning, and continues to align technical resources with business objectives.

Throughout this chapter, we describe in detail the separate components of the information architecture. Some of these concepts will be new to you, and some you will have already encountered as an IS auditor. Together, they will give you a complete overview of the information architecture. With this knowledge, you should be able to review complex business processes and associate the related components, controls, and operational practices. It is important to remember that no matter how complex the technology is, the foundation of standards, practices, and controls remains the same.

Take a basic example that might be familiar to a majority of you: Amazon.com. Amazon uses the same type of transactions and transaction processing that that many e-commerce companies use; it also uses the same base set of controls. The basic components of the systems include a web server to respond to requests and a relational database to manage the transactions. When the customer finds the desired items to purchase, some type of shopping card and payment system is used. The final portions of the system are the inventory management/shipping system and the financial system, which handles all the financial transactions. Overall, the business functions of Amazon.com are not that different. Knowing the individual components, communication protocols, and operational procedures, however, helps the IS auditor evaluate the system to ensure that the organization is using accepted best practices (controls) and that the information architecture is aligned with the business objectives.

Evaluating Hardware Acquisition, Installation, and Maintenance

A significant part of the information architecture is the computing hardware. These systems include the following:

➤ **Processing components**—The central processing unit (CPU). The CPU contains the electrical/electronic components that control or direct all operations in the computer system. A majority of devices within the information architecture are CPUs (supercomputers, mainframes, minicomputer, microcomputer, laptops, and PDAs).

➤ **Input/output components**—The I/O components are used to pass instructions or information to the computer and to generate output from the computer. These types of devices include the keyboard, the mouse (input), and monitors/terminal displays.

Computers logically fall into categories and differ depending on the processing power and size for the organization. The following are the basic categories for computers:

➤ **Supercomputers**—These types of computers have a large capacity of processing speed and power. They are generally used for complex mathematical calculations. Supercomputers generally perform a small number of very specific functions that require extensive processing power (decryption, modeling, and so on). Supercomputers differ from mainframes in that mainframes can use diverse concurrent programs.

➤ **Mainframes**—Mainframes are large general-purpose computers that support large user populations simultaneously. They have a large range of capabilities that are controlled by the operating system. A mainframe environment, as opposed to a client/server environment, is generally more controlled with regard to access and authorization to programs; the entire processing function takes place centrally on the mainframe. Mainframes are multiuser, multithreading, and multiprocessing environments that can support batch and online programs.

➤ **Minicomputer**—Minicomputers are essentially smaller mainframes. They provide similar capabilities but support a smaller user population (less processing power).

➤ **Microcomputer (personal computers)**—Microcomputers are primarily used in the client/server environment. Examples include file/print servers, email servers, web servers, and servers that house database-management systems. Individual workstations also fall into the micro-computer category and are used for word processing, spreadsheet applications, and individual communications (email). Microcomputers are generally inexpensive because they do not have the processing power of larger minicomputers or mainframes.

➤ **Notebook/laptop computers**—Notebook and laptop computers are portable and allow users to take the computing power, applications, and, in some cases, data with them wherever they travel. Notebooks and laptops today have as much computing power as desktop workstations and provide battery power when traditional power is not available. Because of the mobile nature of notebook and laptop computers, they are susceptible to theft. Theft of a laptop computer is certainly the loss of a physical asset, but it also can include the loss of data or unauthorized access to the organization's information resources.

➤ **Personal digital assistants (PDAs)**—PDAs are handheld devices and generally have significantly less processing power, memory, and applications than notebook computers. These devices are battery powered and very portable (most can fit into a jacket pocket). Although the traditional use of a PDA is for individual organization, including the maintenance of tasks, contacts lists, calendars, and expense managers, PDAs are continually adding functionality. As of this writing, a significant number of PDAs provide wireless network access and have either commercial off-the-shelf software or custom software that enables users to access corporate information (sales and inventory, email, and so on). Most PDAs use pen (stylus)–based input instead of the traditional keyboard, effected by using either an onscreen keyboard or handwriting recognition. PDAs are synchronized with laptop/desktop computers through serial interfaces through the use of a cradle or wireless networking (802.11 or Bluetooth). The synchronization can be user initiated or automated, based on the needs of the user.

Earlier in this section, we discussed some of the attributes of computing systems, including multiprocessing, multitasking, and multithreading. These attributes are defined as follows:

➤ **Multitasking**—Multitasking allows computing systems to run two or more applications concurrently. This process enables the systems to allocate a certain amount of processing power to each application. In this instance, the tasks of each application are completed so quickly that it appears to multiple users that there are no disruptions in the process.

➤ **Multiprocessing**—Multiprocessing links more than one processor (CPU) sharing the same memory, to execute programs simultaneously. In today's environment, many servers (mail, web, and so on) contain multiple processors, allowing the operating system to speed the time for instruction execution. The operating system can break up a series of instructions and distribute them among the available processors, effecting quicker instruction execution and response.

➤ **Multithreading**—Multithreading enables operating systems to run several processes in rapid sequence within a single program or to execute (run) different parts, or threads, of a program simultaneously. When a process is run on a computer, that process creates a number of additional tasks and subtasks. All the threads (tasks and subtasks) can run at one time and combine as a rope (entire process). Multithreading can be defined as multitasking within a single program.

Risks and Controls Relating to Hardware Platforms

In aligning the IT strategy with the organizational strategy, IT provides solutions that meet the objectives of the organization. These solutions must be identified, developed, or acquired. As an IS auditor, you will assess this process by reviewing control issues regarding the acquisition, implementation, and maintenance of hardware. Governance of the IT organization and corresponding policies will reduce the risk associated with acquisition, implementation, and maintenance. Configuration management accounts for all IT components, including software. A comprehensive configuration-management program reviews, approves, tracks, and documents all changes to the information architecture. Configuration of the communications network is often the most critical and time-intensive part of network management as a whole. Software development project management involves scheduling, resource management, and progress tracking. Problem management records and monitors incidents and documents them through resolution. The documentation created during the problem-management process can identify inefficient hardware and software, and can be used as a basis for identifying acquisition opportunities that serve the business objectives. Risk management is the process of assessing risk, taking steps to reduce risk to an acceptable level (mitigation) and maintaining that acceptable level of risk. Risk identification and management works across all areas of the organizational and IT processes.

A configuration-management audit should always verify software licensing for authorized use.

The CoBiT framework provides hardware policy areas for IT functions. These policy areas can be used as a basis for control objectives to ensure that the acquisition process is clearly defined and meets the needs of the organization. The CoBiT areas address the following questions:

➤ **Acquisition**—How is hardware acquired from outside vendors?

➤ **Standards**—What are the hardware compatibility standards?

➤ **Performance**—How should computing capabilities be tested?

➤ **Configuration**—Where should client/servers, personal computers, and others be used.

➤ **Service providers**—Should third-party service providers be used?

One of the key challenges facing IT organizations today is the speed of new technology releases in the marketplace and detailed baseline documentation for their organizations. IT organizations need a process for documenting existing hardware and then maintaining that documentation. This documentation supports the acquisition process and ensures that new technologies that meet the business objectives can be thoroughly tested to ensure that they are compatible with the existing information architecture.

Contained within the CoBiT framework regarding hardware and software acquisition, the auditor will consider the control objectives defined in Table 3.1.

Table 3.1 Acquisition Control Objectives	
Identify Automated Solutions	**Control Objective**
1.1 Definition of Information Requirements	The organization's system development life cycle methodology should require that the business requirements for the existing system and the proposed new or modified system (software, data, and infrastructure) are clearly defined before a development, implementation, or modification project is approved. The system development life cycle methodology should specify the solution's functional and operational requirements, including performance, safety, reliability, compatibility, security, and legislation.
1.2 Formulation of Alternative Courses of Action	The organization's system development life cycle should stipulate that alternative courses of action should be analyzed to satisfy the business requirements established for a proposed new or modified system.
1.3 Formulation of Acquisition Strategy	Information systems acquisition, development, and maintenance should be considered in the context of the organization's IT long- and short-range plans. The organization's system development life cycle methodology should provide for a software acquisition strategy plan defining whether the software will be acquired off-the-shelf; developed internally, through contract, or by enhancing the existing software; or developed through a combination of these.
1.4 Third-Party Service Requirements	The organization's system development life cycle methodology should require an evaluation of the requirements and specifications for an RFP (request for proposal) when dealing with a third-party service vendor.
1.5 Technological Feasibility Study	The organization's system development life cycle methodology should require an examination of the technological feasibility of each alternative for satisfying the business requirements established for the development of a proposed new or modified information system project.
1.6 Economic Feasibility Study	In each proposed information systems development, implementation, and modification project, the organization's system development life cycle methodology should require an analysis of the costs

(continued)

Table 3.1 Acquisition Control Objectives *(continued)*	
Identify Automated Solutions	**Control Objective**
	and benefits associated with each alternative being considered for satisfying the established business requirements.
1.7 Information Architecture	Management should ensure that attention is paid to the enterprise data model while solutions are being identified and analyzed for feasibility.
1.8 Risk Analysis Report	In each proposed information system development, implementation, or modification project, the organization's system development life cycle methodology should require an analysis and documentation of the security threats, potential vulnerabilities and impacts, and the feasible security and internal control safeguards for reducing or eliminating the identified risk. This should be realized in line with the overall risk-assessment framework.
1.9 Cost-Effective Security Controls	Management should ensure that the costs and benefits of security are carefully examined in monetary and nonmonetary terms, to guarantee that the costs of controls do not exceed benefits. The decision requires formal management sign-off. All security requirements should be identified at the requirements phase of a project and should be justified, agreed to, and documented as part of the overall business case for an information system. Security requirements for business continuity management should be defined to ensure that the proposed solution supports the planned activation, fallback, and resumption processes.
1.10 Audit Trails Design	The organization's system development life cycle methodology should state that adequate mechanisms for audit trails must be available or developed for the solution identified and selected. The mechanisms should provide the capability to protect sensitive data (for example, user IDs) against discovery and misuse.
1.11 Ergonomics	Management should ensure that the IT function adheres to a standard procedure for identifying all potential system software programs, to satisfy its operational requirements.

(continued)

Table 3.1 Acquisition Control Objectives *(continued)*	
Identify Automated Solutions	**Control Objective**
1.13 Procurement Control	Management should develop and implement a central procurement approach describing a common set of procedures and standards to be followed in the procurement of information technology–related hardware, software, and services. Products should be reviewed and tested before their use and the financial settlement.
1.14 Software Product Acquisition	Software product acquisition should follow the organization's procurement policies.
1.15 Third-Party Software Maintenance	Management should require that before licensed software is acquired from third-party providers, the providers have appropriate procedures to validate, protect, and maintain the software product's integrity rights. Consideration should be given to the support of the product in any maintenance agreement related to the delivered product.
1.16 Contract Application Programming	The organization's system development life cycle methodology should require that the procurement of contract programming services be justified with a written request for services from a designated member of the IT function. The contract should stipulate that the software, documentation, and other deliverables are subject to testing and review before acceptance. In addition, it should require that the end products of completed contract programming services be tested and reviewed according to the related standards by the IT function's quality assurance group and other concerned parties (such as users and project managers) before payment for the work and approval of the end product. Testing to be included in contract specifications should consist of system testing, integration testing, hardware and component testing, procedure testing, load and stress testing, tuning and performance testing, regression testing, user acceptance testing, and, finally, pilot testing of the total system, to avoid any unexpected system failure.
1.17 Acceptance of Facilities	Management should ensure that an acceptance plan for facilities to be provided is agreed upon with the supplier in the contract. This plan should define the

(continued)

Table 3.1 Acquisition Control Objectives *(continued)*	
Identify Automated Solutions	**Control Objective**
	acceptance procedures and criteria. In addition, acceptance tests should be performed to guarantee that the accommodation and environment meet the requirements specified in the contract.
1.18 Acceptance of Technology	Management should ensure that an acceptance plan for specific technology to be provided is agreed upon with the supplier in the contract. This plan should define the acceptance procedures and criteria. In addition, acceptance tests provided for in the plan should include inspection, functionality tests, and workload trials.

The selection of computer hardware requires the organization to define specifications for outside vendors. These specifications should be used in evaluating vendor-proposed solutions. This specification is sometimes called an *invitation to tender* (ITT) or a *request for proposal* (RFP).

Per ISACA, the portion of the ITT pertaining to hardware should include the following:

➤ Information-processing requirements

  ➤ Major existing application systems and future application systems

  ➤ Workload and performance requirements

  ➤ Processing approaches (online/batch, client/server, real-time databases, continuous operation)

➤ Hardware requirements

  ➤ CPU speed

  ➤ Peripheral devices (sequential devices, such as tape drives; direct-access devices, such as magnetic disk drives, printers, CD-ROM drives, and WORM drives)

  ➤ Data-preparation/input devices that accept and convert data for machine processing

  ➤ Direct-entry devices (terminal, point-of-sale terminals, or automated teller machines)

  ➤ Networking capability (Ethernet connections, modems, and ISDN connections)

➤ System software applications

    ➤ Operation systems software (current version and any required upgrades)

    ➤ Compilers

    ➤ Program library software

    ➤ Database-management software and programs

    ➤ Communication software

    ➤ Access-control software

➤ Support requirements

    ➤ System maintenance (for preventative, detective [fault reporting], or corrective purposes)

    ➤ Training (user and technical staff)

    ➤ Backups (daily and disaster)

➤ Adaptability requirements

    ➤ Hardware/software upgrade capabilities

    ➤ Compatibility with existing hardware/software platforms

    ➤ Changeover to other equipment capabilities

➤ Constraints

    ➤ Staffing levels

    ➤ Existing hardware capacity

    ➤ Deliver dates

➤ Conversion requirements

    ➤ Test time for the hardware/software

    ➤ System-conversion facilities

    ➤ Cost/pricing schedule

The acquisition of hardware might be driven by requirements for a new software acquisition, the expansion of existing capabilities, or the scheduled replacement of obsolete hardware. With all these events, senior management must ensure that the acquisition is mapped directly to the strategic goals of the organization. The IT steering committee should guide information systems strategy—and, therefore, that its acquisitions—align with the organization's goals.

In addition, the senior managers of the IT steering committee should receive regular status updates on acquisition projects in progress, the cost of projects, and issues that impact the critical path of those projects. The IT steering committee is responsible for reviewing issues such as new and ongoing projects, major equipment acquisitions, and the review and approval of budget; however, the committee does not usually get involved in the day-to-day operations of the IS department.

The IT organization should have established policies for all phases of the system development life cycle (SDLC) that controls the acquisition, implementation, maintenance, and disposition of information systems. The SDLC should include computer hardware, network devices, communications systems, operating systems, application software, and data. These systems support mission-critical business functions and should maximize the organization's return on investment. The combination of a solid governance framework and defined acquisition process creates a control infrastructure that reduces risk and ensures that IT infrastructure supports the business functions.

As an IS auditor, you will look for evidence of a structured approach to hardware acquisition, implementation, and maintenance. These include written acquisition policies and outline the process for feasibility studies, requirements gathering, and the approval process of the IT steering committee. After hardware is procured, the IT organization must have a defined project-management and change-control process to implement the hardware. All hardware acquired must fall under existing maintenance contracts and procedures, or contracts must be acquired and procedures updated to reflect the new hardware. The hardware should be tested according to written test plans before going into production, and the hardware should be assigned to the appropriate functional areas (such as systems administration) to ensure that production responsibility is clearly defined. The acquired hardware, whether a replacement or new to the IT infrastructure, should be secured (physical, logical) and added to the business continuity plan.

Change Control and Configuration Management Principles for Hardware

The change-control and configuration-management processes detail the formal documented procedures for introducing technology changes into the environment. More specifically, *change control* ensures that changes are documented, approved, and implemented with minimum disruption to the production environment and maximum benefits to the organization.

During the normal operation of the IT infrastructure, there will be changes to hardware and software because of normal maintenance, upgrades, security patches, and changes in network configurations. All changes within the infrastructure need to be documented and must follow change control procedures. In the planning stages the party responsible for the changes (such as end users, line managers or the network administrator) should develop a change-control request. The request should include all systems affected by the change, the length of resources required to implement the change (time and money), and a detailed plan. The plan should include what specific steps will be taken for the change and should include test plans and back-out procedures, in case the change adversely affects the infrastructure. This request should go before the change-control board that votes on the change and normally provides a maintenance window in which the change is to be implemented. When the change is complete and tested, all documentation and procedures that are affected by the change should be updated. The change-control board should maintain a copy of the change request and its review of the implementation of the change.

 Reviewing a diagram of the network topology is often the best first step when auditing IT systems.

The change-control board provides critical oversight for any production IT infrastructure. This board ensures that all affected parties and senior management are aware of both major and minor changes within the IT infrastructure. The change-management process establishes an open line of communication among all affected parties and allows those parties and subject matter experts (SMEs) to provide input that is instrumental in the change process.

In addition to change and configuration control, the IT organization is responsible for capacity planning. A capacity plan and procedures should be developed to ensure the continued monitoring of the network and associated hardware. Capacity planning ensures that the expansion or reduction of resources takes place in parallel with the overall organizational growth or reduction. The audit procedures should include review of the following:

➤ **Hardware performance-monitoring plan**—Includes a review of problem logs, processing schedules, system reports, and job accounting reports.

➤ **Problem log review**—The problem log assists in identifying hardware malfunctions, operator actions, or system resets that negatively affect the performance of the IT infrastructure. The IT organization should regularly monitor the problem log to detect potential IT resource capacity issues.

➤ **Hardware availability and performance reports**—Review and ensure that the services required by the organization (CPU utilization, storage utilization, bandwidth utilization, and system uptime) are available when needed and that maintenance procedures do not negatively impact the organization's operations.

The IT organization should work closely with senior management to ensure that the capacity plan will meet current and future business needs, and to implement hardware-monitoring procedures to ensure that IT services, applications, and data are available. The IT organization should regularly monitor its internal maintenance, job scheduling, and network management to ensure that they are implemented in the most efficient and effective manner.

Computer resources should be carefully monitored to match utilization needs with proper resource capacity levels.

Evaluating Systems Software Development, Acquisition, Implementation, and Maintenance

The development, acquisition, implementation, and maintenance software and hardware support key business practices. The IS auditor must ensure that the organization has controls in place that manage these assets in an effective and efficient manner. A clear understanding of the technology and its operational characteristics are critical to the IS auditor's review.

Understanding Systems Software and Utilities Functionality

We have discussed both hardware and network devices and their important role in today's IT infrastructure. The hardware can be considered a means to an end, but the software is responsible for delivering services and information. A majority of organizations today use client/server software, which enables applications and data to be spread across a number of systems and to serve a variety of operating systems. The advantage of client/server computing is that clients can request data, processing, and services from servers both internal and external to the organization. The servers do the bulk of the work. This technology enables a variety of clients, from workstations to personal digital assistants (PDAs). Client/server computing also enables centralized control of the organization's resources, from access control to continuity.

One level above the hardware we have already discussed is *firmware*. This type of "software" is generally contained on a chip within the component of the hardware (motherboard, video card, modem, and so on). The operating system runs at the next level on top of the hardware and firmware, and is the nucleus of the IT infrastructure. The operating system contains programs that interface among the user, processor, and applications software. Operating systems can be considered the "heart" of the software system. They allow the sharing of CPU processing, memory, application access, data access, data storage, and data processing; they ensure the integrity of the system. The software that is developed for the computer must be compatible with the operating system.

Within the operating system are functions, utilities, and services that control the use and sharing of computer resources. These are the basic functions for the operating system:

➤ Defining user interfaces

➤ Enabling user access to hardware, data, file systems, and applications

➤ Managing the scheduling of resources among users

Along with the never-ending demand for scalability, interoperability, and performance, most operating systems today have parameters that can be customized to fit the organization. These parameters enable administrators to align many different types of functional systems with the performance and security needs of the organization. The selection of parameter settings should be aligned with the organization's workload and control structure. After the parameters are configured, they should be continually monitored to ensure that they do not result in errors, data corruption, unauthorized access, or a degradation of service.

In a client/server model, the server handles the processing of data, and security functions are shared by both workstation and server. The server responds to requests from other computers that are running independently on the network. An example of client/server computing is accessing the Internet via a web browser. An independent machine (workstation) requests data (web pages) from a web server; the web server processes the request, correlates the requested data, and returns it to the requester. The web server might contain static pages (HTML documents), or the HTML pages might contain dynamic data contained within a database-management system (DBMS). In this scenario, the server processes multiple requests, manages the processing, allocates memory, and processes authentication and authorization activities associated with the request. The client/server model enables the integration of applications and data resources.

Client/server architectures differ depending on the needs of organization. An additional component of client/server computing is *middleware*. Middleware provides integration between otherwise distinct applications. As an example of the application of middleware, IT organizations that have legacy applications (mainframe, non–client/server, and so on) can implement web-based front ends that incorporate the application and business logic in a central access point. The web server and its applications (Java servlets, VBScript, and so on) incorporate the business logic and create requests to the legacy systems to provide requested data. In this scenario, the web "front end" acts as middleware between the users and the legacy systems. This type of implementation is useful when multiple legacy systems contain data that is not integrated. The middleware can then respond to requests, correlate the data from multiple legacy applications (accounting, sales, and so on), and present to the client.

Middleware is commonly used to provide the following functionality:

➤ **Transaction-processing (TP) monitors**—These applications or programs monitor and process database transactions.

➤ **Remote procedure calls (RPC)**—An RPC is a function call in client/server computing that enables clients to request that a particular function or set of functions be performed on a remote computer.

➤ **Messaging services**—User requests (messages) can be prioritized, queued, and processed on remote servers.

As an IS auditor, you should assess the use of controls that ensure the confidentiality, integrity, and availability of client/server networks. The development and implementation of client/server applications and middleware should include proper change control and testing of modifications and should ensure that version control is maintained. Lack of proper controls with regard to the authentication, authorization, and data across multiple platforms could result in the loss of data or program integrity.

Organizations use more data today in decision making, customer support, sales, and account management. Data is the lifeblood of any organization.

With the high volume of change, transaction processing, and access, it is important to maintain the confidentiality, availability, and integrity of data according to the organization's business requirements. A DBMS is used to store, maintain, and enforce data integrity, as well provide the capability to convert data into information through the use of relationships and high-availability access. The primary functions of the DBMS are to reduce data redundancy, decrease access time, and provide security over sensitive data (records, fields, and transactions). A typical DBMS can be categorized as a container that stores data. Within the container of related information are multiple smaller containers that comprise logically related data. Figure 3.1 shows a DBMS relational structure for an asset-management system.

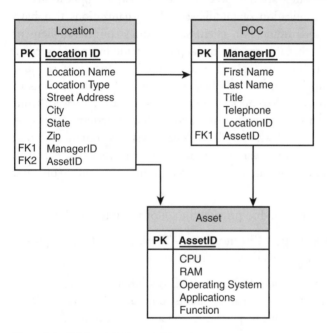

Figure 3.1   Relational database structure.

In Figure 3.1 the location (LocationID) of the asset is related to both the point of contact (POC) and the asset itself. Relational databases use rows (*tuples*, equal to records) and columns (*domains* or *attributes*, which correspond to fields).

A DBMS should include a *data dictionary* that identifies the data elements (fields), their characteristics, and their use. Data dictionaries are used to identify all fields and field types in the DBMS to assist with application development and processing. The data dictionary should contain an index and description of all the items stored in the database.

Three basic database models exist: hierarchical, network, and relational. A *hierarchical* database model establishes a parent-child relationship between tables (entities). It is difficult to manage relationships in this model when children need to relate to more than one parent; this can lead to data redundancy. In the *network* database model, children can relate to more than one parent. This can lead to complexity in relationships, making an ID difficult to understand, modify, and recover in the event of a failure. The *relational* database model separates the data from the database structure, allowing for flexibility in implementing, understanding, and modifying. The relational structure enables new relationships to be built based on business needs.

The key feature of relational databases is *normalization*, which structures data to minimize duplication and inconsistencies. Normalization rules include these:

➤ Each field in a table should represent unique information.

➤ Each table should have a primary key.

➤ You must be able to make changes to the data (other than the primary key) without affecting other fields.

Users access databases through a directory system that describes the location of data and the access method. This system uses a data dictionary, which contains an index and description of all the items stored in the database.

 The directory system of a database-management system describes the location of data and the access method.

In a transaction-processing database, all data transactions to include updating, creating, and deleting are logged to a transaction log. When users update the database, the data contained in the update is written first to the transaction log and then to the database. The purpose of the transaction log is to hold transactions for a short period of time until the database software is ready to commit the transaction to the database. This process ensures that the records associated with the change are ready to accept the entire transactions. In environments with high volumes of transactions, records are locked while transactions are committed (concurrency control), to enable the completion of the transactions. Concurrency controls prevent integrity problems when two processes attempt to update the same data at the same time. The database software checks the log periodically and then commits all transactions contained in the log since the last commit. Atomicity is the process by which data integrity is ensured through the completion of an entire transaction or not at all.

Atomicity enforces data integrity by ensuring that a transaction is completed either in its entirety or not at all. Concurrency controls are used as a countermeasure for potential database corruption when two processes attempt to simultaneously edit or update the same information.

Risks and Controls Related to System Software and Utilities

The software (operating systems, applications, database-management systems, and utilities) must meet the needs of the organization. The challenge facing a majority of IT organizations today is the wide variety of software products and their acquisition, implementation, maintenance, and integration. Organizational software is used to maintain and process the corporate data and enable its availability and integrity. The IT organization is responsible for keeping abreast of new software capabilities to improve business processes and expand services. In addition, the IT organization needs to monitor and maintain existing applications to ensure that they are properly updated, licensed, and supported. A capacity-management plan ensures that software expansion or reduction of resources takes place in parallel with overall business growth or reduction. The IT organization must solicit input from both users and senior management during the development and implementation of the capacity plan, to achieve the business goals in the most efficient and effective manner.

Computer resources should be carefully monitored to match utilization needs with proper resource capacity levels.

Change Control and Configuration Management Principles for System Software

Whether purchased or developed, all software must follow a formal change-control process. This process ensures that software meets the business needs and internal compatibility standards. The existence of a change control process minimizes the possibility that the production network will be disrupted and ensures that appropriate recovery and back-out procedures are in place.

When internal applications are developed and implemented, the IT organization is responsible for maintaining separate development, test, and production libraries. These libraries facilitate effective and efficient management and control of the software inventory, and incorporate security and control procedures for version control and release of software. The library function should be consistent with proper segregation of duties. For example, the system developer may create and alter software logic, but should not be allowed access to information processing or production applications. Source code comparison is an effective method for tracing changes to programs.

Evaluating Network Infrastructure Acquisition, Installation, and Maintenance

The IT organization should have both long- and short-term plans that address maintenance, monitoring, and migration to new software. During the acquisition process, the IT organization needs to map software acquisitions to the organization's strategic plan and ensure that the software meets documented compatibility standards. The IT organization needs to understand copyright laws that apply to the software and must create policies and procedures that guard against unauthorized use or copying of the software without proper approval or licensing agreements. It must maintain a list of all software used in the organization, along with licensing agreements/certificates and support agreements. The IT organization might implement centralized control and automated distribution of software, as well as scan user workstations to ensure adherence to licensing agreements. The following are some key risk indicators related to software acquisition:

➤ Software acquisitions are not mapped to the strategic plan.

➤ No documented policies are aimed at guiding software acquisitions.

➤ No process exists for comparing the "develop vs. purchase" option.

➤ No one is assigned responsibility for the acquisition process.

➤ Affected parties are not involved with assessing requirements and needs.

➤ There is insufficient knowledge of software alternatives.

➤ Security features and internal controls are not assessed.

➤ Benchmarking and performance tests are not carried out.

➤ Integration and scalability issues are not taken into account.

➤ Total cost of ownership is not fully considered.

Understanding Network Components Functionality

The IT infrastructure communication is facilitated by integrated network components. These devices, software, and protocols work together to pass electrical transmissions between systems through analog, digital, or wireless transmission types. It is important to understand the devices and standards involved with networking and telecommunications because they are the most complex part of the information architecture. As you read through this section, keep in mind that we are combining network devices, access media, and networking protocols/standards and how they are used in the network infrastructure. A good starting point for gaining this knowledge is to first understand how computers and other network devices communicate. Understanding communication is key to realizing how devices interoperate to provide network services.

In networking, network standards and protocols facilitate the creation of an integrated environment of application and services communication. For organizations to create these environments and provide centralized troubleshooting, organizations have created reference models for network architectures. Three external organizations develop standards and specifications for protocols used in communications:

➤ The International Organization for Standardization (ISO)

➤ The American Institution of Electrical and Electronic Engineers (IEEE)

➤ The International Telecommunications Union–Telecommunications Sector (ITU-T), formerly the International Telegraph and Telephone Consultative Committee (CCITT)

The ISO developed the Open Systems Interconnect (OSI) model in the early 1980s as a proof-of-concept model that all vendors could use to ensure that their products could communicate and interact. The OSI model was not used as directly as a standard, but it gained acceptance as a framework that a majority of applications and protocols adhere to. The OSI model contains seven layers, each with specific functions. Each layer has its own responsibilities with regard to tasks, processes, and services. The separation of functionality of the layers ensures that the solutions offered by one layer can be updated without affecting the other layers. The goal of the OSI model is to provide the framework for an open network architecture in which no one vendor owns the model, but all vendors can use the model to integrate their technologies. The Transmission Control Protocol/Internet Protocol (TCP/IP) is discussed later in this chapter, but it is important to note that TCP/IP was developed and used for many years before the introduction of the OSI model.

The OSI reference model breaks down the complexities of network communication into seven basic layers of functionality and services. To best illustrate how these seven layers work, we can relate how computers communicate to how humans communicate. The following paragraphs describe how a software application's thought, or data payload, is transferred and prepared for communication by the operating system's communications services. When this is accomplished, we will then look at how the data payload is transported, addressed, and converted from a logical thought into physical signals that can travel across cables or wireless transmissions.

Step 1: Having and Managing a Thought (Data Encapsulation)

As people, we have learned that it is always wise to think before speaking. In other words, we actually need to formulate a thought to communicate (data payload), format the presentation of the thought for the destination, and manage the thought appropriately. For example, sometimes you might be trying to communicate a complex idea to another person, and you find the need to enhance your normal verbal communication with written diagrams or even hand gestures. These types of efforts might not contain new information in and of themselves, but they are used to facilitate the communication of an idea when words alone fail. Computers and other networking devices sometimes need to use such extracurricular thought management as well. So the first step in communicating a data payload between one computer and another is to pass an application's thought to the networking services for further manipulation and management. Within the OSI reference model for networking architecture, these processes are handled within Layers 5, 6, and 7. Table 3.2 looks at each of these layers more closely.

Table 3.2 Open Systems Interconnect (OSI) Model			
OSI Layer	**Purpose**	**Telecommunication Protocol Examples**	**Protocol Data Unit**
7 (Application)	This is the networking layer that interfaces with applications and operating systems. This is where the user (through an application or operating system activity) first passes off information to networking services for telecommunication.	HTTP, Telnet, SMTP, DNS, SNMP	Data
6 (Presentation)	The data might require special formatting techniques, including (but not limited to) preparation according to special presentation protocols for picture and sound, compression, or even encryption.	ASCII, JPG, GIF, MIDI	
5 (Session)	Communicating the data might be a special device-to-device bond, or session, for cooperative multidevice communication efforts, for example.	NetBIOS, RPC, SQL	

Using OSI Layers 7–5 Within the Data PDU

As a user, you will first interface with networking communications by using a network-enabled application. A network-enabled application is capable of utilizing network protocols to send and receive data. Let's take a look at using your web browser to request and view data from an Internet web server. To view a web page, you must enter a URL web address such as http://www. certifiedtechtrainers.com. This simple process tells your web browser to use the Hypertext Transfer Protocol (HTTP) to contact a web server at www.certifiedtechtrainers.com. Neither you nor the browser needs to encapsulate your request for transport, to encapsulate the request with a formal IP address, or even to encapsulate the request appropriately to traverse your connected networking medium, such as an Ethernet cable. HTTP is a management protocol that invokes and coordinates the services of other networking protocols as necessary. That's why HTTP is said to be an OSI Layer 7 protocol, or application-layer protocol. HTTP itself is not an application, but it is the protocol used to interface a desktop application such as a web browser with other necessary communication protocols.

When you enter the URL http://www.certifiedtechtrainers.com into your browser, you unknowingly invoked another application-layer protocol called Domain Name Service (DNS). If we agreed to meet at Certified Tech Trainers office, you would need to know the actual street address of the location, right? Likewise, the www.certifiedtechtrainers.com name maps to an actual IP address designated to the web server you intend the HTTP request to be sent to. DNS queries a DNS server to find out the IP address of www.certifiedtechtrainers.com so it can somewhat transparently reformat your request from http://www.certifiedtechtrainers.com to http://24.227. 60.114. As you can see, these application-layer protocols are more focused on communication management than on actual request transmission. However, there is still more data management necessary. The default web page you are requesting likely has pictures or sounds. HTTP does not know how to present formatted graphics. Rather, the .gif and .jpg picture protocols operate at OSI Layer 6, the presentation layer, to handle the presentation of some common picture formats found on web pages. At some point, you might submit a request for securely encrypted communication by using https:// instead of http:// in your requested URL (this is often done without the user's awareness because requests for such a secure connection are often invoked via a link). By doing so, the browser makes a special request to have the HTTP request encrypted with the Secure Sockets Layer (SSL) encryption protocol. In conjunction with HTTP, SSL operates at OSI Layer 5, or the session layer.

At this point, the top three layers—application, presentation, and session— have been used in managing the request for data. This all occurs before consideration of how to transport or logically address the actual packets that need to be transmitted. Looking at all the activity just described, it would make sense that the data itself (data payload) and all the ancillary HTTP, HTTPS, JPG, GIF, and SSL communication could be considered the "thought" we desire to transmit. The technical term for this networking "thought" is the protocol data unit (PDU), known as data. You now understand how a computer needs to think before it speaks, just as you do.

Using OSI Layer 4 Within the Segment PDU

Now that we have a nicely managed data PDU, we need to package the communication appropriately for transport. As an application-layer protocol, HTTP does not *transport* the data itself. Rather, it manages *transferring* the data using other protocols to do so. The data PDU can now be encapsulated into a segment for transport using an OSI Layer 4 protocol such as the Transmission Control Protocol (TCP).

Just as you must break your thought into sentences and words for transport via your mouth or hands, the computer must encapsulate segments of the data PDU for transmission as well. TCP is a nifty OSI Layer 4 (transport-layer) networking protocol that is especially adept at this task. Not only does it segment the communication, but it does so in a methodical way that allows the receiving host to rebuild the data easily by attaching sequence numbers to its TCP segments. This sequencing information, along with other special TCP transport management communications, is provided in a TCP header within each data segment TCP encapsulates. Other transport-management communications provided by TCP include implementation of confirmation services for ensuring that all segments reach the intended recipient. When you want to be sure a letter is successfully delivered by the postal service, you might pay the additional cost for requiring a return receipt to be delivered to you upon successful delivery of the letter. If you never receive your return receipt, you could mail another copy of the letter and wait for a second confirmation. Without going into technical specifics, TCP can implement a similar system to ensure *reliable* transport. However, if you do not have the money or time to arrange for a return receipt for your letter, you might opt to forgo the assurance that the return receipt provides and send it via regular post, which guarantees only best effort, or *unreliable* delivery.

The technical parallel is to encapsulate the data PDU using the User Datagram Protocol (UDP) at the OSI transport layer instead of TCP. UDP does not implement a system of successful transmission confirmation, and is known as unreliable transport, providing best-effort delivery. The data PDU itself is unchanged either way because it is merely encapsulated by a transport protocol for transmission.

OSI Layer	Purpose	Telecommunication Protocol Examples	Protocol Data Unit
4 (Transport)	Provides for reliable or unreliable delivery. Transport protocols can provide for transmission error detection and correction services.	TCP, UDP	Segment

The transport layer of the TCP/IP protocol suite provides for connection-oriented protocols such as TCP to ensure reliable communication.

Using OSI Layer 3 Within the Packet PDU

We now have a data PDU that has been encapsulated within a segment PDU for transport. However, the segment has no addressing information necessary for determining the best path to the intended recipient. By using an OSI Layer 3, or network-layer, protocol such as Internet Protocol (IP), we can encapsulate the segment into a packet with a logical destination address. In the previous example, the segment needs an IP packet header designating 24.227.60.114 as the logical destination address. IP is a network address protocol especially designed for this purpose because it implements a hierarchical addressing scheme.

Imagine if your computer supported listing filenames but did not support a logical directory structure. You could locate files with no problem, as long as not too many files existed on your hard drive. When you have a great number of files, however, you want to be able to logically organize your files into a directory structure to allow you to quickly and easily navigate to your intended file. In a similar fashion, IP supports network and subnetwork groupings of host addresses, which facilitates logical path determination. This is especially important in a large network with many hosts. For example, a router operates as a network segment junction, or gateway, at OSI Layer 3 using IP and IP routing tables to determine optimal paths for packet forwarding. By using IP's hierarchical addressing, routers can determine which remote routing gateways connect to which remote network or subnetwork host groups. If the network is so small that network groupings of hosts are not necessary, the computers and network devices might not utilize IP at the network layer because doing so would add unnecessary performance overhead, or cost.

OSI Layer	Purpose	Telecommunication Protocol Examples	Protocol Data Unit
3 (Network)	Protocols at this layer provide logical addressing and facilitate path determination.	IP, IPSec, ICMP, RIP, OSPF	Packet

Using OSI Layer 2 Within the Frame PDU

The HTTP data PDU has now been encapsulated within the segment PDU by TCP for transport, and then re-encapsulated within the packet PDU by IP providing an IP address header. Remember that the IP packet can be stripped and rebuilt without affecting the TCP segment, which is a benefit of *data encapsulation*. At this point, we need to re-encapsulate the IP packet into a vehicle that is appropriate for the connected physical medium.

We are now encountering the great transformation of logical processes into physical signals. Just think of it—when you are able to encapsulate your own thoughts into segments with words and sentences, and then address your thoughts by adding your friend's name to the front, a miracle occurs when you are able to transform the logical thoughts and processes into physical vibrations and sound waves that can traverse the air (your connected communication medium). The computer's data needs to make this leap, too. It re-encapsulates the IP packet into a frame that is appropriate for the transmission medium. If Ethernet is being used for the local area network, the IP packet is encapsulated within an Ethernet frame. If the IP packet needs to traverse a point-to-point link to the Internet service provider (via your point-to-point dial-up connection), the packet is encapsulated using PPP. These protocols are used to link the logical data processes with the physical transmission medium. Appropriately, this occurs at OSI Layer 2, or the *data link* layer.

Why does OSI need a data link layer? It needs a separate encapsulation step because physical media can change along a network path. As an Ethernet frame arrives on one side of a routing gateway, it might need to leave the other using PPP. Because you can strip and rebuild a frame without affecting the packet, segment, or data PDUs inside, frame conversion is entirely possible. This is analogous to taking a trip with an airplane. You and your luggage are the data payload. The car you drive to the airport is an appropriate frame type; your locally connected medium is the streets. When you reach the airport, which serves as a junction gateway between land and air travel, you and your luggage are re-encapsulated from your car into a plane because the plane is the appropriate frame type for traveling in air as opposed to traveling on the roads.

Frame headers provide actual physical addressing information as well. Knowing the logical street address of Certified Tech Trainers is helpful to get to the proper city or neighborhood to meet with CTT. Street addresses can change, however, even if the physical geographic latitude and longitude have not. The data link layer manages a flat network address scheme of Media Access Control (MAC) addresses for physical network interface connections. Whereas IP addressing and routes help the packet get to the near proximity of the intended host, MAC addresses are used by the connected network interfaces to know which frames to receive and process, and which frames are intended for other network interfaces.

OSI Layer	Purpose	Telecommunication Protocol Examples	Protocol Data Unit
2 (Data Link)	Protocols at this layer provide access to media (network interface cards, for example) using MAC addresses. They can sometimes also provide transmission error detection, but they cannot provide error correction.	802.3/802.2, HDLC, PPP, Frame Relay	Frame

Using OSI Layer 1 Within the Bits PDU

We have already processed four of the five steps of data encapsulation. Data has been encapsulated into TCP segments at the OSI transport layer. It was re-encapsulated with IP at the OSI network layer and was then further encapsulated with an Ethernet frame at the OSI data link layer. The last step before transmission is to break the frame into electromagnetic digital signals at the OSI *physical* layer, which communicates bits over the connected physical medium. These bits are received at the destination host, which can reconstruct the bits into Ethernet frames and decapsulate the frames back to IP packets. The destination host then can decapsulate the IP packets back to TCP segments, which are then decapsulated and put back together to form data. The data can then be processed by OSI application-, presentation-, and session-layer protocols to make the data available to the destination user or user applications.

Table 3.3 describes the seven OSI layers.

Table 3.3	OSI Reference Model and Data Encapsulation		
OSI Layer	Purpose	Protocol Examples	PDU
7 (Application)	This is the networking layer that interfaces with applications and operating systems. This is	HTTP, Telnet, SMTP, DNS, SNMP	Data

(continued)

Table 3.3 OSI Reference Model and Data Encapsulation (continued)

OSI Layer	Purpose	Protocol Examples	PDU
	where the user (through an application or operating system activity) first passes off information to networking services for telecommunication.		
6 (Presentation)	The data might require special formatting techniques, including (but not limited to) preparation according to special presentation protocols for picture and sound, compression, or even encryption.	ASCII, JPG, GIF, MIDI	
5 (Session)	Communicating the data might a special device-to-device bond, or session, for cooperative multi-device communication efforts, for example.	NetBIOS, RPC, SQL	
4 (Transport)	This layer provides for reliable or unreliable delivery. Transport protocols can provide for transmission error detection and correction services.	TCP, UDP	Segment
2 (Data Link)	Protocols at this layer provide access to media (network interface cards, for example) using MAC addresses. They can sometimes also provide transmission error detection, but they cannot provide error correction.	802.3/802.2, HDLC, PPP, Frame Relay	Frame
1 (Physical)	The purpose of hardware at this level is to move bits between devices. Specifications for voltage, wire speed, and pin-out cables are provided at this layer.	Network cabling, wireless transmissions, microwave transmissions	Bits

Networking Concepts and Devices

Now that we have a better comprehension of network architecture according to the OSI reference model, we have the foundation necessary for discussing various networking concepts, issues, and devices.

A variety of network types are common to most organizations, and are discussed in the following sections.

Local Area Networks (LANs)

Local Area Networks are private or nonpublic packet-based switched networks contained within a limited area providing services within a particular organization or group. Services can include file/print sharing, email, and communications. This structure is similar to a gated community or industrial complex, in that the network of roads is designed to be used primarily by internal residents or employees.

In developing the network architecture, the organization must assess cost, speed, flexibility, and reliability. The IT organization should review what physical media will be used for physically transmitting the data, as well as what methods will be available to access the physical network medium. Additionally, the organization must decide on the topology (physical arrangement) and the network components to be used in that topology.

LANs were originally designed to connect users so they could exchange or share data. The devices and software associated with the transmission of data were originally designed to connect devices that were no more than 3,200 feet (1,000m) apart, but these distances can be extended by special devices and software. If the distance between network devices exceeds the recommended length, the signal will attenuate and cause communication problems. Attenuation is the weakening or degradation of signals during transmission. In addition to attenuation, signals can incur electromagnetic interference (EMI), which is caused by electromagnetic waves created by other devices in the same area as the network cabling.

 Degradation of the communication signal as it meets resistance of a length of network cabling or signal attenuation is a risk that results from utilizing cables that are longer than permitted by the physical media and network topology type.

LANs transmit packets to one or more nodes (computing devices) on the network and include the following types of transmissions:

➤ **Unicast**—A sending station transmits single packets to a receiving station.

➤ **Multicast**—A sending station sends a single packet to a specific number of receiving stations.

➤ **Broadcast**—A sending station sends a single packet to all stations on the network.

Generally, the first step in the development of the network architecture is to define the physical media over which network communications (transmissions) will occur. The physical media specifications are contained at the physical layer within the OSI model (see Table 3.3).

Table 3.3	Physical Layer, OSI Model		
Type	**Use**	**Physical Standards**	**Access Standards**
Copper: twisted pair (Category 3 and 5) Ring)	Short distances (less than 200 feet) Supports voice/data	Ethernet 10Base-T (10Mbps) Ethernet 100Base-T (100Mbps) 10Base-TX (100Mbps) 100Base-T4 (100Mbps 1000Base-T (1000Mbps)	IEEE 802.3/802.3u/802.3z Ethernet/Gigabit (Ethernet/Fast) Ethernet CSMA/CD) IEEE 802.5 (Token
Coaxial cable	Supports voice/data	10Base5 (thick coax 10Mbps) 10Base2 (thin coax 10Mbps)	IEEE 802.3
Fiber optic	Long distances Supports voice/data	10Base-F (10Mbps) 100Base-FX (100Mbps) 1000Base-LX (1000Mbps) 1000Base-CX (1000Mbps)	IEEE 802.3/802.3ae/ 802.3z (Ethernet/Fast Ethernet/Gigabit Ethernet CSMA/CD) IEEE 802.5 (Token Ring) FDDI
Wireless	Short distances Supports voice/data		802.11 (wireless) 802.11b (2.4GHz–11Mbps) 802.11a (5GHz–54Mbps) 802.11g (2.4GHz–54Mbps)

Physical standards dictate both the speed and the reliability of the network. In networking, this is called the media access technology. The IT organization might determine that because all the users and network devices are contained in one physical location (for example, one building), and a majority of the traffic that will be transmitted on the network is voice and data, it will use Ethernet 100Base-T. Ethernet allows multiple devices to communicate on the same network and usually uses a bus or star topology. In the case of 100Base-T, packets are transmitted at 100Mbps.

Ethernet is known as a contention-based network topology. This means that, in an Ethernet network, all devices contend with each other to use the same media (cable). As a result, frames transmitted by one device can potentially collide with frames transmitted by another. Fortunately, the Ethernet standard dictates how computers deal with communications, transmission controls, collisions, and transmission integrity.

Here are some important definitions to help you understand issues common to Ethernet:

➤ **Collisions**—Result when two or more stations try to transmit at the same time

➤ **Collision domain**—A group of devices connected to the same physical media so that if two devices access the media at the same time, a collision of the transmissions can occur

➤ **Broadcast domain**—A group of devices that receive one another's broadcast messages

How Ethernet Deals with Collisions

As a contention-based topology, Ethernet accepts that collisions will occur and has provided two mechanisms to ensure transmission and data integrity. CSMA/CD is a method by which devices on the network can detect collisions and retransmit. When the collision is detected, the source station stops sending the original transmission and sends a signal to all stations that a collision has occurred on the network. All stations then execute what is known as a random collision back-off timer, which delays all transmission on the network, allowing the original sending station to retransmit.

CSMA/CA is a method by which a sending station lets all the stations on the network know that it intends to transmit data. This intent signal lets all other devices know that they should not transmit because there could be a collision, thereby affecting collision avoidance.

As you have learned, collisions are common to an Ethernet network. However, network architecture can be optimized to keep collisions to a minimum. All computers on the same physical network segment are considered to be in the same collision domain because they are competing for the same shared media. High levels of collisions can result from high traffic congestion due to many devices competing on the same network segment. One way to address collision domains and alleviate excessive collisions is to decrease the size of the collision domain (number of competing network devices) by using bridges, switches, or routers (discussed later in the chapter) to segment the network with additional collision domains. As stated earlier, there are unicast, multicast, and broadcast packets that are transmitted on the network. If two networks are separated by a bridge, broadcast traffic, but not collision traffic, is allowed to pass. This reduces the size of the collision domain. Routers are used to segment both collision and broadcast domains by directing traffic and working at Layer 3 of the OSI model.

A separate media-access technology known as token passing can be implemented in place of Ethernet as part of a network architecture. In token passing, a control frame is passed along the network cabling from device to device; all transmissions are made via the token. When a device needs to send network traffic, it waits for the token to arrive and grants it the right to communicate. The token then takes the data, including the routing information (receiving station[s]) and continues from computer to computer. Each computer on the network checks the token's routing information to see if it is the destination station. When the destination station receives its data, it sets a bit in the token to let the sending station know that it received the data. Token-passing methods are used by both Token Ring and FDDI networks. Token-passing networks do not have collisions because only one station at a time can transmit data.

Network Topologies

We have discussed media-access technologies, but you might be asking how these are actually implemented in a network architecture. The connectivity of the network cabling and devices is known as the *topology*. Network topologies fall into the following categories: bus, star, or ring.

Bus Topology

The *bus* topology is primarily used in smaller networks where all devices are connected to a single communication line and all transmissions are received by all devices. This topology requires the minimum amount of cable to connect devices. A repeater can be used to "boost" the signal and extend the bus configuration. A standard bus configuration can encounter performance problems if there is heavy network traffic or a large number of collisions. In addition, each connection to the bus network weakens the electrical signal on the cable. Cable breaks can cause the entire network to stop functioning. Figure 3.2 depicts a bus topology.

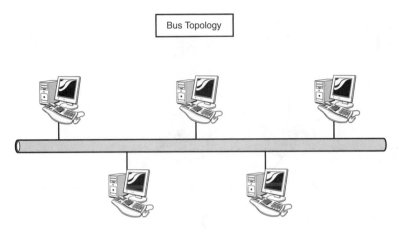

Figure 3.2   Bus topology.

Star Topology

In a *star* topology, each device (node) is linked to a hub or switch, which provides the link between communicating stations. This topology is commonly used in networks today because it provides the capability to add new devices and easily remove old ones. In designing the network, the IT organization needs to ensure that the hubs/switches used will provide enough throughput (speed) for the devices communicating on the network. In contrast to a bus topology, a star topology enables devices to communicate even if a device is not working or is no longer connected to the network. Generally, star networks are more costly because they use significantly more cable and hubs/switches. If the IT organization has not planned correctly, a single failure of a hub/switch can render all stations connected incapable of communicating with the network. To overcome this risk, IT organizations should create a complete or partial mesh configuration, which creates redundant interconnections between network nodes. Figure 3.3 depicts a star topology.

Providing network path redundancy is the best countermeasure or control for potential network device failures. A mesh network topology provides a point-to-point link with every network host. If each host is configured to route and forward communication, this topology provides the greatest redundancy of routes and the greatest network fault tolerance.

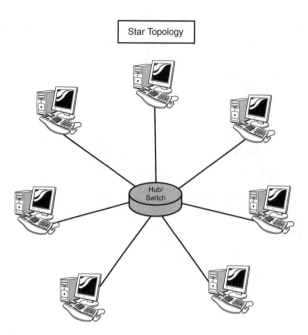

Figure 3.3 Star topology.

Ring Topology

A *ring* configuration is generally used in a Token Ring or FDDI network where all stations are connected to form a closed loop. The stations do not connect to a central device and depend on one another for communications. A ring topology generally provides high performance, but a single device or station can stop the network devices from communicating. In a Token Ring network, a failure might occur when one or more stations start beaconing. In beaconing, a message is passed to the devices on the network that a device is failing. This allows the remaining devices to automatically reconfigure the network, to continue communicating. Figure 3.4 shows a ring topology.

 A simple ring topology is vulnerable to failure if even one device on the ring fails. IBM's Token Ring topology uses dual concentric rings as a more robust ring topology solution.

As an IS auditor, you will look at the network topology and protocols to determine whether they meet the needs of the organization. The IT organization should monitor performance on the LAN to ensure that it is segmented properly (reducing collision/broadcast domains) and that the bandwidth (10/100/1000Mbps) is sufficient for access to network services. The network should be designed in such a manner that device failures do not bring down the network or cause long delays in network communication (redundancy and disaster recovery). IT management should have a configuration-management plan and procedures in place, to establish how the network will function both internally and externally. This includes performance monitoring.

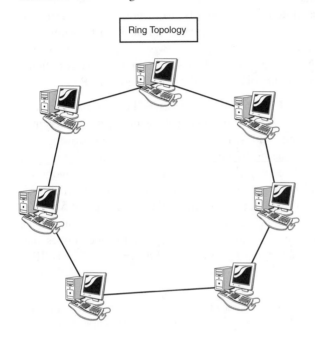

Figure 3.4 Ring topology.

  Configuring the communications network is often the most critical and time-intensive part of network management as a whole.

Wide Area Networks (WANs)

WANs provide connectivity for LANs that are geographically dispersed by providing network connectivity and services across large distances. WANs are similar to the series of interstates (highways) that can be accessed within individual states and are used to cross state boundaries.

The devices and protocols used in WAN communications most commonly work at the physical (Layer 1), data link (Layer 2), and network (Layer 3) layers of the OSI reference model. Communication on WAN links can be either *simplex* (one-way), *half-duplex* (one way at a time), or *full duplex* (separate circuits for communicating both ways at the same time). WAN circuits are usually network communication lines that an organization leases from a telecommunications provider; they can be switched or dedicated circuits. As an example, WAN connectivity could involve an organization with a headquarters in one state (say, Virginia) and smaller satellite offices in other states. The headquarters office could have all servers and their associated services in Virginia (email, file sharing, and so on). One way to enable communication with the satellite offices would be to install a WAN circuit. As with LANs, the WAN circuits utilize standard protocols to transmit messages. WAN can use message switching, packet switching, or circuit switching, or can utilize WAN dial-up services through Integrated Services Digital Network (ISDN) or the Public Switched Telephone Network (PSTN).

Virtual private networking (VPN) enables remote users, business partners, and home users to access the organization's network securely using encrypted packets sent via virtual connections. Encryption involves transforming data into a form that is unreadable by anyone without a secret decryption key. It ensures confidentiality by keeping the information hidden from anyone for whom it was not intended. Organizations use VPNs to allow external business partners to access an extranet or intranet. The advantage of VPNs is that they can use low-cost public networks (Internet) to transmit and receive encrypted data. VPNs rely on tunneling or encapsulation techniques that allow the Internet Protocol (IP) to carry a variety of different protocols (IPX, SNA, and so on).

A virtual private network (VPN) helps to secure access via encrypted tunneled transmission between an enterprise and its partners when communicating over an otherwise unsecured channel such as the Internet.

Metropolitan Area Networks (MANs)

This type of network is larger than a LAN but smaller than a WAN. A MAN can be used to connect users to services within the same city or locality. MANs are similar to the surface roads used to travel from your residence or community to services such as department stores, grocery stores, and your place of business.

Networks exist to facilitate access to application services. The following are some of the common services available within an organization's networking environment:

> **File sharing**—This allows users to share information and resources among one another. File sharing can be facilitated by shared directories or groupware/collaboration applications.

> **Email services**—Email provides the capability for a user population to send unstructured messages to individuals or groups of individuals via a terminal or PC.

➤ **Print services**—Print services enable users to access printers either directly or through print servers (which manage the formatting and scheduling) to execute print requests from terminals or PCs connected to the network.

➤ **Remote-access services**—These services provide remote access capabilities from a user location to where a computing device appears; they emulate a direct connection to the device. Examples include Telnet and remote access through a VPN.

➤ **Terminal-emulation software (TES)**—TES provides remote access capabilities with a user interface as if that user were sitting on the console of the device being accessed. As an example, Microsoft Terminal Services connects to the remote device and displays the desktop of the remote device as if the user were sitting at the console.

➤ **Directory services**—A directory stores information about users, devices, and services available on the network. A directory service enables users to locate information about individuals (such as contact information) or devices/services that are available within the organization.

➤ **Network management**—Network management provides a set of services that control and maintain the network. It generally provides complete information about devices and services with regard to their status. Network-management tools enable you to determine device performance, errors associated with processing, active connections to devices, and so on. These tools are used to ensure network reliability and provide detailed information that enables operators and administrators to take corrective action.

Because of the complex nature of networking and the variety of standards both in use and constantly evolving, implementation and maintenance poses a significant challenge. Managers, engineers, and administrators are tasked to develop and maintain integrated, efficient, reliable, scalable, and secure networks to meet the needs of the organization. Some basic critical success factors apply to these activities:

➤ **Interoperability**—A large number of devices, system types, and standards usually support network communication. All the components must work together efficiently and effectively.

➤ **Availability**—Organizations need continuous, reliable, and secure access to network devices and services.

➤ **Flexibility**—To facilitate scalability, the network architecture must accommodate network expansion for new applications and services.

The TCP/IP Protocol Suite

The Transmission Control Protocol/Internet Protocol Suite (TCP/IP) has become the de facto standard for the Internet, and most organizations use it for network communications. TCP/IP includes both network-communication and application-support protocols. As stated earlier, the TCP/IP protocol suite was developed and in use before the ISO/OSI model was developed and, as such, does not match directly with the layers of the OSI model.

The TCP/IP protocol is defined as follows:

➤ **Remote Terminal Control Protocol (Telnet)**—This terminal-emulation protocol enables users to log into remote systems and use resources as if they were connected locally.

➤ **File Transfer Protocol (FTP)**—FTP enables users and systems to transfer files from one computer to another on the Internet. FTP allows for user and anonymous login based on configuration. FTP can be used to transfer a variety of file types and does not provide secure communication (encryption) during login or file transfer.

➤ **Simple Mail Transfer Protocol (SMTP)**—This protocol provides standard electronic (email) transfer services.

➤ **Domain Name Service (DNS)**—This protocol resolves hostnames to IP addresses and IP addresses to hostnames. That is, www.lmisol.com would resolve to IP address 66.33.202.245. DNS servers have hierarchal distributed database systems that are queried for resolution. The service enables users to remember names instead of having to remember IP addresses.

➤ **Network File System (NFS)**—This protocol allows a computer to access files over a network as if they were on its local disk.

➤ **Transmission Control Protocol (TCP)**—This transport-layer protocol establishes a reliable, full-duplex data-delivery service that many TCP/IP applications use. TCP is a connection-oriented protocol, which means that it guarantees the delivery of data and that the packets will be delivered in the same order as they were sent.

➤ **User Datagram Protocol (UDP)**—This transport-layer protocol provides connectionless delivery of data on the network. UDP does not provide error-recovery services and is primarily used for broadcasting data on the network.

➤ **Internet Protocol (IP)**—This protocol specifies the format of packets (datagrams) that will be transported on the network. IP only defines the format of packets, so it is generally combined with a transport protocol such as TCP to affect delivery.

➤ **Internet Control Message Protocol (ICMP)**—This protocol is an extension of the Internet Protocol (IP). It supports packets that contain error, control, and informational messages. The ping command, used to test network connectivity, uses the ICMP protocol.

➤ **Address Resolution Protocol (ARP)**—This network-layer protocol is used to convert an IP address (logical address) into a physical address (DLC or MAC address). When a host on the network wants to obtain a physical address, it broadcasts an ARP request. The host on the network that has the IP address replies with the physical address.

➤ **X.25**—This is a data communications interface specification developed to describe how data passes into and out of switched packet networks. The X.25 protocol suite defines protocol Layers 1–3.

Firewalls

A *firewall* is a device (hardware/software) that restricts access between networks. These networks might be a combination of an internal and external network (organization's LAN and the Internet) or might be within internal networks (accounting network and the sales network). A firewall is implemented to support the organizational security policy, in that specific restrictions or rules are configured within the firewall to restrict access to services and ports. If configured correctly, the firewall is the gateway through which all traffic will flow. The network traffic (or packets) then is monitored as it comes into the firewall and compared against a set of rules (filters). If the traffic does not meet the requirements of the access control policy, it is not allowed access and might be discarded or redirected.

Firewalls started out as perimeter security devices and protected the organization's internal networks from external (such as, from the Internet) networks, similar to the way a moat was used to protect a castle. Often you will hear of this type of network security that "the network is hard and crunchy on the outside (perimeter firewall), and soft and chewy on the inside (organization's internal network). Perimeter security is an important component of a comprehensive security infrastructure, but it is not the complete answer. Perimeter security assumes that a vast majority of the threats are external to the organization, which is not always the case.

It is important to keep in mind that the firewall can be considered a "choke point" on the network because all traffic must be checked against the rules before gaining access. As a result, the rules that are created for the network must take into account performance as well as security. Firewalls can filter traffic based on a variety of the parameters within the packet:

> ➤ **Source and destination addresses**—The firewall can look at the source or destination address in the packet (or both).

> ➤ **Source and destination ports**—The firewall can look at the source or destination port identifier of the service or application being accessed.

> ➤ **Protocol types**—The firewall might not let certain protocol types access the network.

The level of granularity and types of rules that can be implemented vary among vendors. As an auditor, you will find that a wide variety of parameters can be configured, based on vendor implementation. A number of risk indicators are associated with firewalls:

> ➤ The organization does not employ firewalls.

> ➤ The firewall is poorly configured or misconfigured (affecting performance/security).

> ➤ No audit or testing processes/procedures exist for monitoring firewall security.

> ➤ The organization relies too much on perimeter firewall security.

> ➤ Not all network traffic passes through the firewall (rogue modems, network connectivity, and so on).

Packet-Filtering Firewalls

The first generation of firewalls is known as *packet-filtering firewalls*, or *circuit-level gateways*. This type of firewall uses an *access control list* (ACL) applied at OSI layer 3. An ACL is a set of text-based rules on the firewall that the firewall can apply against incoming packets. A simple access control list could stipulate that all packets coming from a particular network (source address) 192.168.0.0 must be denied and discarded. In this instance, the firewall might have a text-based rule DENY ALL 192.168.0.0. Another type of rule might state that all packets trying to access a particular port, such as a web page request (port 80), be routed to a particular server, in this case, 172.168.1.1. In this instance, the firewall might have a rule that looks like PERMIT FORWARD ALL TCP Port 80 172.168.1.1.

Packet-filtering firewalls can compare the header information in packets only against their rules. As a result, they provide relatively low security compared to other options. The creation of rules in packet filtering involves both permit (or allow) and deny (or block) statements. Permit statements allow packets to be forwarded; deny statements discard the packet. Access lists are sequential: Statements are processed from the top of the list down until a statement condition that matches a packet is found. When the statement is found, no further statements are processed. As an IS auditor, you should review the access lists for completeness and correctness. This example shows both a correct and an incorrect access list:

Access list A (correct):

```
access-list 1 permit host 192.168.32.1
access-list 1 permit host 192.168.32.2
```

Access list B (incorrect):

```
access-list 1 deny 192.168.32.0 0.0.0.255
access-list 1 permit 192.168.32.1
access-list 1 permit 192.168.32.2
access-list 1 deny 192.168.40.0 0.0.255.255
```

In this scenario, we want to permit two IP addresses access to the internal network while denying the remainder of the subnet. In access list A, we allow both 192.168.32.1 and 192.168.32.2 to access the network. By default, routers and firewalls that can be configured to filter based on IP source or destination addresses deny traffic by default, and will not allow traffic unless it has been explicitly permitted. This default characteristic is referred to as the "implicit deny" statement at the end of every access control list. The list will be read in sequence from top to bottom, and because of the implicit deny statement at the end of the access list, any IP addresses that do not meet the criteria of the rules will be denied. In access list B, we are denying the entire subnet of 192.168.32.0, which includes 192.168.32.1 and 192.168.32.2. Because the first statement in access list B would technically match hosts 192.168.32.1 and 192.168.32.2, the later permit statements meant for these hosts would not be processed, and the packets from these source hosts would be discarded. Granular statements must precede global statements. The last rule in access list B is redundant with the first rule in the access list. Because no valid permit statements exist in access list B, no traffic from any source will be permitted due to the implicit deny statement at the end of every access list.

 Improper configuration of traffic rules or access lists is the most common and critical error in firewall implementations.

Stateful Packet-Inspection Firewalls

Stateful packet-inspection firewalls are considered the third generation of fire-wall gateways. They provide additional features, in that they keep track of all packets through all 7 OSI layers until that communication session is closed. The first-generation packet-filtering firewalls receive a packet and match against their rules; the packet is forwarded/discarded and forgotten.

Remember from the discussion of the OSI model that a single communica-tion (such as sending an email) can be broken down into several packets and forwarded to the receiving station. A stateful firewall is a bit more sophisti-cated because it tracks communications (or sessions) from both internal and external sources. A first-generation packet-filtering firewall can be set up to deny all packets from a particular network (as in the previous example), but a stateful firewall with the same rules might allow packets from that denied network if the request came from the internal network.

Proxy Firewalls

Proxy firewalls, or *application-layer gateways*, are used as the "middlemen" in network communications. The difference between a proxy-based firewall and packet filtering is that all packets passing to the network are delivered through the proxy, which is acting on behalf of the receiving computer. The communication is checked for access authorization according to a rulebase, and then passed to the receiving system or discarded. In essence, a proxy impersonates the internal (receiving) system to review packets before for-warding. Any communication that comes from the receiving computer is passed back to the proxy before it is forwarded externally. The actual process that takes place is that the proxy receives each packet, reviews it, and then changes the source address to protect the identity of the receiving computer before forwarding.

Proxies are application-level gateways. They differ from packet filtering in that they can look at all the information in the packet (not just header) all the way to the application layer.

 An application-layer gateway, or proxy firewall, provides the greatest degree of pro-tection and control because it inspects all seven OSI layers of network traffic.

The firewall architecture for the organization depends on the type of pro-tection the organization needs. The architecture might be designed to protect internal networks from external; it might be used to segment different internal departments and might include packet filtering, stateful packet inspection, proxy/application gateways, or a combination of these.

Securing an internal network from external threats requires a firewall to be situated at the perimeter of the network, acting as a gateway for communication between all internal hosts and servers (SMTP, web, and FTP) and external hosts.

In general, there are three basic types of firewall configurations:

> **Bastion host**—A basic firewall architecture in which all internal and external communications must pass through the bastion host. The bastion host is exposed to the external network. Therefore, it must be locked down, removing any unnecessary applications or services. A bastion host can use packet filtering, proxy, or a combination; it is not a specific type of hardware, software, or device. Figure 3.5 shows a basic bastion host configuration.

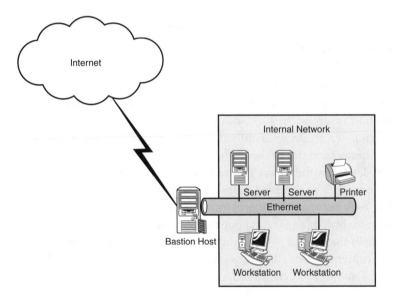

Figure 3.5 Bastion host configuration.

> **Screened host**—A screened host configuration generally consists of a screening router (border router) configured with access control lists. The router employs packet filtering to screen packets, which are then typically passed to the bastion host, and then on to the internal network. The screened host (the bastion host in this example) is the only device

that receives traffic from the border router. This configuration provides an additional layer of protection for the screened host. Figure 3.6 shows a screened host configuration.

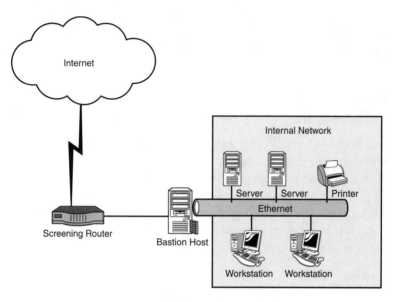

Figure 3.6 Screened host configuration.

➤ **Screened subnet**—A screened subnet is similar to a screened host, with two key differences: The subnet generally contains multiple devices, the bastion host is sandwiched between two routers (the exterior router and the interior router). In this configuration, the exterior router provides packet filtering and passes the traffic to the bastion. After the traffic is processed, the bastion passes the traffic to the interior router for additional filtering. The screened subnet, sometimes called a *DMZ*, provides a buffer zone between the internal and external networks. This configuration is used when an external population needs access to services (web, FTP, email) that can be allowed through the exterior router, but the interior router will not allow those requests to the internal network. Figure 3.7 shows a screened subnet configuration.

 Layering perimeter network protection by configuring the firewall as a screened host in a screened subnet behind the bastion host provides a higher level of protection from external attack.

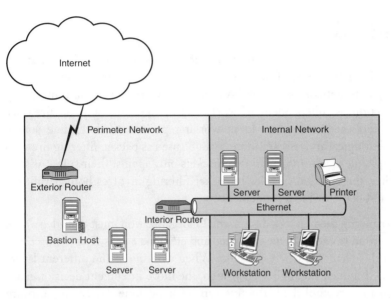

Figure 3.7   Screened subnet configuration.

Firewall architecture is quite varied. The organization might decide on hardware- or software-based firewalls to provide network protection. In the case of software-based firewalls, it is important to remember that they will be installed on top of commercial operating systems, which may have their own vulnerabilities. This type of implementation requires the IT organization to ensure that the operating system is properly locked down and that there is a process in place to ensure continued installation of security patches. Any unnecessary services or applications, as well as unneeded protocols, must be removed or disabled from the operating system.

Because the objective of a firewall is to protect a trusted network from an untrusted network, any organization that uses external communications must implement some level of firewall technology. The firewall architecture should take into consideration the functions and level of security the organization requires. Firewalls are potential bottlenecks because they are responsible for inspecting all incoming and outgoing traffic. Firewalls that are configured at the perimeter of the network provide only limited protection, if any protection, from internal attacks; misconfigured firewall rules could allow unwanted and potentially dangerous traffic on the network.

 Installing firewall software onto an otherwise robust and fully functioning operating system poses a greater risk of firewall compromise. To mitigate this risk, firewall software is often installed onto a system using an operating system that has very limited functionality, providing only the services necessary to support the firewall software.

Routers

Routers are used to direct or route traffic on the network and work at the network layer (Layer 3) of the OSI model. Routers link two or more physically separate network segments. Although they are linked via router, they can function as independent networks. As in the discussion on firewalls, routers look at the headers in networking packets to determine source addresses (logical addresses). Routers can be used as packet-filtering firewalls by comparing header information in packets only against their rules. As stated earlier, the creation of rules in packet filtering involves both permit (or allow) and deny (or block) statements.

In determining the network design, the IT organization must consider where to place routers and leverage the speed and efficiencies of switches (discussed later in this chapter), where possible. When working at the different layers of the OSI model, the higher up you go, the more intelligent decision making is being accomplished. Routers can be standalone devices or software running within or on top of an operating system. They use routing protocols to communicate the available routes on the network. The routing protocols (RIP, BGP, and OSPF) relay information on routers that have gone down on the network, congested routes, or routes that are more economical than others. The information that is passed between routers via the routing protocols are route updates and are stored in a routing table. As packets enter the router, their destination addresses are compared to the routing table, and the packet is forwarded on the most economical route available at the time. As stated earlier in the discussion on firewalls, the fact that routers can look at header information in the packet enables the router to perform filtering capabilities via access lists, which can restrict traffic between networks. The criteria within access control lists can be IP addresses (source and destination), specific ports (such as TCP port 80 for HTTP), or protocols (UDP, TCP, and IP).

Routers are not as fast as hubs or switches for simply forwarding frames, since they need to look at the OSI layer 3 header information in all packets to determine the correct route to the destination address. This creates the possibility for bottlenecks on the network.

Layer 3 of the OSI model, or the network layer, is responsible for logical addressing and routing path determination. Routers operate at Layer 3.

Modems

Modem is short for *modulator-demodulator*. A modem is a device that converts data from digital format to analog format for transmission. Computer information is stored digitally and, when transmitted via the phone line, needs to be converted to analog waves to enable communication. Generally, modems are used for remote access to networks and devices. As a part of the IT infrastructure, modems can be used to access servers or routers to enable routine maintenance or troubleshooting. Users of the organization also can use modems for remote access to data and applications through dial-in virtual private networks (VPN) or to provide terminal services (access to console functions).

In reviewing the IT infrastructure, the IS auditor might find that modems fall outside the security procedures and, in fact, might bypass existing security controls. Modems are susceptible to "war dialing," in which malicious hackers set software to dial a series of telephone numbers, looking for the carrier tone provided by a modem on connection. This technique might allow hackers to enter the network by bypassing existing security controls.

Modems convert analog transmissions to digital, and digital transmission to analog. They are required for analog transmissions to enter a digital network.

A *bridge* works at the data link layer (Layer 2) of the OSI model and connects two separate networks to form a logical network (for example, joining an Ethernet and token network). They can store and forward frames. Bridges examine the media access control (MAC) header of a data packet to determine where to forward the packet; they are transparent to end users. A *MAC address* is the physical address of the device on the network (it resides on the network card [NIC] on the device). As packets pass through it, the bridge determines whether the MAC address resides on its local network; if not, the bridge forwards the packet to the appropriate network segment. Bridges can reduce collisions that result from segment congestion, but they do forward broadcast frames. Bridges are good network devices if used for the right purpose.

Routers often use cut-through or fragment-free forwarding to reproduce and forward frames, whereas switches use the store-and-forward method.

Hubs and Switches

A *hub* operates at the physical layer (Layer 1) of the OSI model and can serve as the center of a star topology. Hubs can be considered concentrators because they concentrate all network communications for the devices attached to them. A hub contains several ports to which clients are directly connected. The hub connects to the network backbone and can be active (repeats signals that are sent through them) or passive (splits signals but does not repeat them).

A *switch* combines the functionality of a multi-port bridge and the signal amplification of a repeater.

Internet, Intranet, and Extranet

The Internet is accessed using the TCP/IP. The Hypertext Transfer Protocol (HTTP) is an application-level protocol that is used to transfer the collection of online documents known as the World Wide Web (WWW). This application service and combines the use of client software (browser) that can request information from web servers. Web-based applications can deliver static and dynamic content in the form of text, graphics, sound, and data; they can be used as an interface to corporate applications. Delivery of information via the Web can include the use of either client-side (servlets or applets) or server-side (common gateway interface scripts [CGI]) applications. The ease of implementation and use of the Web enables a variety of content-rich applications.

An intranet uses the same basic principles of the Internet but is designed for internal users. Intranets are web based and can contain internal calendaring, web email, and information designed specifically for the authorized users of the intranet. Extranets are web based but serve a combination of users. Extranets are commonly used as a place for partners (organization and external partners) to exchange information. A simple example of an extranet is one in which a supplier provides access to its partners to place orders, view inventory, and place support requests. The extranet usually sits outside the corporate border router and might be a screened host or might be maintained on a screened subnet.

With the wide use of web technologies, it is important to develop policies and procedures regarding proper use of the Internet, the intranet, and extranets. The ease of access via the Web opens the door to the organization's network and could allow the download of virus-laden or malicious software. Users in the organization need to be aware of the risks associated with downloading potentially dangerous applets, servlets, and programs. The

IT organization should monitor Internet access to ensure that corporate assets (bandwidth, servers, and workstations) are being used in a productive manner.

Risks and Controls Related to Network Infrastructure

The network infrastructure incorporates all of the organization's data, applications, and communications. The IS auditor must assess the risks associated with the infrastructure and the controls in place to mitigate the risk. It is important to keep in mind that the threats associated with the network are both internal and external; they can include risks from misuse, malicious attack, or natural disaster. The IT organizational controls should mitigate business risk, which is the potential harm or loss in achieving business objectives. The risk-management strategy and risk assessment methodology should address all threats and vulnerabilities and their effect on network assets.

The IT organization should have standards in place for the design and operation of the network architecture. The auditor should identify the following:

➤ LAN topology and network design

➤ Documented network components' functions and locations (servers, routers, modems, and so on)

➤ Network topology that includes interconnections and connections to other public networks

➤ Network uses, including protocols, traffic types, and applications

➤ Documentation of all groups with access to the network (internal and external)

➤ Functions performed by administrators of the network (LAN, security, DBA)

Review of this information enables the IS auditor to make informed decisions with regard to threats to the network and the controls used to mitigate the threats.

Administrative, physical, and technical controls should protect the network and its associated components. The physical controls should protect network hardware and software, permitting physical access to only those individuals who are authorized. When entering restricted areas, individuals with access to sensitive areas should be careful that they do not allow an unauthorized user to follow them in. Known as "piggybacking," this occurs when an unauthorized user follows an authorized user into a restricted area. All hardware devices, software, and manuals should be located in a secure location. Network closets that contain cabling, routers, hubs, and switches should have restricted access. Servers and network components should be locked in racks or should be secured in such a manner that the devices and their components cannot be removed. The network operating manuals and documentation should be secured. All electrical equipment should be protected against the effects of static electricity or power surges (static mats/straps, surge protectors). Network equipment should be equipped with uninterruptible power supplies (UPS), in case of power failure, and facilities should be free of dust, dirt, and water.

Piggybacking can be used to circumvent physical access controls such as locked entryways. Double-doorway monitored entry systems are the preferred countermeasure to such unauthorized access.

The IT organization should have logical controls in place to restrict, identify, and report authorized and unauthorized users of the network. All users should be required to have unique passwords and to change them periodically. Access to applications and data on the network should be based on written authorization and should be granted according to job function (need to know). All login attempts (authorized and unauthorized) should be logged, and the logs should be reviewed regularly. All devices and applications within the network infrastructure should be documented, and the documentation should be updated when changes to hardware, software, configurations, or policies are implemented.

The controls that are implemented on the network should ensure the confidentiality, availability (CIA), and integrity of the network architecture. Confidentiality is the capability to ensure that the necessary level of secrecy is enforced throughout each junction of data processing, to prevent unauthorized disclosure. Integrity ensures accuracy and reliability of data and prevents unauthorized (intentional and unintentional) modification of the data. Availability ensures reliable and timely access to data and network resources for authorized individuals.

As an IS auditor, reviewing the network documentation and logs will provide you with a perspective of the risks associated with the network, but direct observation will provide a more reliable way to determine whether the controls protect the organization. The IS auditor should observe physical security controls and monitor IT resources during daily activities. These results can then be compared against the existing documentation collected to determine adherence.

 An IS auditor usually places more reliance on evidence directly collected, such as through personal observation.

Evaluating IS Operational Practices

As stated in Chapter 2, "Management, Planning, and Organization of IS," the COBIT resources provide a framework for organizations, IT management, and IS auditors to realize best practices to reach business objectives. IS auditors should review the IT organization to ensure the use of formal risk management, project management, and change management associated with the implementation of IT infrastructures.

The COBIT framework provides 11 processes in the management and deployment of IT systems:

1. Develop a strategic plan

2. Articulate the information architecture

3. Find an optimal fit between the IT and the organization's strategy

4. Design the IT function to match the organization's needs

5. Maximize the return on the IT investment

6. Communicate IT policies to the user community

7. Manage the IT workforce

8. Comply with external regulations, laws, and contracts

9. Conduct IT risk assessments

10. Maintain a high-quality systems-development process

11. Incorporate sound project-management techniques

Risks and Controls Related to IS Operational Practices

An IT organization should develop and maintain strategic planning processes (both long and short term) that enable the organization to meet its goals and objectives. The IT organization's policies, procedures, standards, and guidelines are evidence of a detailed reflection of the strategic plan. The IT organization should have a clearly defined structure that outlines authority and responsibility, and should be documented in an organizational chart. Network devices, applications, and data should be maintained, and proper segregation of duties should be implemented. The IT organization should implement proper segregation of incompatible duties, keeping in mind that segregation between computer operators and security administrators, as an example, might not be possible in smaller environments. The use of compensating controls, such as audit trails, might be acceptable to mitigate the risk from improper segregation of duties. The auditor should review information pertaining to the organization structure, to ensure adequate segregation of duties.

 Proper segregation of duties prevents a computer operator (user) from performing security administration duties.

The IS auditor should review policies and procedures because they ensure that organizational objectives are being met. In addition, the IS auditor should review the risk-management process to ensure that the organization is taking steps to reduce risk to an acceptable level (mitigation) and is maintaining that level of risk. The organization's business plan should establish an understanding of the organization's mission and objectives, and should be incorporated into the IT strategic plan. Organizational charts should establish the responsibility and authority of individuals, and job descriptions should define the responsibility of and accountability for employee actions. The policies and procedures should incorporate strategic objectives in operational activities.

Evaluating the Use of System Performance and Monitoring Processes, Tools, and Techniques

To ensure continued availability of both software and hardware, the IT department should implement monitoring processes. These processes should include performance, capacity, and network monitoring. The IT organization should have a performance-monitoring plan that defines service levels of hardware and software. The metrics associated with service levels generally include service availability (uptime), support levels, throughput, and responsiveness. The organization should compare stated service levels against problem logs, processing schedules, job accounting system reports, and preventive maintenance reports, to ensure that hardware availability and utilization meet the stated service levels. As an example, throughput should measure the amount of work that the system performs over a period of time. In looking at an online transaction system, the number of transactions per second/minute can be used as a throughput index.

 Throughput is a performance measure of how many transactions per second an online transaction-processing system is capable of.

The IS auditor might need to review specific reports associated with availability and response. This list identifies log types and characteristics:

➤ System logs identify the activities performed on a system and can be analyzed to determine the existence of unauthorized access to data by a user or program.

➤ The review of abnormal job-termination reports should identify application jobs that terminated before successful completion.

➤ Operator problem reports are used by operators to log computer operations problems and their solutions. Operator work schedules are maintained by IS management to assist in human resource planning.

➤ Capacity-monitoring software to monitor usage patterns and trends enables management to properly allocate resources and ensure continuous efficiency of operations.

➤ Network-monitoring devices are used to capture and inspect network traffic data. The logs from these devices can be used to inspect activities from known or unknown users to find evidence of unauthorized access.

➤ System downtime provides information regarding the effectiveness and adequacy of computer preventive maintenance programs and can be very helpful to an IS auditor when determining the efficacy of a systems-maintenance program.

Exam Prep Questions

1. The offline print spooling feature of print servers should be carefully monitored to ensure that unauthorized viewing access to sensitive information is controlled and prevented. Which of the following issues is an IS auditor MOST concerned with?

   ❏ A. Some users have the technical authority to print documents from the print spooler even though the users are not authorized with the appropriate classification to view the data they can print.

   ❏ B. Some users have the technical authority to modify the print spooler file even though the users do not have the subject classification authority to modify data within the file.

   ❏ C. Some users have the technical authority to delete the print job from the spooler even though the users do not have the authority to modify the data output of the print job.

   ❏ D. Some users have the technical authority to pause the print jobs of certain information even though they do not have the subject classification authority to create, modify, or view the data output of the print job.

   Answer: A. The question focuses on the confidentiality aspect of access control. A user with technical printer administration authority can print jobs from the print spooler, regardless of the user's authorization to view the print output. All other answers are potential compromises of information integrity or availability.

2. When reviewing firewall configuration, which of the following represents the greatest vulnerability for an IS auditor?

   ❏ A. The firewall software has been configured with rules permitting or denying access to systems or networks based upon source and destination networks or systems, protocols, and user authentication.

   ❏ B. The firewall software is configured with an implicit deny rule as the last rule in the rule base.

   ❏ C. The firewall software is installed on a common operating system that is configured with default settings.

   ❏ D. The firewall software is configured as a VPN endpoint for site-to-site VPN connections.

   Answer: C. When auditing any critical application, an IS auditor is always concerned about software or an operating system that is installed according to default settings. Default settings are often published and provide an intruder with predictable configuration information, which allows easier system compromise. Installing firewall software onto an otherwise robust and fully functioning operating system poses a greater risk of firewall compromise. To mitigate this risk, firewall software is often installed onto a system using an operating system that has very limited functionality, providing only the services necessary to support the firewall software. An example of such an operating system is the ISO operating system installed onto Nokia routing/firewall appliances. ISO provides the functionality necessary to support installation of Check Point firewall software but little else. The remaining answers are normal firewall configurations and are not of concern to the IS auditor.

3. An IS auditor strives to ensure that IT is effectively used to support organizational goals and objectives regarding information confidentiality, integrity, and availability. Which of the following processes best supports this mandate?
   - ❑ A. Network monitoring
   - ❑ B. Systems monitoring
   - ❑ C. Staffing monitoring
   - ❑ D. Capacity planning and management

   Answer: D. Computer resources should be carefully monitored to match utilization needs with proper resource capacity levels. Capacity planning and management relies upon network, systems, and staffing monitoring to ensure that organizational goals and objectives regarding information confidentiality, integrity, and availability are met.

4. Which of the following would be the first evidence to review when performing a network audit?
   - ❑ A. Network topology chart
   - ❑ B. Systems inventory
   - ❑ C. Applications inventory
   - ❑ D. Database architecture

   Answer: A. Reviewing a diagram of the network topology is often the best first step when auditing IT systems. This diagram provides the auditor with a foundation-level understanding of how systems, applications, and databases interoperate. Obtaining the systems and applications inventory would be a logical next step. Reviewing the database architecture is much more granular and can be performed only after adequately understanding the basics of how an organization's systems and networks are set up.

5. An IS auditor needs to check for proper software licensing and license management. Which of the following management audits would consider software licensing?
   - ❑ A. Facilities
   - ❑ B. Operations
   - ❑ C. Configuration
   - ❑ D. Hardware

   Answer: C. A configuration-management audit should always verify software licensing for authorized use. The remaining answers do not focus on software licensing.

6. "Dangling tuples" within a database represent a breach in which of the following?

    ❏ A. Attribute integrity

    ❏ B. Referential integrity

    ❏ C. Relational integrity

    ❏ D. Interface integrity

Answer: B. It is important that database referential integrity be enforced, to avoid orphaned references, or "dangling tuples." Relational integrity is enforced more at the record level. The remaining answers are misleading.

7. Which of the following BEST supports communication availability, acting as a countermeasure to the vulnerability of component failure?

    ❏ A. Careful network monitoring with a dynamic real-time alerting system

    ❏ B. Integrated corrective network controls

    ❏ C. Simple component redundancy

    ❏ D. High network throughput rate

Answer: C. Providing network path redundancy is the best countermeasure or control for potential network device failures. Careful monitoring only supports timely response to component failure. Integrated corrective network controls is misleading and loosely describes simple component redundancy. High network throughput rate provides increased performance but does not address component failure.

8. Which of the following firewall types provides the most thorough inspection and control of network traffic?

    ❏ A. Packet-filtering firewall or stateful inspection firewall

    ❏ B. Application-layer gateway or stateful inspection firewall

    ❏ C. Application-layer gateway or circuit-level gateway

    ❏ D. Packet-filtering firewall or circuit-level gateway

Answer: B. An application-layer gateway, or proxy firewall, and stateful inspection firewalls provide the greatest degree of protection and control because both firewall technologies inspect all seven OSI layers of network traffic. A packet-filtering firewall, also known as a circuit-level gateway, reliably inspects only through OSI Layer 3.

9. Decreasing collisions because of network congestion is important for supporting network communications availability. Which of the following devices is best suited for logically segmenting and creating collision domains based upon OSI Layer 2 MAC addressing?

    ❏ A. Router

    ❏ B. Hub

    ❏ C. Repeater

    ❏ D. Switch

Answer: D. A switch is most appropriate for segmenting the network into multiple collision domains to achieve the result of fewer network communications errors because of congestion-related collisions. As OSI Layer 1 devices, repeaters and hubs cannot understand MAC addressing, which is necessary to logically segment collision domains. As an OSI Layer 3 device, a router segments the network according to logical network addressing.

10. Which of the following network configurations BEST supports availability?

   ❑ A. Mesh with host forwarding enabled
   ❑ B. Ring
   ❑ C. Star
   ❑ D. Bus

   Answer: A. Although it is not very practical because of physical implementation constraints, a fully connected mesh with host forwarding enabled provides the most redundancy of network communication paths.

Protection of
Information Assets

Key concepts you will need to understand:

✓ The processes of design, implementation, and monitoring of security (gap analysis baseline, tool selection)

✓ Encryption techniques (DES, RSA)

✓ Public key infrastructure (PKI) components (certification authorities, registration authorities)

✓ Digital signature techniques

✓ Physical security practices

✓ Techniques to identify, authenticate, and restrict users to authorized functions and data (dynamic passwords, challenge/response, menus, profiles)

✓ Security software (single sign-on, intrusion-detection systems [IDS], automated permission, network address translation)

✓ Security testing and assessment tools (penetration testing, vulnerability scanning)

✓ Network and Internet security (SSL, SET, VPN, tunneling)

✓ Voice communications security

✓ Attack/fraud methods and techniques (hacking, spoofing, Trojan horses, denial of service, spamming)

✓ Sources of information regarding threats, standards, evaluation criteria, and practices in regard to information security

✓ Security monitoring, detection, and escalation processes and techniques (audit trails, intrusion detection, computer emergency response team)

✓ Viruses and detection

✓ Environmental protection practices and devices (fire suppression, cooling systems)

Techniques you will need to master:

✓ Evaluate the design, implementation, and monitoring of logical access controls to ensure the integrity, confidentiality, and availability of information assets

✓ Evaluate network infrastructure security to ensure integrity, confidentiality, availability, and authorized use of the network and the information transmitted

✓ Evaluate the design, implementation, and monitoring of environmental controls to prevent and/or minimize potential loss

✓ Evaluate the design, implementation, and monitoring of physical access controls to ensure that the level of protection for assets and facilities is sufficient to meet the organization's business objectives

The IT organization is responsible for ensuring the protection of information assets through effective policy, controls, and standardized procedures and control testing. The security controls implemented within the organization will probably use a *defense-in-depth* strategy. Defense-in-depth strategies provide layered protection for the organization's information systems and data. Realization of this strategy reduces the overall risk of a successful attack in the event of a single control failure using multiple layers of controls to protect an asset. These controls ensure the confidentiality, integrity, and availability of the systems and data, as well as prevent financial losses to the organization.

The organization should have a formalized security function that is responsible for classifying assets and the risks associated with those assets, and mitigating risk through the implementation of security controls. The combination of security controls ensures that the organization's information technology assets and data are protected against both internal and external threats.

The security function protects the IT infrastructure through the use of physical, logical, environmental and administrative (that is, policies, guidelines, standards, and procedures) controls. *Physical* controls guard access to facilities, computers, and telecommunications equipment, and ensure that only authorized users have access to facilities and equipment. Physical security controls can include security guards, biometric devices (retina scanners, hand geometry, fingerprint scanners), keys and locks, and electronic card readers. Physical access controls should be monitored and reviewed periodically to ensure their effectiveness. Physical security controls can be defeated through social engineering, whereby unauthorized persons gain access to the facility by posing as someone they are not. As stated earlier, *social engineering* involves playing psychological tricks on authorized users to gain access to the system. These might include "shoulder surfing," or looking over the shoulder of authorized users to identify key codes that access the building; claiming to have "lost" badges or key cards and persuading an authorized user to permit access; or piggybacking behind an authorized user with a valid key card.

Logical security controls are more complex to implement and maintain. Access controls are security features that control how users and systems communicate or interact with other users and systems. Furthermore, logical controls are the hardware and software tools that are used to restrict access to resources such as the following:

➤ System access

➤ Network architecture

➤ Network access

➤ Encryption and protocols

➤ Systems auditing

Authorization according to the principle of least privilege (need to know) should be applied, meaning that authorized users should have access to only the applications and data they need to perform authorized tasks. In addition, the IT organization should regularly log and monitor logical access to the systems and data. Policies and procedures also should include segregation of duties and access and transaction logs.

Environmental security controls are designed to mitigate the risk associated with naturally occurring events such as storms, earthquakes, hurricanes, tornadoes, and floods. The controls might vary according to the type of event, but the process of classification, mitigation, and monitoring is similar in nature to that of physical and logical security controls.

It is important to remember that unauthorized users can gain access to applications and data from both inside and outside the organization. Unauthorized users might include the following:

➤ Internal employees

➤ Contracted employees

➤ Suppliers or vendors

➤ Cleaning and maintenance contractors

➤ Partners

➤ Remote users

➤ Entities who have access to external information systems (such as general public)

To ensure the effectiveness of the security program and its associated controls, regular penetration tests should be performed. These tests might include breaking into access points through persuasion or brute force, or gaining admission as a visitor and trying to access areas for which someone is not authorized. The combination of regular review, monitoring, and testing of physical, logical, and environmental security controls will identify weaknesses and areas for improvement. In addition to monitoring, the IT organization should define incident response and reporting procedures to react to disruptive events when they occur. The incident response procedures should provide detailed procedures for the identification, notification, evidence collection, continued protection, and reporting of such disruptive events.

Understanding and Evaluating Controls Design, Implementation, and Monitoring

Per ISACA, key elements and roles/responsibilities of security management lead to the successful protection of information systems and assets, reducing losses to the organization:

➤ **Senior management commitment and support**—A successful security-management program requires the full support of senior management.

➤ **Polices and procedures**—Policies and procedures should be created and implemented in alignment with the organizational strategy, and a clear definition of sensitive and critical assets should be created. The confidentiality, integrity, and availability of these assets should be protected through proper risk management and mitigation, including specific guidelines/practices and procedures.

➤ **Organization**—The organization should have both general and specific responsibilities defined for the protection of information assets, as well as clear communication and definition of security roles and responsibilities.

➤ **Security awareness and education**—All employees (internal and external) and third parties should receive appropriate and regular training, as well as updates on the importance of security in organizational policies and procedures. This includes security requirements, legal responsibilities, legal controls, and training on the correct use of information technology resources and organizational data.

➤ **Monitoring and compliance**—The IT organization should implement monitoring and compliance controls that allow for the continuous assessment of the effectiveness of the organization's security programs.

➤ **Incident handling and response**—A formal incident handling and response capability should be established and should include planning and preparation, detection, initiation, response, recovery, closure, post-incident review, and defined key roles and responsibilities.

In addition, the organization should define security management roles and responsibilities. These responsibilities should be considered:

➤ **Process owners**—Ensure that appropriate security measures, consistent with organizational policy, are maintained

➤ **Users**—Follow procedures set out in the organization's security policy

➤ **Information owners**—Are ultimately accountable for how assets and resources are protected, and, therefore, make security decisions, such as determining data-classification levels for information assets so that appropriate levels of control are provided related to their confidentiality, integrity, and availability. Executive management such as the board of directors is an example of information owners.

➤ **IS security committee**—Should constitute a formalized IS security committee formed to support the input of users, executive management, security administration, IS personnel, and legal counsel

➤ **Security specialists/advisors**—Assist with the design, implementation, management, and review of the organization's security policy, standards, and procedures

➤ **IT developers**—Implement information security

➤ **IS auditors**—Provide independent assurance to management of the appropriateness and effectiveness of information security objectives

Logical Access Controls

As described earlier, logical access controls are security features that control how users and systems communicate and interact with other users or systems. These are often the primary safeguards for systems software and data. Three main components of access control exist:

➤ *Access* is the flow of information between a subject and an object.

➤ A *subject* is the requestor of access to a data object.

➤ An *object* is an entity that contains information.

A subject's access rights should be based on the level of trust a company has in a subject and the subject's need to know (principle of least privilege). As a rule, access-control mechanisms should default to "no access," to provide intentional (explicit) access and to ensure that security holes do not go unnoticed.

The access-control model is a framework that dictates how subjects can access objects and defines three types of access:

➤ **Discretionary**—Access to data objects is granted to the subjects at the data owner's discretion.

➤ **Mandatory**—Access to an object is dependent upon security labels.

➤ **Nondiscretionary**—A central authority decides on access to certain objects based upon the organization's security policy.

In implementing *mandatory access control* (*MAC*), every subject and object has a sensitivity label (security label). A mandatory access system is commonly used within the federal government to define access to objects. If a document is assigned a label of top secret, all subjects requesting access to the document must contain a clearance of top-secret or above to view the document. Those containing a lower security label (such as secret or confidential) are denied access to the object. In mandatory access control, all subjects and objects have security labels, and the decision for access is determined by the operating or security system. Mandatory access control is used in organizations where confidentiality is of the utmost concern.

Nondiscretionary access control can use different mechanisms based on the needs of the organization. The first is *role-based access*, in which access to an object(s) is based on the role of the user in the company. In other words, a data entry operator should have create access to a particular database. All data entry operators should have create access based on their role (data entry operator). This type of access is commonly used in environments with high turnover because the access rights apply to a subject's role, not the subject.

Task-based access control is determined by which tasks are assigned to a user. In this scenario, a user is assigned a task and given access to the information system to perform that task. When the task is complete, the access is revoked; if a new task is assigned, the access is granted for the new task.

Lattice-based access is determined by the sensitivity or security label assigned to the user's role. This scenario provides for an upper and lower bound of access capabilities for every subject and object relationship. Consider, for example, that the role of our user is assigned an access level of secret. That user may view all objects that are public (lower bound) and secret (upper bound), as well as those that are confidential (which falls between public and secret). This user's role would not be able to view top-secret documents because they exceed the upper bound of the lattice. Figure 4.1 depicts this access.

Another method of access control is *rule-based access*. The previous discussion of firewalls in Chapter 3, "Technical Infrastructure and Operational Practices and Infrastructure," demonstrated the use of rule-based access implemented through access control lists (ACLs). Rule-based access is generally used between networks or applications. It involves a set of rules from which incoming requests can be matched and either accepted or rejected. Rule-based controls are considered nondiscretionary access controls because the administrator of the system sets the controls rather than the information users.

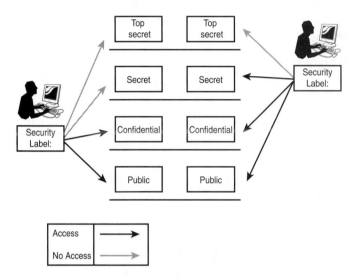

Figure 4.1 Lattice-based access control.

IS auditors should review access control lists (ACL) to determine user permissions that have been granted for a particular resource.

Restricted interfaces are used to control access to both functions and data within applications and through the use of restricted menus or shells. They are commonly used in database views. The database view should be configured so that only that data for which the user is authorized is presented on the screen. A good example of a restricted interface is an Automatic Teller Machine (ATM). When you access your bank account via an ATM, you can perform only certain functions (such as withdraw funds or check an account balance); all of those functions are restricted so that transactions are applied to only your account.

An *access-control matrix* is a single table used to cross-reference rights that have been assigned by subject (subject capabilities) with access rights that are assigned by object (access-control list). The matrix is essentially a combination of a capabilities table and access control list(s). The capability table specifies the rights a subject possesses pertaining to specific objects, bound by subject. The capability corresponds to the subject's row in the access-control matrix. The *access-control list* (*ACL*) is a list of subjects that are authorized to access a specific object. The rights are bound by object. The ACL corresponds to a column of the access-control matrix. Figure 4.2 outlines a simple access-control matrix for a single database and a group of users. It is important to keep in mind that ACLs are generally more granular than the figure.

	Test Database
John	Update (includes read)
Jane	Create/Read

Figure 4.2   Access control list.

In Figure 4.2, John, who is a data entry operator, is responsible for address updates within the test database. He is allowed access to read and update records but does not have access to create new records. Jane is responsible for entering new customers in the database and, therefore, has the capability to read and create new records. Neither John nor Jane can delete records within the database.

The administration of access control can be either *centralized* or *decentralized* and should support the policy, procedures, and standards for the organization. In a centralized access control administration system, a single entity or system is responsible for granting access to all users. In decentralized or distributed administration, the access is given by individuals who are closer to the resources.

As an IS auditor, you will most likely see a combination of access-control and administration methods. It is important to understand what type of access methods and administration are being used within the organization, to determine whether they are providing the necessary control over information resources. In gaining an understanding of the methods used, you will be able to determine the access paths to computerized information. An access path is the logical route an end user or system takes to get to the information resource. A normal access path can include several software and hardware components, which might implement access controls differently. Per ISACA, the IS auditor should evaluate each component for proper implementation and proper physical and logical security. Logical access controls should also be reviewed to ensure that access is granted on a least-privilege basis per the organization's data owners.

Techniques for Identification and Authentication

In gaining access to information resources, the system must know who you are (*identification*) and verify that you are who you say you are (*authentication*). As a user gaining access, you provide a claimed identity (*credentials*), and the system authenticates those credentials before you have *authorization* to utilize the requested object. The most common form of identification is a login ID, in conjunction with a password (authentication), which is used to validate your (subject's) identity. When you provide your credentials (login ID and password), the system can check you (subject) against the system or network you are trying to access (object) and verify that you are allowed access (authorization). The IT organization also should have a method of logging user actions while accessing objects within the information system, to establish accountability (linking individuals to their activities).

Access control involves these components:
1. Identification
2. Authentication
3. Authorization

The most common form of authentication includes the use of passwords, but authentication can take three forms:

➤ **Something you know**—A password.

➤ **Something you have**—A token, ATM bank card, or smart card.

➤ **Something you are**—Unique personal physical characteristic(s) (biometrics). These include fingerprints, retina scans, iris scans, hand geometry, and palm scans.

These forms of authentication can be used together. If two or more are used together, this is known as *strong authentication* or *two-factor authentication*. Two-factor authentication is commonly used with ATMs. To access your account at an ATM, you need two of three forms of authentication. When you walk up to the ATM, you enter your ATM card (something you have); the ATM prompts you for your PIN (something you know). In this instance, you have used two-factor authentication to access your bank account.

Two-factor authentication requires authentication by two of the following three methods: something the user knows, something the user possesses, or something the user is. A smart card requiring the user's PIN is an example of two-factor authentication.

As stated earlier, passwords are the most common form of authentication. Coincidentally, they are also the weakest. Passwords should be implemented in such a way that they are easily remembered but hard to guess. If passwords are initially allocated by an administrator or owner, they should be randomly generated and assigned on an individual basis. If user account and password information is shared between users, all individual accountability for any actions performed under the authority of a shared username has been lost. This is especially critical in a transaction-based environment, such as within financial institutions.

In addition to using randomly generated passwords, administrators should implement alert thresholds within systems to detect and act upon failed login events. The implementation of alert thresholds ensures that if a password is entered incorrectly a predefined number of times, the login ID associated with the password automatically is disabled, either for a specific period of time or permanently. As an IS auditor, you will typically see such a threshold set to 3 (incorrect password attempts); the account will be disabled for a specific period of time (such as 30 minutes) or permanently, in which case the user must contact the security administrator to reactivate the account. Terminating access after three unsuccessful logon attempts is a common best practice for preventing unauthorized dial-up access.

In generating user accounts and passwords, the administrator should have policies regarding password length, how often passwords are required to be changed, and the password lockout policies. As an example, administrators might create user accounts that automatically expire on a predetermined date. This is an effective control for granting temporary access to vendors and external support personnel. Administrators also should ensure that all passwords created are known only to the user. Users should have the authorization to create and change their own passwords.

As a common form of authentication, passwords can be subject to attacks (either internal or external). A common form of password attacks is the dictionary attack, in which an individual uses a dictionary of common words and a program to guess passwords. The dictionaries and programs are widely available on the Internet and are easy to use. The program employed for attack uses each of the words from the dictionary in sequence to guess the password of the logon ID being attacked. Security administrators can mitigate the risk associated with dictionary attacks by enforcing password complexity in the creation of passwords, and also can enforce failed logon attempt password-lockout policies, password length, and periodic password changes. When enforcing password complexity, administrators should extend the required length of passwords (six or more characters) and require the use of numeric characters, upper and lower case, and special characters.

Different types of passwords exist, depending on the implementation. In some systems, the passwords are user created; others use *cognitive passwords*. A cognitive password uses de facto or opinion-based information to verify an individual's identity. Cognitive passwords are commonly used today as security questions associated with an account, in case the user has forgotten the password. During the creation of the user account, a system that uses cognitive passwords might ask one or more security questions: What is your mother's maiden name? What is the name of your favorite pet? What is the elementary school you attended? The user chooses a question and provides the answer, which is stored in the system. If the user forgets the password, the system asks the security question. If it is answered correctly, the system resets the password or sends the existing password via email.

Another type of password is a *one-time*, or *dynamic, password*. One-time passwords provide maximum security because a new password is required for each login. Conversely, a static password is the same for each login. One-time passwords are usually used in conjunction with a token device, which is essentially a password generator. The token can be either synchronous or asynchronous. When using a synchronous token, the generation of the password can be timed (the password changes every *n* seconds or minutes) or event driven (the password is generated on demand with a button). The use of token-based authentication generally incorporates something you know (password) combined with something you have (token) to authenticate. A token device that uses asynchronous authentication uses a challenge-response mechanism to authenticate. In this scenario, the system displays a challenge to the user, which the user then enters into the token device. The token device returns a different value. This value then is entered into the system as the response to be authenticated.

Passwords are used to authenticate users to provide access and authorization. They are the mechanism that allows subjects to access objects within the system. To provide authorization to objects, those objects need to have defined owners that classify the objects or data. Establishing data ownership is an important first step for properly implementing data classification. The data owners are ultimately responsible and accountable for access control of data. Data owners should require written authorization for users to gain access to objects or data. Security administrators should work with the data owners to identify and implement access rules stipulating which users or group of users are authorized to access data or files, along with the level of authorized access (read or update).

Information systems security policies are used as the framework for developing logical access controls. Information systems security policy should be developed and approved by the top management and then should be implemented utilizing access-control lists, password management, and systems configuration files. In addition, data owners might use file encryption to protect confidential data residing on a PC. As stated earlier, authorization of access to objects or data is based on least privilege (need to know) and should incorporate proper segregation of duties. As an example, if a programmer has update access to a live system, IS auditors are more concerned with the programmer's capability to initiate or modify transactions and the capability to access production than the programmer's capability to authorize transactions.

 In a database, system integrity is most often ensured through table link verification and reference checks.

Network Infrastructure Security

As an IS auditor performing detailed network assessments and access control reviews, you first must determine the points of entry to the system and then must review the associated controls. Per ISACA, the following are controls over the communication network:

➤ Network control functions should be performed by technically qualified operators.

➤ Network control functions should be separated, and the duties should be rotated on a regular basis, when possible.

➤ Network-control software must restrict operator access from performing certain functions (such as the capability to amend or delete operator activity logs).

➤ Operations management should periodically review audit trails, to detect any unauthorized network operations activities.

➤ Network operations standards and protocols should be documented and made available to the operations, and should be periodically reviewed to ensure compliance.

➤ Network access by the system engineers should be closely monitored and reviewed to detect unauthorized access to the network.

➤ Analysis should be performed to ensure workload balance, fast response time, and system efficiency.

➤ The communications software should maintain a terminal identification file, to check the authentication of a terminal when it tries to send or receive messages.

➤ When appropriate, data encryption should be used to protect messages from disclosure during transmission.

IS auditors should first determine points of entry when performing a detailed network assessment and access control review.

As stated in Chapter 3, the firewall is a secured network gateway. The firewall protects the organization's resources from unauthorized users (internal or external). As an example, firewalls are used to prevent unauthorized users (usually external) from gaining access to an organization's computer systems through the Internet gateway. A firewall can also be used as an interface to connect authorized users to private trusted network resources. Chapter 3 discussed the implementation of a firewall that works closely with a router to filter all network packets, to determine whether to forward them toward their destination. The router can be configured with outbound traffic filtering that drops outbound packets that contain source addresses from other than the user's organization. Firewalls and filtering routers can be configured to limit services not allowed by policy and can help prevent misuse of the organization's systems. An example of misuse associated with outbound packets is a *distributed denial-of-service attack* (DDoS). In this type of attack, unauthorized persons gain access to an organization's systems and install a *denial-of-service* (DoS) program that is used to launch an attack against other computers. Basically, a large number of systems on different hosts await commands from a central client (unauthorized user). The central client (DDoS client) then sends a message to all the servers (DDoS server program) instructing them to send as much traffic as they can to the target system. In this scenario, the DDoS program distributes the work of flooding the target among all available DoS servers, creating a distributed DoS. The application gateway firewall can be configured to prevent applications such as FTPs from entering the organization's network.

Application gateways, or proxy firewalls, are an effective method for controlling file downloading via FTP. Outbound traffic filtering can help prevent an organization's systems from participating in a distributed denial-of-service (DDoS) attack.

A screened-subnet firewall can be used to create a demilitarized zone (DMZ). This type of firewall utilizes a bastion host that is sandwiched between two packet-filtering routers and is the most secure firewall system. This type of firewall system supports both network and application-level security, while defining a separate demilitarized zone network.

Firewalls can be used to prevent unauthorized access to the internal network from the Internet. A firewall located within a screened subnet is a more secure firewall system.

Employees of the organization, as well as partners and vendors, can connect through a dial-up system to get access to organizational resources. One of the methods implemented for authenticating users is a *callback system*. The callback system works to ensure users are who they say they are by calling back a predefined number to establish a connection. An authorized user calls a remote server through a dial-up line first. Then the server disconnects and dials back to the user machine, based on the user ID and password, using a telephone number from its database. However, it should be noted that callback security can easily be defeated through simple call forwarding.

A callback system is a remote access control whereby the user initially connects to the network systems via dial-up access, only to have the initial connection terminated by the server. The server then subsequently dials the user back at a predetermined number stored in the server's configuration database.

Encryption Techniques

The use of encryption enables companies to digitally protect their most valuable assets: information. The organization's information system contains and processes intellectual property, including organizational strategy, customer lists, and financial data. In fact, a majority of information as well as the transactions associated with this information are stored digitally. This environment requires companies to use encryption to protect the confidentiality and the integrity of information. Organizations should utilize encryption services to ensure reliable authentication of messages, the integrity of documents, and the confidentiality of information that is transmitted and received.

Cryptography is the art and science of hiding the meaning of communication from unintended recipients by encrypting plain text into cipher text. The process of encryption and decryption is performed by a cryptosystem that uses mathematical functions (algorithms) and a special password called a key.

Encryption is used to protect data while in transit over networks, protect data stored on systems, deter and detect accidental or intentional alterations of data, and verify the authenticity of a transaction or document. In other words, encryption provides confidentiality, authenticity, and nonrepudiation. *Nonrepudiation* provides proof of the origin of data and protects the sender against a false denial by the recipient that the data has been received, or to protect the recipient against false denial by the sender that the data has been sent.

The strength of a cryptosystem lies in the attributes of its key components. The first component is the *algorithm*, which is a mathematical-based function that performs encryption and decryption. The second component is the *key* that is used in conjunction with the algorithm; each key makes the encryption/decryption process unique. To decrypt a message that has been encrypted, the receiver must use the correct key; if an incorrect key is used, the message is unreadable. The key length, which is predetermined, is important to reduce the possibility of a brute-force attack to decrypt an encrypted message. The longer the key is, the more difficult it is to decrypt a message because of the amount of computation required to try all possible key combinations (work factor). Cryptanalysis is the science of studying and breaking the secrecy of encryption algorithms and their necessary pieces. The work factor involved in brute-forcing encrypted messages relies significantly on the computing power of the machines that are brute-forcing the message.

The strength of a cryptosystem is determined by a combination of key length, initial input vectors, and the complexity of the data-encryption algorithm that uses the key.

As an example, the Data Encryption Standard (DES) was selected as an official cipher (method of encrypting information) under the Federal Information Processing Standard (FIPS) for the United States in 1976. When introduced, DES used a 56-bit key length. It is now considered to be insecure for many applications because they have been broken into in less than 24 hours. A 24-hour time frame to break a cryptographic key is considered a very low work factor. In 1998, the Electronic Frontier Foundation (EFF) spent approximately $250,000 and created a DES-cracker to show that DES was breakable. The machine brute-forced a DES key in a little more than two days, proving that the work factor involved was small and that DES was, therefore, insecure. Fortunately, there is a version of DES named Triple DES (3DES) that uses a 168-bit key (three 56-bit keys) and provides greater security than its predecessor. As a point of interest, you should note that the

U.S. Federal Government has ended support for the DES cryptosystem in favor of the new Advanced Encryption Standard (AES).

The cryptographic algorithms use either symmetric keys or asymmetric keys. *Symmetric* keys are also known as *secret keys* or *shared secret keys* because both parties in a transaction use the same key for encryption and decryption. The ability of users to keep the key secret is one of the weaknesses in a symmetric key system. If a key is compromised, all messages using this key can be decrypted. In addition, the secure delivery of keys poses a problem when adding new devices or users to a symmetric key system. Acceptable methods of delivery can include placing the key on a floppy and hand delivering it or delivering the key through the use of a secure courier or via postal mail. Protecting the exchange of symmetric shared keys through the use of asymmetric or hybrid cryptosystems is another option that is described in more detail later in this chapter.

A variety of symmetric encryption algorithms exists, as shown in Table 4.1.

Table 4.1 Symmetric Encryption Algorithms	
Algorithm	**Notes**
Data Encryption Standard (DES)	Low work factor—has been broken once Provides confidentiality but not nonrepudiation Low work factor Provides confidentiality but not nonrepudiation
Advanced Encryption Standard (AES)	High work factor Provides confidentiality but not nonrepudiation
International Data Encryption Algorithm (IDEA)	High work factor Provides confidentiality but not nonrepudiation
Rivest Cipher 5 (RC5)	High work factor Provides confidentiality but not nonrepudiation

Symmetric keys are fast because the algorithms are not burdened with providing authentication services, and they are difficult to break if they use a large key size. However, symmetric keys are more difficult to distribute securely.

Figure 4.3 shows the symmetric key process. Both the sending and receiving parties use the same key.

Symmetric encryption's security is based on how well users protect the private key. If the private key is compromised, all messages encrypted with the private key can be decrypted by an unauthorized third party. The advantage of symmetric encryption is speed.

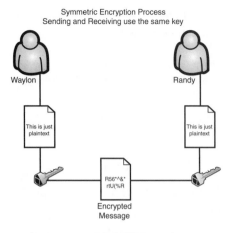

Symmetric Encryption Process
Sending and Receiving use the same key

Waylon

Randy

This is just plaintext

This is just plaintext

R56*^&*
rtU(%R

Encrypted
Message

Figure 4.3   Symmetric encryption process.

Asymmetric Encryption (Public-Key Cryptography)

In using symmetric key encryption, a single shared secret key is used between parties. In asymmetric encryption, otherwise known as public-key cryptography, each party has a respective key pair. These asymmetric keys are mathematically related and are known as *public* and *private keys*. When messages are encrypted by one key, the other key is required for decryption. Public keys can be shared and are known to everyone, hence the definition *public*. Private keys are known only to the owner of the key. These keys make up the key pair in public key encryption.

Before public-key cryptography can be used, both the sender and the recipient need to exchange one another's public keys. If a sender wants to encrypt a message to another recipient, the sender encrypts a message using his private key (known only to him), and the recipient decrypts the message using the sender's public key (known to everyone). Because the keys are mathematically linked, the recipient is assured that the message truly came from the original sender. This is known as authentication or authenticity because the sender is the only party who should have the private key to encrypt content in a way that can be decrypted by the sender's public key. It is important to keep in mind that anyone who has the sender's public key can decrypt this message at this point, so this initial encryption does not provide confidentiality. If the sender wants the message to be confidential, he should then re-encrypt his message using the recipient's public key. This requires the recipient to use his own private key (known only to him) to initially decrypt the message and then to use the sender's public key to decrypt the remainder. In this scenario, the sender is assured that only the recipient can decrypt the message (protecting confidentiality), and the recipient is assured that the message came from Waylon (proof of authenticity). This type of data encryption provides message confidentiality and authentication.

 With public key encryption, or asymmetric encryption, data is encrypted by the sender using the recipient's public key. The data is then decrypted using the recipient's private key.

The following is a review of basic asymmetric encryption flow:

1. A clear-text message is encrypted by the sender with the sender's private key, to ensure authenticity only.

2. The message is re-encrypted with the recipient's public key, to ensure confidentiality.

3. The message is initially decrypted by the recipient using the recipient's own private key, rendering a message that remains encrypted with sender's private key.

4. The message is then decrypted by the recipient using the sender's public key. If this is successful, the receiver can be sure that the message truly came from the original sender.

Figure 4.4 outlines asymmetric encryption to ensure both authenticity and confidentiality.

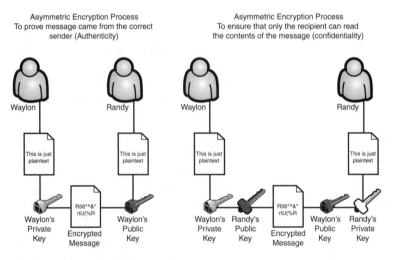

Figure 4.4   Asymmetric encryption process.

The advantages of an asymmetric key encryption system are the ease of secure key distribution and the capability to provide authenticity, confidentiality, and nonrepudiation. The disadvantages of asymmetric encryption systems are the increase in overhead processing and, therefore, cost.

 An elliptic curve cryptosystem has a much higher computation speed than RSA encryption.

A variety of asymmetric encryption algorithms are used, as shown in Table 4.2.

Table 4.2 Encryption Algorithms		
Algorithm	**Use**	**Notes**
Rivest, Shamir, Adleman (RSA)	Encryption Digital signature	Security comes from the difficulty of factoring large prime numbers.
Elliptic Curve Cryptosystem (ECC)	Encryption Digital signature	Rich mathematical structures are used for efficiency. ECC can provide the same level of protection as RSA, but with a key size that is smaller than what RSA requires.
Digital Signature Algorithm (DSA)	Digital signature	Security comes from the difficulty of factoring discrete algorithms in a finite space.

 A long asymmetric encryption key increases encryption overhead and cost.

We have examined both symmetric and asymmetric cryptography, and each has advantages and disadvantages. Symmetric cryptography is fast, but if the shared secret key is compromised, the encrypted messages might be compromised. There are challenges in distributing the shared secret keys securely. Asymmetric processing provides authenticity, confidentiality, and nonrepudiation but requires higher overhead because processing is slower. If we combine the two encryption methods in a hybrid approach, we can use public key cryptography.

Public and private key cryptography use algorithms and keys to encrypt messages. In private (shared) key cryptography, there are significant challenges in distributing keys securely. In public key cryptography, the challenge lies in ensuring that the owner of the public key is who he says he is, and trusted notification if the key is invalid because of compromise.

Public Key Infrastructure (PKI)

A *public key infrastructure* (*PKI*) incorporates public key cryptography, security policies, and standards that enable key maintenance (including user identification, distribution, and revocation) through the use of certificates. The goal of PKI is to answer the question "How do I know this key is truly your public key?" PKI provides access control, authentication, confidentiality, nonrepudiation, and integrity for the exchange of messages through use of *Certificate Authorities* (CA) and *digital certificates*. PKI uses a combination of public-key cryptography and digital certificates to provide some of the strongest overall control over data confidentiality, reliability, and integrity for Internet transactions.

The CA maintains, issues, and revokes public key certificates, which ensure an individual's identity. If a user (Randy) receives a message from Waylon that contains Waylon's public key, he can request authentication of Waylon's key from the CA. When the CA has responded that this is Waylon's public key, Randy can communicate with Waylon, knowing that he is who he says he is. The other advantage of the CA is the maintenance of a *certificate revocation list* (*CRL*), which lists all certificates that have been revoked. Certificates can be revoked if the private key has been comprised or the certificate has expired. As an example, imagine that Waylon found that his private key had been compromised and had a list of 150 people to whom he had distributed his public key. He would need to contact all 150 and tell them to discard the existing public key they had for him. He would then need to distribute a new public key to all those he communicates with. In using PKI, Waylon could contact the CA, provide a new public key (establish a new certificate), and place the old public key on the CRL. This is a more efficient way to deal with key distribution because a central authority is providing key maintenance services.

A Certificate Authority manages the certificate life cycle and certificate revocation list (CRL).

The certificates used by the CAs incorporate identity information, certificate serial numbers, certificate version numbers, algorithm information, lifetime dates, and the signature of the issuing authority (CA). The most widely used certificate types are the Version 3 X.509 certificates. The X.509 certificates are commonly used in secure web transactions via Secure Sockets Layer (SSL).

This example provides a view of the contents of an X.509 certificate and includes the lifetime dates, who the certificate is issued to, who the certificate is issued by, and the communication and encryption protocols that are used. Digital certificates are considered the most reliable sender-authentication control. In this case, PKI provides nonrepudiation services for e-commerce transactions. This e-commerce hosting organization uses asymmetric encryption along with digital certificates to verify the authenticity of the organization and its transaction communications for its customers.

A Certifying Authority (CA) can delegate the processes of establishing a link between the requesting entity and its public key to a *Registration Authority* (*RA*). An RA performs certification and registration duties to offload some of the work from the CAs. The RA can confirm individual identities, distribute keys, and perform maintenance functions, but it cannot issue certificates. The CA still manages the digital certificate life cycle, to ensure that adequate security and controls exist.

Digital Signature Techniques

Digital signatures provide integrity in addition to message source authentication because the digital signature of a signed message changes every time a single bit of the document changes. This ensures that a signed document cannot be altered without being detected. Depending on the mechanism chosen to implement a digital signature, the mechanism might be capable of ensuring data confidentiality or even timeliness, but this is not guaranteed.

A digital signature is a cryptographic method that ensures data integrity, authentication of the message, and nonrepudiation. The primary purpose of digital signatures is to provide authentication and integrity of data. In common electronic transactions, (a digital signature is created by the sender to prove message integrity and authenticity by initially using a hashing algorithm to produce a hash value, or message digest, from the entire message contents. The sender provides a mechanism to authenticate the message contents by encrypting the message digest using the sender's own private key. If the recipient can decrypt the message using the sender's public key, which has been validated by a third-party Certificate Authority, the recipient can rest assured that the message digest was indeed created by the original sender. Upon receiving the data and decrypting the message digest, the recipient can independently create a message digest from the data using the same publicly available hashing algorithm for data comparison and integrity validation.

The following is the flow of a digital signature:

1. The sender and recipient exchange public keys:

   ➤ These public keys are validated via a third-party Certificate Authority (CA).

   ➤ A Registration Authority (sometimes separate from the CA) manages the certificate application and procurement procedures.

2. The sender uses a digital signature hashing algorithm to compute a hash value of the entire message (called a message digest).

3. The sender "signs" the message digest by encrypting it with the sender's private key.

4. The recipient validates authenticity of the message digest by decrypting it with the sender's validated public key.

5. The recipient then validates the message integrity by computing a message digest of the message and compares the message digest value to the recently decrypted message digest provided by the sender.

With digital signatures, a hash of the data is encrypted with the sender's private key, to ensure data integrity.

A key distinction between encryption and hashing algorithms is that hashing algorithms are irreversible. A message digest is the result of using a one-way hash that creates a fingerprint of the message. If the message is altered, a comparison of the message digest to the hash of the altered message will show that the message has been changed. The hashing algorithms are publicly known and differ from encryption algorithms in that they are one-way functions and are never used in reverse. The sender runs a hash against a message to produce the message digest, and the receiver runs the same hash to produce a second message digest. The message digests are compared; if they are different, the message has been altered. The sender can use a digital signature to provide message authentication, integrity, and nonrepudiation by first creating a message digest from the entire message by using an irreversible hashing algorithm, and then "signing" the message digest by encrypting the message digest with the sender's private key. Confidentiality is added by then re-encrypting the message with the recipient's public key.

 Digital signatures require the sender to "sign" the message by encrypting the message digest, or hash of the message, with the sender's private key. The encrypted message digest is then decrypted by the recipient using the sender's public key that has been shared with the recipient.

Within the Digital Signature Standard (DSS) the RSA and Digital Signature Algorithm (DSA) are the most popular.

Each component of cryptography provides separate functions. An encrypted message can provide confidentiality. If the message contains a digital signature, this is a guarantee of the authentication and integrity of the message. As an example, a message that contains a digital signature that encrypts a message digest with the sender's private key provides strong assurance of message authenticity and integrity.

Network and Internet Security

As an IS auditor, you need to understand network connectivity, security, and encryption mechanisms on the organization's network. The use of layer security (also known as defense-in-depth) reduces the risks associated with the theft of or damage to computer systems, data, or the organization's network. Proper security policies and procedures, combined with strong internal and external access-control mechanisms, reduce risk to the organization and ensure the confidentiality, integrity, and availability of services and data.

As stated earlier in Chapter 3, firewalls can be used to protect the organization's assets against both internal and external threats. Firewalls can be used as perimeter security between the organization and the Internet, to protect critical systems and data from external hackers or internally from untrusted users (internal hackers).

Per ISACA, organizations that have implemented firewalls face these problems:

➤ A false sense of security, with management feeling that no further security checks or controls are needed on the internal network (that is, the majority of incidents are cause by insiders, who are not controlled by firewalls).

➤ Circumventing firewalls through the use of modems might connect users directly to Internet service providers. Management should ensure that the use of modems when a firewall exists is strictly controlled or prohibited altogether.

➤ Misconfigured firewalls might allow unknown and dangerous services to pass through freely.

➤ What constitutes a firewall might be misunderstood (companies claiming to have a firewall might have merely a screening router).

➤ Monitoring activities might not occur on a regular basis (for example, log settings might not be appropriately applied and reviewed).

➤ Firewall policies might not be maintained regularly.

An initial step in creating a proper firewall policy is identifying network applications, such as mail, web, or FTP servers to be externally accessed. When reviewing a firewall, an IS auditor should be primarily concerned with proper firewall configuration, which supports enforcement of the security policy.

Working in concert with firewalls are the methods of access and encryption of data and user sessions on the network. A vast majority of organizations have users who are geographically dispersed, who work from home, or who travel as part of their job (road warriors). In addition, organizations allow vendors, suppliers, or support personnel access to their internal network. Virtual private networks (VPNs) provide a secure and economical method for WAN connectivity. This access can be provided via a VPN or via a public site for which traffic is encapsulated or encrypted.

VPNs use a combination of tunneling encapsulation and encryption to ensure communication security. The protocols used to provide secure connectivity might vary by the vendor and implementation. A *tunneling protocol* creates a virtual path through public and private networks. Network protocols such as IPSec often encrypt and encapsulate data in the OSI network layer.

 Data encryption is an effective control against confidentiality vulnerabilities associated with connectivity to remote sites.

PPTP is a protocol that provides encapsulation between a client and a server. PPTP works at the data link layer of the OSI model and provides encryption and encapsulation over the private link. Because it is designed to work from a client to a server, it sets up a single connection and transmits only over

IP networks. In negotiating a PPTP connection, the client initiates a connection to a network either by using dial-in services or coming across the Internet. A weakness associated with PPTP is that the initial negotiation of IP address, username, and password are sent in clear text (not encrypted); after the connection is established, the remainder of communication is encapsulated and encrypted. This is a weakness in the protocol and might allow unauthorized parties to use a network sniffer to see initial negotiations passed in the clear.

 VPNs use tunneling and encryption to hide information from sniffers on the Internet.

IPSec works at the network layer and protects and authenticates packets through two modes: transport and tunnel. IPSec transport mode encrypts only the data portion of each packet, not the header. For more robust security, tunnel mode encrypts both the original header and the data portion of the packet. IPSec supports only IP networks and can handle multiple connections at the same time.

In addition to protocols associated with establishing private links, tunneling, and encrypting data, protocols are used to facilitate secure web and client/server communication. The Secure Sockets Layer (SSL) protocol provides confidentiality through symmetric encryption such as the Data Encryption Standard (DES) and is an application/session-layer protocol used for communication between web browsers and servers. When a session is established, SSL achieves secure authentication and integrity of data through the use of a public key infrastructure (PKI). The services provided by SSL ensure confidentiality, integrity, authenticity, and nonrepudiation. SSL is most commonly used in e-commerce transactions to provide security for all transactions within the HTTP session.

The complexity associated with the implementation of encryption and secure transmission protocols requires the IT organization to pay careful attention to ensure that the protocols are being configured, implemented, and tested properly. In addition, careful attention should be paid to the secrecy and length of keys, as well as the randomness of key generation.

Security Software

Intrusion-detection systems (IDS) are used to gather evidence of system or network attacks. An IDS can be either be signature based or statistical anomaly based. Generally, statistical anomaly–based IDSs are more likely to generate false alarms. A network-based IDS works in concert with the routers and firewalls by monitoring network usage to detect anomalies at different levels within the network.

The first type of IDS is a network-based IDS. Network IDSs are generally placed between the firewall and the internal network, and on every sensitive network segment to monitor traffic looking for attack patterns or suspicious activity. If these patterns are recognized, the IDS alerts administrators or, in later generations of IDS, protects the network by denying access to the attacking addresses or dropping all packets associated with the attack. Host-based IDSs operate on a host and can monitor system resources (CPU, memory, and file system) to identify attack patterns.

The latest generation of IDSs can detect either misuse or anomalies by gathering and analyzing information and comparing it to large databases of attack signatures. In this case, the specific attack or misuse must have already occurred and been documented. This type of IDS is only as good as the database of attack signatures. If the IDS is using anomaly detection, the administrator should identify and document (within the IDS) a baseline; when the IDS detects patterns that fall outside the baseline (anomalies), it performs a certain action (alerts, stops traffic, shuts down applications or network devices). If the IDS is not baselined or configured correctly, the system could detect and alert on false positives. A false positive occurs when a system detects and alerts on an act that does not really exist. If a system detects a high number of false positives, the risk is that either the alerts will be ignored or that the particular rule associated with the alert will be turned off completely. If the IDS is a passive system, it will detect potential anomalies, log the information, and alert administrators. In a reactive system, the IDS takes direct action to protect assets on the network. These actions can include dropping packets from the attacking IP address, reprogramming the firewall to block the offending traffic or all traffic, or shutting down devices or applications that are being attacked.

A common issue with intrusion-detection systems is the detection of false positives (an attack is reported that is not actually an attack).

The firewall and IDS work together to achieve network security. The firewall can be viewed as a preventative measure because the firewall limits the access between networks to prevent intrusion but does not signal an attack. An IDS evaluates a suspected intrusion after it has taken place and sends an alert.

Single sign-on (SSO) systems are used to centralize authentication and authorization access within an information system. With specialization of applications, the average user accesses multiple applications while performing his duties. Some applications might allow users to authenticate once and access multiple applications (usually the same vendor), but most do not. SSO allows users to authenticate once, usually with a single login ID and password, and get authorization to work on multiple applications. SSO can apply to one network or can span multiple networks and applications. It is sometimes referred to as federated identity management. When implementing a single sign-on system, the organization must ensure that the authentication systems are redundant and secure.

Single sign-on authentication systems are prone to the vulnerability of having a single point of failure for authentication. In addition, if all the users internal and external to the organization and their authorization rights are located in one system, the impact of compromised authentication and subsequent unauthorized access is magnified. If one user within a single sign-on system or directory is compromised, all users, passwords, and access rights might have been compromised.

Voice Communications Security

Most people use the phone in day-to-day business and do not think about the security required within the telecommunications network. In fact, for many years, both telecommunications companies and organizations focused on the aspect of availability and did not consider integrity and confidentiality. When someone places a phone call from home or work, the call moves through any number of telephone switches before reaching its destination. These switches connect businesses within cities, cities to states, and countries to countries.

One of the systems in use in most business is the Private Branch Exchange (PBX). The PBX is similar to the telecommunications company switches, in that it routes calls within the company and passes calls to the external telecommunication provider. Organizations might have a variety of devices connected to the PBX, including telephones, modems (remote-access and vendor-maintenance lines), and computer systems. The lack of proper controls within the PBX and associated devices increases both unauthorized access vulnerabilities and outages (availability) in the organization's voice telecommunications network.

These vulnerabilities include the following:

➤ **Theft of service**—An example is toll fraud, in which attackers gain access to the PBX to make "free" phone calls.

➤ **Disclosure of information**—Organizational data is disclosed without authorization, through either malicious acts or error. Telephone conversations might be intentionally or unintentionally overheard by unauthorized individuals, or access might be gained to telephone routing or address data.

➤ **Information modification**—Organizational data contained within the PBX or a system connected to the PBX might be altered through deletion or modification. An unauthorized person might alter billing information or modify system information to gain access to additional services.

➤ **Unauthorized access**—Unauthorized users gain access to system resources or privileges.

➤ **Denial of service**—Unauthorized persons intentionally or unintentionally prevent the system from functioning as intended.

➤ **Traffic analysis**—Unauthorized persons observe information about calls and make informed guesses based on source and destination numbers or call frequency. As an example, an unauthorized person might see a high volume of calls between the CEO of an organization and a competitor's CEO or legal department, and infer that the organizations are looking to merge.

To reduce the risk associated with these vulnerabilities, administrators should remove all default passwords from the PBX system and ensure that access control within the system applies the rule of least privilege. All modems associated with maintenance should be disabled unless they are needed, and modems that employees use for remote access should employ additional hardware or software for access control. All phone numbers that are not in use should be disabled, and users who need to access voice mail should have a password policy that requires the use of strong passwords and periodic password changes. In addition, administrators should enable logging on the system and review both the PBX access and telephone call logs periodically.

Environmental Protection Practices and Devices

Environmental controls mitigate the risks associated with naturally occurring events. The most common of these are power sags, spikes, surges, and reduced voltage, but they also include tornadoes, hurricanes, earthquakes, floods, and other types of weather conditions. Per ISACA, power failures can be grouped into four distinct categories, based on the duration and relative severity of the failure:

➤ **Total failure**—A complete loss of electrical power, which might involve a single area building up to an entire geographic area. This is often caused by weather conditions (such as a storm or earthquake) or the incapability of an electrical utility company to meet user demands (such as during summer months).

➤ **Severely reduced voltage (brownout)**—The failure of an electrical utility company to supply power within an acceptable range (108–125 volts AC in the United States). Such failure places a strain on electrical equipment and could limit its operational life or even cause permanent damage.

➤ **Sags, spikes, and surges**—Temporary and rapid decreases (sags) or increases (spikes and surges) in voltage levels. These anomalies can cause loss of data, data corruption, network transmission errors, or even physical damage to hardware devices such as hard disks or memory chips.

➤ **Electromagnetic interference (EMI)**—Interference caused by electrical storms or noisy elective equipment (such as motors, fluorescent lighting, or radio transmitters). This interference could cause computer systems to hang or crash, and could result in damages similar to those caused by sags, spikes, and surges.

To reduce the risks associated with power sags, spikes, and surges, the organization should deploy surge protectors for all electrical equipment. The additional implementation of an *uninterruptible power supply* (*UPS*) can provide enough power to either shut down systems gracefully in the event of a power failure or provide enough power to keep mission-critical systems operating until power returns. A UPS can be either implemented on a system-by-system basis (portable) or deployed as part of the overall IT infrastructure. A UPS contains batteries that continue to charge as the system has power and provides battery backup power in case of a failure. Generally, smaller portable UPS systems provide between 30 minutes and 3 hours of power; larger systems (a permanent UPS) can provide power for multiple days.

The organization can provide a complete power system, which would include the UPS, a *power conditioning system* (*PCS*), and a generator. The PCS is used to prevent sags, spikes, and surges from reaching the electrical equipment by conditioning the incoming power to reduce voltage deviations and provide steady-state voltage regulation. The PCS ensures that all power falls within acceptable levels for the electrical devices it is serving. The organization might employ a generator in concert with the UPS. In most cases, the generator and UPS are controlled by the same system, allowing the generator to power up when the battery power in the UPS falls below a certain threshold.

In addition to the issues surrounding electrical power, organizations must deploy environmental controls for the overall health of the hardware and software, as well as preventative, detective, and corrective measures in case of an emergency. Within the design of the IT infrastructure, the organization must determine the best place for the core servers and network devices. This location is sometimes referred to as the LAN room or computer room. It should be implemented with climate controls, fire-suppression systems, and power-control systems. The computer room should be located in a place that is not threatened by *electromagnetic interference* (*EMI*) or the possibility of flooding.

Electrical equipment must operate in climate-controlled facilities that ensure proper temperature and humidity levels. Relative humidity should be between 40% and 60%, and the temperature should be between 70°F and 74°F. Both extremely low and extremely high temperatures can cause electrical component damage. High humidity can cause corrosion in electrical components, reducing their overall efficiency or permanently damaging the equipment; low humidity can introduce static electricity, which can short out electrical components. Proper ventilation should be employed to maintain clean air free of contaminants. A positive pressurization system ensures that air flows out of instead of into the computer room. If you have ever entered a building and opened the door to feel the air pushing out toward you, you have entered a building that is positively pressurized. This pressurization ensures that contaminants from the outside do not flow into the room or building. Water detectors should be placed near drains in the computer room to detect water leaks and sound audible alarms.

One of the most serious threats facing both computing equipment and people is fire. A variety of systems are available to prevent, detect, and suppress fire.

A number of fire-detection systems are activated by heat, smoke, or flame. These systems should provide an audible signal and should be linked to a monitoring system that can contact the fire department.

> ➤ **Smoke detectors**—Placed both above and below the ceiling tiles. They use optical detectors that detect the change in light intensity when there is a presence of smoke.

> ➤ **Heat-activated detectors**—Detect a rise in temperature. They can be configured to sound an alarm when the temperature exceeds a certain level.

➤ **Flame-activated detectors**—Sense infrared energy or the light patterns associated with the pulsating flames of a fire.

Fire-suppression systems can be either automatic (chemical or water) or manual (fire extinguishers) and are designed to suppress fire using different methods. Table 4.3 outlines suppression agents and their method of extinguishing different types of fires.

Table 4.3 Fire-Suppression Agents		
Suppression Agent	Used to Control	Method of Extinguishing
Water	Common combustibles	Reducing temperatures
CO^2	Liquid and electrical fires	Removing fuel and oxygen
Soda acid	Liquid and electrical fires	Removing fuel and oxygen
Gas	Chemical fires	Interfering with the chemical reaction necessary for fire

The following are automatic fire suppression systems:

➤ **Water sprinklers**—These are effective in fire suppression, but they will damage electrical equipment.

➤ **Water dry pipe**—A dry-pipe sprinkler system suppresses fire via water that is released from a main valve, to be delivered via a system of dry pipes that fill with water when the fire alarm activates the water pumps. A dry-pipe system detects the risk of leakage.

Water-based suppression systems are an acceptable means of fire suppression, but they should be combined with an automatic power shut-off system.

Although many methods of fire suppression exist, dry-pipe sprinklers are considered to be the most environmentally friendly because they are water based as opposed to chemical based in the case of halon or CO^2.

➤ **Halon**—Pressurized halon gas is released, which interferes with the chemical reaction of a fire. Halon damages the ozone and, therefore, is banned, but replacement chemicals include FM-200, NAF SIII, and NAF PIII.

➤ **CO^2**—Carbon dioxide replaces oxygen. Although it is environmentally acceptable, it cannot be used in sites that are staffed because it is a threat to human life.

The threat of a fire can be mitigated through the use of detection and suppression systems, but personnel also should be properly trained on how to react in case of a fire. This should include the use of manual fire alarms, fire extinguishers, and evacuation procedures.

Physical Access

Physical security supports confidentiality, integrity, and availability by ensuring that the organization is protected from unauthorized persons accessing the physical facility. The type of physical security controls depends on the risk associated with the asset.

In auditing a facility, the IS auditor should ensure that there are physical access restrictions governing employees, visitors, partners/vendors, and unauthorized persons (intruders). All facilities associated with the organization, including off-site computing and storage facilities, should be reviewed. An organization's facilities are similar to those of a city, in that there are different physical access controls based on the assets being protected. In a city, the physical access controls for a corner store, for instance, might include a lock and key, whereas a bank might employ physical security guards, lock and key, and additional stronger internal controls, such as a vault. This type of layered security can include administrative controls such as access policies, visitor logging, and controlled visitor access.

> ➤ **Access policies**—Individuals internal and external to the organization are identified, along with the areas of the facility to which they are allowed access.

> ➤ **Visitor logging**—Visitors provide identification and are signed into the facility; they indicate the purpose of their visit, their name, and their company.

> ➤ **Controlled visitor access**—Individuals must be escorted by an employee while in the facility.

Personally escorting visitors is a preferred form of physical access control for guests.

In addition to administrative controls, the facility might employ biometric access controls, physical intrusion detection (alarms, motion sensors, glass break alarms, and so on), and electronic surveillance (cameras, electronic logging, and so on). Technical controls often provide the capability to create audit logs that show access attempts into the facility. Audit logs should include the point of entry, date and time of access, ID use during access, and both successful and unsuccessful attempts to access. These logs should be reviewed periodically to ensure that only authorized persons are gaining access to the facility and should take note of any modifications of access rights.

Similar to the review of the organization's network, the IS auditor should review facilities to determine paths of physical entry and should evaluate those paths for the proper level of security. Access paths include external doors, glass windows, suspended ceilings (plenum space), and maintenance access panels and ventilation systems.

Physical Security Practices

The previous section discussed authentication methods that are used in gaining access to IT systems. Authentication can be in the form of something you know (passwords), something you have (smart card), something you are, or unique personal characteristics (fingerprints, retina patterns, iris patterns, hand geometry, and palm patterns). The "what you are" of authentication is referred to as *biometrics*. This involves authenticating an individual's identity by a unique personal attribute. When implementing biometric systems, the individuals provide a sample of a personal attribute (known as enrollment), such as a fingerprint, which will be used for comparison when access is requested. Although biometrics provides only single-factor authentication, many consider it to be an excellent method for user authentication and an excellent physical access control.

A biometric system by itself is advanced and very sensitive. This sensitivity can make biometrics prone to error. These errors fall into two categories:

➤ **False Rejection Rate (FRR) Type I error**—The biometric system rejects an individual who is authorized to access the system.

➤ **False Acceptance Rate (FAR) Type II error**—The biometric system accepts unauthorized individuals who should be rejected.

Most biometric systems have sensitivity levels associated with them. When the sensitivity level is increased, the rate of rejection errors increases (authorized users are rejected). When the sensitivity level is decreased, the rate of acceptance (unauthorized users are accepted) increases. Biometric devices use a comparison metric called the *Equal Error Rate (EER)*, which is the rate at which the FAR and FRR are equal or cross over. In general, the lower the EER is, the more accurate and reliable the biometric device is. Organizations with a higher need for confidentiality are more concerned with a biometric access control False Acceptance Rate (FAR) than its False Rejection Rate (FRR) or Equal Error Rate (EER).

 When evaluating biometric access controls, a low Equal Error Rate (EER) is preferred because Equal Error Rates (EERs) are used as the best overall measure of a biometric system's effectiveness.

Intrusion Methods and Techniques

Most organizations today have opened their systems or a portion of their systems to partners, vendors, and the general public. The explosive growth of the Internet has enabled organizations to provide information, sell goods and services, exchange and update information, and transmit data between geographically dispersed offices. This "openness" provides the perfect opportunity for hackers or intruders to gain unauthorized access to private networks and data.

The terms hacker and *cracker* are commonly used today to describe individuals who use either social engineering or technical skills to gain unauthorized access to networks. In the not-too-distant past, a hacker was someone who was interested in the way things worked (such as computers and programs) and used skills to find out very detailed information on what made them tick. These individuals, called hackers, were not malicious, but curious. Today the term *hacker* refers to an individual who is trying to gain unauthorized access to or compromise the integrity and availability of computer systems and data. For the purposes of this book, we replace the term *hacker* with the term *intruder* because it is more appropriate. Intruders can be either internal or external to the organization and might try to gain access to systems with the intent of causing harm to the systems or data, invading others' privacy, or stealing proprietary information. The IS auditor should understand both the internal and external risks to ensure that proper security controls are in place to protect the organization's assets.

Passive and Active Attacks

Intruders have access to detailed instructions, tools, and methods via the Internet. Intruders use this collection of information and programs to gain a better understanding of an organization's computer systems and network topography, and to circumvent access controls. Attack types include both passive and active attacks, and can be either internal or external to the organization's network. Passive attacks are generally used to probe network devices and applications, in an attempt to learn more about the vulnerabilities of those systems. An intruder might utilize scanning tools, eavesdropping, and traffic analysis to create a profile of the network:

➤ **Scanning**—This attack uses automated tools to scan systems and network devices, to determine systems that are on the network and network ports (services) that are listening on those systems.

➤ **Eavesdropping**—In this attack, also known as sniffing or packet analysis, the intruder uses automated tools to collect packets on the network. These packets can be reassembled into messages and can include email, names and passwords, and system information.

➤ **Traffic analysis**—In traffic analysis, an intruder uses tools capable of monitoring network traffic to determine traffic volume, patterns, and start and end points. This analysis gives intruders a better understanding of the communication points and potential vulnerabilities.

Traffic analysis is a passive attack method intruders use to determine potential network vulnerabilities.

Active attacks involve using programs to either bypass access controls or negatively impact the availability of network devices and services. Active attacks include brute-force attack, masquerading, packet replay, message modification, unauthorized access through the Internet or web-based services, denial of service, dial-in penetration attacks, email bombing and spamming, and email spoofing:

➤ **Brute-force attack**—An intruder uses automated tools and electronic dictionaries to try to guess user and system passwords. These automated tools try thousands of words or character combinations per hour in an attempt to gain unauthorized access to the system.

➤ **Denial of service**—Any method an intruder uses to hinder or prevent the delivery of information services to authorized users is considered a denial-of-service (DoS) attack. As an example, an intruder inundates (floods) the system with requests. In the process of responding to a high volume of requests, the system is rendered useless to authorized users. These types of attacks generally intend to exhaust all available CPU or memory.

The "ping of death" is a common denial-of-service (DoS) attack that entails using a ping with a packet size higher than 65Kb with the "no fragmentation" flag on. When the system receives the oversize packet that exceeds the acceptable length (higher than 65Kb), it causes the system to freeze, reboot, or crash.

➤ **Spamming**—Spam is common on the Internet today, but the act of spamming or email bombing is the capability of sending messages in bulk. Spamming can be used to overload individual email boxes on servers, which fills up the hard drives and causes system freezes and crashes.

When an intruder gains access to the system, he might tamper with existing programs to add a *Trojan* horse. A Trojan horse is a program that masquerades as another program or is even embedded within a program. Trojan horse programs or code can delete files, shut down the systems, or send system and network information to an email or Internet address. Trojan horse programs are a common form of Internet attack.

In addition to active and passive attacks, intruders might use social engineering to gain information that opens access to physical facilities and network systems. Social engineering is the use of psychological tricks on authorized users to gain access. Intruders might use techniques such as calling on the phone to authorized users and posing as help-desk personnel, to coerce an authorized user into divulging his password. Social engineering is the art of using social "con" skills to obtain passwords without the use of computer tools or programs.

Using social skills to obtain unauthorized access to company assets is called social engineering. Security-awareness programs are used to address the risk of unauthorized access resulting from social engineering attacks.

Viruses

A *virus* is computer program that infects systems by inserting copies of itself into executable code on a computer system. In addition to damaging computer systems through reconfiguration and file deletion, viruses are self-replicating, similar to a biological virus. When executed, a virus spreads itself across computer systems. A *worm* is another type of computer program that is often incorrectly called a virus. The difference between a virus and a worm is that the virus relies on the host (infected) system for further propagation because it inserts itself into applications or programs so that it can replicate and perform its functions. Worms are malicious programs that can run independently and can propagate without the aid of a carrier program such as email. Worms can delete files, fill up the hard drive and memory, or consume valuable network bandwidth.

Viruses come in many shapes and sizes. As an example, the *polymorphic virus* has the capability of changing its own code, enabling it to have many different variants. The capability of a polymorphic virus to change its signature pattern enables it to replicate and makes it more difficult for antivirus systems to detect it. Another type of malicious code is a *logic bomb*, which is a program or string of code that executes when a sequence of events or a prespecified time or date occurs. A stealth virus is a virus that hides itself by intercepting disk access requests.

Adopting and communicating a comprehensive antivirus policy is a fundamental step in preventing virus attacks. Antivirus software is considered a preventive control. Antivirus software products are applications that detect, prevent, and sometimes remove all the virus files located within a computing system. IS auditors should look for the existence of antivirus programs on all systems within the organization. In addition, users within the IT infrastructure should understand the risks of downloading programs, code, and ActiveX and Java applets from unknown sources. The primary restlessness seeded with virus programs is their ability to replicate across a variety of platforms very quickly.

Integrity checkers are programs that detect changes to systems, applications, and data. Integrity checkers compute a binary number for each selected program called a cyclical redundancy check (CRC). When initially installed, an integrity checker scans the system and places these results in a database file. Before the execution of each program, the checker recomputes the CRC and compares it to the value stored in the database. If the values do not match, the program is not executed because the integrity checker has determined that the application file might have been modified. Similar to antivirus programs, integrity checkers can be used to detect and prevent the use of virus-infected programs.

Security Testing and Assessment Tools

To ensure that the organization's security controls are functioning properly, both the IT organization and the IS auditor should use the same techniques that hackers use in an attempt to bypass access controls.

A *vulnerability assessment* is used to determine potential risks to the organization's systems and data. *Penetration testing* is used to test controls implemented as countermeasures to vulnerabilities. Penetration tests performed by the organization are sometimes called intrusion tests or ethical hacking. The penetration test team uses public sources to gain information on an organization's network, systems, and data. Known as discovery, this includes passive scanning techniques to discover the perimeter systems' OS and applications that are listening for network connections (ports). It might also include the review of public websites, partner websites, and news groups, to discover information on applications and network connectivity. One example of discovery is the use of newsgroups. System administrators often post questions to newsgroups on the Internet to solve problems they are having with applications or network devices. An intruder can search newsgroups using the domain name of the organization to find potential vulnerabilities.

When the discovery process is complete, the penetration test team should develop a list of potential vulnerabilities on the network. They should then systematically attempt to bypass the access controls by attempting to guess passwords (using automated password-cracking tools and dictionaries), searching for back doors into the system, or exploiting known vulnerabilities based on the type of servers and applications within the organization. Penetration testing is intended to use the same techniques and tools intruders use. Penetration testing can be performed against both internal (applications) and external (firewalls) devices. It should be performed by qualified and authorized individuals. The penetration team should develop a penetration test plan and use caution when performing penetration tests on production systems. The penetration test plan should include methods by which vulnerabilities will be identified, documented, and communicated upon conclusion of the penetration testing period.

 Authorized penetration testing is often performed using the same network diagnostic tools hackers commonly use.

The IT organization should implement regular vulnerability scanning in addition to penetration testing. Similar to virus-protection programs, vulnerability scanners combined with firewall and IDS logs ensure that the IT infrastructure is protected against both new and existing vulnerabilities. Vulnerability scanning is implemented using automated tools that periodically scan network devices looking for known vulnerabilities. These tools maintain a vulnerability database that is periodically updated as new vulnerabilities are discovered. The vulnerability scans produce reports and generally categorize vulnerabilities into three categories of risk (high, medium, low). The more sophisticated scanning tools provide a list of the vulnerabilities found on the network by device or application, as well as the remediation of that risk. One of the more popular tools used for vulnerability scanning is Nessus (www.nessus.org), an open-source scanner that maintains a vulnerability database (which can be updated via the Internet). An example of a Nessus vulnerability report is shown here (this example does not include the entire report):

Scan Details

Hosts that were alive and responding during test	9
Number of security holes found	54
Number of security warnings found	113

Host List

Host(s)	Possible Issue
10.163.156.10	Security hole(s) found

Security Issues and Fixes: 10.163.156.10

Type	Port	Issue and Fix
Warning	echo (7/tcp)	The echo port is open. This port is not of any use nowadays and could be a source of problems because it can be used along with other ports to perform a denial of service. You should really disable this service. Risk factor: Low Solution: Comment out 'echo' in /etc/inetd.conf CVE: CVE-1999-0103 Nessus ID: 10061
Informational	echo (7/tcp)	An echo server is running on this port Nessus ID: 10330
Vulnerability	telnet (23/tcp)	The Telnet server does not return an expected number of replies when it receives a long sequence of "Are You There" commands. This probably means that it overflows one of its internal buffers and crashes. It is likely that an attacker could abuse this bug to gain control over the remote host's superuser. For more information, see www.team-teso.net/advisories/teso-advisory-011.tar.gz. Solution: Comment out the telnet line in /etc/inetd.conf. Risk factor: High CVE: CVE-2001-0554 BID: 3064 Nessus ID: 10709
Vulnerability	ssh (22/tcp)	You are running a version of OpenSSH that is older than 3.0.2.

Security Issues and Fixes: 10.163.156.10

Type	Port	Issue and Fix
		Versions older than 3.0.2 are vulnerable to an environment variable's export, which can allow a local user to execute a command with root privileges. This problem affects only versions earlier than 3.0.2 and when the UseLogin feature is enabled (usually disabled by default).
		Solution: Upgrade to OpenSSH 3.0.2 or apply the patch for older versions. (Available at ftp://ftp.openbsd.org/pub/OpenBSD/OpenSSH.)
		Risk factor: High (if UseLogin is enabled, and locally)
		CVE: CVE-2001-0872
		BID: 3614
		Nessus ID: 10823

The Nessus report shows the machine address, vulnerability (port/service), a text description of the vulnerability, the solution, and the *Common Vulnerability and Exposure* (*CVE*) ID. As public vulnerabilities are discovered, they are maintained in databases to provide naming and documentation standards. One such free public database is maintained by the MITRE Corporation (http://cve.mitre.org) and can be used to review known vulnerabilities and their remediation.

In addition to vulnerability testing, the organization can employ tools that are designed to entice and trap intruders. *Honey pots* are computer systems that are expressly set up to attract and trap individuals who attempt to penetrate other individuals' computer systems. Honey pots generally are placed in an area of the network that is publicly accessible and that contain known vulnerabilities. The concept of a honey pot is to learn from an intruder's actions by monitoring the methods and techniques employed by a hacker attempting to gain access to a system.

Honey pots are often used as a detection and deterrent control against Internet attacks.

The most significant vulnerability in any organization is the user. The use of appropriate access controls can sometimes be inconvenient or cumbersome for the user population. To ensure that the organization's security controls are effective, a comprehensive security program should be implemented. The security program should include these components:

➤ Continuous user awareness training

➤ Continuous monitoring and auditing of IT processes and management

➤ Enforcement of acceptable use policies and information security controls

Sources of Information on Information Security

Security professionals use a variety of sources to improve their knowledge of defense and mitigation strategies and to stay up-to-date on known vulnerabilities or intrusion techniques. The following list contains some of the publicly available sources of information:

➤ **The CERT Coordination Center (www.cert.org)**—Established in 1988, the CERT Coordination Center (CERT/CC) is a center of Internet security expertise. It is located at the Software Engineering Institute, a federally funded research and development center operated by Carnegie Mellon University.

➤ **The Forum of Incident Response and Security Teams (FIRST) (www.first.org)**—FIRST brings together a variety of computer security incident response teams from government, commercial, and educational organizations. FIRST aims to foster cooperation and coordination in incident prevention, to stimulate rapid reaction to incidents, and to promote information sharing among members and the community at large.

➤ **The SANS Institute (www.sans.org)**—SANS (SysAdmin, Audit, Network, Security) develops, maintains, and makes available at no cost the largest collection of research documents about various aspects of information security. It operates the Internet's early warning system, the Internet Storm Center. The SANS Institute was established in 1989 as a cooperative research and education organization. At the heart of SANS are the many security practitioners in government agencies, corporations, and universities around the world who invest hundreds of hours each year in research and teaching to help the entire information security community.

➤ **The Computer Crime and Intellectual Property Section (CCIPS) (www.cybercrime.gov)**—CCIPS is a department of the Criminal Division of the U.S. Department of Justice. It provides information on topics such as computer crime, intellectual property crime, cybercrime documents, and cybernetics.

In addition, there are a number of security portals:

➤ **Insecure (www.insecure.org)**—Insecure.org is the home of Nmap (security scanning tool) and provides information on security tools, techniques, and news.

➤ **Information Systems Security (http://infosyssec.com)**—Infosyssec was originally created by students for students, to help locate and consolidate resources on the Internet that would assist them in their study of information system security. It has become a favorite bookmark of information security professionals.

Security Monitoring, Detection, and Escalation Processes and Techniques

The IT organization should have clear policies and procedures for incident response, including how disruptive incidents are detected, corrected or restored, and managed. Both policies and procedures should outline how specific incidents are to be handled and how the systems, applications, and data involved in the incident can be restored to normal operation. The main goal of an incident-response plan is to restore systems damaged during the incident and to prevent any further damage. The incident-response plan should define a central authority (incident response team) and the procedures for training employees to understand an incident. The incident response team should ensure the following:

➤ Systems involved in the incident are segregated from the network so they do not cause further damage.

➤ Appropriate procedures for notification and escalation are followed.

➤ Evidence associated with the incident is preserved.

➤ Documented procedures to recover systems, applications, and data are followed.

An *intrusion-detection system* (*IDS*) should be part of the security infrastructure of the organization, to monitor the organization's systems and data to detect misuse. The IDS can be either network based or host based, and it operates continuously to alert administrators when it detects a threat. Both types of IDSs can use knowledge-based (signature-based) or behavior-based (statistical, neural) programs to detect network attacks. A network-based IDS can be placed between the Internet and the firewall, to detect attack attempts. A host-based IDS should be configured to run on a specific host and monitor the resources associated with the host system. Host-based IDSs can be used to monitor file systems, memory, CPU, and network traffic to the host system. Both network- and host-based IDSs use sensors to collect data for review.

An IDS can be signature based, statistical based, or a neural network. A signature-based IDS monitors and detects known intrusion patterns. A signature-based IDS has a database of signature files (known attack types) to which it compares incoming data from the sensors. If it detects a match, it alerts administrators. A statistical-based IDS compares data from sensors against an established baseline (created by the administrator). If the data from the sensors exceeds the thresholds in the baseline, it alerts an administrator. As an example, security administrators can monitor and review unsuccessful logon attempts to detect potential intrusion attempts. Neural networks monitor patterns of activity or traffic on a network. This self-learning process enables the IDS to create a database (baseline) of activity for comparison to future activity.

The correct implementation of an IDS is critical. If the type of IDS or the configuration of the IDS creates a large number of alerts that are not intrusions (false positives), the administrators might disregard alerts or turn off the rule(s) associated with the alert. The opposite might occur if the type of IDS does not fit the needs of the organization or is misconfigured, and intrusion activity might not be detected. The IT organization must continue to adjust the rules and signatures associated with the IDS, to ensure optimum performance.

The Processes of Design, Implementation, and Monitoring of Security

The IS auditor does not generally review the effectiveness and utilization of assets during a security audit. Security audits primarily focus on the evaluation of the policies and procedures that ensure the confidentiality, integrity, and availability of data. During an audit of security, the IS auditor normally reviews access to assets and validates the physical and environmental controls to the extent necessary to satisfy the audit requirements. The IS auditor also should review logical access policies and compare them to job profiles, to ensure that excessive access has not been granted, and evaluate asset safe-guards and procedures to prevent unauthorized access to assets.

 Rather than simply reviewing the effectiveness and utilization of assets, an IS audi-tor is more concerned with adequate access control, appropriate access policies, and the effectiveness of safeguards and procedures.

Network performance-monitoring tools are used to measure and ensure proper network capacity management and availability of services. Proper implementation and incident-handling procedures ensure network connec-tivity and the availability of network services.

The IT organization should have policies and procedures outlining proper patch-management procedures. The application of patches reduces known vulnerabilities to operating systems and applications, but systems adminis-trators should always assess the impact of patches before installation. System administrators should immediately evaluate patches as they become available and should understand the effect they will have within their environment. Any patch management methodology should also include extensive testing on the effects of the patch implemented.

The data owners, who are responsible for the use and reporting of informa-tion under their control, should provide written authorization for users to gain access to that information. The data owner should periodically review and evaluate authorized (granted) access to ensure that these authorizations are still valid.

 Data owners are ultimately responsible and accountable for reviewing user access to systems.

Intrusion-detection systems (IDS) are used to identify intrusion attempts to a network. However, work should be implemented in concert with firewalls and routers because they *detect* intrusion attempts instead of prevent against attack.

Per ISACA, the IS auditor should review the following when auditing secu-rity management, logical access issues, and exposures.

Review Written Policies, Procedures, and Standards

Policies and procedures provide the framework and guidelines for maintaining proper operation in control. The IS auditor should review the policies and procedures to determine whether they set the tone for proper security and provide a means for assigning responsibility for maintaining a secured computer processing environment.

Logical Access Security Policy

These policies should encourage limiting logical access on a need-to-know basis and should reasonably assess the exposure to the identified concerns.

Formal Security Awareness and Training

Promoting security awareness is a preventive control. Through this process, employees become aware of their responsibility for maintaining good physical and logical security.

Per ISACA, assimilation of the framework and intent of a written security policy by the users of the systems is critical to the successful implementation and maintenance of security policy. You might have a good password system, but if the users of the system keep passwords written on their table, the password system is of little value. Management support and commitment is no doubt important, but for successful implementation and maintenance of security policy, user education on the critical nature of security is of paramount importance. The stringent implementation, monitoring, and enforcing of rules by the security officer through access-control software, and the provision for punitive actions when security rules are violated also are required.

Data Ownership

Data ownership refers to the classification of data elements and the allocation of responsibility for ensuring that they are kept confidential, complete, and accurate. The key point of ownership is that by assigning responsibility for protecting the organization's data to a particular person, you establish accountability for appropriate protection of confidentiality, integrity, and availability of the data.

Security Administrators

Security administrators are responsible for providing adequate physical and logical security for the IS programs, data, and equipment.

Access Standards

The IS auditor should review access standards to ensure that they meet organizational objectives for separating duties, preventing fraud or error, and that they meet policy requirements for minimizing the risk of unauthorized access.

Auditing Logical Access

When evaluating logical access controls, the highest order should be as follows:

➤ Obtain a general understanding of the security risks facing information processing, through a review of relevant documentation, inquiry, observation, risk assessment, and evaluation techniques

➤ Document and evaluate controls over potential access paths to the system, to assess their adequacy, efficiency and effectiveness, by reviewing appropriate hardware and software security features in identifying any deficiencies

➤ Test controls over access paths, to determine whether they are functioning and effective, by applying appropriate audit techniques

➤ Evaluate the access control environment, to determine whether the control objectives are achieved, by analyzing test results and other audit evidence

➤ Evaluate the security environment, to assess its adequacy, by reviewing written policies, observing practices and procedures, and comparing them to appropriate security standards or practices and procedures used by other organizations

Exam Prep Questions

1. Which of the following controls is MOST effective for protecting software and access to sensitive data?

   ❑   A. Security policies

   ❑   B. Biometric physical access control for the server room

   ❑   C. Fault tolerance with complete systems and data redundancy

   ❑   D. Logical access controls for the operating systems, applications, and data

   Answer: D. Logical access controls are often the primary safeguards for authorized access to systems software and data. All the other controls complement logical access control to applications and data.

2. Which of the following would an IS auditor review to BEST determine user access to systems or data?

   ❑   A. Access-control lists (ACLs)

   ❑   B. User account management

   ❑   C. Systems logs

   ❑   D. Applications logs

   Answer: A. IS auditors should review access-control lists (ACLs) to determine user permissions that have been granted for a particular resource.

3. Which of the following is ultimately accountable for protecting and securing sensitive data?

   ❑   A. Data users

   ❑   B. Security administrators

   ❑   C. Data owners

   ❑   D. Data custodians

   Answer: C. Data owners, such as corporate officers, are ultimately responsible and accountable for access control of data. Although security administrators are indeed responsible for securing data, they do so at the direction of the data owners. A security administrator is an example of a data custodian. Data users access and utilize the data for authorized tasks.

4. A review of logical access controls is performed primarily to:

   ❑   A. Ensure that organizational security policies conform to the logical access design and architecture

   ❑   B. Ensure that the technical implementation of access controls is performed as intended by security administration

   ❑   C. Ensure that the technical implementation of access controls is performed as intended by the data owners

   ❑   D. Understand how access control has been implemented

Answer: C. Logical access controls should be reviewed to ensure that access is granted on a least-privilege basis, per the organization's data owners. Logical access design and architecture should conform to policies, not vice versa. Understanding how access control has been implemented is an essential element of a logical access controls review, but the ultimate purpose of the review is to make sure that access controls adequately support and protect the organizational needs of the data owners.

5. Authorization is BEST characterized as:

 ❑ A. Providing access to a resource according to the principle of least privilege

 ❑ B. A user providing an identity and a password

 ❑ C. Authenticating a user's identity with a password

 ❑ D. Certifying a user's authority

Answer: A. Authorization is the process of providing a user with access to a resource based upon the specific needs of the user to perform an authorized task. This process relies upon a verified understanding of the user's identity. Therefore, a user must provide a claim of identity, which is then verified through an authentication process. Following the authentication process, access can be authorized according to the principle of least privilege.

6. Data classification must begin with:

 ❑ A. Determining specific data sensitivity according to organizational and legal requirements for data confidentiality and integrity

 ❑ B. Determining data ownership

 ❑ C. A review of organizational security policies

 ❑ D. A review of logical access controls

Answer: B. Data classification is a process that allows an organization to implement appropriate controls according to data sensitivity. Before data sensitivity can be determined by the data owners, data ownership must be established. Logical access controls and organizational security policies are controlled and driven by the data owners.

7. Which of the following firewalls can be configured to MOST reliably control FTP traffic between the organization's network and the Internet?

 ❑ A. Packet-filtering firewall

 ❑ B. Application-layer gateway or a stateful inspection firewall

 ❑ C. A router configured as a firewall with access-control lists

 ❑ D. Circuit-level firewall

Answer: B. FTP is a network protocol that operates at the application layer of the OSI model. Of the choices available, only an application-layer gateway or a stateful inspection firewall can reliably filter all the way through to the application layer. The remaining answers are examples of a firewall that can reliably filter only through OSI Layer 3, the network layer.

8. An IS auditor wants to ensure that the organization's network is adequately protected from network-based intrusion via the Internet and the World Wide Web. A firewall that is properly configured as a gateway to the Internet protects against such intrusion by:

   ❏ A. Preventing external users from accessing the network via internal rogue modems

   ❏ B. Preventing unauthorized access to the Internet by internal users

   ❏ C. Preventing unauthorized access to the network by external users via ad-hoc wireless networking

   ❏ D. Preventing unauthorized access by external users to the internal network via the firewalled gateway

   Answer: D. Firewalls are used to prevent unauthorized access to the internal network from the Internet. Firewalls provide little protection from users who do not need to access the network via the firewall, such as via internal rogue modems or via peer-to-peer ad-hoc wireless network connections. Preventing unauthorized access to the Internet by internal users is the opposite of the goal stated in the question.

9. Various cryptosystems offer differing levels of compromise between services provided versus computational speed and potential throughput. Which of the following cryptosystems would provide services including confidentiality, authentication, and nonrepudiation at the cost of throughput performance?

   ❏ A. Symmetric encryption

   ❏ B. Asymmetric encryption

   ❏ C. Shared-key cryptography

   ❏ D. Digital signatures

   Answer: B. Through the use of key pairs, asymmetric encryption algorithms can provide confidentiality and authentication. By providing authentication, nonrepudiation is also supported. Symmetric encryption, also known as shared-key cryptography, uses only a single shared key. Because the key is shared, there is no sole ownership of the key, which precludes its use as an authentication tool. Digital signatures are used to verify authenticity and data integrity only.

10. The organization desires to ensure integrity, authenticity, and nonre-pudiation of emails for sensitive communications between security administration and network administration personnel through the use of digitally signed emails. Which of the following is a valid step in signing an email with keys from a digital certificate?

❑ A. The sender encrypts the email using the sender's public key.

❑ B. The sender creates a message digest of the email and attachments using the sender's private key.

❑ C. The sender creates a message digest of the email and attachments using a common hashing algorithm, such as DSA.

❑ D. The sender encrypts the message digest using the sender's public key.

Answer: C. A digital signature provides the recipient with a mechanism for validating the integrity of the email and its attachments by creating a message digest as a result of the application of a common hashing algorithm such as MD5 or DSA. The message digest is then "signed" by encrypting it with the sender's private key. The recipient uses the sender's public key to decrypt the message digest and then uses the same hashing algorithm as the sender of the email and attachments. If the decrypted message digest matches that created independently by the recipient, the recipient can rest assured that the message has not been tampered with since transmission by the sender.

Disaster Recovery and Business Continuity

Key concepts you will need to understand:

✓ Knowledge of crisis management and business impact analysis techniques

✓ Knowledge of disaster recovery and business continuity planning and processes

✓ Knowledge of backup and storage methods and practices

✓ Knowledge of disaster recovery and business continuity testing approaches and methods

✓ Knowledge of insurance in relation to business continuity and disaster recovery

✓ Knowledge of human resource issues (such as evacuation planning and response teams)

Techniques you will need to master:

✓ Evaluate the adequacy of backup and recovery provisions to ensure the resumption of normal information processing in the event of a short-term disruption or the need to rerun or restart a process

✓ Evaluate the organization's capability to continue to provide information system–processing capabilities in the event that the primary information-processing facilities are not available

✓ Evaluate the organization's capability to ensure business continuity in the event of a business disruption

Understanding and Evaluating Process Development

Disaster recovery for systems typically focuses on making alternative processes and resources available for transaction processing. A *disaster recovery plan* (*DRP*) should reduce the length of recovery time necessary and also the costs associated with recovery. Proper planning will mitigate the risk and impact of a major business interruption. Although DRP results in an increase of pre- and post-incident operational costs, the extra costs are more than offset by reduced recovery and business impact costs. A *disaster* can be classified as a disruption that causes critical information resources to be inoperative for a period of time, adversely affecting business operations. *Business continuity plans* (*BCP*) are the result of a process of plan creation to ensure that critical business functions can withstand a variety of emergencies. Disaster-recovery plans deal with the immediate restoration of the organization's business systems while the business continuity plan also deals with the long-term issues before, during, and after the disaster. The BCP should include getting employees to the appropriate facilities; communicating with the public, partners, and customers; and making the transition from emergency recovery back to normal operations. The DRP is a part of the BCP and is the responsibility of senior management.

A disaster can be caused by naturally occurring events such as floods, tornadoes, fire, or earthquakes, but it can include anything that causes disruption to information processing. Other types of disasters include loss of electrical power or telecommunications, or direct or indirect attacks on the organization's systems or facilities (such as a terrorist attack or hacking). These are the attributes of a disaster:

➤ Unplanned and unanticipated

➤ Impacts critical business functions

➤ Has the capacity for significant loss

According to the United Nation's International Decade for Natural Disasters Reduction, natural disasters kill one million people around the world each decade and leave millions more homeless each year. In addition, economic damages from natural disasters have tripled in the past 30 years, rising from $40 billion in the 1960s to $120 billion in the 1980s. In the past year, more than a dozen worldwide disasters have caused billion-dollar losses. Table 5.1 provides a snapshot of the costs resulting from natural disasters from 1983 to 1994.

Table 5.1 Costs of Natural Disasters from 1983 to 1994	
Hurricane Alicia (USA, 1983)	$1.65 billion
Winter storm Herta (Europe, 1990)	$1.90 billion
Forest fire (USA, 1991)	$2 billion
Winter storm Wiebke (Europe, 1990)	$2.25 billion
Hurricane Iniki (Hawaii, 1992)	$3.00 billion
Winter storm Vivian (Europe, 1990)	$3.25 billion
Winter gale (Western Europe, 1987)	$3.70 billion
Blizzard (USA, 1993)	$5.00 billion
Typhoon Mireille (Japan, 1991)	$6.00 billion
Winter storm Daria (Europe, 1990)	$6.80 billion
Hurricane Hugo (USA, Caribbean, 1989)	$9.00 billion
Floods (USA, 1993)	$12.00 billion
Northridge Earthquake (USA, 1994)	$30.00 billion
Hurricane Andrew (USA, 1991)	$30.00 billion

Source: World Health Organization

During the initiation of the business continuity planning process, the BCP team should prepare for a meeting with senior management to define the project goals and objectives, present the project schedule, and review the proposed interview schedule (resources required). In preparation for this meeting, the BCP team should do the following:

➤ Review the organizational structure to determine what resources will be assigned to the team

➤ Review existing disaster-planning policies, strategies, and procedures

➤ Review existing continuity plans

➤ Research any events that have occurred previously (severe weather, fires, equipment or facility failures, and so on) and that had or could have a negative effect on the organization

➤ Create a draft project schedule and associated documents (timing, resources, interview questionnaires, roles and responsibilities, and so on)

Per ISACA, the business continuity planning process can be divided into the following phases:

➤ Analyze the business impact

➤ Develop business-recovery strategies

➤ Develop a detailed plan

➤ Implement the plan

➤ Test and maintain the plan

The development of an effective business-continuity plan will take all threats (disasters) into account during development. Some of these threats might affect systems only for minutes or hours, but the plan should include recovery from these events as well. The recovery might be simply restoring data from backups or moving personnel and equipment to a new facility to continue business operations.

Crisis Management and Business Impact Analysis Techniques

A *business impact analysis* (*BIA*) is used to identify threats that can impact continuity of operations. These threats might be natural or man-made and should encompass everything from a telecommunications outage to a fire or hurricane. The results of the BIA should provide a clear picture of the continuity impact in terms of the impact to human and financial resources, as well as the reputation of the organization. To assess the risks associated with continuity, the BIA team should have a clear understanding of the organization, key business processes, and IT resources that support those processes. The BIA team should work with senior management, IT personnel, and end users to identify all resources used during normal operations. These resources might include both automated and manual processes. Although BCP and DRP are often implemented and tested by middle management and end users, the ultimate responsibility and accountability for the plans remains with executive management, such as the board of directors. The following steps can be used for the framework of business impact assessment:

➤ Gather business impact analysis data

  ➤ Questionnaires or interviews

➤ Review the BIA results

  ➤ Check for completeness and consistency

  ➤ Follow up with interviews for areas of ambiguity or missing information

➤ Establish the recovery time for operations, processes, and systems

➤ Define recovery alternatives and costs

The BIA will help the organization understand the degree of loss associated with the business functions and associated systems. This covers financial loss as well as loss of customer confidence and damage to the organization's reputation. The BIA questionnaire and interviews should gather the following information from the business units:

➤ Financial impacts resulting from the incapability to operate for prolonged periods of time

➤ Operational impacts within each business unit

➤ Expenses associated with continuing operations after a disruption

➤ Current policies and procedures to resume operations in the event of a disruption

➤ Technical requirements for recovery

 End-user involvement is critical during the business impact assessment phase of business continuity planning.

The BIA should include both quantitative and qualitative questions. *Quantitative* questions generally describe the economic or financial impacts of a potential disruption. These types of disruptions are measured in monetary terms, including both loss of income and expenses incurred during and after recovery. Quantitative impacts might include loss of revenue or sales, interest paid on loans, penalties for late payments to vendors, fines or penalties associated with contractual obligations, unavailability of operating funds, delayed or canceled orders, and so on. Expenses might include use of third-party services, emergency purchases related to recovery, rental or lease equipment, and relocation of employees. *Qualitative* impacts are impacts that cannot be quantified in monetary terms. These types of impacts are generally associated with the business impact of a disaster and include damage to reputation and loss of confidence in customer services or products. Although DRP results in an increase of pre- and post-incident operational costs, the extra costs are more than offset by reduced recovery and business impact costs.

A couple approaches can be taken to a BIA: The team might develop questionnaires for senior management and end users, or might gather information during an interview process. The important part of the process is to identify, sequence, and prioritize mission-critical processes. During the information-gathering phase of the BIA, the team will generally get information from individual business units. In addition to the information gathered from the business units, the team should identify the IT resources required for each process and the current disaster-recovery procedures. When the questionnaires are complete, the BCP team should conduct interviews to clarify information contained in the questionnaires, to ensure that the organization has identified time-sensitive business operations and services, financial risks, correct time frames for the resumption of operations, and estimates of the resources required for successful recovery. A sample of a BIA questionnaire is shown in Figure 5.1.

Organization:	Date Complete:
Business Unit:	BIA POC:

A. Business Function and Dependencies

Identification of Business Unit Function - Description of the function being performed.

Function Dependencies - Description of the dependencies of the function.

Business Records – What business records are needed, and are they automated or manual? If required, are they backed up? How often?

B. Disruption Impacts

Financial Impacts – What and when would the financial impact be to the business if the function was not performed?

Operational Impacts – What and when would the operational impact be to the business if the function was not performed?

Business Disruption – Has the business unit experienced a disruption in the past? What type of disruption? How was it handled (recovery, operations, etc)?

C. Recovery Resources

Recovery - What type of resources are needed to support the function, how many are needed, and how soon are they needed after a disruption (personnel, office space, telephones, etc)?

Identify System Resources - What technology resources are required to support the function (include quantity and type)?

Hardware/Software

Figure 5.1 BIA questionnaire.

When the BIA questionnaires and the interviews are complete, the BIA team should begin to document the results in the form of a BIA recommendation report. This report should allow for the prioritization of recovery among the business functions, and also give the team an overall view of potential recovery scenarios within the organization. This overall view might highlight gaps where additional information is required. When the initial draft is complete, the BIA team should develop a summary sheet to send back to the interviewees for confirmation. This allows the interviewees to review the information and add information that might have come up since the initial questionnaire or interview. The BIA is an important step in business continuity planning because all future decisions are based on the information gathered during the BIA. It is important to ensure that the information is as accurate as possible and that individual business units and end users are closely tied to the development of the business continuity plan.

During the creation of the recommendation report, the BIA team must define time-critical business functions and processes and their interdependencies among the business units. The development of recovery scenarios depends on the clear definition of time-critical processes and the financial and operational impacts gathered during the BIA. Before the development of a BCP/DRP, the BIA team should develop a recommendation or findings report for senior management. The purpose of this report is to provide senior management with a draft priority list of the business unit service and support recovery, as well as the financial and operational impacts that drive the prioritization. This step will give senior management the opportunity to approve the recovery priorities and prepare them for the next phase, in which they will review the recovery solutions and associated costs.

The objective of a BCP is to ensure that the organization can continue operations and keep the costs associated with both downtime and recovery to a minimum. In reviewing the information gathered during the BIA, the team should determine what the critical information resources are related to the organization's critical business processes. This relationship is important because the disruption of an information resource is not a disaster unless that resource is critical to a business process. Per ISACA, each resource should be assessed to determine criticality. Indications of criticality might include these:

➤ The process supports lives or people's health and safety.

➤ Disruption of the process would cause a loss of income to the organization or exceptional costs that are unacceptable.

➤ The process must meet legal or statutory requirements.

An important factor is the time period in which critical information resources must resume processing before significant or unacceptable losses are suffered. These time periods will depend on the type of business. As an example, the technology resources (hardware, software, network, and so on) that are used in completing stock transactions would probably be deemed critical, and the disruption or delay in resumption of any component of these services would result in large financial losses for that organization. In contrast, a smaller organization, such as a nonprofit organization, might be able to go without technology resources for hours or a few days without significant impact to the organization.

In making this determination, the BIA team should consider two cost factors. The first is the cost associated with downtime. This cost is defined in terms of hours per days, and the cost usually increases quickly over time to a certain point at which it stops growing. The stop in growth reflects the point in time when the business can no longer function. The costs associated with downtime vary based on the organization but might include a drop in order transactions, the cost of idle resources, the cost associated with the incapability to invoice customers or collect billing information, and qualitative costs associated with damage to reputation, goodwill, or the loss of market share. The second cost factor is the cost associated with recovery or resumption of services by implementing the business continuity plan. These costs include the cost of the development and maintenance of the continuity plan, off-site premises, insurance, and resources associated with recovery and resumption. As stated earlier, an optimal BCP and associated strategies should be based on the point in time when both cost factors are at a minimum. As an example of balancing these costs, the business might be capable of sustaining a longer recovery time, which will generally be less expensive but will incur more downtime costs than a shorter recovery. The combination of these costs should be taken into consideration when developing the recovery strategies.

The BIA is used to help business units understand the impact of a disruptive event and should include the execution of a vulnerability assessment for critical business processes to identify natural, man-made, and technical threats. The implementation of the BIA requires a high level of support from senior management and requires extensive involvement from IT and end-user personnel. The information collected during the BIA is used to develop the actual business continuity plan, which includes plan implementation, testing, and maintenance.

Disaster Recovery and Business Continuity Planning and Processes

The next step in developing the business continuity plan is to identify recovery strategies and select the strategy or strategies that best meet the organization's needs. It is important to remember that the strategy should include the technologies required for recovery and that the policies and procedures should include specific sequencing. The sequence in which systems are recovered is important for ensuring that the organization can function effectively following a disaster. As an example, the organization might need access to the accounting systems and associated accounting functions to facilitate the purchase of equipment associated with a recovery. If the accounting personnel and systems are not brought online first, this could delay the recovery process. Using the results of the BIA, the BCP team should identify both manual and automated processes that are required for the organization to resume business operations. These processes might include notifying personnel and moving them to processing facilities; notifying partners, customers, and shareholders of a disaster; and bringing hardware, software, and data online for use in processing.

Per ISACA, the classification matrix shown in Table 5.2 can be used to classify the criticality of systems to be recovered. This matrix will help the BCP team identify the best recovery strategies and alternative recovery strategies to be presented to senior management. The selection of the recovery strategy is based on the following:

➤ The criticality of the business process and the applications supporting the process

➤ The cost of the downtime and recovery

➤ Time required to recovery

➤ Security

Table 5.2 System Classification	
Classification	**Description**
Critical	These functions cannot be performed unless they are replaced by identical capabilities. Critical applications cannot be replaced by manual methods. Tolerance to interruption is very low; therefore, cost of interruption is very high.
Vital	These functions can be performed manually, but only for a brief period of time. There is a higher tolerance of interruption than with critical systems and, therefore, somewhat lower costs of interruption, provided that functions are restored within a certain time frame (usually five days or less).
Sensitive	These functions can be performed manually, at a tolerable cost and for an extended period of time. Although they can be performed manually, it usually is a difficult process and requires additional staff to perform.
Noncritical	These functions can be interrupted for an extended period of time, at little or no cost to the company, and require little or no catching up when restored.

A variety of strategies exist for the recovery of critical business processes and their associated systems. The best strategy is one that takes into account the cost of downtime and recovery, the criticality of the system, and the likelihood of occurrence determined during the BIA. In addition to actual recovery procedures, the organization should implement different levels of redundancy so that a relatively small event does not escalate to a full-blown disaster. An example of this type of control is to use redundant routing or fully meshed wide area networks. This redundancy would ensure that network communication will continue if portions of the wide area network are lost. This type of redundancy acts to either remove the threat altogether or minimize the likelihood or the effect of occurrence. These types of controls should be evaluated when developing the business-recovery strategies.

The recovery solution might include the use of different types of physical processing facilities and should include agreements and the costs associated with the facility both before and during use.

Hot Sites

A *hot site* is a facility that is basically a mirror image of the organization's current processing facility. It can be ready for use within a short period of time and contains the equipment, network, operating systems, and applications that are compatible with the primary facility being backed up. When hot sites are used, the staff, data files, and documentation are the only additional items needed in the facility. A hot site is generally the highest cost among recovery options, but it can be justified when critical applications and data need to resume operations in a short period of time. The costs associated include subscription costs, monthly fees, testing costs, activation costs, and hourly or daily charges (when activated). The use of a hot site generally includes connectivity over public networks (WAN or Internet) to enable regular backups and periodic testing to ensure that the hardware and software are compatible.

As with any recovery plan, the hot site should be part of the testing and maintenance procedures. The organization will incur costs associated with a live recovery, which requires the organization's personnel to work onsite at the hot site facility to test the recovery of applications and data. Generally, hot sites are to be used for a relatively short recovery time; they would be used only for a period of a week to several weeks while the primary facility is repaired. The physical facility should incorporate the same level of security as the primary facility and should not be easily identifiable externally (with signs or company logos, for example). This type of external identification creates an additional vulnerability for sabotage. In addition, this facility should not be subject to the same natural disaster that could affect the originating site and, thus, should not be located in proximity to the original site.

Although hot sites are the most expensive type of alternate processing redundancy, they are very appropriate for operations that require immediate or very short recovery times.

Warm Sites

Warm sites are sites that contain only a portion of the equipment and applications required for recovery. In a warm site recovery, it is assumed that computer equipment and operating software can be procured quickly in the event of a disaster. The warm site might contain some computing equipment that is generally of a lower capacity than the equipment at the primary facility. The contracting and use of a warm site are generally lower cost than a hot site but take longer to get critical business functions back online. Because of the requirement of ordering, receiving, and installing equipment and operating systems, a warm site might be operational in days or weeks, as opposed to hours with a hot site. The costs associated with a warm site are similar to but lower than those of a hot site and include subscription costs, monthly fees, testing costs, activation costs, and hourly or daily charges (when activated).

Cold Site

A *cold site* can be considered a basic recovery site, in that it has the required space for equipment and environmental controls (air conditioning, heating, power, and so on) but does not contain any equipment of connectivity. A cold site is ready to receive the equipment necessary for a recovery but will take several weeks to activate. Of the three major types of off-site processing facilities (hot, warm, and cold), a cold site is characterized by at least providing for electricity and HVAC. A warm site improves upon this by providing for redundant equipment and software that can be made operational within a short time.

A cold site is often an acceptable solution for preparing for recovery of noncritical systems and data.

Duplicate Processing Facilities

Duplicate processing facilities are similar to hot site facilities, with the exception that they are completely dedicated, self-developed recovery facilities. An example of duplicate processing facilities is large organizations that have multiple geographic locations. The organization might have a primary site in Washington, D.C., and might designate a duplicate site at one of its own facilities in Utah. The duplicate facility would have the same equipment, operating systems, and applications and might have regularly synchronized data. In this example, the facility can be activated in a relatively short period of time and does not require the organization to notify a third party for activation. Per ISACA, several principles must be in place to ensure the viability of this approach:

➤ The site chosen should not be subject to the same natural disaster(s) as the original (primary) site.

➤ There must be a coordination of hardware and software strategies. A reasonable degree of compatibility must exist to serve as a basis for backup.

➤ Resource availability must be ensured. The workloads of the sites must be monitored to ensure that availability for emergency backup use will not be impaired.

➤ There must be agreement on the priority of adding applications (workloads) until the recovery resources are fully utilized.

➤ Regular testing is necessary. Even though duplicate sites are under common ownership, and even if the sites are under the same management, testing of the backup operation is necessary.

Reciprocal Agreements

Reciprocal agreements are arrangements between two or more organizations with similar equipment and applications. In this type of agreement, the organizations agree to provide computer time (and sometimes facility space) to one another in the event of an emergency. These types of agreements are generally low cost and can be used between organizations that have unique hardware or software that cannot be maintained at a hot or warm site. The disadvantage of reciprocal agreements is that they are not enforceable, hardware and software changes are generally not communicated over time (requiring significant reconfiguration in the event of an emergency), and the sites generally do not employ capacity planning, which may render them useless in the event of an emergency. ISACA recommends that organizations considering a reciprocal agreement ensure the terms of the agreement by answering the following questions:

➤ How much time will be available at the host computer site?

➤ What facilities and equipment will be available?

➤ Will staff assistance be provided?

➤ How quickly can access be gained to the host recovery facility?

➤ How long can the emergency operation continue?

➤ How frequently can the system(s) be tested for compatibility?

➤ How will the confidentiality of data be maintained?

➤ What type of security will be afforded for information systems operations and data?

➤ How much advance notice is required for using the facility?

➤ Are there certain times of the year or month when the partner's facilities are not available?

 A reciprocal agreement is not usually appropriate as an alternate processing solution for organizations with large databases or live transaction processing.

In reviewing the recovery options, the BCP team should review both the agreements and the facilities to be used in recovery to ensure that they will meet the demands of the organization. The facility should have the capacity (space, network, and infrastructure) to support a recovery and should not be oversubscribed. If a facility is oversubscribed and multiple companies declare a disaster at or near the same time, the facility would not be capable of supporting recovery. The vendor that owns the facility should be able to attest to the reliability of the site to include UPS, number of subscribers, diverse network connectivity, and guarantees of space and availability.

The organization must define procedures and put in place agreements to ensure that needed hardware and software will be available. This might include the use of emergency credit lines or credit cards with banks, agreements with hardware and software vendors, and agreements for backup data. A majority of hardware vendors provide high-response services that guarantee hardware and software availability times. These agreements must be in place before the declaration of an emergency. If the organization maintains off-site backup media, there should be an agreement in place for the procurement and shipping of media to the recovery facility.

The BCP team should develop a detailed plan for recovery. This plan should include roles and responsibilities as well as specific procedures associated with the recovery. The following factors should be considered when developing the detailed plan:

➤ Predisaster readiness: Contracts, maintenance and testing, policies, and procedures

➤ Evacuation procedures: Personnel, required company information

➤ Disaster declaration: What defines a disaster? Who is responsible for declaring?

➤ Identification of critical business processes and key personnel (business and IT)

➤ Plan responsibilities: Plan objectives

➤ Roles and responsibilities: Who is responsible for what?

➤ Contract information: Who maintains it, and where is it?

➤ Procedures for recovery: Step-by-step procedures with defined responsibilities

➤ Resource identification: Hardware, software, and personnel required for recovery

The BCP should be written in clear, simple language and should be understandable to all in the organization. It is important to remember that the plan will be implemented under the worst of circumstances, personnel who are assigned duties may not be available, and those who are available could be under significant emotional stress. When the plan is complete, a copy should be maintained off-site and should be easily accessible.

When the primary components of the plan are in place, it is time to organize the plan. The plan should be organized to address response, resumption, recovery, and restoration. The resources required for a successful recovery include the following:

➤ **People**—Team members, vendors, partners, customers, clients, shareholders, employees, and services

➤ **Places**—Alternative recovery sites, processing locations, off-site storage facilities, vaults, and so on

➤ **Things**—Supplies, equipment (computing, office, voice and data communications), and vital records (data, software, documentation, forms, contracts)

The organization of the plan should be prepared to define step-by-step procedures that will take place when a disaster is declared and notification of the necessary personnel who are responsible for the timely resumption of critical business processes and systems. During the organization, the BCP team should incorporate existing policies, procedures, and recovery plans. In addition, the team should define specific training for both key personnel (BCP teams) and employees.

The business continuity plan should be created to minimize the effect of disruptions. The process associated with the development of the plan should include the following steps:

➤ Perform a business impact analysis to determine the effect of disruptions on critical business processes

➤ Identify, prioritize, and sequence resources (systems and personnel) required to support critical business processes in the event of a disruption

➤ Identify recovery strategies that meet the needs of the organization in resumption of critical business functions until permanent facilities are available

➤ Develop the detailed disaster-recovery plan for the IT systems and data that support the critical business functions

➤ Test both the business continuity and disaster recovery plans

➤ Maintain the plan and ensure that changes in business process, critical business functions, and systems assets, such as replacement of hardware, are immediately recorded within the business continuity plan

As an IS auditor, you should review the plan to ensure that it will allow the organization to resume its critical business functions in the event of a disaster. ISACA states the IS Auditors tasks include the following:

➤ Evaluating the business continuity plans to determine their adequacy and currency, by reviewing the plans and comparing them to appropriate standards or government regulations

➤ Verifying that the business continuity plans are effective, by reviewing the results from previous tests performed by both IT and end-user personnel

➤ Evaluating off-site storage to ensure its adequacy, by inspecting the facility and reviewing its contents, security, and environmental controls

➤ Evaluating the ability of IT and user personnel to respond effectively in emergency situations, by reviewing emergency procedures, employee training, and results of their tests and drills

Backup and Storage Methods and Practices

The backup of both software and data varies among organizations, and both the methods and technology used in backing up data and software will affect recovery time. The organization's critical data should be stored both onsite, for quick recovery in nondisaster situations, and off-site, in case of a disaster. The Storage Networking Industry Association defines a *backup* as follows:

A collection of data stored on (usually removable) nonvolatile storage media for purposes of recovery in case the original copy of data is lost or becomes inaccessible. Also called a backup copy. To be useful for recovery, a backup must be made by copying the source data image when it is in a consistent state ... or contains elements and information enabling a consistent state to be recovered.

Organizations continue to rely on the availability of computer services and corporate data. The IT department is responsible for ensuring that systems and data are available, and that the organization is capable of recovering from disasters, to enable continuity of operations. There are a variety of threats to systems and data, ranging from the accidental deletion of corporate data to a disaster that affects the physical facilities and the systems contained within that facility. The evolution of the corporate computing environment has led to tighter integration of systems and applications. In this environment, the database, file, web, communications, and messaging servers are components of a larger system. A failure of any component affects the system as a whole. Most organizations have implemented a centralized backup scheme that incorporates enterprise backup software, tape libraries, and specific storage requirements. To ensure minimum downtime, it is important to understand the different types of backups and their effect on recovery time.

Backup Definitions

Three backup methods are used:

➤ **Full backup**—In a full backup, all the files (in some cases, applications) are backed up by copying them to a tape or other storage medium. This type of backup is the easiest backup to perform but requires the most time and space on the backup media.

> **Differential backup**—A differential backup is a procedure that backs up only the files that have been changed or added since the last full backup. This type of backup reduces the time and media required.

> **Incremental backup**—An incremental backup is a procedure that backs up only the files that have been added or changed since the last backup (whether full or differential).

The method of backup depends on factors that include the cost of media, the speed of restoration, and the time allocated for backups. For instance, the organization might choose to perform a single full weekly backup combined with daily incremental backups. This method decreases the time and media required for the daily backups but increases restoration time. This type of restoration requires more steps and, therefore, more time because the administrator will have to restore the full backup first and then apply the incremental backups sequentially until all the data is restored.

A variety of vendors provide centralized enterprise backup software, and their products generally work off the same basic premise—that is, to back up systems over the network to a server that has some sort of storage device attached. Generally, a central server controls the enterprise backup environment. The backup software incorporates backup schedules, indexes, backup groups, and communication with the client software. In addition, the central server logs its activities to include communication, backup start and end times and dates, and any errors incurred during the backup. To effect communication with clients, a backup agent (client software) is installed on all systems that will be backed up through the central server. The client software listens for connections from the central server and assists in the transfer of data from the client to the central server.

Tape backup media is a magnetic medium and, as such, is susceptible to damage from both the environment in which it is stored (temperature, humidity, and so on) and physical damage to the tape through excessive use. For this reason, administrators use backup schemes that allow tapes to be regularly rotated and eventually retired from backup service. One popular scheme is the grandfather, father, and son scheme (GFS), in which the central server writes to a single tape or tape set per backup. When using the GFS scheme, the backup sets are daily (son), weekly (father), and monthly (grandfather). Daily backups come first. The four backup tapes are usually labeled (Mon–Thur) and used on their corresponding day. The tape rotation is based on how long the organization wants to maintain file history. If a file history for one week is required, tapes are overwritten each week; if history is required for three weeks, each tape is overwritten every three weeks (requiring 12 tapes). The five (some months have five weeks) father tapes are used for full weekly backups (Friday tapes). If one month of history is being kept, tapes are overwritten monthly. The three grandfather tapes are used as full monthly backups and are typically overwritten quarterly or yearly.

Based on its retention/rotation, the tape is then retained for a period of time; when the tape has reached its expiration date, it can be put back into the rotation and used again. One of the disadvantages of this scheme is that sometimes the full capacity of the media is not used. As an example, if the administrator is using an 80GB tape that backs up 25GB of data, the tape will be rotated out, and when it expires, it will be rewritten from the beginning (with 25GB), leaving the remaining 55GB unused. All tapes within the backup scheme will be saved based on the retention period assigned to them. Creating a retention schedule ensures that an organization maintains historical records for an appropriate period of time, in compliance with business requirements and any regulations pertaining to business operations. This retention schedule also ensures that unnecessary records are disposed of in a controlled manner. A retention schedule should include all the types of records, period of retention, description of the records, disposition (destroy, transfer, and so on), and retention requirement.

Tape Storage

Two types of tape storage are used:

> **Onsite storage**—One copy of the backup tapes should be stored onsite to effect quick recovery of critical files. Another copy should be moved to an off-site location as redundant storage. Tapes should be stored in environmentally controlled facilities that incorporate physical access controls that are commensurate with the requirements of the data being stored. Onsite tapes should be stored in a secure fireproof vault, and all access to tapes should be logged.

> **Off-site storage**—The organization could contract with a reputable records storage company for off-site tape storage, or could maintain the facility themselves. The physical and environmental controls for the off-site facility should be equal to those of the organization. The contract should stipulate who from the organization will have the authority to provide and pick up tapes, as well as the time frame in which tapes can be delivered in the event of a disaster.

In addition to tape backup options, organizations can employ storage area networks (SAN) or electronic vaulting options. A SAN is a special-purpose network in which different types of data storage are associated with servers and users. A SAN can either interconnect attached storage on servers into a storage array or connect the servers and users to a storage device that contains disk arrays. The SAN can be implemented locally or can use disk arrays at a redundant facility. The enterprise backup software either can back up the entire array to a separate storage medium or, in the case of an off-site SAN, can instruct the SAN itself to create a snapshot of the local volumes and then move the snapshot to the off-site SAN.

Storage Area Networks and Electronic Vaulting

If the organization cannot implement an off-site SAN, it might opt for an electronic vaulting option. With this option, the organization contracts with a vaulting provider that provides disk arrays for the backup and storage of the organization's applications and data. Generally, the organization installs an agent on all the servers and workstations that require a backup and identifies the files to be included in the backup. The agent then performs full and incremental backups, and moves that data via a broadband connection to the electronic vault. Organizations that have a significant amount of data or high levels of change might incur issues in moving large amounts of data across a broadband connection.

As with all IT procedures, proper security should be implemented to enforce segregation of duties and ensure the integrity of the backup media and data. The backup administration should be responsible for backup scheduling and adding machines and drives to the backup schedule. A tape operator should be responsible for adding and removing tapes from the various devices and tape libraries in a data center, but should not be allowed access to change client definitions or backup schedules. A systems operator should be responsible for checking backup status and ensuring that the central server's OS is up-to-date and operating correctly.

The objective of having backups is to ensure recovery in the event of a failure or disaster. The organization should perform regular disaster-recovery testing to ensure that data can be restored within the time frame required in the BCP. The organization should utilize off-site storage facilities to maintain redundancy of current and critical information within backup files. The off-site data backup and storage should be geographically separate, to mitigate the risk of a widespread physical disaster such as a hurricane or earthquake.

Disaster Recovery and Business Continuity Testing Approaches and Methods

As a part of regular testing and maintenance, organizations can opt to perform either full or partial testing of recovery and continuity plans, though most organizations do not perform full-scale tests because of resource constraints. To continue to improve recovery and continuity plans, organizations can perform a paper, walk-through, or preparedness test. Tests should be scheduled during a time that causes minimal disruption to the normal operations of the organization. It is important that all key team members participate in testing and that the test process addresses all critical areas of the plan. The testing methods employed by the organization will vary from simple to complex, and each method has its own objectives and benefits. The following sections give examples of testing methods.

Paper Test

A *paper test* is the least complex test that can be performed. This test helps ensure that the plan is complete and that all team members are familiar with their responsibilities within the plan. With this type of test, the BCP/DRP plan documents are simply distributed to appropriate managers and BCP/DRP team members for review, markup, and comment.

Walk-Through Testing

A *walk-through test* is an extension of the paper testing, in that the appropriate managers and BCP/DRP team members actually meet to discuss and walk through procedures of the plan, individual training needs, and clarification of critical plan elements.

 Of the three major types of BCP tests (paper, walk-through, and preparedness), a walk-through test requires only that representatives from each operational area meet to review the plan.

Preparedness Test (Full Test)

A *preparedness test* is a localized version of the full test in which the team members and participants simulate an actual outage or disaster and simulate performing the steps necessary to effect recovery and continuity. This test can be performed against specific areas of the plan instead of the entire plan. This test validates response capability, demonstrates skills and training, and practices decision-making capabilities. Only the preparedness test actually takes the primary resources offline to test the capabilities of the backup resources and processing.

 Of the three major types of BCP tests (paper, walkthrough, and preparedness), only the preparedness test uses actual resources to simulate a system crash and validate the plan's effectiveness.

Full Operational Test

A *full operational test* is the most comprehensive test and includes all team members and participants in the plan. The BCP team and participants should have multiple paper and preparedness tests completed before performing a full operational test. This test involves the mobilization of personnel, and disrupts and restores operations just as an outage or disaster would. This test extends the preparedness test by including actual notification, mobilization of resources, processing of data, and utilization of backup media for restoration.

Per ISACA, the test should strive to accomplish the following tasks:

➤ Verify the completeness and precision of the business continuity plan

➤ Evaluate the performance of the personnel involved in the exercise

➤ Appraise the training and awareness of the nonbusiness continuity members

➤ Evaluate the coordination among the business continuity team and external vendors and suppliers

➤ Measure the capability and capacity of the backup site to perform prescribed processing

➤ Assess the vital records retrieval capability

➤ Evaluate the state and quantity of equipment and supplies that have been related to the recovery site

➤ Measure the overall performance of operational and information systems–processing activities related to maintaining the business entity

During the test, detailed documentation and observations should be maintained. This documentation should include any problems incurred and suggested solutions. This documentation should be used during analysis of the test, with the success of the plan measured against plan objectives. During this analysis, team members and management should be able to evaluate against specific or general measurements associated with the plan. Per ISACA, these measurements might include the following:

> ➤ **Time**—The elapsed time for completion of prescribed tasks, delivery of equipment, assembly of personnel, and arrival at a predetermined site.

> ➤ **Amount**—Amount of work performed at the backup site by clerical personnel and information systems processing operations.

> ➤ **Count**—The number of vital records successfully carried to the backup site versus the required number, and the number of supplies and equipment requested versus those actually received. Also, the number of critical systems successfully recovered can be measured with the number of transactions processed.

> ➤ **Accuracy**—Accuracy of the data entry at the recovery site versus normal accuracy. Also, the accuracy of actual processing cycles can be determined by comparing output results with those for the same period processed under normal conditions.

It is important for organizations to remember that a BCP plan is a living document and will change according to the needs of the organization. The testing, maintenance, and analysis will provide the organization with a BCP plan that is viable in the event of a disaster. The plan should include a regular review and testing schedule to allow for changes in business strategy, the introduction of new applications, vendor or contract changes, and the disposition of applications or systems. The organization should appoint a business continuity coordinator to ensure that periodic testing and maintenance of the plan are implemented. The coordinator should also ensure that team members and participants receive regular training associated with their duties in the BCP and maintain records and results of testing.

The organization should implement an independent party (internal or external IS auditor) to review the adequacy of the business continuity process, to ensure that the board and management expectations are met. The independent review should include assessing the identification of critical business processes, team and individual skill sets, testing scenarios and schedules, and the communication of test results and recommendations. The IS auditor should directly observe tests and training, and report on the effectiveness of the BCP.

Understanding and Evaluating Business Continuity Planning, Documentation, Processes, and Maintenance

In reviewing the organization's business continuity planning process, the IS auditor should look for evidence of a structured process in developing the business continuity plan. The planning process should include identifying and prioritizing resources and systems that are required to maintain continuity of critical business processes and strategies for recovery. Senior management is responsible for ensuring that the plan reduces the organization's risk associated with an unexpected disruption of critical business functions. During the audit, you should review test plans as well as the results of previous tests to ensure the adequacy of the BCP. The BCP should define key personnel and their tasks. Key personnel should have a clear understanding of their tasks and should have detailed documentation on how to perform those tasks.

Evaluating the Organization's Capability to Ensure Business Continuity in the Event of a Business Disruption

As an IS auditor, you should review the BCP for adequacy and currency by reviewing the plans and possibly participating in plan testing or reviewing the results of previous tests. In addition, the IS Auditor should review procedures associated with backups to ensure that systems required for critical business processes are included along with storage (onsite and off-site), rotation, and retention procedures. The IS Auditor should also review individual team members to ensure that their skill sets are adequate to perform their duties as described in the plan. Team members should have training specific to these duties, and personnel within the organization should be trained on their roles and responsibilities in the event of a disaster.

Per ISACA, the audit procedures for BCP review include the following:

➤ Obtaining a current copy of the business continuity plan or manual.

➤ Sampling the distributed copies of the manual and verifying that they are current.

➤ Evaluating the effectiveness of the document procedures for the initiation of the BCP.

➤ Reviewing the identification, priorities, and planned support of critical applications, including PC-based or end user–developed systems.

➤ Determining whether all applications have been reviewed for their level of tolerance in the event of a disaster.

➤ Determining whether all critical applications (including PC applications) have been identified.

➤ Determining whether the hot site (if required) has the correct versions of all system software. Also, verifying that all the software is compatible; otherwise, the system will not be capable of processing production data during the disaster recovery.

➤ Reviewing the list of BCP personnel, emergency alternate site contacts, vendor contacts, and so on for appropriateness and completeness.

➤ Calling a sample of the people indicated and verifying that their phone numbers and addresses are correct, as indicated, and that they possess a current copy of the BCP.

➤ Interviewing them for an understanding of their assigned responsibilities in a disaster situation.

➤ Evaluating the procedures for documenting tests.

➤ Evaluating the procedure for updating the manual. Are updates applied and distributed in a timely manner? Are specific responsibilities for maintenance of the manual documented?

The currency and viability of the plan are important, and the IS auditor should ensure that the business continuity coordinator performs regular tests of the plan and updates the plan to mitigate weaknesses discovered during testing. In addition, you will need to ensure that the tests are thorough and performed often enough to incorporate changes in strategy and critical business functions. All contracts associated with the business continuity plan should be included in a regular review, to ensure that response times, capacity, and security procedures are in accordance with the business continuity plan. The purpose of business continuity planning and disaster-recovery planning is to mitigate, or reduce, the risk and impact of a business interruption or disaster.

Evaluating Backup and Recovery Provisions in the Event of a Short-Term Disruption

Business disruptions, as opposed to disasters, can be caused by a variety of internal and external factors, including these:

➤ Equipment failure (processors, hard drives, memory, and so on)

➤ Service failures (telecommunications outages, power outages, external application failure, and so on)

➤ Application or data corruption

In addition to the disaster-recovery plan, the IT department should have policies and procedures for backup, storage of backup media (onsite and off-site), defined roles and responsibilities, and recovery. The IS auditor should review the following to ensure that the organization can recover data and applications in the event of a short-term disruption:

➤ **Backup procedures**—The procedures identify the backup scheme and define responsibilities for implementing backups. The procedures should identify how often (weekly or daily) backups are performed, as well as the type of backup (full, differential, or incremental). In addition, the plan should include a retention and rotation schedule to ensure that critical data is in compliance with internal and external guidelines and that tapes are rotated to reduce the chance of error from overuse.

➤ **Onsite storage**—All storage media should be stored in environmentally controlled facilities and should be secured in a fire rated safe. Procedures should exist for the inventory of all onsite storage media as well as physical access controls and logging of media check-in and check-out. All storage media should have a record of information regarding the contents, version, and location of data.

➤ **Off-site storage**—The off-site storage facility should have environmental and security controls that equal those of the onsite storage facility. The contract with the off-site facility should contain the points of contact within the organization that have the authority to check storage media in and out of the facility, as well as clearly defined response times for the delivery of storage media in the event of a disaster. An inventory of all storage media at the off-site facility should be maintained and should include the dataset name, the volume serial number, the date created, the accounting period, and the off-site storage bin number.

Off-site data storage should be kept synchronized when preparing for the recovery of time-sensitive data such as that resulting from transaction processing.

In addition, the plan should include procedures for the restoration of hardware, operating systems, applications, and data. The IS auditor should review all contracts associated with hardware, software, or services, to ensure that the service-level agreements are in accordance with recovery times and that specific points of contact for both the third party and the organization are accurate and up-to-date. All contracts associated with hardware replacement should identify response times to get replacement hardware onsite, support levels, and escalation procedures. The IS Auditor should review previous tests to ensure that the restoration of applications and data meets time requirements of the critical business functions. All documents associated with recovery or restoration should be stored off-site and kept up-to-date in the event of a facility failure.

Although some business continuity plans focus on the procedures regarding major disasters, the recovery of minor disruptions should not be overlooked during planning. The lack of proper backup and restoration procedures associated with a minor disruption can allow the disruption to escalate to a major disruption that may affect the organization's critical business processes.

Evaluating the Capability to Continue Information System Processing in the Event That the Primary Information-Processing Facilities Are Not Available

The off-site facility should have the same level of access control and security as the originating site. This should include physical access controls such as locked doors and human surveillance. The off-site facility should not be easily identified from the outside (with signs, for example) and should not be subject to the same natural disaster that could affect the originating site. The organization should have procedures associated with the notification and transportation of personnel and the procurement of the necessary hardware, software, and data. The off-site facility should have the same environmental monitoring and controls of the originating site. Per ISACA, the following questions can be considered in reviewing the off-site facility:

➤ Does the plan adequately address the movement to the recovery site?

➤ Does the plan include the items necessary for the reconstruction of the information-processing facility, such as blueprints, hardware inventory, and wiring diagrams?

➤ Does the plan identify rendezvous points for the disaster-management committee or emergency-management team to meet and decide whether business continuity should be initiated?

➤ Does the plan address relocation into a new information-processing facility in the event that the original center cannot be restored?

➤ Is there adequate documentation to perform a recovery?

➤ Does the alternative site contract meet the recovery needs of the organization?

➤ Is the contract written and clearly understandable?

➤ Is the organization's agreement clear with rules that apply to sites shared with other subscribers? The following rules apply to these sites:

  ➤ Ensure that insurance coverage ties in with and covers all (or most) expenses of the disaster

  ➤ Ensure that tests can be performed at the site at regular intervals

  ➤ Review and evaluate communications requirements for the site

  ➤ Ensure that enforceable source code escrow is reviewed by a lawyer specializing in such contracts

  ➤ Determine the limitation recourse tolerance in the event of a breached agreement

In addition to answering these questions, the IS auditor should review the plan to ensure that there are clear guidelines and responsibilities for the declaration of disaster, the movement to the off-site facility, and the restoration of normal business operations when the disaster is over. Both the facility and the contracts should be tested, reviewed, and updated to meet the needs of the organization. All personnel associated with the BCP, particularly the implementation of the disaster-recovery site, should be trained and should participate in regular testing in the off-site facility.

Insurance in Relation to Business Continuity and Disaster Recovery

The organization's insurance coverage should take into account the actual cost of recovery and should include coverage for media damage, business interruption, and business continuity processing. Mitigating the risk and impact of a disaster or business interruption usually takes priority over transferring the risk to a third party such as an insurer, but the organization should ensure that the amount of coverage will provide for the recovery of income and equipment in the event of a disaster. The amount of coverage as well as the items covered will vary depending on whom the organization has a policy with. There are two general types of insurance: property and liability.

Property Insurance

Property insurance can protect the organization from a wide variety of losses, including these:

➤ Buildings

➤ Personal property owned by the organization (tables, desks, chairs, and equipment)

➤ Loss of income

➤ Earthquake

➤ Flood (usually an additional rider on the policy)

Property insurance can be structured to cover computer equipment, software, and vital records, as well as the loss of income that would result from disruptions or disasters.

Liability Insurance

A general liability policy is designed to provide coverage for the following:

➤ Personal injury

➤ Fire liability

➤ Medical expenses

➤ General liability for accidents occurring on the organization premises

The organization must ensure that all costs associated with a disaster and the recoveries are included in its insurance policies. It might be necessary to purchase additional insurance policies to extend coverage (sometimes called umbrella policies) or purchase specific insurance coverage (flood or terrorism, for example) based on the needs of the organization.

Human Resource Issues (Evacuation Planning, Response Teams)

The BCP team should define key personnel within the business units and IT to implement the plan. These personnel should be a part of the planning, testing, and maintenance of the BCP. Key personnel should have alternates to function in their place, where necessary. Per ISACA, response team structures within the BCP might include the following:

➤ **Emergency action team**—These are the first responders and deal with the immediate effects of the disaster. One of their primary functions is to evacuate personnel and secure human life.

➤ **Damage-assessment team**—This team assesses the damage immediately following the disaster, to provide the estimate of time to recover.

➤ **Emergency-management team**—This team is the primary coordinator for the recovery efforts. It handles key decision making and directs recovery teams and business personnel. It also handles financial arrangement, public relations, and media inquiries.

The emergency-management team should coordinate the following activities:

➤ Retrieving critical data from off-site storage facilities

➤ Installing and testing systems software and applications at the system-recovery site

➤ Identifying, purchasing, and installing hardware at the system-recovery site

➤ Operating from the system-recovery site

➤ Rerouting network communication traffic

➤ Re-establishing the user/system network

➤ Transporting users to the recovery facility

➤ Reconstructing databases

➤ Supplying necessary office goods, such as special forms, check stock, paper, and so on

➤ Arranging and paying for employee relocation expenses at the recovery facility

➤ Coordinating systems use and employee work schedules

➤ **Off-site storage team**—This team is responsible for obtaining, packaging, and shipping media and records to the recovery facilities, as well as establishing and overseeing an off-site storage schedule for information created during operations at the recovery site.

➤ **Software team**—This team is responsible for restoring system service packs, loading and testing operating systems software, and resolving system-level problems.

➤ **Applications team**—This team travels to the systems-recovery site and restores user packs and application programs on the backup system. As the recovery progresses, this team might have the responsibility of monitoring application performance and database integrity.

➤ **Security team**—This team continually monitors the security of system and communication links, resolves any security conflicts that impede the expeditious recovery of the system, and ensures the proper installation and functioning of the security software package.

➤ **Emergency operations team**—This team consists of shift operations and shift supervisors who will reside at the systems-recovery site and manage system operations during the duration of the disaster and recovery projects. Another responsibility might be coordinating hardware installation, if a hot site or other equipment-ready facility has not been designated as the recovery center.

➤ **Network-recovery team**—This team is responsible for rerouting wide-area voice and data communications traffic, re-establishing host network control and access at the system-recovery site, providing ongoing support for data communications, and overseeing communications integrity.

➤ **Communications team**—This team travels to the recovery site, where its members work in conjunction with the remote network-recovery team to establish a user/system network. This team also is responsible for soliciting and installing communication hardware at the recovery site, and working with the local exchange carriers and gateway vendors in the rerouting of local service and gateway access.

➤ **Transportation team**—This team serves as a facilities team to locate a recovery site, if one has not been predetermined, and is responsible for coordinating the transport of company employees to a distant recovery site. It also might assist in contacting employees to inform them of new work locations and scheduling and arranging employees' lodging.

➤ **User hardware team**—This team locates and coordinates the delivery and installation of user terminals, printers, typewriters, photocopiers, and other necessary equipment. This team also offers support to the communication team and to any hardware and facilities salvage efforts.

➤ **Data preparation and records team**—This team works from a terminal that connects to the user recovery site and updates the applications database. The team also oversees additional data-entry personnel and assists in record-salvage efforts in acquiring primary documents and other input information sources

➤ **Administrative support team**—This team provides clerical support to the other teams and serves as a message center for the user-recovery site. This team also might control accounting and payroll functions, as well as ongoing facilities management.

➤ **Supplies team**—This team supports the efforts of the user hardware team by contacting vendors and coordinating logistics for an ongoing supply of necessary office and computer supplies.

➤ **Salvage team**—This team manages the relocation project. It also makes a more detailed assessment of the damage to the facilities and equipment than was performed initially, provides the emergency-management team with the information required to determine whether planning should be directed toward reconstruction or relocation, provides information necessary for filling out insurance claims, and coordinates the efforts necessary for immediate records salvage, such as restoring paper documents and electronic media.

➤ **Relocation team**—This team coordinates the process of moving from the hot site to a new location or to the restored original location. This involves relocating the information systems–processing operations, communications traffic, and user operations. This team also monitors the transition to normal service levels.

The response teams are responsible for the tasks associated with everything from evacuating personnel and securing human life, to relocating and resuming critical business functions. Each individual on the response team should have clearly defined responsibilities and documented procedures on how to perform their tasks.

Exam Prep Questions

1. Disaster recovery planning is a critical component of protecting data availability and integrity. Which of the following is the MOST important consideration of a disaster recovery plan?

   ❑ A. Alternative processing capability

   ❑ B. Protection and redundancy of data

   ❑ C. Protection of human life

   ❑ D. Ensuring that the disaster-recovery plan effectively supports organizational goals and objectives

   Answer: C. Although all the answers are important considerations of disaster recovery planning, the primary objective is to protect human life.

2. Disaster recovery planning often comes down to a compromise between cost and target recovery times. Which of the following statements is true regarding this compromise?

   ❑ A. Disaster-recovery duration times and costs should decrease.

   ❑ B. Disaster-recovery duration times should decrease, but recovery costs will necessarily increase.

   ❑ C. Disaster-recovery duration times should remain constant, but recovery costs should decrease.

   ❑ D. Disaster-recovery times should remain constant, but recovery costs should increase.

   Answer: A. Effective recovery-control planning incorporates a control feasibility study, including a cost/benefit analysis. The objective of DRP is to reduce the financial business impact of a disaster or disruptive event to a greater extent than the cost of implementing a disaster-recovery control. Therefore, a control that decreases the recovery time and associated net recovery costs of the disaster is accepted and implemented.

3. Which of the following is ultimately accountable for effective business continuity and disaster-recovery controls?

   ❑ A. Stockholders

   ❑ B. Security administrators

   ❑ C. Network administrators

   ❑ D. Executive officers

   Answer: D. The executive officers of an organization are ultimately accountable corporate governance, which includes decisions to have or forego BCP/DRP controls. Although security administrators and network administrators might actually implement the controls that the executive officers or the board of directors approves, stockholders hold executive management accountable for making sure organizational viability is protected.

4. Which of the following BCP/DRP processes MOST requires end-user participation for effective business continuity and disaster-recovery planning?

❑ A. Development of recovery strategies

❑ B. Business impact assessment (BIA)

❑ C. Development of the BCP/DRP plan documents

❑ D. Final testing of the BCP and DRP

Answer: B. As the initial step of effective business continuity and disaster-recovery planning, a business impact assessment (BIA) must be accurate to effectively perform an additional BCP/DRP processes. Therefore, end-user involvement is most critical to the BIA phase, to make sure that continuity risks are fully understood and properly assessed.

5. Regarding alternate site data-processing facilities, which of the following best practices is MOST important?

❑ A. The facility is not clearly identified as belonging to the company.

❑ B. The facility is clearly identified as belonging to the company.

❑ C. Primary-site recovery teams can reach the facility within an hour to ensure minimal business impact from the disruptive event.

❑ D. The facility does not provide any external windows.

Answer: A. Because a potential disruptive event could be facility sabotage or bomb threat, the alternate processing facility should *not* be easily identified as belonging to the company. Because off-site facilities mitigate the risk of widespread natural disasters such as hurricanes and earthquakes, the facilities should be geographically distant from the primary site. External windows should be avoided because such windows expose the facility to unauthorized physical access, as well as storm damage. However, this best practice is not considered as important as answer A.

6. When should a business continuity or disaster plan be updated?

❑ A. Annually

❑ B. Biannually

❑ C. Semiannually

❑ D. Upon any significant change to the organization, such as asset acquisition or release

Answer: D. Business continuity and disaster recovery planning should be an ongoing program that is event-triggered rather than simply a periodic project. After all, newly acquired assets should be protected sooner rather than later.

7. Hot-site off-site processing facilities are characterized by:

□   A.   High implementation and maintenance costs

□   B.   Reduced recovery time

□   C.   Decreased disaster preparation costs

□   D.   Both answers A and B

□   E.   Both answers B and C

Answer: D. Hot sites are the most expensive type of alternate processing redundancy, but they are very appropriate for operations that require immediate or very short recovery times.

8. Which of the following is the MOST important control aspect of maintaining data backup at off-site storage facilities?

□   A.   The security of the storage facility is as secure as or more secure than the primary site.

□   B.   The data backups are always tested for accuracy and reliability.

□   C.   Critical and time-sensitive data is kept current at the off-site storage facility.

□   D.   Applications for processing the data are backed up to the off-site storage facility along with critical data.

Answer: C. Organizations should use off-site storage facilities to maintain redundancy of current and critical information within backup files. All other answers are important, too, but answer C is considered most important.

9. Critical real-time data such as that associated with transaction processing requires special backup procedures. Which of the following is recommended for backing up transaction-processing files?

□   A.   Duplicate logging of transactions

□   B.   Time stamping of transactions and communications data

□   C.   Use of before-and-after images of master records

□   D.   All of the above

Answer: D. Duplicate logging of transactions, use of before-and-after images of master records, and time stamping of transactions and communications data are all recommended best practices for establishing effective redundancy of transaction databases.

10. Which of the following is considered MOST appropriate for backing up real-time transaction databases?

□   A.   Periodic imaging of transaction database master records, along with automated periodic incremental tape backups

□   B.   Electronic vaulting

□   C.   Remote journaling

□   D.   Answers A and C

□   E.   Answers B and C

Answer: E. Electronic vaulting and remote journaling are both considered effective redundancy controls for backing up real-time transaction databases. Periodic imaging of transaction database master records along with automated periodic incremental tape-backups does not support immediate or short recovery times.

Business Application System Development, Acquisition, Implementation, and Maintenance

Key concepts you will need to understand:

- ✓ System-development methodologies and tools (prototyping, RAD, SDLC, object-oriented design techniques)
- ✓ Documentation and charting methods
- ✓ Application implementation practices (piloting, parallel run)
- ✓ Software quality-assurance methods
- ✓ Application architecture (client/server applications, object-oriented design, data warehousing, web-based applications, interfaces)
- ✓ Testing principles, methods, and practices

- ✓ Project-management principles, methods, and practices (PERT, CPM, estimation techniques)
- ✓ Application system-acquisition processes (evaluation of vendors, preparation of contracts, vendor management, escrow)
- ✓ Application-maintenance principles (versioning, packaging, change request)
- ✓ System migration and data-conversion tools, techniques, and procedures
- ✓ Application change-control and emergency change-management procedures
- ✓ Post-implementation review techniques

Techniques you will need to master:

- ✓ Evaluate the processes by which application systems are developed and implemented to ensure that they contribute to the organization's business objectives
- ✓ Evaluate the processes by which application systems are acquired and implemented to

ensure that they contribute to the organization's business objectives
- ✓ Evaluate the processes by which application systems are maintained to ensure the continued support of the organization's business objectives

Evaluating Application Systems Development and Implementation

Organizations invest heavily in the development, acquisition, implementation, and maintenance of applications and their associated systems. These applications are developed or acquired in support of key business functions. The IT department should have clearly defined processes to control the resources associated with the development, acquisition, and implementation of applications. This process, called the systems-development life cycle (SDLC), encompasses a structured approach to do the following:

➤ Minimize risk and maximize return on investment

➤ Reduce software business risk, the likelihood that the new system will not meet the application user's business expectations

The lack of a formal documented software-development process can result in software projects that are not on time or on budget, or do not meet user or business needs. The IS auditor should look for evidence of a structured approach to application development, acquisition, implementation, and maintenance. The IS auditor also should review policies and procedures to ensure that the objectives of the strategic plan are being met. The SDLC should have clearly defined life-cycle phases and progression points, to allow the IS auditor to identify each phase in the process and ensure adherence to planned objectives and company procedures.

As discussed in Chapter 1, "The Information Systems (IS) Audit Process," all significant IT projects should have a project sponsor and project steering committee. The project sponsor is ultimately responsible for providing requirement specifications to the software-development team. The project steering committee is responsible for the overall direction, costs, and time-tables for systems-development projects.

The IS auditor is responsible for advising the project-management team and senior management if processes are disorderly (informal) or lack sufficient controls. A primary high-level goal for an auditor who is reviewing a systems-development project is to ensure that business objectives are achieved. This objective guides all other systems-development objectives. In addition to auditing projects, the IS auditor should be included within a systems-development project in an advisory capacity to ensure that adequate controls are incorporated into the system during development and to ensure that adequate and complete documentation exists for all projects.

System-Development Methodologies and Tools

A *Software Development Life Cycle* is a logical process that systems analysts and systems developers use to develop software (applications). The SDLC should produce high-quality software that meets or exceeds business and user requirements, is produced within time and cost estimates, is efficient and effective, and provides for cost-effective maintenance and enhancement. The most common SDLC is the *Classic Life Cycle Model*, which can be either the *Linear Sequential Model* or the *Waterfall Method*. The SDLC is a framework, and specific activities in the framework will vary by organization. Figure 6.1 shows the high-level phases associated with a waterfall SDLC.

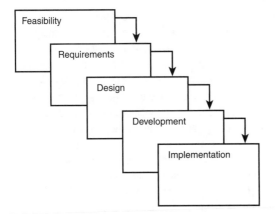

Figure 6.1   The Waterfall SDLC.

The waterfall methodology is the oldest and most commonly used approach. It begins with the feasibility study and progresses through requirements, design, development, implementation, and post-implementation. It is important to remember that, in using this approach, the subsequent step does not begin until all tasks in the previous step are completed. When the process has moved to the next step, it does not go back to the previous step.

The waterfall approach is best used in environments where the organization's requirements will remain stable and the system architecture is known early in the development process. Per ISACA, Table 6.1 describes the phases associated with the traditional systems-development life cycle approach.

Table 6.1 Phases of the Traditional Systems-Development Life Cycle	
SDLC Phase	**General Description**
Phase 1: Feasibility	Determine the strategic benefits of implementing the system either in productivity gains or in future cost avoidance, identify and quantify the cost savings of a new system, and estimate a payback schedule for costs incurred in implementing the system. This business case provides the justification for proceeding to the next phase.
Phase 2: Requirements	Define the problem or need that requires resolution, and define the functional and quality requirements of the solution system. This can be either a customized approach or a vendor-supplied software package, which would entail following a defined and documented acquisition process. In either case, the user needs to be actively involved.
Phase 3: Design	Based on the requirements defined, establish a baseline of system and subsystem specifications that describe the parts of the system, how they interact, and how the system will be implemented using the chosen hardware, software, and network facilities. (During the design phase of an application-development project, the IS auditor should strive to ensure that all necessary controls are included in the initial design.) Generally, the design also includes both program and database specifications, and a security plan. (Application controls should be considered as early as possible in the system-development process, even in the development of the project's functional specifications.) Additionally, a formal change-control process is established to prevent uncontrolled entry of new requirements into the development process.
Phase 4: Development	Use the design specifications to begin programming and formalizing supporting operational processes of the system. Various levels of testing also occur in this phase to verify and validate what has been developed.
Phase 5: Implementation	The actual operation of the new information system is established, with final user acceptance testing conducted in this environment. (Acceptance testing is used to ensure that the system meets user and business needs.) The system also may go through a certification and accreditation process to assess the effectiveness of the business application in mitigating risks to an appropriate level, and providing management accountability over the effectiveness of the system in meeting its intended objectives and in establishing an appropriate level of internal control.

In addition to following a structured approach to systems development, the IT organization must have a sound IT management methodology that includes the following:

➤ **Project management**—Utilizes knowledge, tools, and techniques to reach the goals of the project

➤ **IT organizational policies**—Ensures that organizational goals are fulfilled and business risks are reduced

➤ **Steering committee**—Ensures that the IS department closely supports the corporate mission and objectives

➤ **Change-management process**—Ensures that there is not uncontrolled entry of new requirements into the development process or existing systems

To improve software life-cycle processes and software-processing capability, the organization can implement the *Software Capability Maturity Model* (CMM), developed by Carnegie Melon's Software Engineering Institute. Software process maturity is the extent to which a specific process is explicitly defined, managed, measured, controlled, and effective. The more mature an organization's software process is, the higher the productivity and quality are of the software products produced. As software process maturity increases, the organization institutionalizes its software process via policies, standards, and organizational structures. This institutionalization entails building an infrastructure and a corporate culture that support the methods, practices, and procedures of the business so that they endure after those who originally defined them have gone. Figure 6.2 shows the CMM maturity levels.

A standard software-development process is included within Level 3 (defined) of the Software Capability Maturity Model (CMM).

For the organization to ensure the production of high-quality software that meets or exceeds business and user requirements, it must be produced within time and cost estimates, be efficient and effective, and provide for cost-effective maintenance. This can be accomplished only with an efficient SDLC process.

In addition to the life-cycle phases, the organization must utilize formal programming methods, techniques, languages, and library control software.

The utilization of formal coding standards ensures the quality of programming activities and enhances future maintenance capabilities. Program coding standards serve as a control that enables clear communication among members of the programming team and between the programming team and the users. These standards should include methods of source code documentation, methods of data declaration, and naming standards.

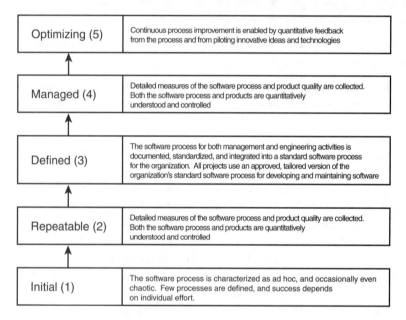

Figure 6.2 CMM maturity levels.

 Coding standards promote compliance with accepted field-naming conventions.

In application development, programs are coded into statements that are then translated by the compiler into machine language. The language chosen will vary by the organization and will be based on the existing environment, skills sets, and application requirements. These are the commonly used programming languages and their attributes:

➤ **Common Business Orientated Language (COBOL) and C programming Language**—High-level general-purpose languages.

➤ **C++ and Java**—Object-oriented languages.

➤ **SH (Shell), Perl, JavaScript, VBScript**—Scripting languages; primarily used in web development.

➤ **4GL**—Fourth-generation high-level programming languages; are object-oriented but lack the lower-level detail commands.

 Fourth-generation languages (4GLs) are most appropriate for designing the application's graphical user interface (GUI). They are inappropriate for designing any intensive data-calculation procedures.

Throughout the SDLC, it is important to protect the integrity of source code and executables. This integrity is maintained through the use of production source code and production libraries. The library control software provides access control to ensure, as an example, that source code is accessible only in a read-only state. The organization should have procedures in place to ensure proper access levels and segregation of duties. As an example, users and application programmers should not have access to the production source code.

Per ISACA, IS auditors should perform the following functions during the design and development SDLC phases:

➤ Review the system flowcharts for adherence to the general design. Verify that the appropriate approvals were obtained for any changes and that all changes were discussed and approved by appropriate user management.

➤ Review the input, processing, and output controls designed into the system for appropriateness.

➤ Interview the key users of the system to determine their understanding of how the system will operate, and assess their level of input into the design of screen formats and output reports.

➤ Assess the adequacy of audit trails to provide traceability and accountability of system transactions.

➤ Verify the integrity of key calculations and processes.

➤ Verify that the system can identify and process erroneous data correctly.

➤ Review the quality-assurance results of the programs developed during this phase.

➤ Verify that all recommended corrections to programming errors were made and that the recommended audit trails or embedded modules were coded into the appropriate programs.

Prototyping

Prototyping is the process of developing a system through the rapid development and testing of code. This process uses trial and error to reduce the level of risks in developing the system. In general, prototyping reduces the time required to deploy applications through iterative development and testing. The developers create high-level code (mostly 4G languages) based on the design requirements and then provide them to the end users for review and testing. The end users can then see a high-level view of the system (generally screens and reports) and provide input on changes or gaps between the code and requirements. A couple major challenges are associated with prototyping:

➤ The use of prototyping to develop applications systems often results in overly optimistic expectations of project timelines.

➤ Change control becomes much more complicated because changes in design and requirements happen so quickly that they are seldom documented or approved.

➤ Because of the iterative process, end users might define functions or extras that were not originally defined during the requirements phase. If not properly managed through a review and approval process, it can extend the cost and time required for the project.

The IS auditor should be aware of risks associated with prototyping and ensure that the organization has implemented the proper controls to ensure that the project continues to meet the needs of the organization while providing a return on investment. These controls should be found in the project-management process as well as the change-control process. Both processes should have controls for the regular review and approval of changes in requirements, schedule, or cost.

RAD

Rapid application development (RAD) is used to develop strategically important systems faster, reduce development costs, and still maintain high quality. The organization should use a prototype that can be updated continually to meet changing user or business requirements. According to ISACA, this is achieved by using a series of proven application-development techniques within a well-defined methodology:

➤ Small, well-trained development teams

➤ Evolutionary prototypes

➤ Integrated power tools that support modeling, prototyping, and component reusability

➤ A central repository

➤ Interactive requirements and design workshops

➤ Rigid limits on development time frames

Although RAD supports analysis, design, development, and implementation, the initial development is based on requirements that are best understood. This reduces the time associated with traditional requirements gathering and documentation. The requirements (specification), development, and implementation are intertwined, allowing for the delivery of the application in phases. Most organizations have built their processes around a waterfall method of development and might not have the specialized skill sets or supporting processes required for RAD development. The IS auditor must ensure that the processes and skill sets support RAD development.

The Phases of the SDLC

As stated earlier, there are five distinct phases in the SDLC. In the Waterfall Model, each of these phases has specific tasks and outcomes; the next phase does not start until the tasks and outcomes of the previous phase have been completed. The SDLC helps to ensure the software will meet user and business needs. Therefore, failing to adopt a systematic approach to application development such as that illustrated by the SDLC increases the risk that the system will not ultimately meet business and user needs.

The following sections discuss the detailed tasks and outcomes associated with the five phases of the SDLC.

Phase 1: Feasibility

In this phase, the cost savings of a new system are identified and quantified, and the payback schedule for costs incurred in implementing the system is estimated.

This provides the justification for proceeding to Phase 2.

Phase 2: Requirements Definition

The need that requires resolution is defined and then mapped to the major requirements of the solution.

It is critical to involve all management and the end-user business function in this phase, to make sure the new system supports business needs:

➤ Users specify automated and nonautomated resource needs (access controls, regulatory restrictions, interface requirements, and so on) and how they want to have them addressed in the new system.

➤ The IS auditor should verify that requirements are complete, consistent, unambiguous, verifiable, modifiable, testable, and traceable.

➤ IS auditors should determine whether adequate security requirements have been defined for the new system.

Plans for testing for user acceptance are usually prepared in the requirements-definition phase of the systems-development project.

Phase 3: Design

Based on the requirements defined in Phase 2, a baseline of specifications for systems is established (application users need not be judiciously involved in this phase). The IS auditor should be allowed to participate in the design phase of the software in an overseeing advisory capacity: Establishing the baseline of specifications is one control used to prevent scope creep during the development phase. Scope creep occurs when new requirements are gradually added and exceed the requirements stated in the baseline of specifications. Although individual new requirements might appear small, they can have a cumulative effect on the cost or time associated with the project (scope creep).

➤ A formal change-control process is established to prevent entry of new requirements into the development process.

➤ Test plans are developed:

   ➤ Unit (program)

   ➤ Subsystem (module)

   ➤ Integration (system)

   ➤ Interface with other systems

   ➤ Loading and initializing files

   ➤ Security, backup, and recovery

➤ The IS auditor is involved to ensure that an adequate system of controls is incorporated into the system specs and test plans, and to ensure that continuous online auditing functions are built into the system.

Procedures to prevent scope creep are baselined in the design phase of the system's SDLC model.

Phase 4: Development

Programming and testing of the new system occurs in this phase. The tests verify and validate what has been developed. The responsibilities in this phase rest primarily with programmers and systems analysts who are building the system:

➤ Program coding standards are essential to simply and clearly reading and understanding code without requiring review of specifications.

➤ More cohesion (dedication to a single function) and less coupling (interaction with other functions) result in less troubleshooting and software-maintenance effort.

➤ Logic path monitors can provide programmers with clues on logic errors.

➤ Output analyzers validate processing accuracy.

➤ Online programming facilities can increase programming productivity but can also increase risk of inappropriate access. An online programming facility stores the program library on a server, and developers use individual PC workstations to download code to develop, modify, and test.

Online programming can lower development costs, reduce response time, and expand programming resources available. Its disadvantages, however, include reduced integrity of programming and processing; in addition, version control and valid changes can be overwritten by invalid changes.

Test plans identify specific portions of the application that will be tested, as well as the approach to testing:

➤ Bottom-up approach

   ➤ Start testing with programs or modules, and progress toward testing the entire system.

   ➤ Testing can be started before the entire system is complete.

   ➤ Errors in critical modules are found early.

➤ Top-down approach

  ➤ Tests of major functions or processes are conducted early.

  ➤ Interface errors can be detected sooner.

Testing levels identify the specific level of testing that will occur and are usually based on the size and complexity of the application:

➤ Unit testing

➤ Interface or integration testing

➤ System testing

➤ Recovery testing

➤ Security testing

➤ Stress/volume testing

➤ Performance testing

➤ Final acceptance testing

Phase 5: Implementation
Actual operation of the new system is established. Final user acceptance testing is conducted in this environment:

➤ May include certification and accreditation processes

➤ Includes implementation and migration plans. Implementation plans include procedures for setting up the production environment, connectivity and transaction testing, and user training. The migration plan includes data cleansing and conversion.

Project-Management Principles, Methods, and Practices

The organization must include formal project-management techniques in addition to the SDLC to ensure that the software-development project meets the stated objectives. The project-management team should follow the phases of the project life cycle (initiating, planning, executing, controlling, and project closing). The project-management team should develop a detailed plan and report all project activity against the plan, to ensure corrective action where needed. The software-development project should be assigned a project manager who is experienced in the area of software development and has skills associated with managing projects. The successful use of sound project-management techniques will help ensure a successful implementation and minimize the risk of failure because of late delivery, cost overruns, lack of functionality, or poor quality.

During the planning phase, the project-management team should set the time, cost, and scope of the project. In developing the project plan for a software-development project, the project-management team must determine the relative physical size of the software to be developed. In a software project, the planning team and project manager should determine the relative physical size of the software to be developed; this can be used as a guide for allocating and budgeting resources. The project-management team can use function point analysis (FPA) to provide an estimate of the size of an information system based on the number and complexity of a system's inputs, outputs, and files. Per ISACA, function points (FPs) are computed by first completing a table (see Table 6.2) to determine whether a particular task is simple, average, or complex. There are a total of five FP count values, which include the number of user inputs, user outputs, user inquiries, files, and external interfaces. Table 6.2 shows the formula for computing FP metrics.

Table 6.2 Computing Function Point Metrics					
Measurement Parameter	Count		Weighing Factor		
		Simple	Average	Complex	Results
Number of user inputs	× 3	4	6		=
Number of user outputs	× 4	5	7		=
Number of user inquiries	× 3	4	6		=
Number of files	× 7	10	15		=
Number of external interfaces	× 5	7	10		=
Count total:					

NOTE

Organizations that use FP methods develop criteria for determining whether a particular entry is simple, average, or complex.

After the table entries are completed, the organization can use the count totals and compute them through an algorithm. The results of this computation, which takes into account complexity values specific to the organization, are used to measure cost, schedule, productivity, and quality metrics (that is, productivity = FP/person-month, quality = defects/FP, and cost = $/FP).

When the size of the software-development project is determined, the project team should identify the resources required to complete each task. The project team then should develop a *work breakdown structure* that identifies specific tasks and the resources assigned those tasks, as well as project milestones and dependencies. The team should create Gantt charts to show timelines, milestones, and dependencies. A Gantt chart is a graphic representation of the timing and duration of the project phases; it typically includes start date, end date, and task duration.

Determining time and resource requirements for an application-development project is often the most difficult part of initial efforts in application development.

In addition, the project team should perform a *program evaluation review technique* (PERT).

PERT is the preferred tool for formulating an estimate of development project duration. A *PERT chart* depicts task, duration, and dependency information. The beginning of each chart starts with the first task, which branches out via a connecting line that contains three estimates:

➤ The first is the most optimistic time for completing the task.

➤ The second is the most likely scenario.

➤The third is the most pessimistic, or "worst case," scenario.

The line then is terminated to another node (identifying the start of another task). The chart is completed by connecting predecessor to successor from a network of tasks and connecting lines. The completed chart should depict all tasks coming together at the completion node. All tasks, including milestones, review points, and checkpoints, should be depicted on the chart to correctly estimate the total time associated with the plan. Figure 6.3 depicts an example of a PERT chart.

The calculation of PERT time uses the following formula:

Optimistic + pessimistic + (4 × most likely) / 6

So if you wanted to calculate the PERT time for the project using task 1 terminating at 2, you would apply the formula in this manner:

Task 1 to 2 – (2 + (4 × 5) + 7) / 6 = 4.8

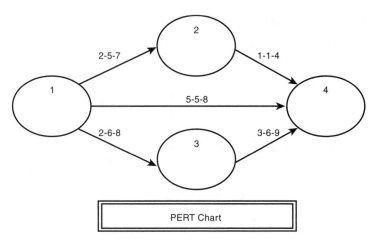

Figure 6.3 A PERT chart.

The numbers represent days, so the PERT time for task 1 would be 4.8 days.

  PERT considers different scenarios for planning and control projects.

After the project teams complete the project plan, they should monitor the progress of the project against the baseline plan using benchmarks, milestones, and deliverables. Any deviations from the plan must be addressed immediately to ensure that the project does not exceed the time and cost estimates.

Many factors can affect the time, cost, and, ultimately, success of a project. And IS auditor can look for some risk indicators in reviewing the project plan and implementation.

The Critical Path Methodology (CPM) is a project-management technique that analyzes successive activities within a project plan to determine the time required to complete a project and which activities are critical in maintaining the schedule. Critical activities have the least amount of flexibility, meaning that the completion time cannot be changed because it would delay the completion of the overall project. The successive critical activities are known as the critical path. The computation of all successive activities along the critical path predicts the required time to complete the project. The critical path of a project can be graphically represented with a diagram showing the relationship of critical activities.

The following are project planning risk indicators:

➤ The organization does not utilize a formal project-management methodology.

➤ The assigned project managers do not have the experience or skill sets to plan and manage software-development projects.

➤ The project has not been reviewed and approved by a steering committee, or does not have senior management support.

➤ Reviews of previous projects indicate that they have not met the business need or that they exceed time and cost estimates.

Application-Maintenance Principles

In conjunction with a formal SDLC and project-management activities, the organization must implement change-management processes, which include change-control procedures both for software-development projects and for the production environment. The change-management process, usually facilitated by the *change-control board* (CCB), reviews all changes associated with the software-development project. The CCB has the authority to accept, deny, or postpone a requested change. The change-management process ensures that any deviations from the original requirements are approved before being added to the project. This process ensures that all changes meet the needs of the organization and that any additional resources (time, money, or personnel) are balanced against the existing project requirements and approved resources. In addition, the change-management process provides a formal environment for the documentation of changes and the decision process.

A change request can generally be submitted by anyone associated with the development project, including the end users. The submitter of the change request should specify the change as well as the justification for the change. The users of the system should be part of the approval process. User approvals of program changes ensure that changes are correct as specified by the user and that they are authorized.

The presence of a change-management process ensures that subject matter experts (organization managers, IT management, security, and so on) are aware of proposed changes and their impact on current resources and the IT environment.

Programmers should perform unit, module, and full regression testing following any changes to an application or system.

The organization should implement *quality control* (QC) procedures to ensure that proper testing is performed through the development life cycle. The QC team is responsible for conducting code reviews and tests to ensure that software is free of defects and meets user expectations. Unit, module, and regression testing ensure that the specific unit or module is complete, performs as expected, and meets requirements. Regression testing should be required for all changes introduced into the system, whether in development or in production. The purpose of regression testing is to ensure that the change introduced does not negatively impact the system as a whole.

Post-Implementation Review Techniques

After development, testing, and implementation have been completed and the new system is part of the production environment, a formal post-implementation review should be performed. When reviewing an organization's systems-development process, the auditor should first compare established formal standards to actual observed procedures. The IS auditor should carefully review the functional requirements to ensure that the project objectives and requirements were met. The IS auditor should review the functional requirements and, based on the evidence found, perform other testing to confirm that the necessary controls and functionality are in place. The development of test transactions also can be performed, if necessary. During the review the IS auditor should look at system utilization, end user satisfaction with the system, and error logs to determine whether there are resource or operating problems. A system fails to meet the needs of the business and users most commonly because of inadequate user participation during the systems-requirements definition.

If the organization determined the cost benefit or performed ROI assessments as part of the feasibility study, the IS auditor should ensure that the metrics associated with the production system are being measured, analyzed, and reported. Overall, the post-implementation review should determine whether the development project achieved stated objectives and whether the process of development was performed in an efficient and effective manner. In addition, the post-implementation review should allow the organization to identify areas of improvement through lessons learned. When these improvements are implemented, they improve the overall capability and maturity of the organization's software-development process, thus maximizing benefits and reducing costs and risks.

Evaluating Application Systems Acquisition and Implementation

The IT organization is responsible for ensuring that the acquired solutions meet the objectives of the organization and reduce risk to the organization through the use of formal acquisition and implementation processes. The IS auditor should assess this process by reviewing control issues regarding acquisition and implementation. A comprehensive acquisition process should include clearly defined procedures for requirements gathering, feasibility studies, proposal creation, and vendor selection. Implementation of the applications should follow a documented system life-cycle development process (SDLC), as well as defined project-management and change-control procedures.

Application-Implementation Practices

The primary concern for an organization is to ensure that projects are consistently managed through a formal documented process. This process includes the SDLC, project management, change control, and policies/procedures aligned with the strategic plan. The introduction of new software, whether developed in-house or acquired, can affect systems and services if not implemented properly. All software should follow rigorous testing procedures and meet existing standards before being put into production. Before being added to the production environment, the software should undergo vulnerability testing to validate controls and to document and correct any deficiencies. The software should be added to existing procedures (backup, vulnerability testing, and patch/upgrade schedules) to ensure continued confidentiality, integrity, and availability of the software and its associated data. If an IS auditor observes that an IS department fails to use formal documented methodologies, policies, and standards, the auditor should at least document the informal standards and policies, and test for compliance. Furthermore, the IS auditor should recommend to management that formal documented policies be developed and implemented.

Application System-Acquisition Processes

The acquisition of software is driven by business requirements. The IT organization should have clearly defined acquisition procedures, including procedures for performing the feasibility study and requirements gathering. In conjunction with managers, the IT organization should analyze the requirements and create the feasibility study. This study helps determine whether the organization will "buy" or "build" the software to meet the needs of the organization. Although software acquisition is not part of the SDLC, it should have a formal documented process. According to ISACA, the project team, technical support staff, and key users should be asked to write a *request for proposal* (RFP). This RFP should be sent to a variety of vendors, and their responses (proposals) should be reviewed to determine which vendor's products offer the best solution.

 "Make vs. buy" decisions are typically made during the feasibility study phase of the software- or systems-development project.

After the vendors respond to the RFP with their proposals, the project team should review them for completeness and determine whether a single vendor can be chosen. If a vendor cannot be chosen based on the proposals, the project team should narrow the list to two or three vendors through a suitable methodology. This methodology should ensure that the same criteria are used in evaluating the vendors. This might require the project team to obtain additional information from the vendors (additional documentation or demonstrations) and to use a scoring methodology to determine which vendor is the best fit for the organization.

After the project team makes the selection, it must negotiate and sign a contract. Per ISACA, the contract should include the following items:

➤ A specific description of deliverables and their costs.

➤ Commitment dates for deliverables.

➤ Commitments for the delivery of documentation, fixes, upgrades, new release notifications, and training.

➤ Allowance for a software escrow agreement, if the deliverables do not include source code. (A clause for requiring source code escrow in an application vendor agreement is important to ensure that the source code remains available even if the application vendor goes out of business.)

➤ Description of the support to be provided during installation.

➤ Provision for a reasonable acceptance testing period, before the commitment to purchase is made.

➤ Allowance for changes to be made by the purchasing company.

➤ A maintenance agreement.

➤ Allowance for copying software for use in business continuity efforts and for test purposes.

➤ Payment schedule linked to actual delivery dates.

As an IS auditor, you should look for evidence of a structured approach to software acquisition. This includes acquisition procedures, defines the process for feasibility studies, and outlines a suitable methodology for the evaluation of proposals. After the software is acquired, there should be a project-management and change-control process to implement the software. All software acquired should be added to existing maintenance contracts, or a new maintenance contract should be acquired. Before being introduced into the production environment, the software should be tested according to written test plans, and responsibilities for the production software should be clearly defined. The software should be secured (physical, logical) and added to the business continuity plan.

Application Change Control and Emergency Change-Management Procedures

As stated in an earlier section, the change-management process ensures that any deviations from the original requirements are approved (or denied) and, if approved, are added to the project. There is one exception to the normal change-management process: the emergency change request used to correct immediate system problems that might affect critical services or processing. The difference between emergency changes and regular change requests is that the emergency change is corrected immediately and the change request (with supporting documentation) is completed after the fact. The organization should use emergency IDs to enable programmers and analysts to log in to the system and correct emergency problems. These IDs should be monitored and logged, and used only in the event of any emergency. The code associated with emergency changes should be stored in an emergency library until the change-control board has reviewed the request. When complete, the code should be moved to the production library. The IS auditor should review emergency change requests as well as the program change log to ensure that only authorized program changes were made.

Evaluating Application Systems

The IS auditor should review the application system to ensure the control aspects of the system development and implementation process meet the needs of the users as well as management objectives. IS auditors performing this audit should be independent and should not be involved in the system-development process. The IS auditor should assess whether the prescribed project management, SDLC, and change-management processes were followed. The IS auditor should ensure that proper testing procedures were used to validate user requirements and that the system's internal controls are working as intended.

Application Architecture

In addition to ensuring that systems within the application architecture meet the requirements and objectives of the organization, the IS auditor should review them to ensure that controls protect the confidentiality, integrity, and availability of both applications and data. In reviewing the application architecture, the application controls should ensure that information stored, delivered, and processed by applications is complete, accurate, and authorized. In developing control objectives, the IS auditor should keep in mind the following control categories:

➤ Security

➤ Input

➤ Processing

➤ Output

➤ Databases

➤ Backup and recovery

Section AI5 of COBIT ("Install and Accredit Systems") provides specific activities that an IS auditor should perform to ensure the effectiveness, efficiency, confidentiality, integrity, availability, compliance, and reliability of the IT system. Accreditation is a process by which an organization, through internal or third parties, IT services, or systems ensures adequate security and control exist. The COBIT activities associated with this objective are listed next.

The IS auditor should obtain the following:

➤ Organizational policies and procedures relating to system-development life cycle planning

➤ IT policies and procedures relating to security policies and committees; systems-development life cycle planning; systems-development testing procedures for programs, unit, and system test plans; training of users; migration of systems from test to production; and quality assurance and training

➤ System-development life cycle plan and schedule, and system-development life cycle programming standards, including the following:

➤ Change-request process

➤ Sample system-development effort status reports

➤ Post-implementation reports from earlier developmental efforts

In reviewing this information, the IS auditor should consider whether the following are true:

➤ Policies and procedures relating to the system-development life cycle process exist.

➤ A formal system-development life cycle methodology is in place for system installation and accreditation, including, but not limited to, a phased approach of training, performance sizing, conversion plan, testing of programs, groups of programs (units) and the total system, a parallel or prototype test plan, acceptance testing, security testing and accreditation, operational testing, change controls, and implementation and post-implementation review and modification.

➤ User training as part of each developmental effort is occurring.

➤ Program and system controls are consistent with security standards of the organization and IT policies, procedures, and standards.

➤ Various development, test, and production libraries exist for in-process systems.

➤ Predetermined criteria exist for testing success, failure, and termination of further efforts.

➤ The quality-assurance process includes independent migration of development into production libraries and completeness of required user and operations groups' acceptance.

➤ Test plans for simulation of volumes, processing intervals, and output availability, installation, and accreditation are part of the process.

➤ A training program associated with a sample of several system-development efforts contains the difference from the prior system, including changes affecting input, entry, processing, scheduling, distribution, interfaces to other systems, and errors and error resolution.

➤ Automated tools optimize systems developed, once in production, and these tools are being used for efficiency opportunities.

➤ Problem resolution is occurring, relating to less than optimal performance.

➤ User involvement and formal approval exist at each phase of the system-development process.

➤ A test plan is in place for programs, units, systems (including parallel or prototype), conversion, and implementation and post-implementation review.

➤ Appropriate consistency is being maintained with security and internal control standards.

➤ Appropriate data-conversion tasks and schedules exist.

➤ Testing occurs independently from development, modification, or maintenance of the system.

➤ Formal user acceptance of system functionality, security, integrity, and remaining risk has been obtained.

➤ Operations manuals include procedures for scheduling, running, restoring/restarting, backing up/backing out, and handling error resolution.

➤ Production libraries are physically and logically separate from development or test libraries.

Test and development environments should be separated to control the stability of the test environment.

Software Quality-Assurance Methods

The organization should ensure quality during the SDLC through testing. Testing should take place at a variety of levels and degrees, but the testing process should follow an accepted methodology. The testing process can be either a bottom-up or a top-down approach. Bottom-up testing starts at the smallest level of the application (modules and components) and works up through the application until full system testing is completed. The advantage of bottom-up testing is that it provides the capability to test single modules or components before the system is complete and allows for the early detection of errors. Top-down testing is usually used in RAD or prototype development and provides the capability to test complete functions within the system. It also allows for the early correction of interface errors. The approach for testing should include the following:

➤ **Development of a test plan**—Should include specific information on testing (I/O tests, length of test, expected results).

➤ **Testing**—Utilizes personnel and testing software, and then provides testing reports that compare actual results against expected results. Testing results remain part of the system documentation throughout the SDLC.

➤ **Defect management**—Defects are logged and corrected. Test plans are revised, if required, and testing continues until the tests produce acceptable results.

In addition to testing, the quality-assurance activities include ensuring that the processes associated with the SDLC meet prescribed standards. These standards can include documentation, coding, and management standards. The IS auditor should ensure that all activities associated with the SDLC meet the quality-assurance standards of the organization.

 Using a bottom-up approach to software testing often allows earlier detection of errors in critical modules.

Testing Principles, Methods, and Practices

To ensure that applications function as expected, meet the requirements of the organization, and implement proper controls, they must be tested. These tests ensure that both the modules and the entire system function as designed and that individual modules will not malfunction, negatively affecting the system. Whenever an application is modified, the entire program, including any interface systems with other applications or systems, should be tested to determine the full impact of the change. The following are the general testing levels:

➤ **Unit testing**—Used for testing individual modules, and tests the control structure and design of the module. Unit testing pertains to components within a system; system testing pertains to interfaces between application programs.

➤ **Interface/integration testing**—Used for testing modules that pass data between them. These test are used to validate the interchange of data and the connection among multiple system components.

➤ **System testing**—Used for testing all components of the system, and usually comprised of a series of tests. System testing is typically performed in a nonproduction environment by a test team.

➤ **Final acceptance testing**—Used to test two areas of quality assurance. Quality assurance testing (QAT) tests the technical functions of the system, and user acceptance testing (UAT) tests the functional areas of the system. These tests are generally performed independently from one another because they have different objectives.

 Above almost all other concerns, failing to perform user acceptance testing often results in the greatest negative impact on the implementation of new application software.

It is important for an IS auditor to know the testing levels as well as the different types of tests that can be performed. As part of an audit, the auditor should review test results that dictate a specific type of test to be performed, to ensure that controls are operating per the specification. As an example, you might observe that individual modules of a system perform correctly during development testing. You would then inform management of the positive results and recommend further comprehensive integration testing. Testing at different levels and with separate testing elements ensures that the system meets the detailed requirements, does not malfunction, and meets the needs of the users. The following are some of the specific types of tests that can be performed within the testing levels:

➤ **Whitebox testing**—Logical paths through the software are tested using test cases that exercise specific sets of conditions and loops. Whitebox testing is used to examine the internal structure of an application module during normal unit testing.

➤ **Blackbox testing**—This testing examines an aspect of the system with regard to the internal logical structure of the software. As an example of blackbox testing, the tester might know the inputs and expected outputs, but not system logic that derives the outputs. Whereas a whitebox test is appropriate for application unit testing, blackbox testing is used for dynamically testing software modules.

➤ **Regression testing**—A portion of the test scenario is rerun to ensure that changes or corrections have not introduced new errors, that bugs have been fixed, and that the changes do not adversely affect existing system modules. Regression testing should use data from previous tests to obtain accurate conclusions regarding the effects of changes or corrections to a program, and to ensure that those changes and corrections have not introduced new errors.

Regression testing is used in program development and change management to determine whether new changes have introduced any errors in the remaining unchanged code.

Exam Prep Questions

1. Software library control ensures that application programmers never have access to production application processing and that users do not have access to source code. Which of the following statements is NOT true regarding the software librarian's access to code or data?

   ❏ A. The software librarian does not have read-write access to application source code used by programmers.

   ❏ B. The software librarian has read-only access to application production code.

   ❏ C. The software librarian does not have access to live data.

   ❏ D. The software librarian has read access to test data.

   Answer: B. Library control software restricts source code to read-only access. All other statements are true.

2. The use of decision trees implemented by leading users through a series of questions or choices from a knowledge base to compute a logical finding is implemented by which of the following?

   ❏ A. Expert systems

   ❏ B. Artificial neural networks (ANN)

   ❏ C. Critical path analysis

   ❏ D. Function point analysis

   Answer: A. Decision trees use questionnaires to lead the user through a series of choices to reach a conclusion. Artificial neural networks attempt to emulate human thinking by analyzing many attributes of knowledge to reach a conclusion. Critical path analysis is used in project management. Function point analysis is used in determining a proposed software application's size for development planning purposes.

3. Which of the following goals is MOST important to a system-development project?

   ❏ A. The system to be developed makes the most efficient use of current IT resources.

   ❏ B. The system to be developed does not compromise the security of existing systems and controls.

   ❏ C. The system to be developed meets organizational goals and objectives.

   ❏ D. The system to be developed is approved by the project feasibility committee.

   Answer: C. A primary high-level goal for an auditor who is reviewing a system-development project is to ensure that business objectives are achieved. This objective guides all other systems-development objectives.

4. When analyzing and developing a new system, when should security first be considered?

- ❏ A. During the feasibility study of the proposed system
- ❏ B. During the development of the software project's functional specifications
- ❏ C. During user acceptance testing
- ❏ D. During the system development

Answer: B. Application controls should be considered as early as possible in the system-development process, even in the development of the project's functional specifications. Success of all other phases relies upon proactive security controls planning.

5. An IS auditor is reviewing an organization's change-development process and finds that the development calls for using fourth-generation programming languages (4GLs). Which of the following statements is NOT true regarding 4GLs?

- ❏ A. 4GLs provide extensive lower-level detail commands necessary to perform data-intensive or online operations.
- ❏ B. 4GLs can use simple language subsets, which can be utilized by lesser-skilled users.
- ❏ C. 4GLs make extensive use of object-oriented programming concepts.
- ❏ D. 4GLs are often platform portable.

Answer: A. Fourth-generation languages (4GLs) are most appropriate for designing the application's graphical user interface (GUI). They are inappropriate for designing any intensive data-calculation procedures. All other statements are true.

6. Within the Software Capability Maturity Model, Level 3, "Defined" best describes which of the following?

- ❏ A. Develop and apply quantitative managed control over software-development processes.
- ❏ B. Management processes are established to oversee the project to plan and track cost, schedule, and functionality. Successfully defined and applied processes can be repeated on another project of similar size and scope.
- ❏ C. The organization improves upon managed development by implementing continuous process-improvement strategies facilitated by innovative solutions and state-of-the-art technologies.
- ❏ D. Repeatable processes are used to develop a standard software-development process across the organization.

Answer: D. A standard software-development process is included within Level 3 (Defined) of the software capability maturity model (CMM). Answer A describes CMM phase 4, "Managed." Answer B describes CMM phase 2, "Repeatable." Answer C describes CMM phase 5, "Optimized."

7. An organization's software-development projects are planned according to formal software Development Life Cycle (SDLC) processes. In which of the following phases would the software-development project's baselines and scope be established?

- ❏ A. Feasibility
- ❏ B. Requirements definition
- ❏ C. Design
- ❏ D. Development
- ❏ E. Implementation

Answer: C. Although all answers are valid SDLC phases, procedures to prevent scope creep are baselined in the design phase of the systems-development life cycle (SDLC) model.

8. In planning a new software-application development project, function point analysis (FPA) can be used to understand the potential size of a projected application. Which of the following best describes how FPA works?

- ❏ A. Based upon the number of function lines of source code, FPA can estimate the size of a software application.
- ❏ B. Based upon the number of functional intersections of source code design, FPA can estimate the size of a software application.
- ❏ C. Based upon the number of function application calls within an application, FPA can estimate the size of a software application.
- ❏ D. Based upon the number and complexity of inputs and files that a user interacts with, FPA can estimate the size of a software application.

Answer: D. Function point analysis (FPA) provides an estimate of the size of an information system based on the number and complexity of a system's inputs, outputs, and files. All other answers are misleaders.

9. When assessing the potential scope of an application-development project, which of the following provides the most reliable estimate of the size of an information system?

- ❏ A. Critical path analysis
- ❏ B. Function point analysis
- ❏ C. Program evaluation review technique
- ❏ D. Rapid application development

Answer: B. A function point analysis (FPA) is a reliable technique for estimating the scope and cost of a software-development project. PERT is used in both the planning and control of projects for network management. RAD is a methodology that enables organizations to develop strategically important systems more quickly and to reduce development costs. Critical path analysis is a process for finding the shortest project duration by optimizing utilization of project resources.

10. When auditing software change-control practices, which of the following is considered MOST important to the IS auditor?

 ❏ A. Change requests are well documented with thorough specifications.

 ❏ B. Change requests provide need justification.

 ❏ C. Appropriate business process user approval is obtained before change implementation.

 ❏ D. Business process users are informed about the change before implementation.

Answer: C. Although all answers are recognized as good practices, the IS auditor is primarily concerned with having the change properly evaluated and approved by business process users before implementation.

Business Process Evaluation and Risk Management

Key concepts you will need to understand:

- ✓ Methods and approaches for designing and improving business procedures (e-business, B2B, BPR)
- ✓ Business process controls (management, automated, and manual controls)
- ✓ Business performance indicators (balanced scorecard, key performance indicators [KPI])

- ✓ Business project organization, management, and control practices
- ✓ Project progress monitoring and reporting mechanisms
- ✓ Project success criteria and pitfalls
- ✓ Corporate governance risk and control frameworks

Techniques you will need to master:

- ✓ Evaluate the efficiency and effectiveness of information systems in supporting business processes, through techniques such as benchmarking, best practice analysis, or business process re-engineering (BPR), to ensure optimization of business results
- ✓ Evaluate the design and implementation of programmed and manual controls to

ensure that identified risks to business processes are at an acceptable level
- ✓ Evaluate business process change projects to ensure that they are properly organized, staffed, managed, and controlled
- ✓ Evaluate the organization's implementation of risk management and governance

Evaluating IS Efficiency and Effectiveness of Information Systems in Supporting Business Processes

The evaluation of the efficiency and effectiveness of an organization's IT program involves reviewing the IT governance structure as well as its alignment with the organization's strategy. The IT organization must also manage the risks associated with ongoing development and operations. The IT organization should have a risk-management program that utilizes internal controls and best practices to mitigate risks to an acceptable level. As a part of risk management, the IT organization should have formal documented methodologies for managing business process change to include organization, management, controls, and measurement. The IS auditor should ensure that IT is aligned with corporate goals and that the benefit of IT is maximized while risk is minimized.

Methods and Approaches for Designing and Improving Business Procedures

The standard approach to improving business processes is to identify specific areas to be reviewed, document the existing baseline process(es), and identify areas for improvement. After improvement areas have been identified, they should be presented to senior management for prioritization and implementation. Upon implementation of the business processes, the organization should monitor the new processes against the baseline and establish a continuous improvement process. Known as *business process re-engineering* (BPR), this usually successfully reduces manual interventions and controls within the organization.

Benchmarking

ISACA defines *benchmarking* as the continuous, systematic process of evaluating the products, services, and work processes of organizations, recognized as representing best practices for the purpose of organizational improvement. The purpose of identifying a benchmarking partner is to find a work process in your industry that is identified as having the qualities that your organization would like to re-engineer to (success, quality, excellence, and so on). ISACA outlines the following steps in a benchmarking exercise:

1. **Plan.** In the planning stage, critical processes are identified for the benchmarking exercise. The benchmarking team should identify the critical processes and understand how they are measured, what kind of data is needed, and how that data needs to be collected.

2. **Research.** The team should collect baseline data about its own processes before collecting this data about others. The next step is to identify the benchmarking partners through sources such as business newspapers and magazines, quality award winners, and trade journals.

3. **Observe.** The next step is to collect data and visit the benchmarking partner. There should be an agreement with the partner organization, a data-collection plan, and a method to facilitate proper observation.

4. **Analyze.** This step involves summarizing and interpreting the data collected, analyzing the gaps between an organization's process and its partner's process, and converting key findings into new operational goals.

5. **Adapt.** Adapting the results of benchmarking can be the most difficult step. In this step, the team needs to translate the findings into a few core principles and work down from the principles to strategies and action plans.

6. **Improve.** Continuous improvement is the key focus in a benchmarking exercise. Benchmarking links each process in an organization with an improvement strategy and organizational goals.

Benchmarking partners are identified in the research stage of the benchmarking process.

The IS auditor must ensure that the change efforts are consistent with the culture and strategic plan of the organization, and that the change efforts reduce negative impact on the organization's staff. In addition, the auditor must ensure that key controls, if required, are engineered into the new process. If key controls are removed as a part of the re-engineering effort, the IS auditor must ensure that all risks associated with these controls are communicated to and accepted by management.

This benchmarking methodology assumes that organizations will be able to find partner organizations that will agree to review and observation. In today's competitive market, most organizations turn to professional consulting companies that have performed business process re-engineering across industries and use the information gathered during those engagements to compare to their organization.

Business Process Re-engineering (BPR)

In today's competitive landscape, the continuous improvement of business processes no longer ensures an organization's survival. Business change is primarily driven by customer needs for new and improved products and services. If an organization cannot provide these products and services, customers have the option of turning to other organizations that can provide these products and services. Business process re-engineering (BPR) provides an accelerated means of process improvement by assuming that existing business processes do not work; therefore, the re-engineering effort can focus on a new processes by defining a future state (to be).

After the future state has been defined, the re-engineering team can create an action plan based on the gap between current processes and the future state. The re-engineering team and management then can create the transition plan and begin to implement the changes. To help ensure the success of the re-engineering effort, determining the scope of areas to be reviewed should be the first step in the business process re-engineering project. In defining specific areas for improvement, the organization can ensure that the effort focuses on value and customer requirements.

As organizations work to drive time and cost out of business processes, they often turn to technology as a solution. The advent of new technologies such as the Internet has allowed organizations to rapidly bring new capabilities that dramatically improve business processes. The availability of new technologies and the drive for rapid implementation could put the organization at risk by driving key controls out of improved business processes and lacking key controls in new business processes. An IS auditor should always make sure that a re-engineered business process has not inadvertently removed key controls from the previous control environment.

 Whenever business processes have been re-engineered, the IS auditor should attempt to identify and quantify the impact of any controls that have been removed, or controls that might not work as effectively after a business process changes.

The implementation of BPR affects the culture, structure, and direction of the organization. Generally, the largest impact of re-engineering is on the staff. The organization should have a change-management process and teams that can evaluate possible issues or problems that might arise and that can provide solutions. The change-management team should monitor the re-engineering process to ensure that it is meeting the strategic plan and goals of the organization. As the re-engineering is implemented, the organization should see improvements in products, services, and profitability. The proper implementation of technology should reduce manual intervention and controls, producing an accelerated production and delivery of products and services.

Business process re-engineering often results in increased automation, which results in a greater number of people using technology.

A couple emerging business and technology trends illustrate these improvements. The first is *customer relationship management* (CRM), which focuses on managing detailed customer information. This might include previous transactions and customer requirements, allowing organizations to match customer needs to products and services. A CRM system usually integrates a database, web technologies, telephony, accounting, and fulfillment systems. This integration enables organizations to capture transaction data, customer preferences, order status, and demographic information. This gives an organization a complete view of its customers across all business units and product lines, and enables it to proactively identify which products or services the customer might need.

The second, *supply chain management* (SCM), is the improvement of an organization's product and service design, purchasing, invoicing, distribution, and customer service. The implementation of SCM involves streamlining the supply chain through the collaboration of entities in real time and the realization of *just-in-time* (JIT) delivery. JIT delivery reduces the overall cycle time associated with manufacture and inventory by creating products and services based on customer demand.

One of the technologies associated with SCM is the process of *electronic funds transfer* (EFT). EFT is an electronic payment process between buyers and sellers that is very efficient because it reduces paper transactions and manual intervention.

EFT systems are more efficient than traditional paper checks for accounts payable disbursements.

Business Performance Indicators

After an organization has developed a strategic plan and defined its goals, it must measure its progress toward these goals. *Key performance indicators* (KPI) are quantifiable measurements that are developed and accepted by senior management. Key performance indicators vary by organization but are created as long-term measurements of an organization's operational activities against its goals. The organization uses quantifiable measurements that ensure the measurement of expected outcomes as opposed to activities. As an example of a goal, the IT organization would expect to deliver services in accordance with *service-level agreements* (SLA). The IT organization would measure actual service levels against the SLA, identify gaps, and define controls to proactively reduce the service-level failures to meet the SLA.

Some organizations tend to measure things that are easy to measure instead of those that are critical to the organization meeting its goals. These types of measurements might include the number of events but not the expected outcome from the events. To ensure that KPIs are understandable and do not detract from the organization's mission, they should be kept to a minimum of three to five. The use of KPIs provides management with a compass that allows for course corrections in meeting organizational goals and a communication tool for the entire organization defining the importance of achieving these goals.

Another way to measure organizational performance is the balanced scorecard. The balanced scorecard is a management tool that clarifies an organization's goals, and defines actions and the measurement of those actions to meet goals. The balanced scorecard differs from previous methodologies, in that it combines measurement of all business processes. This allows managers to see the organization from many different perspectives and identify areas for improvement. The balanced scorecard incorporates measurements of financial performance, customer satisfaction, business processes, and the capability to improve business processes. ISACA defines the application of the balanced scorecard to IT as a three-layered structure that addresses the four perspectives through the following.

Mission:

➤ To be a preferred supplier of information systems

➤ To deliver effective and efficient applications and services

➤ To obtain reasonable business contribution of IT investments

➤ To develop opportunities to answer future challenges

Strategies:

➤ Use preferred suppliers of application and operations

➤ Foster user partnerships and greater customer service

➤ Pursue efficient and economical developments and operations

➤ Control IT objectives

➤ Provide business value to IT projects

➤ Provide new business capabilities

➤ Train and educate IT staff, and promote excellence

➤ Provide support for research and development

Measures:

➤ Provide a balanced set of metrics to guide business-oriented IT decisions

Table 7.1 integrates the ISACA example and shows some possible measures associated with a balanced scorecard.

Table 7.1	Balanced Scorecard Perspectives, Objectives, and Measures	
Perspective	**Objective**	**Measure**
Customer	• Use preferred suppliers of information systems, applications, and operations • Foster user partnerships and greater customer service	Client/customer satisfaction Service-level agreements met Systems, applications, and operations controls meet control objectives
Financial	• Deliver efficient and effective applications and services • Obtain reasonable business contribution of IT investments • Pursue efficient and economical development and operations	Total operational and development costs Commitments met, project estimates Requirements met, post-implementation review
Internal business processes	• Provide support for research and development • Control IT Objectives • Provide business value to IT projects • Develop opportunities to answer future challenges	Best practices adopted New opportunities realized IT strategic plan aligned with business strategy

(continued)

Table 7.1 Balanced Scorecard Perspectives, Objectives, and Measures *(continued)*		
Perspective	Objective	Measure
Growth and learning	• Provide new business capabilities • Train and educate IT personnel, and promote excellence • Provide a balanced set of metrics to guide business-oriented IT decisions	Employees in developmental assignments Employee satisfaction Core competency profile IT mission and strategy clearly defined

Evaluating the Design and Implementation of Programmed and Manual Controls

Chapter 6, "Business Application System Development, Acquisition, Implementation, and Maintenance," discussed the review of general controls, which include the controls over project and change management, systems development, operations and maintenance, and network operations. This section discusses *application controls*, which relate directly to the functions (input, processing, and output) performed by applications. Application controls are used to ensure that only accurate, complete, and authorized data is entered into a system. These controls can be either manual or automated and ensure the following:

➤ Valid, accurate, and complete data is entered into the system.

➤ Processing of data is accurate and performs the function(s) it was created for.

➤ The processing of data and results meet expectations.

➤ The data is maintained to ensure validity, accuracy, and completeness.

Manual controls include checks performed by IT staff and IS auditors such as the review of error logs, reconciliations, and exception reports. *Automated controls* include programming logic, validation and edit checks, and programmed control functions.

ISACA recommends that the testing of automated controls include the use of manual procedures to ensure proper investigation of exceptions and that the IS auditor's tasks include the following:

➤ Identifying application components and transaction flow through those components, and gaining an understanding of the system by reviewing system documentation and performing interviews

➤ Applying the appropriate audit procedures to test control strengths and weaknesses, and evaluate the impact of control weaknesses

➤ Analyzing test results and audit evidence to determine whether the control objectives were achieved within the control environment

➤ Ensuring the application's operational effectiveness and efficiency by comparing the application with efficient programming standards, and comparing systems functionality to management objectives for the system

Business Process Controls

The IS auditor should use a combination of manual review (system documentation and logs), observations, integrated test facilities, and embedded audit modules. The IS auditor must review application controls, data integrity controls, and controls associated with business systems and components. These components might include electronic data interchange (EDI) and electronic funds transfers (EFT).

In reviewing application controls, the IS auditor should review the following areas:

➤ Input/output controls

  ➤ Input authorization

  ➤ Batch controls

➤ Processing control procedures

  ➤ Processing

  ➤ Validation

  ➤ Editing

➤ Output controls

  ➤ Critical forms logging and security

  ➤ Negotiable instruments logging and security (signatures)

  ➤ Report distribution

  ➤ Balancing and reconciliation

➤ Output error handling

➤ Output report retention

An IS auditor must first understand relative business processes before performing an application audit. This can be accomplished by reviewing the business plan, the IT strategic plan (long and short term), and organizational goals.

Input/Output Controls

In auditing input and output controls, the auditor must ensure that all transactions have been received, processed, and recorded accurately, and that the transactions are valid and authorized. The auditor should review access controls and validation and edit checks. It is important to remember that in an integrated environment, the output of one system could be the input to another system. Input/output controls should be implemented for both the sending and receiving applications.

Input Authorization

Input can be either automated or manual, and it ensures that only authorized transactions are entered into the system for processing. Manual controls can include reports generated by the system that list transactions requiring manual authorization or source documents containing signatures. Some systems employ an automated control to provide authorization for data exceptions. An example is a sales transaction in which the price of the product is being reduced. The salesperson might not be authorized to reduce the price, but an automated request could be sent to a supervisor. The supervisor would then log in with a second-level password to authorize the price change.

A second-level password is an automated process to facilitate the approval of transaction data exceptions.

When using manual controls, the organization must ensure that all documents are controlled and that procedures exist to ensure that they have been accounted for. Automated access controls include the following:

➤ **Online controls**—Authorized individuals or systems are authenticated before performing sensitive functions

➤ **Client identification**—Specific workstations and individuals are authenticated before performing sensitive functions

Batch Controls

A batch control transaction summarizes totals of transactions within a batch. This transaction can be based on monetary amount, total items, total documents, or hash totals. These totals can be compared to the source documents to ensure that all items have accurate input. In addition, control totals ensure that the data input is complete and should be implemented as early as data preparation to support data integrity. Hash totals are generated by selecting specific fields in a series of transactions or records. If a later summation does not produce the number, this indicates that records have been lost, entered or transmitted incorrectly, or duplicated.

Hash totals are used as a control to detect loss, corruption, or duplication of data.

Processing, Validation, and Editing

Data validation is used to identify errors in data regarding completeness, inconsistencies, duplicates, and reasonableness. Edit controls perform the same function as data-validation controls but are generally used after data has been entered but before it is processed. Table 7.2, created by ISACA, describes edit checks.

Table 7.2 Data-Validation Edits and Controls	
Validation Edits	**Description**
Sequence check	A sequence check ensures that data falls within a range sequence and that no values are missing or outside the sequence range. The sequence check uses the last known valid number as the first number and the last number in the sequence, and ensures that data falls sequentially within that range. An example would be to ensure that all check numbers in a system fall within an acceptable range (such as 1–100) and that all checks fall within that range, with no missing checks.
Limit check	A limit check verifies that the data in the transaction does not exceed a predetermined limit.
Range check	A range check verifies that data is within a predetermined range of values. An example would be a check to ensure that the data falls between two dates (such as 1/1/2005 and 6/1/2005).

(continued)

Table 7.2   Data-Validation Edits and Controls *(continued)*

Validation Edits	Description
Validity check	A validity check uses predetermined criteria to check data validity.
Reasonableness check	A reasonableness check is a data-validation edit control that matches input data to an occurrence rate. In other words, the data is within reasonable limits.
Table look-ups	This check ensures that data entered complies with predetermined values in a corresponding table.
Existence check	An existence check ensures that required data is entered correctly according to predetermined criteria.
Key verification	Key verification is an edit check ensuring input integrity by having initial input re-entered by a second employee before the transaction can occur.
Check digit	A check digit is an effective edit check to detect data transposition and transcription errors. A check digit is a sum of the numeric value of the data and is appended to the data to ensure that the original data has not been altered or is not incorrect.
Completeness check	A completeness check is an edit check to determine whether a field contains valid data and is not null or filled with zeros or blanks.
Duplicate check	A duplicate check ensures that the new data being input does not already exist as a prior transaction.
Logical relationship check	A logical relationship utilizes logic, in that if a particular condition is true, one or more additional conditions or data-input relationships might be required to be true. Performing a check for logical relationships is useful for detecting errors such as incorrect birth dates or marriage dates.

Data edits are implemented before processing and are considered preventative integrity controls.

During the review of input processing, the IS auditor can compare the transaction journal to authorized source documents. The transaction journal records all transaction activity and provides the information necessary for detecting unauthorized input from a terminal and completeness of transactions.

Processing Control Procedures

Processing controls ensure that data is accurate and complete, and is processed only through authorized routines. The processing controls can be programmed controls that detect and initiate corrective action, or edit checks that ensure completeness, accuracy, and validity. Processing controls also include manual controls, such as these:

➤ **Manual recalculation**—Periodic sample transaction groups can be recalculated to ensure that processing is performing as expected.

➤ **Run-to-run totals**—These verify data values throughout the various stages of application processing. They are an effective control to detect accidental record deletion in transaction-based applications.

Output Controls

Output controls ensure that information resulting from processing will be delivered in a consistent and secure manner to authorized persons. Per ISACA, output controls include the following:

➤ Logging and storage of negotiable, sensitive, and critical forms in a secure place. These types of forms should be properly logged and secured to protect against theft or damage.

➤ Computer generation of negotiable instruments, forms, and signatures. This type of output should be properly controlled. The organization should enable logging to provide a detailed listing of generation, and it should be compared with the forms received.

➤ Report distribution. Reports can be distributed manually or automatically, but they should follow authorized distribution procedures. All reports should be logged. When automatic reports are distributed either electronically or to print devices, access-control procedures should ensure that only authorized personnel have access to the reports.

➤ Balancing and reconciling. All output from applications should be logged via transaction logs. The output should be routinely balanced to control totals.

➤ Output error handling. Procedures should exist for the controlling, logging, and reporting of output errors. The output transaction originators should be notified of errors in a timely manner for review and error correction.

➤ Output report retention. Policies and procedures regarding record retention should be adhered to. The retention policy should ensure compliance with any legal regulations.

Data Integrity Controls

Data is stored in the form of files and databases. Data integrity testing ensures the completeness, accuracy, consistency, and authorization of data. This differs from application testing because it tests data that is stored within a system after input and processing. The testing of stored data might uncover weaknesses in input/output or processing controls. Two types of tests are associated with data integrity:

➤ **Referential integrity tests**—Referential integrity works within a relational data model within a database and ensures that the relationships between two or more references are consistent. If the data in one reference is inserted, deleted, or updated, the integrity to the second reference is maintained through the use of primary and foreign keys. Disabling referential integrity controls can result in invalid transactions, such as a payment to a vendor that is never recorded to the vendor payment database.

➤ **Relational integrity tests**—These tests ensure that validation (either application or database) routines check data before entry into the database.

Electronic Data Interchange (EDI)

The purpose of EDI is to promote a more efficient and effective data-exchange process by reducing paper, errors, and delays. In using EDI, organizations with dissimilar computer systems facilitate the exchange and transmittal of information such as product orders, invoices, and business documents. This is accomplished through standardizing the format of data and transmitting the data between systems. Organizations must ensure proper authentication techniques for sending and receiving data between EDI systems, to prevent unauthorized transactions. Transaction authorization is a primary security concern in EDI environments.

Traditionally, EDI systems contain the following components:

➤ **Communications handler**—A process for transmitting and receiving electronic documents between trading partners via dial-up lines, the Public Switched Telephone Network (PSTN), multiple dedicated lines, or value-added networks.

A communications handler is an EDI component that transmits and receives documents.

➤ **EDI interface**—This manipulates and routes data between the application system and the communications handler.

➤ **EDI translator**—This translates between data formats.

➤ **Applications interface**—This moves transactions to or from the application systems and performs data mapping. The EDI interface can ensure the validity of transactions and trading partners by checking information against a trading partner master file. After validation, the EDI interface generates and sends a *functional acknowledgment*. A functional acknowledgment is a message transmitted from the receiver of an electronic submission to the sender; it notifies the sender that the document was received/processed or was not processed. Functional acknowledgments provide an audit trail for EDI transactions.

Functional acknowledgments can be implemented in the EDI interface to provide efficient data mapping.

➤ **Application system**—This processes the data sent to or received from a trading partner.

When reviewing an EDI environment, it is important to remember that the EDI environment consists of software that transmits, translates, and stores transactions for processing. Network environments can often add to the complexity of program-to-program communication, making application systems implementation and maintenance more difficult.

Organizations that exchange data via EDI should have a trading partner agreement. The trading partner agreement defines the responsibilities of both organizations with regard to the handling and processing of transactions. The IS auditor should ensure that all transactions are accurately sent and received, translated, processed once, and accessed by authorized parties.

ISACA recommends the following tasks for the IS auditor in reviewing EDI controls:

➤ Inbound EDI transactions that use public Internet infrastructures should utilize encryption to ensure confidentiality, authenticity, and integrity.

➤ All inbound EDI transactions should be logged. Edit checks should be used to identify erroneous, unusual, or invalid transactions.

➤ Inbound and outbound transaction message counts (sent/received) should be logged and periodically reconciled between trading partners.

➤ Outbound EDI transactions should be compared to the trading partner master file before transmission, to ensure that transactions are being sent to authorized trading partners.

➤ Authority to initiate, authorize, and transmit transactions should be properly segregated.

Evaluating Business Process Change Projects

In evaluating business process change projects, the IS auditor should ensure that the change efforts meet the goals defined in the strategic plan, as well as the culture of the organization. The IS auditor should ensure that the organization has clearly defined the areas for review, and developed a project plan organization that will use proper project and change management processes.

The project plan should ensure that the goals of the business process re-engineering effort are met and fulfill organizational goals. The project should have a detailed plan with an assigned project manager who is experienced with business process re-engineering. A change-management team and plan should be established with mitigation plans for possible issues or problems during the re-engineering effort. The change-management team should assist the staff in transitioning to the re-engineered business process, as well as monitoring the project's progress toward the re-engineering goals and strategic plan.

As stated in the section "IS Project-Management Strategies and Policies" in Chapter 2, "Management, Planning, and Organization of IS," the IS auditor should look for the following risk indicators when auditing the business process re-engineering project:

➤ BPR project leaders have insufficient domain expertise.

➤ BPR project teams are unqualified to handle project size/complexity.

➤ BPR project team members are dissatisfied.

➤ The BPT project does not include input from all affected parties.

➤ BPR project recipients are dissatisfied with project outcomes.

➤ The BPR project has a high staff turnover rate.

Evaluating the Implementation of Risk Management and Governance

IT governance encompasses the information systems, strategy, and people. This control helps ensure that IT is aligned with the organization's strategy and goals. The board of directors and executive officers are ultimately accountable for functionality, reliability, and security within IT governance.

Within the IT governance structure, there should be clearly defined roles and responsibilities. The IT department should implement best practices in its operational and development methodology and should have a structured approach to project and change management. Overall, the IT governance structure ensures the efficient and effective use of resources in the secure and reliable deployment and maintenance of information systems.

An important area of IT governance is risk management. Risk management is the process that enables IT managers to balance the operational and economic costs of protective measures, and achieve gains in mission objectives by protecting the IT systems and data that support business objectives. In the development of a risk-management plan, ISACA states that the organization must do the following:

➤ Establish the purpose of the risk-management program. In establishing the purpose for the program, the organization will be better prepared to evaluate the results and determine its effectiveness.

➤ Assign responsibility for the risk-management plan. To ensure the success of the risk-management plan, the organization should designate an individual or team responsible for developing and implementing the risk-management plan. The team should coordinate efforts across the organization in identifying risks and defining strategies to mitigate the risk.

As stated in Chapter 1, "The Information Systems (IS) Audit Process," risk can be defined as the possibility of something adverse happening. Risk management is the process of assessing risk, taking steps to reduce risk to an acceptable level (mitigation), and maintaining that level of risk. In developing the risk-management plan, the organization should identify organizational assets as well as the threats and vulnerabilities associated with these assets. After identifying potential vulnerabilities, the IS auditor should perform a business impact analysis (BIA) of the threats that would exploit the vulnerabilities.

Threats exploit vulnerabilities to cause loss or damage to the organization and its assets.

The IS auditor can use qualitative or quantitative analysis during the BIA to assess the potential impacts, or degree of loss, associated with the assets. *Quantitative* impacts are easily measured because they can result in a direct loss of money, opportunity, or disruption. *Qualitative* impacts are harder to measure because they result in losses associated with damage to reputation, endangerment of staff, or breach of confidence. In other words, a quantitative approach attempts to assign real numbers to the cost of threats and the amount of damage, whereas a qualitative approach uses a ranking method to analyze the seriousness of the threat against the sensitivity of the asset.

Quantitative risk analysis is not always possible because the IS auditor is attempting to calculate risk using nonquantifiable threats and potential losses. In this event, a qualitative risk assessment is more appropriate.

When the BIA is complete, the organization must determine whether the risk is acceptable. If not, the IS auditor can evaluate the existing controls or design new controls to reduce the vulnerabilities to an acceptable level of risk. The controls, called countermeasures, can be actions, devices, procedures, or techniques. After the organization has applied controls to the asset, the remaining risk is called *residual risk*. The organization's management sets acceptable risk levels; if the residual risk falls below that level, further controls are not required. The IS auditor can evaluate this control to see whether an excessive level of control is being used. The removal of excessive controls can result in cost savings to the organization. The organization's acceptance of residual risk takes into account the organizational policy, risk-management plan and measurement, and the cost-effectiveness of implementing controls.

The risk-management process provides management with an effective method of understanding risk and achieving a cost-effective balance when applying countermeasures. The risk-management program must be supported by senior management and must have a designated individual or team to be successful.

In most organizations, the executive director works with the board of directors to define the purpose for the risk-management program. In clearly defining the risk-management program goals, senior management can evaluate the results of risk management and determine its effectiveness. The risk-management team should be utilized at all levels within the organization and needs the help of the operations staff and board members to identify areas of risk and to develop suitable mitigation strategies.

Exam Prep Questions

1. Which of the following processes is MOST important to ensure that implementation of applications and systems is optimized to the organization's goals and objectives?

   ❑ A. Obtaining a comprehensive network diagram

   ❑ B. Reviewing the organization's IT policies and procedures

   ❑ C. Obtaining a thorough understanding of the organization's business processes

   ❑ D. Performing compliance testing on current controls

   Answer: C. An IS auditor must first understand relative business processes before performing a systems or application audit. All other answers describe processes to be performed after obtaining a thorough understanding of the organization's business processes.

2. Processing controls should ensure that:

   ❑ A. All data is accurate

   ❑ B. All data is complete

   ❑ C. All transactions are authorized

   ❑ D. All of the above

   Answer: D. Processing controls ensure that data is accurate and complete, and is processed only through authorized routines.

3. Which of the following must be proven to ensure message or transaction nonrepudiation?

   ❑ A. The integrity of the message or transaction cannot have been compromised after it was last controlled by the party sending the message or performing the transaction.

   ❑ B. The level of nonrepudiation is tightly linked to the strength of authentication of the party sending the message or performing the transaction.

   ❑ C. Both A and B are true.

   ❑ D. Neither A nor B is true.

   Answer: C. Nonrepudiation is provided by having proof that an action occurred and proof of the identity of the party performing the action.

4. These are steps included in business process re-engineering:

   a. Gain an understanding of the business process to be reviewed

   b. Establish a continuous improvement process

   c. Redesign and streamline the process

   d. Define the areas to be reviewed

   e. Implement and monitor the new process

   f. Develop a project plan

What is the proper sequence of these steps?

- ❏ A. d, f, a, c, e, b
- ❏ B. a, f, d, c, e, b
- ❏ C. f, a, d, c, e, b
- ❏ D. d, a, f, c, e, b

Answer: A. Answer A describes the correct sequence of steps performed in business process re-engineering. All other answers are out of proper sequence.

5. An organization has automated data transfer between two database applications. How should controls be implemented to ensure data integrity?

- ❏ A. Input controls on the application sending the data, and output controls on the application receiving the data
- ❏ B. Input and output controls on both the sending and receiving applications
- ❏ C. Output controls on the application sending the data, and input controls on the application receiving the data
- ❏ D. Input and output controls in the application sending the data, but only input controls are necessary on the application receiving the data

Answer: B. Input and output controls should be implemented for both the sending and receiving applications in an integrated systems environment.

6. Data mining is a technique that BEST detects which of the following?

- ❏ A. Fraudulent transactions
- ❏ B. Password compromise
- ❏ C. Malicious network traffic
- ❏ D. Malicious code

Answer: A. By comparing and cross-indexing transaction data from multiple databases, data mining can be used to determine suspicious transactions that fall outside the norm. Data-mining techniques can be used to support investigation of a password compromise, but this is still more appropriate for answer A. Network-based intrusion detection is better suited for detecting malicious network traffic. Host-based intrusion detection, code auditing, and antivirus software are better suited for detecting malicious code.

7. A company is backing up its transactional database to an offsite location. Which of the following is the MOST important issue if the backups are not kept up-to-date and fully synchronized with the live transaction-processing databases?

❑ A. The capability of the primary data to survive disruptive events without losing accuracy

❑ B. The capability of the primary data to survive disruptive events without losing completeness

❑ C. The capability of the primary data to survive disruptive events without losing availability

❑ D. The capability of the primary data to survive disruptive events without losing confidentiality

Answer: B. When storing data archives offsite, data must be synchronized to ensure backup data completeness. Failure to maintain backup synchronization in a live transaction-based processing environment could result in the incapability to restore *all* transactional data lost in the event of primary data or systems failure. Failure to synchronize does not affect the accuracy, availability, or confidentiality of the data that exists in backup.

8. When a business attempts to streamline its business processes through business process re-engineering (BPR), utilization of technology often:

❑ A. Increases

❑ B. Decreases

❑ C. Stays the same

❑ D. Is a waste of money

Answer: A. Business process re-engineering often results in increased automation, which results in a greater number of people using technology. Cost-effectiveness is evaluated within BPR and should *not* be negatively affected by BPR.

9. To which of the following should an IS auditor give the MOST consideration when auditing systems affected by a recent business process re-engineering (BPR) project?

❑ A. Cultural feasibility of the re-engineered business process incorporates input from affected end users.

❑ B. Financial feasibility of the re-engineered business process was properly conducted by appropriate parties.

❑ C. The technical feasibility of the re-engineered business process was properly evaluated by the appropriate parties.

❑ D. The re-engineered business process incorporates new internal controls where appropriate, and does not inadvertently negate prior internal controls.

Answer: D. An IS auditor should always check to make sure that a re-engineered business process has not inadvertently removed key controls from the previous control environment, and has taken newly introduced risks and corresponding controls into consideration. For example:

BPR often results in higher levels of automation, so the human resources staff is often consolidated. This can easily result in improper segregation of duties by users, which can result in unauthorized activity. The re-engineered business process planning should recognize this and implement appropriate new compensatory internal controls.

10. When attempting to assess financial risk when accurate financial impact cannot be determined, which of the following is the MOST appropriate approach to risk assessment?

   ❑ A. Quantitative risk assessment
   ❑ B. Decision support system approach
   ❑ C. Qualitative risk assessment approach
   ❑ D. Quantum risk assessment approach

Answer: C. Quantitative risk assessment is not always possible because the IS auditor is attempting to calculate risk using nonquantifiable threats and potential losses. In this event, a qualitative risk assessment is more appropriate. Answers B and D are invalid and are misleading.

Practice Exam 1

1. The traditional role of an IS auditor in a control self-assessment (CSA) should be that of a(n):
   - ❑ A. Implementor
   - ❑ B. Facilitator
   - ❑ C. Developer
   - ❑ D. Sponsor

2. What is the primary objective of a control self-assessment (CSA) program?
   - ❑ A. Enhancement of the audit responsibility
   - ❑ B. Elimination of the audit responsibility
   - ❑ C. Replacement of the audit responsibility
   - ❑ D. Integrity of the audit responsibility

3. IS auditors are MOST likely to perform compliance tests of internal controls if, after their initial evaluation of the controls, they conclude that control risks are within the acceptable limits. True or false?
   - ❑ A. True
   - ❑ B. False

4. As compared to understanding an organization's IT process from evidence directly collected, how valuable are prior audit reports as evidence?
   - ❑ A. The same value.
   - ❑ B. Greater value.
   - ❑ C. Lesser value.
   - ❑ D. Prior audit reports are not relevant.

5. What is the PRIMARY purpose of audit trails?

❑ A. To document auditing efforts

❑ B. To correct data integrity errors

❑ C. To establish accountability and responsibility for processed transactions

❑ D. To prevent unauthorized access to data

6. How does the process of systems auditing benefit from using a risk-based approach to audit planning?

❑ A. Controls testing starts earlier.

❑ B. Auditing resources are allocated to the areas of highest concern.

❑ C. Auditing risk is reduced.

❑ D. Controls testing is more thorough.

7. After an IS auditor has identified threats and potential impacts, the auditor should:

❑ A. Identify and evaluate the existing controls

❑ B. Conduct a business impact analysis (BIA)

❑ C. Report on existing controls

❑ D. Propose new controls

8. The use of statistical sampling procedures helps minimize:

❑ A. Detection risk

❑ B. Business risk

❑ C. Controls risk

❑ D. Compliance risk

9. What type of risk results when an IS auditor uses an inadequate test procedure and concludes that material errors do not exist when errors actually exist?

❑ A. Business risk

❑ B. Detection risk

❑ C. Residual risk

❑ D. Inherent risk

10. A primary benefit derived from an organization employing control self-assessment (CSA) techniques is that it can:

❑ A. Identify high-risk areas that might need a detailed review later

❑ B. Reduce audit costs

❑ C. Reduce audit time

❑ D. Increase audit accuracy

11. What type of approach to the development of organizational policies is often driven by risk assessment?

❑ A. Bottom-up

❑ B. Top-down

❑ C. Comprehensive

❑ D. Integrated

12. Who is accountable for maintaining appropriate security measures over information assets?

   ❑   A. Data and systems owners
   ❑   B. Data and systems users
   ❑   C. Data and systems custodians
   ❑   D. Data and systems auditors

13. Proper segregation of duties prohibits a system analyst from performing quality-assurance functions. True or false?

   ❑   A. True
   ❑   B. False

14. What should an IS auditor do if he or she observes that project-approval procedures do not exist?

   ❑   A. Advise senior management to invest in project-management training for the staff
   ❑   B. Create project-approval procedures for future project implementations
   ❑   C. Assign project leaders
   ❑   D. Recommend to management that formal approval procedures be adopted and documented

15. Who is ultimately accountable for the development of an IS security policy?

   ❑   A. The board of directors
   ❑   B. Middle management
   ❑   C. Security administrators
   ❑   D. Network administrators

16. Proper segregation of duties normally does not prohibit a LAN administrator from also having programming responsibilities. True or false?

   ❑   A. True
   ❑   B. False

17. A core tenant of an IS strategy is that it must:

   ❑   A. Be inexpensive
   ❑   B. Be protected as sensitive confidential information
   ❑   C. Protect information confidentiality, integrity, and availability
   ❑   D. Support the business objectives of the organization

18. Batch control reconciliation is a _____(fill in the blank) control for mitigating risk of inadequate segregation of duties.

   ❑   A. Detective
   ❑   B. Corrective
   ❑   C. Preventative
   ❑   D. Compensatory

19. Key verification is one of the best controls for ensuring that:
    - ❏ A. Data is entered correctly
    - ❏ B. Only authorized cryptographic keys are used
    - ❏ C. Input is authorized
    - ❏ D. Database indexing is performed properly

20. If senior management is not committed to strategic planning, how likely is it that a company's implementation of IT will be successful?
    - ❏ A. IT cannot be implemented if senior management is not committed to strategic planning.
    - ❏ B. More likely.
    - ❏ C. Less likely.
    - ❏ D. Strategic planning does not affect the success of a company's implementation of IT.

21. Which of the following could lead to an unintentional loss of confidentiality? Choose the BEST answer.
    - ❏ A. Lack of employee awareness of a company's information security policy
    - ❏ B. Failure to comply with a company's information security policy
    - ❏ C. A momentary lapse of reason
    - ❏ D. Lack of security policy enforcement procedures

22. What topology provides the greatest redundancy of routes and the greatest network fault tolerance?
    - ❏ A. A star network topology
    - ❏ B. A mesh network topology with packet forwarding enabled at each host
    - ❏ C. A bus network topology
    - ❏ D. A ring network topology

23. An IS auditor usually places more reliance on evidence directly collected. What is an example of such evidence?
    - ❏ A. Evidence collected through personal observation
    - ❏ B. Evidence collected through systems logs provided by the organization's security administration
    - ❏ C. Evidence collected through surveys collected from internal staff
    - ❏ D. Evidence collected through transaction reports provided by the organization's IT administration

24. What kind of protocols does the OSI Transport Layer of the TCP/IP protocol suite provide to ensure reliable communication?
    - ❏ A. Non–connection-oriented protocols
    - ❏ B. Connection-oriented protocols
    - ❏ C. Session-oriented protocols
    - ❏ D. Non–session-oriented protocols

25. How is the time required for transaction processing review usually affected by properly implemented Electronic Data Interface (EDI)?
    - ❏ A. EDI usually decreases the time necessary for review.
    - ❏ B. EDI usually increases the time necessary for review.
    - ❏ C. Cannot be determined.
    - ❏ D. EDI does not affect the time necessary for review.

26. What would an IS auditor expect to find in the console log? Choose the BEST answer.
    - ❏ A. Evidence of password spoofing
    - ❏ B. System errors
    - ❏ C. Evidence of data copy activities
    - ❏ D. Evidence of password sharing

27. Atomicity enforces data integrity by ensuring that a transaction is either completed in its entirely or not at all. Atomicity is part of the ACID test reference for transaction processing. True or false?
    - ❏ A. True
    - ❏ B. False

28. Why does the IS auditor often review the system logs?
    - ❏ A. To get evidence of password spoofing
    - ❏ B. To get evidence of data copy activities
    - ❏ C. To determine the existence of unauthorized access to data by a user or program
    - ❏ D. To get evidence of password sharing

29. What is essential for the IS auditor to obtain a clear understanding of network management?
    - ❏ A. Security administrator access to systems
    - ❏ B. Systems logs of all hosts providing application services
    - ❏ C. A graphical map of the network topology
    - ❏ D. Administrator access to systems

30. How is risk affected if users have direct access to a database at the system level?
    - ❏ A. Risk of unauthorized access increases, but risk of untraceable changes to the database decreases.
    - ❏ B. Risk of unauthorized and untraceable changes to the database increases.
    - ❏ C. Risk of unauthorized access decreases, but risk of untraceable changes to the database increases.
    - ❏ D. Risk of unauthorized and untraceable changes to the database decreases.

31. What is the most common purpose of a virtual private network implementation?

  ❑ A. A virtual private network (VPN) helps to secure access between an enterprise and its partners when communicating over an otherwise unsecured channel such as the Internet.

  ❑ B. A virtual private network (VPN) helps to secure access between an enterprise and its partners when communicating over a dedicated T1 connection.

  ❑ C. A virtual private network (VPN) helps to secure access within an enterprise when communicating over a dedicated T1 connection between network segments within the same facility.

  ❑ D. A virtual private network (VPN) helps to secure access between an enterprise and its partners when communicating over a wireless connection.

32. What benefit does using capacity-monitoring software to monitor usage patterns and trends provide to management? Choose the BEST answer.

  ❑ A. The software can dynamically readjust network traffic capabilities based upon current usage.

  ❑ B. The software produces nice reports that really impress management.

  ❑ C. It allows users to properly allocate resources and ensure continuous efficiency of operations.

  ❑ D. It allows management to properly allocate resources and ensure continuous efficiency of operations.

33. What can be very helpful to an IS auditor when determining the efficacy of a systems maintenance program? Choose the BEST answer.

  ❑ A. Network-monitoring software

  ❑ B. A system downtime log

  ❑ C. Administration activity reports

  ❑ D. Help-desk utilization trend reports

34. What are used as a countermeasure for potential database corruption when two processes attempt to simultaneously edit or update the same information? Choose the BEST answer.

  ❑ A. Referential integrity controls

  ❑ B. Normalization controls

  ❑ C. Concurrency controls

  ❑ D. Run-to-run totals

35. What increases encryption overhead and cost the most?

  ❑ A. A long symmetric encryption key

  ❑ B. A long asymmetric encryption key

  ❑ C. A long Advance Encryption Standard (AES) key

  ❑ D. A long Data Encryption Standard (DES) key

36. Which of the following best characterizes "worms"?

    ❑ A. Malicious programs that can run independently and can propagate without the aid of a carrier program such as email

    ❑ B. Programming code errors that cause a program to repeatedly dump data

    ❑ C. Malicious programs that require the aid of a carrier program such as email

    ❑ D. Malicious programs that masquerade as common applications such as screensavers or macro-enabled Word documents

37. What is an initial step in creating a proper firewall policy?

    ❑ A. Assigning access to users according to the principle of least privilege

    ❑ B. Determining appropriate firewall hardware and software

    ❑ C. Identifying network applications such as mail, web, or FTP servers

    ❑ D. Configuring firewall access rules

38. What type of cryptosystem is characterized by data being encrypted by the sender using the recipient's public key, and the data then being decrypted using the recipient's private key?

    ❑ A. With public-key encryption, or symmetric encryption

    ❑ B. With public-key encryption, or asymmetric encryption

    ❑ C. With shared-key encryption, or symmetric encryption

    ❑ D. With shared-key encryption, or asymmetric encryption

39. How does the SSL network protocol provide confidentiality?

    ❑ A. Through symmetric encryption such as RSA

    ❑ B. Through asymmetric encryption such as Data Encryption Standard, or DES

    ❑ C. Through asymmetric encryption such as Advanced Encryption Standard, or AES

    ❑ D. Through symmetric encryption such as Data Encryption Standard, or DES

40. What are used as the framework for developing logical access controls?

    ❑ A. Information systems security policies

    ❑ B. Organizational security policies

    ❑ C. Access Control Lists (ACL)

    ❑ D. Organizational charts for identifying roles and responsibilities

41. Which of the following are effective controls for detecting duplicate transactions such as payments made or received?

    ❑ A. Concurrency controls

    ❑ B. Reasonableness checks

    ❑ C. Time stamps

    ❑ D. Referential integrity controls

42. Which of the following is a good control for protecting confidential data residing on a PC?

   ❑ A. Personal firewall

   ❑ B. File encapsulation

   ❑ C. File encryption

   ❑ D. Host-based intrusion detection

43. Which of the following is a guiding best practice for implementing logical access controls?

   ❑ A. Implementing the Biba Integrity Model

   ❑ B. Access is granted on a least-privilege basis, per the organization's data owners

   ❑ C. Implementing the Take-Grant access control model

   ❑ D. Classifying data according to the subject's requirements

44. What does PKI use to provide some of the strongest overall control over data confidentiality, reliability, and integrity for Internet transactions?

   ❑ A. A combination of public-key cryptography and digital certificates and two-factor authentication

   ❑ B. A combination of public-key cryptography and two-factor authentication

   ❑ C. A combination of public-key cryptography and digital certificates

   ❑ D. A combination of digital certificates and two-factor authentication

45. Which of the following do digital signatures provide?

   ❑ A. Authentication and integrity of data

   ❑ B. Authentication and confidentiality of data

   ❑ C. Confidentiality and integrity of data

   ❑ D. Authentication and availability of data

46. Regarding digital signature implementation, which of the following answers is correct?

   ❑ A. A digital signature is created by the sender to prove message integrity by encrypting the message with the sender's private key. Upon receiving the data, the recipient can decrypt the data using the sender's public key.

   ❑ B. A digital signature is created by the sender to prove message integrity by encrypting the message with the recipient's public key. Upon receiving the data, the recipient can decrypt the data using the recipient's public key.

   ❑ C. A digital signature is created by the sender to prove message integrity by initially using a hashing algorithm to produce a hash value or message digest from the entire message contents. Upon receiving the data, the recipient can independently create it.

   ❑ D. A digital signature is created by the sender to prove message integrity by encrypting the message with the sender's public key. Upon receiving the data, the recipient can decrypt the data using the recipient's private key.

47. Which of the following would provide the highest degree of server access control?

 ❏ A. A mantrap-monitored entryway to the server room
 ❏ B. Host-based intrusion detection combined with CCTV
 ❏ C. Network-based intrusion detection
 ❏ D. A fingerprint scanner facilitating biometric access control

48. What are often the primary safeguards for systems software and data?

 ❏ A. Administrative access controls
 ❏ B. Logical access controls
 ❏ C. Physical access controls
 ❏ D. Detective access controls

49. Which of the following is often used as a detection and deterrent control against Internet attacks?

 ❏ A. Honeypots
 ❏ B. CCTV
 ❏ C. VPN
 ❏ D. VLAN

50. Which of the following BEST characterizes a mantrap or deadman door, which is used as a deterrent control for the vulnerability of piggybacking?

 ❏ A. A monitored double-doorway entry system
 ❏ B. A monitored turnstile entry system
 ❏ C. A monitored doorway entry system
 ❏ D. A one-way door that does not allow exit after entry

51. Which of the following is an effective method for controlling downloading of files via FTP? Choose the BEST answer.

 ❏ A. An application-layer gateway, or proxy firewall, but not stateful inspection firewalls
 ❏ B. An application-layer gateway, or proxy firewall
 ❏ C. A circuit-level gateway
 ❏ D. A first-generation packet-filtering firewall

52. Which of the following provides the strongest authentication for physical access control?

 ❏ A. Sign-in logs
 ❏ B. Dynamic passwords
 ❏ C. Key verification
 ❏ D. Biometrics

53. What is an effective countermeasure for the vulnerability of data entry operators potentially leaving their computers without logging off? Choose the BEST answer.
    - ❏ A. Employee security awareness training
    - ❏ B. Administrator alerts
    - ❏ C. Screensaver passwords
    - ❏ D. Close supervision

54. What can ISPs use to implement inbound traffic filtering as a control to identify IP packets transmitted from unauthorized sources? Choose the BEST answer.
    - ❏ A. OSI Layer 2 switches with packet filtering enabled
    - ❏ B. Virtual Private Networks
    - ❏ C. Access Control Lists (ACL)
    - ❏ D. Point-to-Point Tunneling Protocol

55. What is the key distinction between encryption and hashing algorithms?
    - ❏ A. Hashing algorithms ensure data confidentiality.
    - ❏ B. Hashing algorithms are irreversible.
    - ❏ C. Encryption algorithms ensure data integrity.
    - ❏ D. Encryption algorithms are not irreversible.

56. Which of the following is BEST characterized by unauthorized modification of data before or during systems data entry?
    - ❏ A. Data diddling
    - ❏ B. Skimming
    - ❏ C. Data corruption
    - ❏ D. Salami attack

57. Which of the following is used to evaluate biometric access controls?
    - ❏ A. FAR
    - ❏ B. EER
    - ❏ C. ERR
    - ❏ D. FRR

58. Who is ultimately responsible and accountable for reviewing user access to systems?
    - ❏ A. Systems security administrators
    - ❏ B. Data custodians
    - ❏ C. Data owners
    - ❏ D. Information systems auditors

59. Establishing data ownership is an important first step for which of the following processes? Choose the BEST answer.
    - ❏ A. Assigning user access privileges
    - ❏ B. Developing organizational security policies
    - ❏ C. Creating roles and responsibilities
    - ❏ D. Classifying data

60. Which of the following is MOST is critical during the business impact assessment phase of business continuity planning?
    - ❑ A. End-user involvement
    - ❑ B. Senior management involvement
    - ❑ C. Security administration involvement
    - ❑ D. IS auditing involvement

61. What type of BCP test uses actual resources to simulate a system crash and validate the plan's effectiveness?
    - ❑ A. Paper
    - ❑ B. Preparedness
    - ❑ C. Walk-through
    - ❑ D. Parallel

62. Which of the following typically focuses on making alternative processes and resources available for transaction processing?
    - ❑ A. Cold-site facilities
    - ❑ B. Disaster recovery for networks
    - ❑ C. Diverse processing
    - ❑ D. Disaster recovery for systems

63. Which type of major BCP test only requires representatives from each operational area to meet to review the plan?
    - ❑ A. Parallel
    - ❑ B. Preparedness
    - ❑ C. Walk-thorough
    - ❑ D. Paper

64. What influences decisions regarding criticality of assets?
    - ❑ A. The business criticality of the data to be protected
    - ❑ B. Internal corporate politics
    - ❑ C. The business criticality of the data to be protected, and the scope of the impact upon the organization as a whole
    - ❑ D. The business impact analysis

65. Of the three major types of off-site processing facilities, what type is characterized by at least providing for electricity and HVAC?
    - ❑ A. Cold site
    - ❑ B. Alternate site
    - ❑ C. Hot site
    - ❑ D. Warm site

66. With the objective of mitigating the risk and impact of a major business interruption, a disaster-recovery plan should endeavor to reduce the length of recovery time necessary, as well as costs associated with recovery. Although DRP results in an increase of pre- and post-incident operational costs, the extra costs are more than offset by reduced recovery and business impact costs. True or false?

   ❏ A. True
   ❏ B. False

67. Of the three major types of off-site processing facilities, what type is often an acceptable solution for preparing for recovery of noncritical systems and data?

   ❏ A. Cold site
   ❏ B. Hot site
   ❏ C. Alternate site
   ❏ D. Warm site

68. Any changes in systems assets, such as replacement of hardware, should be immediately recorded within the assets inventory of which of the following? Choose the BEST answer.

   ❏ A. IT strategic plan
   ❏ B. Business continuity plan
   ❏ C. Business impact analysis
   ❏ D. Incident response plan

69. Although BCP and DRP are often implemented and tested by middle management and end users, the ultimate responsibility and accountability for the plans remain with executive management, such as the _____. (fill-in-the-blank)

   ❏ A. Security administrator
   ❏ B. Systems auditor
   ❏ C. Board of directors
   ❏ D. Financial auditor

70. Obtaining user approval of program changes is very effective for controlling application changes and maintenance. True or false?

   ❏ A. True
   ❏ B. False

71. Library control software restricts source code to:

   ❏ A. Read-only access
   ❏ B. Write-only access
   ❏ C. Full access
   ❏ D. Read-write access

72. When is regression testing used to determine whether new application changes have introduced any errors in the remaining unchanged code?

  ❑ A. In program development and change management
  ❑ B. In program feasibility studies
  ❑ C. In program development
  ❑ D. In change management

73. What is often the most difficult part of initial efforts in application development? Choose the BEST answer.

  ❑ A. Configuring software
  ❑ B. Planning security
  ❑ C. Determining time and resource requirements
  ❑ D. Configuring hardware

74. What is a primary high-level goal for an auditor who is reviewing a system development project?

  ❑ A. To ensure that programming and processing environments are segregated
  ❑ B. To ensure that proper approval for the project has been obtained
  ❑ C. To ensure that business objectives are achieved
  ❑ D. To ensure that projects are monitored and administrated effectively

75. Whenever an application is modified, what should be tested to determine the full impact of the change? Choose the BEST answer.

  ❑ A. Interface systems with other applications or systems
  ❑ B. The entire program, including any interface systems with other applications or systems
  ❑ C. All programs, including interface systems with other applications or systems
  ❑ D. Mission-critical functions and any interface systems with other applications or systems

76. The quality of the metadata produced from a data warehouse is _____ in the warehouse's design. Choose the BEST answer.

  ❑ A. Often hard to determine because the data is derived from a heterogeneous data environment
  ❑ B. The most important consideration
  ❑ C. Independent of the quality of the warehoused databases
  ❑ D. Of secondary importance to data warehouse content

77. Function Point Analysis (FPA) provides an estimate of the size of an information system based only on the number and complexity of a system's inputs and outputs. True or false?

  ❑ A. True
  ❑ B. False

78. Who assumes ownership of a systems-development project and the resulting system?
    - ❑ A. User management
    - ❑ B. Project steering committee
    - ❑ C. IT management
    - ❑ D. Systems developers

79. If an IS auditor observes that individual modules of a system perform correctly in development project tests, the auditor should inform management of the positive results and recommend further:
    - ❑ A. Documentation development
    - ❑ B. Comprehensive integration testing
    - ❑ C. Full unit testing
    - ❑ D. Full regression testing

80. When participating in a systems-development project, an IS auditor should focus on system controls rather than ensuring that adequate and complete documentation exists for all projects. True or false?
    - ❑ A. True
    - ❑ B. False

81. What is a reliable technique for estimating the scope and cost of a software-development project?
    - ❑ A. Function point analysis (FPA)
    - ❑ B. Feature point analysis (FPA)
    - ❑ C. GANTT
    - ❑ D. PERT

82. Which of the following is a program evaluation review technique that considers different scenarios for planning and control projects?
    - ❑ A. Function Point Analysis (FPA)
    - ❑ B. GANTT
    - ❑ C. Rapid Application Development (RAD)
    - ❑ D. PERT

83. If an IS auditor observes that an IS department fails to use formal documented methodologies, policies, and standards, what should the auditor do? Choose the BEST answer.

    ❑ A. Lack of IT documentation is not usually material to the controls tested in an IT audit.

    ❑ B. The auditor should at least document the informal standards and policies. Furthermore, the IS auditor should create formal documented policies to be implemented.

    ❑ C. The auditor should at least document the informal standards and policies, and test for compliance. Furthermore, the IS auditor should recommend to management that formal documented policies be developed and implemented.

    ❑ D. The auditor should at least document the informal standards and policies, and test for compliance. Furthermore, the IS auditor should create formal documented policies to be implemented.

84. What often results in project scope creep when functional requirements are not defined as well as they could be?

    ❑ A. Inadequate software baselining

    ❑ B. Insufficient strategic planning

    ❑ C. Inaccurate resource allocation

    ❑ D. Project delays

85. Fourth-Generation Languages (4GLs) are most appropriate for designing the application's graphical user interface (GUI). They are inappropriate for designing any intensive data-calculation procedures. True or false?

    ❑ A. True

    ❑ B. False

86. Run-to-run totals can verify data through which stage(s) of application processing?

    ❑ A. Initial

    ❑ B. Various

    ❑ C. Final

    ❑ D. Output

87. _____ (fill in the blank) is/are are ultimately accountable for the functionality, reliability, and security within IT governance. Choose the BEST answer.

    ❑ A. Data custodians

    ❑ B. The board of directors and executive officers

    ❑ C. IT security administration

    ❑ D. Business unit managers

88. What can be used to help identify and investigate unauthorized transactions? Choose the BEST answer.
    - ❏ A. Postmortem review
    - ❏ B. Reasonableness checks
    - ❏ C. Data-mining techniques
    - ❏ D. Expert systems

89. Network environments often add to the complexity of program-to-program communication, making the implementation and maintenance of application systems more difficult. True or false?
    - ❏ A. True
    - ❏ B. False

90. _____ risk analysis is not always possible because the IS auditor is attempting to calculate risk using nonquantifiable threats and potential losses. In this event, a _____ risk assessment is more appropriate. Fill in the blanks.
    - ❏ A. Quantitative; qualitative
    - ❏ B. Qualitative; quantitative
    - ❏ C. Residual; subjective
    - ❏ D. Quantitative; subjective

91. What must an IS auditor understand before performing an application audit? Choose the BEST answer.
    - ❏ A. The potential business impact of application risks.
    - ❏ B. Application risks must first be identified.
    - ❏ C. Relative business processes.
    - ❏ D. Relevant application risks.

92. What is the first step in a business process re-engineering project?
    - ❏ A. Identifying current business processes
    - ❏ B. Forming a BPR steering committee
    - ❏ C. Defining the scope of areas to be reviewed
    - ❏ D. Reviewing the organizational strategic plan

93. When storing data archives off-site, what must be done with the data to ensure data completeness?
    - ❏ A. The data must be normalized.
    - ❏ B. The data must be validated.
    - ❏ C. The data must be parallel-tested.
    - ❏ D. The data must be synchronized.

94. Which of the following can help detect transmission errors by appending specially calculated bits onto the end of each segment of data?
    - ❏ A. Redundancy check
    - ❏ B. Completeness check
    - ❏ C. Accuracy check
    - ❏ D. Parity check

95. What is an edit check to determine whether a field contains valid data?
    - ❏ A. Completeness check
    - ❏ B. Accuracy check
    - ❏ C. Redundancy check
    - ❏ D. Reasonableness check

96. A transaction journal provides the information necessary for detecting unauthorized _____ (fill in the blank) from a terminal.
    - ❏ A. Deletion
    - ❏ B. Input
    - ❏ C. Access
    - ❏ D. Duplication

97. An intentional or unintentional disclosure of a password is likely to be evident within control logs. True or false?
    - ❏ A. True
    - ❏ B. False

98. When are benchmarking partners identified within the benchmarking process?
    - ❏ A. In the design stage
    - ❏ B. In the testing stage
    - ❏ C. In the research stage
    - ❏ D. In the development stage

99. A check digit is an effective edit check to:
    - ❏ A. Detect data-transcription errors
    - ❏ B. Detect data-transposition and transcription errors
    - ❏ C. Detect data-transposition, transcription, and substitution errors
    - ❏ D. Detect data-transposition errors

100. Parity bits are a control used to validate:
    - ❏ A. Data authentication
    - ❏ B. Data completeness
    - ❏ C. Data source
    - ❏ D. Data accuracy

Answer Key 1

1. B	**18.** D	**35.** B
2. A	**19.** A	**36.** A
3. A	**20.** C	**37.** C
4. C	**21.** A	**38.** B
5. C	**22.** B	**39.** D
6. B	**23.** A	**40.** A
7. A	**24.** B	**41.** C
8. A	**25.** A	**42.** C
9. B	**26.** B	**43.** B
10. A	**27.** A	**44.** C
11. A	**28.** C	**45.** A
12. A	**29.** C	**46.** C
13. A	**30.** B	**47.** D
14. D	**31.** A	**48.** B
15. A	**32.** D	**49.** A
16. B	**33.** B	**50.** A
17. D	**34.** C	**51.** B

52. D	69. C	86. B
53. C	70. A	87. B
54. C	71. A	88. C
55. B	72. A	89. A
56. A	73. C	90. A
57. B	74. C	91. C
58. C	75. B	92. C
59. D	76. B	93. D
60. A	77. B	94. A
61. B	78. A	95. A
62. D	79. B	96. B
63. C	80. B	97. B
64. C	81. A	98. C
65. A	82. D	99. B
66. A	83. C	100. B
67. A	84. A	
68. B	85. A	

Question 1

Answer B is correct. The traditional role of an IS auditor in a control self-assessment (CSA) should be that of a facilitator.

Question 2

Answer A is correct. Audit responsibility enhancement is an objective of a control self-assessment (CSA) program.

Question 3

Answer A is correct. IS auditors are *most* likely to perform compliance tests of internal controls if, after their initial evaluation of the controls, they conclude that control risks are within the acceptable limits. Think of it this way: If any reliance is placed on internal controls, that reliance must be validated through compliance testing. High control risk results in little reliance on internal controls, which results in additional *substantive* testing.

Question 4

Answer C is correct. Prior audit reports are considered of lesser value to an IS auditor attempting to gain an understanding of an organization's IT process than evidence directly collected.

Question 5

Answer C is correct. The primary purpose of audit trails is to establish accountability and responsibility for processed transactions.

Question 6

Answer B is correct. Allocation of auditing resources to the areas of highest concern is a benefit of a risk-based approach to audit planning.

Question 7

Answer A is correct. After an IS auditor has identified threats and potential impacts, the auditor should then identify and evaluate the existing controls.

Question 8

Answer A is correct. The use of statistical sampling procedures helps minimize detection risk.

Question 9

Answer B is correct. Detection risk results when an IS auditor uses an inadequate test procedure and concludes that material errors do not exist when errors actually exist.

Question 10

Answer A is correct. A primary benefit derived from an organization employing control self-assessment (CSA) techniques is that it can identify high-risk areas that might need a detailed review later.

Question 11

Answer A is correct. A bottom-up approach to the development of organizational policies is often driven by risk assessment.

Question 12

Answer A is correct. Data and systems owners are accountable for maintaining appropriate security measures over information assets.

Question 13

Answer A is correct. Proper segregation of duties prohibits a system analyst from performing quality-assurance functions.

Question 14

Answer D is correct. If an IS auditor observes that project-approval procedures do not exist, the IS auditor should recommend to management that formal approval procedures be adopted and documented.

Question 15

Answer A is correct. The board of directors is ultimately accountable for the development of an IS security policy.

Question 16

Answer B is correct. Proper segregation of duties normally prohibits a LAN administrator from also having programming responsibilities.

Question 17

Answer D is correct. Above all else, an IS strategy must support the business objectives of the organization.

Question 18

Answer D is correct. Batch control reconciliations is a compensatory control for mitigating risk of inadequate segregation of duties.

Question 19

Answer A is correct. Key verification is one of the best controls for ensuring that data is entered correctly.

Question 20

Answer C is correct. A company's implementation of IT will be less likely to succeed if senior management is not committed to strategic planning.

Question 21

Answer A is correct. Lack of employee awareness of a company's information security policy could lead to an unintentional loss of confidentiality.

Question 22

Answer B is correct. A mesh network topology provides a point-to-point link between every network host. If each host is configured to route and forward communication, this topology provides the greatest redundancy of routes and the greatest network fault tolerance.

Question 23

Answer A is correct. An IS auditor usually places more reliance on evidence directly collected, such as through personal observation.

Question 24

Answer B is correct. The transport layer of the TCP/IP protocol suite provides for connection-oriented protocols to ensure reliable communication.

Question 25

Answer A is correct. Electronic data interface (EDI) supports intervendor communication while decreasing the time necessary for review because it is usually configured to readily identify errors requiring follow-up.

Question 26

Answer B is correct. An IS auditor can expect to find system errors to be detailed in the console log.

Question 27

Answer A is correct. Atomicity enforces data integrity by ensuring that a transaction is either completed in its entirely or not at all. Atomicity is part of the ACID test reference for transaction processing.

Question 28

Answer C is correct. When trying to determine the existence of unauthorized access to data by a user or program, the IS auditor will often review the system logs.

Question 29

Answer C is correct. A graphical interface to the map of the network topology is essential for the IS auditor to obtain a clear understanding of network management.

Question 30

Answer B is correct. If users have direct access to a database at the system level, risk of unauthorized and untraceable changes to the database increases.

Question 31

Answer A is correct. A virtual private network (VPN) helps to secure access between an enterprise and its partners when communicating over an otherwise unsecured channel such as the Internet.

Question 32

Answer D is correct. Using capacity-monitoring software to monitor usage patterns and trends enables management to properly allocate resources and ensure continuous efficiency of operations.

Question 33

Answer B is correct. A system downtime log can be very helpful to an IS auditor when determining the efficacy of a systems maintenance program.

Question 34

Answer C is correct. Concurrency controls are used as a countermeasure for potential database corruption when two processes attempt to simultaneously edit or update the same information.

Question 35

Answer B is correct. A long asymmetric encryption key (public key encryption) increases encryption overhead and cost. All other answers are single shared symmetric keys.

Question 36

Answer A is correct. Worms are malicious programs that can run independently and can propagate without the aid of a carrier program such as email.

Question 37

Answer C is correct. Identifying network applications such as mail, web, or FTP servers to be externally accessed is an initial step in creating a proper firewall policy.

Question 38

Answer B is correct. With public key encryption or asymmetric encryption, data is encrypted by the sender using the recipient's public key; the data is then decrypted using the recipient's private key.

Question 39

Answer D is correct. The SSL protocol provides confidentiality through symmetric encryption such as Data Encryption Standard, or DES.

Question 40

Answer A is correct. Information systems security policies are used as the framework for developing logical access controls.

Question 41

Answer C is correct. Time stamps are an effective control for detecting duplicate transactions such as payments made or received.

Question 42

Answer C is correct. File encryption is a good control for protecting confidential data residing on a PC.

Question 43

Answer B is correct. Logical access controls should be reviewed to ensure that access is granted on a least-privilege basis, per the organization's data owners.

Question 44

Answer C is correct. PKI uses a combination of public-key cryptography and digital certificates to provide some of the strongest overall control over data confidentiality, reliability, and integrity for Internet transactions.

Question 45

Answer A is correct. The primary purpose of digital signatures is to provide authentication and integrity of data.

Question 46

Answer C is correct. A digital signature is created by the sender to prove message integrity by initially using a hashing algorithm to produce a hash value, or message digest, from the entire message contents. Upon receiving the data, the recipient can independently create its own message digest from the data for comparison and data integrity validation. Public and private keys are used to enforce confidentiality. Hashing algorithms are used to enforce integrity.

Question 47

Answer D is correct. A fingerprint scanner facilitating biometric access control can provide a very high degree of server access control.

Question 48

Answer B is correct. Logical access controls are often the primary safeguards for systems software and data.

Question 49

Answer A is correct. Honeypots are often used as a detection and deterrent control against Internet attacks.

Question 50

Answer A is correct. A monitored double-doorway entry system, also referred to as a mantrap or deadman door, is used as a deterrent control for the vulnerability of piggybacking.

Question 51

Answer B is correct. Application-layer gateways, or proxy firewalls, are an effective method for controlling downloading of files via FTP. Because FTP is an OSI application-layer protocol, the most effective firewall needs to be capable of inspecting through the application layer.

Question 52

Answer D is correct. Biometrics can be used to provide excellent physical access control.

Question 53

Answer C is correct. Screensaver passwords are an effective control to implement as a countermeasure for the vulnerability of data entry operators potentially leaving their computers without logging off.

Question 54

Answer C is correct. ISPs can use access control lists to implement inbound traffic filtering as a control to identify IP packets transmitted from unauthorized sources.

Question 55

Answer B is correct. A key distinction between encryption and hashing algorithms is that hashing algorithms are irreversible.

Question 56

Answer A is correct. Data diddling involves modifying data before or during systems data entry.

Question 57

Answer B is correct. When evaluating biometric access controls, a low equal error rate (EER) is preferred. EER is also called the crossover error rate (CER).

Question 58

Answer C is correct. Data owners are ultimately responsible and accountable for reviewing user access to systems.

Question 59

Answer D is correct. To properly implement data classification, establishing data ownership is an important first step.

Question 60

Answer A is correct. End-user involvement is critical during the business impact assessment phase of business continuity planning.

Question 61

Answer B is correct. Of the three major types of BCP tests (paper, walk-through, and preparedness), only the preparedness test uses actual resources to simulate a system crash and validate the plan's effectiveness.

Question 62

Answer D is correct. Disaster recovery for systems typically focuses on making alternative processes and resources available for transaction processing.

Question 63

Answer C is correct. Of the three major types of BCP tests (paper, walk-through, and preparedness), a walk-through test requires only that representatives from each operational area meet to review the plan.

Question 64

Answer C is correct. Criticality of assets is often influenced by the business criticality of the data to be protected and by the scope of the impact upon the organization as a whole. For example, the loss of a network backbone creates a much greater impact on the organization as a whole than the loss of data on a typical user's workstation.

Question 65

Answer A is correct. Of the three major types of off-site processing facilities (hot, warm, and cold), a cold site is characterized by at least providing for electricity and HVAC. A warm site improves upon this by providing for redundant equipment and software that can be made operational within a short time.

Question 66

Answer A is correct. With the objective of mitigating the risk and impact of a major business interruption, a disaster-recovery plan should endeavor to reduce the length of recovery time necessary and the costs associated with recovery. Although DRP results in an increase of pre- and post-incident operational costs, the extra costs are more than offset by reduced recovery and business impact costs.

Question 67

Answer A is correct. A cold site is often an acceptable solution for preparing for recovery of noncritical systems and data.

Question 68

Answer B is correct. Any changes in systems assets, such as replacement of hardware, should be immediately recorded within the assets inventory of a business continuity plan.

Question 69

Answer C is correct. Although BCP and DRP are often implemented and tested by middle management and end users, the ultimate responsibility and accountability for the plans remain with executive management, such as the board of directors.

Question 70

Answer A is correct. Obtaining user approval of program changes is very effective for controlling application changes and maintenance.

Question 71

Answer A is correct. Library control software restricts source code to read-only access.

Question 72

Answer A is correct. Regression testing is used in program development and change management to determine whether new changes have introduced any errors in the remaining unchanged code.

Question 73

Answer C is correct. Determining time and resource requirements for an application-development project is often the most difficult part of initial efforts in application development.

Question 74

Answer C is correct. A primary high-level goal for an auditor who is reviewing a systems-development project is to ensure that business objectives are achieved. This objective guides all other systems development objectives.

Question 75

Answer B is correct. Whenever an application is modified, the entire program, including any interface systems with other applications or systems, should be tested to determine the full impact of the change.

Question 76

Answer B is correct. The quality of the metadata produced from a data warehouse is the most important consideration in the warehouse's design.

Question 77

Answer B is correct. Function point analysis (FPA) provides an estimate of the size of an information system based on the number and complexity of a system's inputs, outputs, and files.

Question 78

Answer A is correct. User management assumes ownership of a systems-development project and the resulting system.

Question 79

Answer B is correct. If an IS auditor observes that individual modules of a system perform correctly in development project tests, the auditor should inform management of the positive results and recommend further comprehensive integration testing.

Question 80

Answer B is correct. When participating in a systems-development project, an IS auditor should also strive to ensure that adequate and complete documentation exists for all projects.

Question 81

Answer A is correct. A function point analysis (FPA) is a reliable technique for estimating the scope and cost of a software-development project.

Question 82

Answer D is correct. PERT is a program-evaluation review technique that considers different scenarios for planning and control projects.

Question 83

Answer C is correct. If an IS auditor observes that an IS department fails to use formal documented methodologies, policies, and standards, the auditor should at least document the informal standards and policies, and test for compliance. Furthermore, the IS auditor should recommend to management that formal documented policies be developed and implemented.

Question 84

Answer A is correct. Inadequate software baselining often results in project scope creep because functional requirements are not defined as well as they could be.

Question 85

Answer A is correct. Fourth-generation languages (4GLs) are most appropriate for designing the application's graphical user interface (GUI). They are inappropriate for designing any intensive data-calculation procedures.

Question 86

Answer B is correct. Run-to-run totals can verify data through various stages of application processing.

Question 87

Answer B is correct. The board of directors and executive officers are ultimately accountable for the functionality, reliability, and security within IT governance.

Question 88

Answer C is correct. Data-mining techniques can be used to help identify and investigate unauthorized transactions.

Question 89

Answer A is correct. Network environments often add to the complexity of program-to-program communication, making application systems implementation and maintenance more difficult.

Question 90

Answer A is correct. Quantitative risk analysis is not always possible because the IS auditor is attempting to calculate risk using nonquantifiable threats and potential losses. In this event, a qualitative risk assessment is more appropriate.

Question 91

Answer C is correct. An IS auditor must first understand relative business processes before performing an application audit.

Question 92

Answer C is correct. Defining the scope of areas to be reviewed is the first step in a business process re-engineering project.

Question 93

Answer D is correct. When storing data archives off-site, data must be synchronized to ensure data completeness.

Question 94

Answer A is correct. A redundancy check can help detect transmission errors by appending especially calculated bits onto the end of each segment of data.

Question 95

Answer A is correct. A completeness check is an edit check to determine whether a field contains valid data.

Question 96

Answer B is correct. A transaction journal provides the information necessary for detecting unauthorized input from a terminal.

Question 97

Answer B is correct. An intentional or unintentional disclosure of a password is not likely to be evident within control logs.

Question 98

Answer C is correct. Benchmarking partners are identified in the research stage of the benchmarking process.

Question 99

Answer B is correct. A check digit is an effective edit check to detect data-transposition and transcription errors.

Question 100

Answer B is correct. Parity bits are a control used to validate data completeness.

Practice Exam 2

1. An IS auditor is using a statistical sample to inventory the tape library. What type of test would this be considered?
   - ❏ A. Substantive
   - ❏ B. Compliance
   - ❏ C. Integrated
   - ❏ D. Continuous audit

2. Which of the following would prevent accountability for an action performed, thus allowing nonrepudiation?
   - ❏ A. Proper authentication
   - ❏ B. Proper identification AND authentication
   - ❏ C. Proper identification
   - ❏ D. Proper identification, authentication, AND authorization

3. Which of the following is the MOST critical step in planning an audit?
   - ❏ A. Implementing a prescribed auditing framework such as COBIT
   - ❏ B. Identifying current controls
   - ❏ C. Identifying high-risk audit targets
   - ❏ D. Testing controls

4. To properly evaluate the collective effect of preventative, detective, or corrective controls within a process, an IS auditor should be aware of which of the following? Choose the BEST answer.
   - ❏ A. The business objectives of the organization
   - ❏ B. The effect of segregation of duties on internal controls
   - ❏ C. The point at which controls are exercised as data flows through the system
   - ❏ D. Organizational control policies

5. What is the recommended initial step for an IS auditor to implement continuous-monitoring systems?

- ❏ A. Document existing internal controls
- ❏ B. Perform compliance testing on internal controls
- ❏ C. Establish a controls-monitoring steering committee
- ❏ D. Identify high-risk areas within the organization

6. What type of risk is associated with authorized program exits (trap doors)? Choose the BEST answer.

- ❏ A. Business risk
- ❏ B. Audit risk
- ❏ C. Detective risk
- ❏ D. Inherent risk

7. Which of the following is best suited for searching for address field duplications?

- ❏ A. Text search forensic utility software
- ❏ B. Generalized audit software
- ❏ C. Productivity audit software
- ❏ D. Manual review

8. Which of the following is of greatest concern to the IS auditor?

- ❏ A. Failure to report a successful attack on the network
- ❏ B. Failure to prevent a successful attack on the network
- ❏ C. Failure to recover from a successful attack on the network
- ❏ D. Failure to detect a successful attack on the network

9. An integrated test facility is not considered a useful audit tool because it cannot compare processing output with independently calculated data. True or false?

- ❏ A. True
- ❏ B. False

10. An advantage of a continuous audit approach is that it can improve system security when used in time-sharing environments that process a large number of transactions. True or false?

- ❏ A. True
- ❏ B. False

11. If an IS auditor finds evidence of risk involved in not implementing proper segregation of duties, such as having the security administrator perform an operations function, what is the auditor's primary responsibility?

- ❏ A. To advise senior management.
- ❏ B. To reassign job functions to eliminate potential fraud.
- ❏ C. To implement compensator controls.
- ❏ D. Segregation of duties is an administrative control not considered by an IS auditor.

12. Who is responsible for implementing cost-effective controls in an automated system?

❏ A. Security policy administrators
❏ B. Business unit management
❏ C. Senior management
❏ D. Board of directors

13. Why does an IS auditor review an organization chart?

❏ A. To optimize the responsibilities and authority of individuals
❏ B. To control the responsibilities and authority of individuals
❏ C. To better understand the responsibilities and authority of individuals
❏ D. To identify project sponsors

14. Ensuring that security and control policies support business and IT objectives is a primary objective of:

❏ A. An IT security policies audit
❏ B. A processing audit
❏ C. A software audit
❏ D. A vulnerability assessment

15. When auditing third-party service providers, an IS auditor should be concerned with which of the following? Choose the BEST answer.

❏ A. Ownership of the programs and files
❏ B. A statement of due care and confidentiality, and the capability for continued service of the service provider in the event of a disaster
❏ C. A statement of due care
❏ D. Ownership of programs and files, a statement of due care and confidentiality, and the capability for continued service of the service provider in the event of a disaster

16. When performing an IS strategy audit, an IS auditor should review both short-term (one-year) and long-term (three- to five-year) IS strategies, interview appropriate corporate management personnel, and ensure that the external environment has been considered. The auditor should especially focus on procedures in an audit of IS strategy. True or false?

❏ A. True
❏ B. False

17. What process allows IS management to determine whether the activities of the organization differ from the planned or expected levels? Choose the BEST answer.

❏ A. Business impact assessment
❏ B. Risk assessment
❏ C. IS assessment methods
❏ D. Key performance indicators (KPIs)

18. When should reviewing an audit client's business plan be performed relative to reviewing an organization's IT strategic plan?

□ A. Reviewing an audit client's business plan should be performed before reviewing an organization's IT strategic plan.

□ B. Reviewing an audit client's business plan should be performed after reviewing an organization's IT strategic plan.

□ C. Reviewing an audit client's business plan should be performed during the review of an organization's IT strategic plan.

□ D. Reviewing an audit client's business plan should be performed without regard to an organization's IT strategic plan.

19. Allowing application programmers to directly patch or change code in production programs increases risk of fraud. True or false?

□ A. True

□ B. False

20. Who should be responsible for network security operations?

□ A. Business unit managers

□ B. Security administrators

□ C. Network administrators

□ D. IS auditors

21. Proper segregation of duties does not prohibit a quality control administrator from also being responsible for change control and problem management. True or false?

□ A. True

□ B. False

22. What can be implemented to provide the highest level of protection from external attack?

□ A. Layering perimeter network protection by configuring the firewall as a screened host in a screened subnet behind the bastion host

□ B. Configuring the firewall as a screened host behind a router

□ C. Configuring the firewall as the protecting bastion host

□ D. Configuring two load-sharing firewalls facilitating VPN access from external hosts to internal hosts

23. The directory system of a database-management system describes:

□ A. The access method to the data

□ B. The location of data AND the access method

□ C. The location of data

□ D. Neither the location of data NOR the access method

24. How is the risk of improper file access affected upon implementing a database system?

□ A. Risk varies.

□ B. Risk is reduced.

□ C. Risk is not affected.

□ D. Risk is increased.

25. In order to properly protect against unauthorized disclosure of sensitive data, how should hard disks be sanitized?

   ❑   A. The data should be deleted and overwritten with binary 0s.
   ❑   B. The data should be demagnetized.
   ❑   C. The data should be low-level formatted.
   ❑   D. The data should be deleted.

26. When reviewing print systems spooling, an IS auditor is MOST concerned with which of the following vulnerabilities?

   ❑   A. The potential for unauthorized deletion of report copies
   ❑   B. The potential for unauthorized modification of report copies
   ❑   C. The potential for unauthorized printing of report copies
   ❑   D. The potential for unauthorized editing of report copies

27. Why is the WAP gateway a component warranting critical concern and review for the IS auditor when auditing and testing controls enforcing message confidentiality?

   ❑   A. WAP is often configured by default settings and is thus insecure.
   ❑   B. WAP provides weak encryption for wireless traffic.
   ❑   C. WAP functions as a protocol-conversion gateway for wireless TLS to Internet SSL.
   ❑   D. WAP often interfaces critical IT systems.

28. Proper segregation of duties prevents a computer operator (user) from performing security administration duties. True or false?

   ❑   A. True
   ❑   B. False

29. How do modems (modulation/demodulation) function to facilitate analog transmissions to enter a digital network?

   ❑   A. Modems convert analog transmissions to digital, and digital transmission to analog.
   ❑   B. Modems encapsulate analog transmissions within digital, and digital transmissions within analog.
   ❑   C. Modems convert digital transmissions to analog, and analog transmissions to digital.
   ❑   D. Modems encapsulate digital transmissions within analog, and analog transmissions within digital.

30. Which of the following are effective in detecting fraud because they have the capability to consider a large number of variables when trying to resolve a problem? Choose the BEST answer.

   ❑   A. Expert systems
   ❑   B. Neural networks
   ❑   C. Integrated synchronized systems
   ❑   D. Multitasking applications

31. What supports data transmission through split cable facilities or duplicate cable facilities?
    - ❏ A. Diverse routing
    - ❏ B. Dual routing
    - ❏ C. Alternate routing
    - ❏ D. Redundant routing

32. What type(s) of firewalls provide(s) the greatest degree of protection and control because both firewall technologies inspect all seven OSI layers of network traffic?
    - ❏ A. A first-generation packet-filtering firewall
    - ❏ B. A circuit-level gateway
    - ❏ C. An application-layer gateway, or proxy firewall, and stateful-inspection firewalls
    - ❏ D. An application-layer gateway, or proxy firewall, but not stateful-inspection firewalls

33. Which of the following can degrade network performance? Choose the BEST answer.
    - ❏ A. Superfluous use of redundant load-sharing gateways
    - ❏ B. Increasing traffic collisions due to host congestion by creating new collision domains
    - ❏ C. Inefficient and superfluous use of network devices such as switches
    - ❏ D. Inefficient and superfluous use of network devices such as hubs

34. Which of the following provide(s) near-immediate recoverability for time-sensitive systems and transaction processing?
    - ❏ A. Automated electronic journaling and parallel processing
    - ❏ B. Data mirroring and parallel processing
    - ❏ C. Data mirroring
    - ❏ D. Parallel processing

35. What is an effective control for granting temporary access to vendors and external support personnel? Choose the BEST answer.
    - ❏ A. Creating user accounts that automatically expire by a predetermined date
    - ❏ B. Creating permanent guest accounts for temporary use
    - ❏ C. Creating user accounts that restrict logon access to certain hours of the day
    - ❏ D. Creating a single shared vendor administrator account on the basis of least-privileged access

36. Which of the following help(s) prevent an organization's systems from participating in a distributed denial-of-service (DDoS) attack? Choose the BEST answer.
    - ❏ A. Inbound traffic filtering
    - ❏ B. Using access control lists (ACLs) to restrict inbound connection attempts
    - ❏ C. Outbound traffic filtering
    - ❏ D. Recentralizing distributed systems

37. What is a common vulnerability, allowing denial-of-service attacks?

❑ A. Assigning access to users according to the principle of least privilege

❑ B. Lack of employee awareness of organizational security policies

❑ C. Improperly configured routers and router access lists

❑ D. Configuring firewall access rules

38. What are trojan horse programs? Choose the BEST answer.

❑ A. A common form of internal attack

❑ B. Malicious programs that require the aid of a carrier program such as email

❑ C. Malicious programs that can run independently and can propagate without the aid of a carrier program such as email

❑ D. A common form of Internet attack

39. What is/are used to measure and ensure proper network capacity management and availability of services? Choose the BEST answer.

❑ A. Network performance-monitoring tools

❑ B. Network component redundancy

❑ C. Syslog reporting

❑ D. IT strategic planning

40. What can be used to gather evidence of network attacks?

❑ A. Access control lists (ACL)

❑ B. Intrusion-detection systems (IDS)

❑ C. Syslog reporting

❑ D. Antivirus programs

41. Which of the following is a passive attack method used by intruders to determine potential network vulnerabilities?

❑ A. Traffic analysis

❑ B. SYN flood

❑ C. Denial of service (DoS)

❑ D. Distributed denial of service (DoS)

42. Which of the following fire-suppression methods is considered to be the most environmentally friendly?

❑ A. Halon gas

❑ B. Deluge sprinklers

❑ C. Dry-pipe sprinklers

❑ D. Wet-pipe sprinklers

43. What is a callback system?

   ❑ A. It is a remote-access system whereby the remote-access server immediately calls the user back at a predetermined number if the dial-in connection fails.

   ❑ B. It is a remote-access system whereby the user's application automatically redials the remote-access server if the initial connection attempt fails.

   ❑ C. It is a remote-access control whereby the user initially connects to the network systems via dial-up access, only to have the initial connection terminated by the server, which then subsequently dials the user back at a predetermined number stored in the server's configuration database.

   ❑ D. It is a remote-access control whereby the user initially connects to the network systems via dial-up access, only to have the initial connection terminated by the server, which then subsequently allows the user to call back at an approved number for a limited period of time.

44. What type of fire-suppression system suppresses fire via water that is released from a main valve to be delivered via a system of dry pipes installed throughout the facilities?

   ❑ A. A dry-pipe sprinkler system

   ❑ B. A deluge sprinkler system

   ❑ C. A wet-pipe system

   ❑ D. A halon sprinkler system

45. Digital signatures require the sender to "sign" the data by encrypting the data with the sender's public key, to then be decrypted by the recipient using the recipient's private key. True or false?

   ❑ A. False

   ❑ B. True

46. Which of the following provides the BEST single-factor authentication?

   ❑ A. Biometrics

   ❑ B. Password

   ❑ C. Token

   ❑ D. PIN

47. What is used to provide authentication of the website and can also be used to successfully authenticate keys used for data encryption?

   ❑ A. An organizational certificate

   ❑ B. A user certificate

   ❑ C. A website certificate

   ❑ D. Authenticode

48. What determines the strength of a secret key within a symmetric key cryptosystem?

- ❑ A. A combination of key length, degree of permutation, and the complexity of the data-encryption algorithm that uses the key
- ❑ B. A combination of key length, initial input vectors, and the complexity of the data-encryption algorithm that uses the key
- ❑ C. A combination of key length and the complexity of the data-encryption algorithm that uses the key
- ❑ D. Initial input vectors and the complexity of the data-encryption algorithm that uses the key

49. What process is used to validate a subject's identity?

- ❑ A. Identification
- ❑ B. Nonrepudiation
- ❑ C. Authorization
- ❑ D. Authentication

50. What is often assured through table link verification and reference checks?

- ❑ A. Database integrity
- ❑ B. Database synchronization
- ❑ C. Database normalcy
- ❑ D. Database accuracy

51. Which of the following should an IS auditor review to determine user permissions that have been granted for a particular resource? Choose the BEST answer.

- ❑ A. Systems logs
- ❑ B. Access control lists (ACL)
- ❑ C. Application logs
- ❑ D. Error logs

52. What should IS auditors always check when auditing password files?

- ❑ A. That deleting password files is protected
- ❑ B. That password files are encrypted
- ❑ C. That password files are not accessible over the network
- ❑ D. That password files are archived

53. Using the OSI reference model, what layer(s) is/are used to encrypt data?

- ❑ A. Transport layer
- ❑ B. Session layer
- ❑ C. Session and transport layers
- ❑ D. Data link layer

54. When should systems administrators first assess the impact of applications or systems patches?
    - ❑ A. Within five business days following installation
    - ❑ B. Prior to installation
    - ❑ C. No sooner than five business days following installation
    - ❑ D. Immediately following installation

55. Which of the following is the most fundamental step in preventing virus attacks?
    - ❑ A. Adopting and communicating a comprehensive antivirus policy
    - ❑ B. Implementing antivirus protection software on users' desktop computers
    - ❑ C. Implementing antivirus content checking at all network-to-Internet gateways
    - ❑ D. Inoculating systems with antivirus code

56. Which of the following is of greatest concern when performing an IS audit?
    - ❑ A. Users' ability to directly modify the database
    - ❑ B. Users' ability to submit queries to the database
    - ❑ C. Users' ability to indirectly modify the database
    - ❑ D. Users' ability to directly view the database

57. What are intrusion-detection systems (IDS) primarily used for?
    - ❑ A. To identify AND prevent intrusion attempts to a network
    - ❑ B. To prevent intrusion attempts to a network
    - ❑ C. Forensic incident response
    - ❑ D. To identify intrusion attempts to a network

58. Rather than simply reviewing the adequacy of access control, appropriateness of access policies, and effectiveness of safeguards and procedures, the IS auditor is more concerned with effectiveness and utilization of assets. True or false?
    - ❑ A. True
    - ❑ B. False

59. If a programmer has update access to a live system, IS auditors are more concerned with the programmer's ability to initiate or modify transactions and the ability to access production than with the programmer's ability to authorize transactions. True or false?
    - ❑ A. True
    - ❑ B. False

60. Organizations should use off-site storage facilities to maintain
    _____ (fill in the blank) of current and critical informa-
    tion within backup files. Choose the BEST answer.

    ❏ A. Confidentiality
    ❏ B. Integrity
    ❏ C. Redundancy
    ❏ D. Concurrency

61. The purpose of business continuity planning and disaster-recovery
    planning is to:

    ❏ A. Transfer the risk and impact of a business interruption or disaster
    ❏ B. Mitigate, or reduce, the risk and impact of a business interruption or
         disaster
    ❏ C. Accept the risk and impact of a business
    ❏ D. Eliminate the risk and impact of a business interruption or disaster

62. If a database is restored from information backed up before the last
    system image, which of the following is recommended?

    ❏ A. The system should be restarted after the last transaction.
    ❏ B. The system should be restarted before the last transaction.
    ❏ C. The system should be restarted at the first transaction.
    ❏ D. The system should be restarted on the last transaction.

63. An off-site processing facility should be easily identifiable externally
    because easy identification helps ensure smoother recovery. True or
    false?

    ❏ A. True
    ❏ B. False

64. Which of the following is the dominating objective of BCP and DRP?

    ❏ A. To protect human life
    ❏ B. To mitigate the risk and impact of a business interruption
    ❏ C. To eliminate the risk and impact of a business interruption
    ❏ D. To transfer the risk and impact of a business interruption

65. How can minimizing single points of failure or vulnerabilities of a
    common disaster best be controlled?

    ❏ A. By implementing redundant systems and applications onsite
    ❏ B. By geographically dispersing resources
    ❏ C. By retaining onsite data backup in fireproof vaults
    ❏ D. By preparing BCP and DRP documents for commonly identified
         disasters

66. Mitigating the risk and impact of a disaster or business interruption
    usually takes priority over transference of risk to a third party such as
    an insurer. True or false?

    ❏ A. True
    ❏ B. False

67. Off-site data storage should be kept synchronized when preparing for recovery of time-sensitive data such as that resulting from which of the following? Choose the BEST answer.

  ❑ A. Financial reporting
  ❑ B. Sales reporting
  ❑ C. Inventory reporting
  ❑ D. Transaction processing

68. What is an acceptable recovery mechanism for extremely time-sensitive transaction processing?

  ❑ A. Off-site remote journaling
  ❑ B. Electronic vaulting
  ❑ C. Shadow file processing
  ❑ D. Storage area network

69. Off-site data backup and storage should be geographically separated so as to _____ (fill in the blank) the risk of a widespread physical disaster such as a hurricane or earthquake.

  ❑ A. Accept
  ❑ B. Eliminate
  ❑ C. Transfer
  ❑ D. Mitigate

70. Why is a clause for requiring source code escrow in an application vendor agreement important?

  ❑ A. To segregate systems development and live environments
  ❑ B. To protect the organization from copyright disputes
  ❑ C. To ensure that sufficient code is available when needed
  ❑ D. To ensure that the source code remains available even if the application vendor goes out of business

71. What uses questionnaires to lead the user through a series of choices to reach a conclusion? Choose the BEST answer.

  ❑ A. Logic trees
  ❑ B. Decision trees
  ❑ C. Decision algorithms
  ❑ D. Logic algorithms

72. What protects an application purchaser's ability to fix or change an application in case the application vendor goes out of business?

  ❑ A. Assigning copyright to the organization
  ❑ B. Program back doors
  ❑ C. Source code escrow
  ❑ D. Internal programming expertise

73. Who is ultimately responsible for providing requirement specifications to the software-development team?

   ❑ A. The project sponsor
   ❑ B. The project members
   ❑ C. The project leader
   ❑ D. The project steering committee

74. What should regression testing use to obtain accurate conclusions regarding the effects of changes or corrections to a program, and ensuring that those changes and corrections have not introduced new errors?

   ❑ A. Contrived data
   ❑ B. Independently created data
   ❑ C. Live data
   ❑ D. Data from previous tests

75. An IS auditor should carefully review the functional requirements in a systems-development project to ensure that the project is designed to:

   ❑ A. Meet business objectives
   ❑ B. Enforce data security
   ❑ C. Be culturally feasible
   ❑ D. Be financially feasible

76. Which of the following processes are performed during the design phase of the systems-development life cycle (SDLC) model?

   ❑ A. Develop test plans.
   ❑ B. Baseline procedures to prevent scope creep.
   ❑ C. Define the need that requires resolution, and map to the major requirements of the solution.
   ❑ D. Program and test the new system. The tests verify and validate what has been developed.

77. When should application controls be considered within the system-development process?

   ❑ A. After application unit testing
   ❑ B. After application module testing
   ❑ C. After applications systems testing
   ❑ D. As early as possible, even in the development of the project's functional specifications

78. What is used to develop strategically important systems faster, reduce development costs, and still maintain high quality? Choose the BEST answer.

   ❑ A. Rapid application development (RAD)
   ❑ B. GANTT
   ❑ C. PERT
   ❑ D. Decision trees

79. Test and development environments should be separated. True or false?

 ❑ A. True
 ❑ B. False

80. What kind of testing should programmers perform following any changes to an application or system?

 ❑ A. Unit, module, and full regression testing
 ❑ B. Module testing
 ❑ C. Unit testing
 ❑ D. Regression testing

81. Which of the following uses a prototype that can be updated continually to meet changing user or business requirements?

 ❑ A. PERT
 ❑ B. Rapid application development (RAD)
 ❑ C. Function point analysis (FPA)
 ❑ D. GANTT

82. What is the most common reason for information systems to fail to meet the needs of users? Choose the BEST answer.

 ❑ A. Lack of funding
 ❑ B. Inadequate user participation during system requirements definition
 ❑ C. Inadequate senior management participation during system requirements definition
 ❑ D. Poor IT strategic planning

83. Who is responsible for the overall direction, costs, and timetables for systems-development projects?

 ❑ A. The project sponsor
 ❑ B. The project steering committee
 ❑ C. Senior management
 ❑ D. The project team leader

84. When should plans for testing for user acceptance be prepared? Choose the BEST answer.

 ❑ A. In the requirements definition phase of the systems-development project
 ❑ B. In the feasibility phase of the systems-development project
 ❑ C. In the design phase of the systems-development project
 ❑ D. In the development phase of the systems-development project

85. Above almost all other concerns, what often results in the greatest negative impact on the implementation of new application software?

 ❑ A. Failing to perform user acceptance testing
 ❑ B. Lack of user training for the new system
 ❑ C. Lack of software documentation and run manuals
 ❑ D. Insufficient unit, module, and systems testing

86. Input/output controls should be implemented for which applications in an integrated systems environment?

    ❑ A. The receiving application

    ❑ B. The sending application

    ❑ C. Both the sending and receiving applications

    ❑ D. Output on the sending application and input on the receiving application

87. Authentication techniques for sending and receiving data between EDI systems is crucial to prevent which of the following? Choose the BEST answer.

    ❑ A. Unsynchronized transactions

    ❑ B. Unauthorized transactions

    ❑ C. Inaccurate transactions

    ❑ D. Incomplete transactions

88. After identifying potential security vulnerabilities, what should be the IS auditor's next step?

    ❑ A. To evaluate potential countermeasures and compensatory controls

    ❑ B. To implement effective countermeasures and compensatory controls

    ❑ C. To perform a business impact analysis of the threats that would exploit the vulnerabilities

    ❑ D. To immediately advise senior management of the findings

89. What is the primary security concern for EDI environments? Choose the BEST answer.

    ❑ A. Transaction authentication

    ❑ B. Transaction completeness

    ❑ C. Transaction accuracy

    ❑ D. Transaction authorization

90. Which of the following exploit vulnerabilities to cause loss or damage to the organization and its assets?

    ❑ A. Exposures

    ❑ B. Threats

    ❑ C. Hazards

    ❑ D. Insufficient controls

91. Business process re-engineering often results in _____ automation, which results in _____ number of people using technology. Fill in the blanks.

    ❑ A. Increased; a greater

    ❑ B. Increased; a fewer

    ❑ C. Less; a fewer

    ❑ D. Increased; the same

92. Whenever business processes have been re-engineered, the IS auditor attempts to identify and quantify the impact of any controls that might have been removed, or controls that might not work as effectively after business process changes. True or false?

   ❑ A. True
   ❑ B. False

93. When should an application-level edit check to verify that availability of funds was completed at the electronic funds transfer (EFT) interface?

   ❑ A. Before transaction completion
   ❑ B. Immediately after an EFT is initiated
   ❑ C. During run-to-run total testing
   ❑ D. Before an EFT is initiated

94. _____ (fill in the blank) should be implemented as early as data preparation to support data integrity at the earliest point possible.

   ❑ A. Control totals
   ❑ B. Authentication controls
   ❑ C. Parity bits
   ❑ D. Authorization controls

95. What is used as a control to detect loss, corruption, or duplication of data?

   ❑ A. Redundancy check
   ❑ B. Reasonableness check
   ❑ C. Hash totals
   ❑ D. Accuracy check

96. Data edits are implemented before processing and are considered which of the following? Choose the BEST answer.

   ❑ A. Deterrent integrity controls
   ❑ B. Detective integrity controls
   ❑ C. Corrective integrity controls
   ❑ D. Preventative integrity controls

97. In small office environments, it is not always possible to maintain proper segregation of duties for programmers. If a programmer has access to production data or applications, compensatory controls such as the reviewing of transaction results to approved input might be necessary. True or false?

   ❑ A. True
   ❑ B. False

98. Processing controls ensure that data is accurate and complete, and is processed only through which of the following? Choose the BEST answer.

   ❑   A. Documented routines
   ❑   B. Authorized routines
   ❑   C. Accepted routines
   ❑   D. Approved routines

99. What is a data validation edit control that matches input data to an occurrence rate? Choose the BEST answer.

   ❑   A. Accuracy check
   ❑   B. Completeness check
   ❑   C. Reasonableness check
   ❑   D. Redundancy check

100. Database snapshots can provide an excellent audit trail for an IS auditor. True or false?

   ❑   A. True
   ❑   B. False

Answer Key 2

1. A	**18.** A	**35.** A
2. B	**19.** A	**36.** C
3. C	**20.** B	**37.** C
4. C	**21.** A	**38.** D
5. D	**22.** A	**39.** A
6. D	**23.** B	**40.** B
7. B	**24.** D	**41.** A
8. A	**25.** B	**42.** C
9. B	**26.** C	**43.** C
10. A	**27.** C	**44.** A
11. A	**28.** A	**45.** A
12. B	**29.** A	**46.** A
13. C	**30.** B	**47.** C
14. A	**31.** A	**48.** B
15. D	**32.** C	**49.** C
16. B	**33.** D	**50.** A
17. C	**34.** B	**51.** B

52. B	69. D	86. C
53. C	70. D	87. B
54. B	71. B	88. C
55. A	72. C	89. D
56. A	73. A	90. B
57. D	74. D	91. A
58. B	75. A	92. A
59. A	76. B	93. D
60. C	77. D	94. A
61. B	78. A	95. C
62. B	79. A	96. D
63. B	80. A	97. A
64. A	81. B	98. B
65. B	82. B	99. C
66. A	83. B	100. A
67. D	84. A	
68. C	85. A	

Question 1

Answer A is correct. Using a statistical sample to inventory the tape library is an example of a substantive test.

Question 2

Answer B is correct. If proper identification and authentication are not performed during access control, no accountability can exist for any action performed.

Question 3

Answer C is correct. In planning an audit, the *most* critical step is identifying the areas of high risk.

Question 4

Answer C is correct. When evaluating the collective effect of preventive, detective, or corrective controls within a process, an IS auditor should be aware of the point at which controls are exercised as data flows through the system.

Question 5

Answer D is correct. When implementing continuous-monitoring systems, an IS auditor's first step is to identify high-risk areas within the organization.

Question 6

Answer D is correct. Inherent risk is associated with authorized program exits (trap doors).

Question 7

Answer B is correct. Generalized audit software can be used to search for address field duplications.

Question 8

Answer A is correct. Lack of reporting of a successful attack on the network is a great concern to an IS auditor.

Question 9

Answer B is correct. An integrated test facility is considered a useful audit tool because it compares processing output with independently calculated data.

Question 10

Answer A is correct. It is true that an advantage of a continuous audit approach is that it can improve system security when used in time-sharing environments that process a large number of transactions.

Question 11

Answer A is correct. An IS auditor's primary responsibility is to advise senior management of the risk involved in not implementing proper segregation of duties, such as having the security administrator perform an operations function.

Question 12

Answer B is correct. Business unit management is responsible for implementing cost-effective controls in an automated system.

Question 13

Answer C is correct. The primary reason an IS auditor reviews an organization chart is to better understand the responsibilities and authority of individuals.

Question 14

Answer A is correct. Ensuring that security and control policies support business and IT objectives is a primary objective of an IT security policies audit.

Question 15

Answer D is correct. When auditing third-party service providers, an auditor should be concerned with ownership of programs and files, a statement of due care and confidentiality, and the capability for continued service of the service provider in the event of a disaster.

Question 16

Answer B is correct. When performing an IS strategy audit, an IS auditor should review both short-term (one-year) and long-term (three- to five-year) IS strategies, interview appropriate corporate management personnel, and ensure that the external environment has been considered.

Question 17

Answer C is correct. IS assessment methods allow IS management to determine whether the activities of the organization differ from the planned or expected levels.

Question 18

Answer A is correct. Reviewing an audit client's business plan should be performed before reviewing an organization's IT strategic plan.

Question 19

Answer A is correct. Allowing application programmers to directly patch or change code in production programs increases risk of fraud.

Question 20

Answer B is correct. Security administrators are usually responsible for network security operations.

Question 21

Answer A is correct. Proper segregation of duties does not prohibit a quality-control administrator from also being responsible for change control and problem management.

Question 22

Answer A is correct. Layering perimeter network protection by configuring the firewall as a screened host in a screened subnet behind the bastion host provides a higher level of protection from external attack than all other answers.

Question 23

Answer B is correct. The directory system of a database-management system describes the location of data and the access method.

Question 24

Answer D is correct. Improper file access becomes a greater risk when implementing a database system.

Question 25

Answer B is correct. To properly protect against unauthorized disclosure of sensitive data, hard disks should be demagnetized before disposal or release.

Question 26

Answer C is correct. When reviewing print systems spooling, an IS auditor is most concerned with the potential for unauthorized printing of report copies.

Question 27

Answer C is correct. Functioning as a protocol-conversion gateway for wireless TLS to Internet SSL, the WAP gateway is a component warranting critical concern and review for the IS auditor when auditing and testing controls that enforce message confidentiality.

Question 28

Answer A is correct. Proper segregation of duties prevents a computer operator (user) from performing security administration duties.

Question 29

Answer A is correct. Modems (modulation/demodulation) convert analog transmissions to digital, and digital transmissions to analog, and are required for analog transmissions to enter a digital network.

Question 30

Answer B is correct. Neural networks are effective in detecting fraud because they have the capability to consider a large number of variables when trying to resolve a problem.

Question 31

Answer A is correct. Diverse routing supports data transmission through split cable facilities, or duplicate cable facilities.

Question 32

Answer C is correct. An application-layer gateway, or proxy firewall, and stateful-inspection firewalls provide the greatest degree of protection and control because both firewall technologies inspect all seven OSI layers of network traffic.

Question 33

Answer D is correct. Inefficient and superfluous use of network devices such as hubs can degrade network performance.

Question 34

Answer B is correct. Data mirroring and parallel processing are both used to provide near-immediate recoverability for time-sensitive systems and transaction processing.

Question 35

Answer A is correct. Creating user accounts that automatically expire by a predetermined date is an effective control for granting temporary access to vendors and external support personnel.

Question 36

Answer C is correct. Outbound traffic filtering can help prevent an organization's systems from participating in a distributed denial-of-service (DDoS) attack.

Question 37

Answer C is correct. Improperly configured routers and router access lists are a common vulnerability for denial-of-service attacks.

Question 38

Answer D is correct. Trojan horse programs are a common form of Internet attack.

Question 39

Answer A is correct. Network performance-monitoring tools are used to measure and ensure proper network capacity management and availability of services.

Question 40

Answer B is correct. Intrusion-detection systems (IDS) are used to gather evidence of network attacks.

Question 41

Answer A is correct. Traffic analysis is a passive attack method used by intruders to determine potential network vulnerabilities. All others are active attacks.

Question 42

Answer C is correct. Although many methods of fire suppression exist, dry-pipe sprinklers are considered to be the most environmentally friendly.

Question 43

Answer C is correct. A callback system is a remote-access control whereby the user initially connects to the network systems via dial-up access, only to have the initial connection terminated by the server, which then subsequently dials the user back at a predetermined number stored in the server's configuration database.

Question 44

Answer A is correct. A dry-pipe sprinkler system suppresses fire via water that is released from a main valve to be delivered via a system of dry pipes installed throughout the facilities.

Question 45

Answer A is correct. Digital signatures require the sender to "sign" the data by encrypting the data with the sender's private key, to then be decrypted by the recipient using the sender's public key.

Question 46

Answer A is correct. Although biometrics provides only single-factor authentication, many consider it to be an excellent method for user authentication.

Question 47

Answer C is correct. A website certificate is used to provide authentication of the website and can also be used to successfully authenticate keys used for data encryption.

Question 48

Answer B is correct. The strength of a secret key within a symmetric key cryptosystem is determined by a combination of key length, initial input vectors, and the complexity of the data-encryption algorithm that uses the key.

Question 49

Answer D is correct. Authentication is used to validate a subject's identity.

Question 50

Answer A is correct. Database integrity is most often ensured through table link verification and reference checks.

Question 51

Answer B is correct. IS auditors should review access-control lists (ACL) to determine user permissions that have been granted for a particular resource.

Question 52

Answer B is correct. IS auditors should always check to ensure that password files are encrypted.

Question 53

Answer C is correct. User applications often encrypt and encapsulate data using protocols within the OSI session layer or farther down in the transport layer.

Question 54

Answer B is correct. Systems administrators should always assess the impact of patches before installation.

Question 55

Answer A is correct. Adopting and communicating a comprehensive antivirus policy is the most fundamental step in preventing virus attacks. All other antivirus prevention efforts rely upon decisions established and communicated via policy.

Question 56

Answer A is correct. A major IS audit concern is users' ability to directly modify the database.

Question 57

Answer D is correct. Intrusion-detection systems (IDS) are used to identify intrusion attempts on a network.

Question 58

Answer B is correct. Instead of simply reviewing the effectiveness and utilization of assets, an IS auditor is more concerned with adequate access control, appropriate access policies, and effectiveness of safeguards and procedures.

Question 59

Answer A is correct. If a programmer has update access to a live system, IS auditors are more concerned with the programmer's ability to initiate or modify transactions and the ability to access production than with the pro-grammer's ability to authorize transactions.

Question 60

Answer C is correct. Redundancy is the best answer because it provides both integrity and availability. Organizations should use off-site storage facilities to maintain redundancy of current and critical information within backup files.

Question 61

Answer B is correct. The primary purpose of business continuity planning and disaster-recovery planning is to mitigate, or reduce, the risk and impact of a business interruption or disaster. Total elimination of risk is impossible.

Question 62

Answer B is correct. If a database is restored from information backed up before the last system image, the system should be restarted before the last transaction because the final transaction must be reprocessed.

Question 63

Answer B is correct. An off-site processing facility should *not* be easily identifiable externally because easy identification would create an additional vulnerability for sabotage.

Question 64

Answer A is correct. Although the primary business objective of BCP and DRP is to mitigate the risk and impact of a business interruption, the dominating objective remains the protection of human life.

Question 65

Answer B is correct. Minimizing single points of failure or vulnerabilities of a common disaster is mitigated by geographically dispersing resources.

Question 66

Answer A is correct. Mitigating the risk and impact of a disaster or business interruption usually takes priority over transferring risk to a third party such as an insurer.

Question 67

Answer D is correct. Off-site data storage should be kept synchronized when preparing for the recovery of time-sensitive data such as that resulting from transaction processing.

Question 68

Answer C is correct. Shadow file processing can be implemented as a recovery mechanism for extremely time-sensitive transaction processing.

Question 69

Answer D is correct. Off-site data backup and storage should be geographically separated, to mitigate the risk of a widespread physical disaster such as a hurricane or an earthquake.

Question 70

Answer D is correct. A clause for requiring source code escrow in an application vendor agreement is important to ensure that the source code remains available even if the application vendor goes out of business.

Question 71

Answer B is correct. Decision trees use questionnaires to lead the user through a series of choices to reach a conclusion.

Question 72

Answer C is correct. Source code escrow protects an application purchaser's ability to fix or change an application in case the application vendor goes out of business.

Question 73

Answer A is correct. The project sponsor is ultimately responsible for providing requirement specifications to the software-development team.

Question 74

Answer D is correct. Regression testing should use data from previous tests to obtain accurate conclusions regarding the effects of changes or corrections to a program, and ensuring that those changes and corrections have not introduced new errors.

Question 75

Answer A is correct. An IS auditor should carefully review the functional requirements in a systems-development project to ensure that the project is designed to meet business objectives.

Question 76

Answer B is correct. Procedures to prevent scope creep are baselined in the design phase of the systems-development life cycle (SDLC) model.

Question 77

Answer D is correct. Application controls should be considered as early as possible in the system-development process, even in the development of the project's functional specifications.

Question 78

Answer A is correct. Rapid application development (RAD) is used to develop strategically important systems faster, reduce development costs, and still maintain high quality.

Question 79

Answer A is correct. Test and development environments should be separated, to control the stability of the test environment.

Question 80

Answer A is correct. Programmers should perform unit, module, and full regression testing following any changes to an application or system.

Question 81

Answer B is correct. Rapid application development (RAD) uses a prototype that can be updated continually to meet changing user or business requirements.

Question 82

Answer B is correct. Inadequate user participation during system requirements definition is the most common reason for information systems to fail to meet the needs of users.

Question 83

Answer B is correct. The project steering committee is responsible for the overall direction, costs, and timetables for systems-development projects.

Question 84

Answer A is correct. Plans for testing for user acceptance are usually prepared in the requirements definition phase of the systems-development project.

Question 85

Answer A is correct. Above almost all other concerns, failing to perform user acceptance testing often results in the greatest negative impact on the implementation of new application software.

Question 86

Answer C is correct. Input/output controls should be implemented for both the sending and receiving applications in an integrated systems environment

Question 87

Answer B is correct. Authentication techniques for sending and receiving data between EDI systems are crucial to prevent unauthorized transactions.

Question 88

Answer C is correct. After identifying potential security vulnerabilities, the IS auditor's next step is to perform a business impact analysis of the threats that would exploit the vulnerabilities.

Question 89

Answer D is correct. Transaction authorization is the primary security concern for EDI environments.

Question 90

Answer B is correct. Threats exploit vulnerabilities to cause loss or damage to the organization and its assets.

Question 91

Answer A is correct. Business process re-engineering often results in increased automation, which results in a greater number of people using technology.

Question 92

Answer A is correct. Whenever business processes have been re-engineered, the IS auditor should attempt to identify and quantify the impact of any controls that might have been removed, or controls that might not work as effectively after business process changes.

Question 93

Answer D is correct. An application-level edit check to verify availability of funds should be completed at the electronic funds transfer (EFT) interface before an EFT is initiated.

Question 94

Answer A is correct. Control totals should be implemented as early as data preparation to support data integrity at the earliest point possible.

Question 95

Answer C is correct. Hash totals are used as a control to detect loss, corruption, or duplication of data.

Question 96

Answer D is correct. Data edits are implemented before processing and are considered preventive integrity controls.

Question 97

Answer A is correct. In small office environments, it is not always possible to maintain proper segregation of duties for programmers. If a programmer has access to production data or applications, compensatory controls such as the review of transaction results to approved input might be necessary.

Question 98

Answer B is correct. Processing controls ensure that data is accurate and complete, and is processed only through authorized routines.

Question 99

Answer C is correct. A reasonableness check is a data validation edit control that matches input data to an occurrence rate.

Question 100

Answer A is correct. Database snapshots can provide an excellent audit trail for an IS auditor.

CD Contents and Installation Instructions

The CD features an innovative practice test engine powered by Certified Tech Trainers, giving you yet another effective tool to assess your readiness for the exam. The CD also includes a helpful "Need to Know More?" appendix that breaks down by chapter extra resources to use if some of the topics in this book are still unclear to you.

Multiple Test Modes

Certified Tech Trainers practice tests are available in Custom Exam mode and a comprehensive All-Module mode. For all exams, you can choose to grade each question as you take it, or you can choose to grade the exam at the end.

Wrong Answer Feedback

If you answer a question wrong, the exam engine can provide feedback on which answer is correct and often provides more explanation. Additionally, the feedback provides you with a link to view an audiovisual presentation specific to the question.

When you complete an exam, your results are automatically recorded to the history files. You can use this history to track your learning progress or to even retake an exam.

Retake a Previous Exam from Your Exam History

You can choose to retake an exam directly from the Exam Center administration page, or you can choose to retake an exam displayed on your Exam History screen. If you choose to retake an exam displayed on your Exam History screen, you automatically are forwarded to the Exam Center administration screen, and the exam you selected from the history is preselected in Custom Exam mode for you to begin.

Configure Your Own Custom Exam

You can choose to select modules to be included from the Exam Options dialog box. Don't forget to indicate how many questions you want for your custom exam. The exam engine automatically proportionately and randomly draws questions from your selections to create your custom exam.

Tests administered in Custom Exam mode enable you to choose predefined groups of questions, create your own test, or retake a previous exam. You request the correct answer(s) and explanation for each question during the test. These tests are not timed. You can modify the testing environment *during* the test by clicking the Options button.

Start Your Exam from a Predefined Set of Questions

The default total exam pool is 200 questions. You can choose to take a predefined selection of exam questions from the total pool from Exam Question Groups Section 1 through Section 5. Each predefined section is automatically created as a unique comprehensive exam that includes questions from all course topic areas. Each predefined section contains approximately 20% (40 questions) of the entire question pool.

Custom Exam Mode

Custom mode enables you to specify your preferred testing environment. Use this mode to specify the objectives you want to include in your test, the timer length, and other test properties. You can also modify the testing environment *during* the test by clicking the Options button.

Question Types

The practice question types simulate the real exam experience and provide a unique and novel learning opportunity through mentored audiovisual question explanations by author Allen Keele.

Random Questions and Order of Answers

This feature helps you learn the material without memorizing questions and answers. Each time you take a practice test, the questions and answers appear in a different randomized order.

Detailed Explanations of Correct and Incorrect Answers

You'll receive automatic feedback on all correct and incorrect answers. The detailed answer explanations are a superb learning tool in their own right. Additionally, Certified Tech Trainers tests provide special question-specific audiovisual feedback to give you the context and special instructor-led mentoring you need to sharpen your test-taking skills.

Attention to Exam Objectives

Certified Tech Trainers practice tests are designed to appropriately balance the questions over each technical area covered by a specific exam.

Installing the CD

The minimum system requirements for the CD-ROM are listed here:

➤ Free disk space: 230MB is typical for the program installation.

➤ Microsoft Internet Explorer (IE) 6.*x* or later. If you do not have Internet Explorer 6.*x* or later, you can choose to upgrade your Internet Explorer online directly with Microsoft at http://windowsupdate.microsoft.com/.

➤ Microsoft Media Player. If you do not have Microsoft Media Player, you can choose to upgrade your Internet Explorer online directly with Microsoft at windowsupdate.microsoft.com/ or www.microsoft.com/ windows/windowsmedia/download/default.asp.

➤ Functioning sound card and speakers (internal or external)

➤ Audio volume, controlled through your computer's normal audio controls. Advanced audio controls sometimes provide separate controls for different audio input types.

➤ SVGA Video with 256 colors recommended.

NOTE

If you need technical support, contact Certified Tech Trainers by email at cisa.support@CertifiedTechTrainers.com. Additionally, you'll find frequently asked questions (FAQs) at www.CertifiedTechTrainers.com.

To install the CD-ROM, follow these instructions:

1. Close all applications before beginning this installation.

2. Insert the CD into your CD-ROM drive. A menu should start automatically. Select Install Program. If Setup starts automatically, go to step 6. If Setup does not start automatically, continue with step 3.

3. From the Start menu, select Run.

4. Click Browse to locate the Certified Tech Trainers CD. In the Browse dialog box, from the Look In drop-down list, select the CD-ROM drive.

5. In the Browse dialog box, double-click Setup.exe. In the Run dialog box, click OK to begin the installation.

6. On the Installation Welcome Screen, click Next.

7. To agree to the Software License Agreement, click Yes.

8. On the Choose Destination Location screen, click Next to install the software to default locations.

9. On the Setup Type screen, select Individual Typical Setup. Click Next to continue.

10. When the installation is complete, you might be asked whether you want to restart your computer. If so, verify that the option Yes, I Want to Restart My Computer Now is selected. If you select No, I Will

Restart My Computer Later, you will not be able to use the program until you restart your computer.

11. Click Finish.

12. After you restart your computer, choose Start, Programs, Certified Tech Trainers/CISA Exam Cram 2.

Technical Support

If you encounter problems with the Certified Tech Trainers test engine on the CD-ROM, you can contact Certified Tech Trainers by email at cisa.support@CertifiedTechTrainers.com. Technical support hours are from 8:30 a.m. to 5:00 p.m. EST Monday through Friday. Additionally, you'll find frequently asked questions (FAQs) at www.CertifiedTechTrainers.com.

If you would like to learn about additional Certified Tech Trainers products, you can visit the Certified Tech Trainers website at www.certifiedtechtrainers.com.

CISA Glossary

access-control matrix
A single table used to cross-reference access rights that have been assigned to subjects (subject capabilities) with access rights that are assigned per objects (access control list).

access-control model
A framework that dictates how subjects can access objects. Three access-control modes can be defined: discretionary, mandatory, and nondiscretionary.

access controls
Controls that ensure confidentiality, integrity, and availability of information systems and their associated data by limiting access to computer systems.

access path
The logical route an end user or system takes to get to the information resource.

accreditation
The authorization and approval granted to an information system to process in an operational environment within a predefined control environment.

Address Resolution Protocol (ARP)
TCP/IP network-layer protocol used to convert an IP address (logical address) into a physical address (DLC or MAC address).

administrative audit
A type of audit that assesses issues related to the efficiency of operational productivity.

administrative controls
Procedures that are used to ensure compliance with management policy.

alert thresholds

Processes within systems to detect and act upon failed login events by automatically disabling the login either for a specific period of time or permanently.

algorithm

A mathematical-based function that performs encryption and decryption.

antivirus software

Programs that detect, prevent, and sometimes remove virus files located within a computing system.

application

A program or set of programs specifically designed to perform a function or series of functions.

application programming

The act of developing, updating, and maintaining programs.

assets

Resources, processes, products, or computer infrastructures that an organization has determined must be protected.

asymmetric encryption

Also known as public-key cryptography, in which each party has respective key pairs that are mathematically related and known as public and private keys.

atomicity

The process by which data integrity is ensured through the completion of an entire transaction or not at all.

attenuation

The weakening or degradation of communication signals during transmission.

attestation

An assurance by an auditor on something for which the client is responsible.

attribute sampling

The technique used for the selection or a sample containing certain attributes from a population for audit testing.

audit methodology

A set of documented audit procedures that ensures that the auditor achieves the planned audit objectives.

audit objective

Objective that outlines the specific goals associated with an audit.

audit risk

The risk that the information of financial reports might contain material errors or that the IS auditor might not detect an error that has occurred.

audit trail

A trail of evidence that enables one to trace a series of events or information back to the source.

auditor's report

A report from an independent auditor that generally contains a description of the relevant policies and procedures, control objectives, and results of the auditor's tests, and may result in an opinion on operating effectiveness, efficiency, and security of the organization.

authentication

The verification of a user's identification.

authorization

The determination of whether a subject is allowed to have access to a particular resource. Generally, an authenticated user is compared against an access list to determine what level of access is authorized.

availability

The reliable and timely access to information by authorized users, programs, or processes.

backup (system)

A collection of data stored on (usually removable) nonvolatile storage media for purposes of recovery, in case the original copy of data is lost or becomes inaccessible.

balanced scorecard

A management tool that clarifies an organization's goals, and defines actions and the measurement of those actions to meet goals.

bastion host

A basic network architecture in which all internal and external communications must pass through the perimeter bastion host, which is exposed to the external network.

benchmarking

The continuous, systematic process of evaluating the products, services, and work processes of organizations recognized as representing best practices for the purpose of organizational improvement.

biometrics

A means of access control in which an individual's identity is authenticated by a unique personal attribute, such as a fingerprint, retina scan, or hand geometry.

blackbox testing

Testing that examines an aspect of the system with regard to the internal logical structure of the software.

bridge

A networking component that works at the data link layer (Layer 2) of the OSI model and connects two separate networks to form a logical network. Bridges examine the media access control (MAC) header of a data packet to determine where to forward the packet.

broadcast

A network communication process in which a sending station sends a single packet to all stations on the network.

brute-force attack

A type of system attack in which an intruder uses automated tools and electronic dictionaries to try to guess user and system passwords in an attempt to gain unauthorized access to the system.

bus topology

Topology primarily used in smaller networks in which all devices are connected to a single communication line and all transmissions are received by all devices.

business continuity plan (BCP)

The identification of personnel, equipment, and detailed recovery procedures to ensure that the impact of an event to the business function is minimized.

business impact analysis (BIA)

A process used to identify an attempt to quantify the loss (over time) that can impact an asset from a given threat.

business process re-engineering (BPR)

Provides an accelerated means of business process improvement through identifying, baselining, and prioritizing areas for improvement and implementing improvements.

business risk

The risk that a business will not achieve its stated business goals or objectives.

callback system

Process used during remote access in which an authorized user calls a remote server through a dial-up line, and the server disconnects and dials back to the user machine, based on the user ID and password, using a telephone number from its database.

capability maturity model (CMM)

Model that provides a framework for improving software life-cycle processes and specific metrics to improve the software process. The CMM was developed by Carnegie Melon's Software Engineering Institute.

capacity plan

The continued monitoring of the network and associated hardware, to ensure that the expansion or reduction of resources takes place in parallel with the overall organizational growth or reduction.

carrier sense multiple access/ collision avoidance (CSMA/CA)

Method employed on Ethernet networks in which a sending station lets all the stations on the network know that it intends to transmit data to avoid collisions.

carrier sense multiple access/ collision detection (CSMA/CD)

Method employed on an Ethernet network in which devices on the network can detect collisions and retransmit if they occur.

central processing unit (CPU)

The electrical/electronic components that control or direct all operations in the computer system.

centralized access control

Utilizes a single entity or system that is responsible for granting access to all users.

Certificate Authority (CA)

Maintains, issues, and revokes digital certificates that authenticate an individual's identity.

certificate revocation list (CRL)

A list maintained by a Certificate Authority that lists all digital certificates that have been revoked.

certification

The technical evaluation that establishes the extent to which a computer system, application, or network design and implementation meets a prespecified set of security requirements in a certain operating environment.

change control

Ensures that changes are documented, approved, and implemented with minimal disruption to the production environment and maximum benefits to the organization.

change-control board (CCB)

A governance structure that ensures that all affected parties and senior management are aware of both major and minor changes within the IT infrastructure.

change-control process (CCP)

Implemented in organizations as a way to provide a formal review and change-management process for systems and associated documentation.

change request (CR)

Contains information associated with a change to the information system (that is, applications,

network devices, documentation, policies, and so on). The information contained in the CR is used to evaluate the change's impacts in the current environment.

client/server

A group of networked computers in which the server responds to requests from clients that are running independently on the network.

CO^2

A type of fire-suppression system in which CO_2, a chemical formula of carbon dioxide, is released, thereby reducing the oxygen content of the protected area below the point that it can support combustion.

cognitive password

Password that uses de facto or opinion-based information to verify an individual's identity. Cognitive passwords are commonly used today as security questions associated with an account, in case the user has forgotten the password.

cold site

A basic recovery site, in that it has the required space for equipment and environmental controls (air conditioning, heating, power, and so on), but does not contain any equipment of connectivity.

collision

The result when two or more stations on a network transmit at the same time.

collision domain

A group of network devices connected to the same physical medium in such a way that if two devices access the media at the same time, a collision of the transmissions can occur.

common vulnerability and exposure (CVE)

A public database of discovered vulnerabilities according to naming and documentation standards.

compensating control

A control that is used to reduce the risk or weakness within an existing control.

compliance audit

Involves an integrated series of activities focused on investigating and confirming whether products or services comply with internal policy or external guidelines or laws.

compliance testing

The evaluation of controls to ensure that they are being applied in a manner that complies with the internal or external guidelines.

concurrency controls

Controls within a database to prevent integrity problems when two processes attempt to update the same data at the same time.

confidentiality

The assurance that the information will not be disclosed to unauthorized individuals, programs, or processes.

confidentiality agreement

An agreement between employee and employer or, in some cases, partners that stipulates that the parties agree not to divulge confidential information that they might come in contact with during the course of the agreement.

continuity of operations

Continued service in the event of a disaster.

continuity risk

The risk associated with systems availability and its capability to utilize backups to recover.

contract

An agreement between or among two or more persons or entities (business, organizations, or government agencies) to do, or to abstain from doing, something in return for an exchange of consideration.

Control Objectives for Information and Related Technology (COBIT)

An audit framework that provides good practices for the management of IT governance internal controls and processes.

control risk

The risk that a material error exists that would not be prevented or detected on a timely basis by the system of internal controls.

control self-assessment (CSA)

A formal, documented, collaborative process in which management or work teams are directly involved in judging and monitoring the effectiveness of controls.

corrective controls

Controls designed to minimize the impact of a threat by identifying the cause of a problem and modifying the system to correct it.

cryptoanalysis

The science of studying and breaking the secrecy of encryption algorithms and their necessary pieces.

cryptography

The art and science of hiding the meaning of communication from unintended recipients by encrypting plain text into cipher text.

cryptosystem

A system that uses mathematical functions (algorithms) and a key to encrypt and decrypt messages.

customer relationship management (CRM)

An information system that focuses on managing detailed customer information, which can include previous transactions and customer needs and requirements, allowing organizations to match customer needs to products and services.

data dictionary

A document that identifies the data elements (fields), their characteristics, and their use.

Data Encryption Standard (DES)

An encryption cipher (method of encrypting information) that uses a 56-bit key length.

data ownership

The allocation of responsibility over data elements to ensure that they are kept confidential, complete, and accurate.

database administrator (DBA)

The individual responsible for defining data structures and for maintaining those structures in the organization's database systems.

database-management system (DBMS)

The primary functions of the DBMS are to reduce data redundancy, decrease access time, and provide security over sensitive data (records, fields, and transactions).

decentralized access control

In decentralized or distributed administration, user and system access is given by individuals who are closer to the resources.

defense-in-depth strategies

A defense methodology that is based on layered sets of compensating controls to reduce the risk of threats associated with assets.

demilitarized zone (DMZ)

Defines a zone that has an "intermediate" level of security between a secure zone (normally the internal network) and an insecure zone (typically the Internet).

denial-of-service attack

Any method an intruder uses to hinder or prevent the delivery of information services to authorized users.

detection risk

Risk that results when an IS auditor uses an inadequate test procedure and concludes that material errors do not exist, when, in fact, they do.

detective controls

Controls that are designed to detect and report the occurrence of an error, an omission, or malicious acts.

dictionary attack

A common form of password attack in which an intruder uses a dictionary of common words and a computer program to guess passwords.

differential backup

A procedure that backs up the files that have been changed or added since the last full backup.

digital signature

A cryptographic method that ensures data integrity, authentication of the message, and nonrepudiation.

disaster-recovery planning (DRP)

The plan followed by IS to recover an IT processing facility, or by business units to recover an operational facility.

discovery agreement

An agreement between two parties that identifies the ownership of discoveries during the period of time that the two parties work together. A discovery agreement can be between partner companies or between employer and employee.

discretionary

An access-control model in which access to data objects is granted to the subject at the data owner's discretion.

domain name service (DNS)

TCP/IP protocol that resolves hostnames to IP addresses and IP addresses to hostnames through the use of domain name servers. Domain name servers have hierarchal distributed database systems that are queried for resolution.

duplicate processing facilities

Types of facilities similar to hot site facilities, with the exception that they are completely dedicated, self-developed recovery facilities.

electromagnetic interference (EMI)

The introduction of electromagnetic waves that interfere with electronic signals.

electronic data interchange (EDI)

The electronic exchange of information, reducing paper, errors, and delays to promote a more efficient and effective data-exchange process.

electronic funds transfer (EFT)

An electronic payment process between buyers and sellers that reduces paper transactions and manual intervention.

electronic vaulting

Enables organizations to back up data directly from their systems to an electronic storage facility using computer programs (agents) and public networks (such as the Internet).

encryption

The process of transforming data into a form that is unreadable by anyone without a secret decryption key. Encryption is used to protect data while in transit over networks, protect data stored on systems, deter and detect accidental or intentional alterations of data, and verify the authenticity of a transaction or document.

environmental security controls

Controls that are designed to mitigate the risk associated with naturally occurring events such as storms, earthquakes, hurricanes, tornadoes, and floods.

evidence

Information that is sufficient, reliable, relevant, and useful to achieve the audit objectives relating to the audit area.

extranets

A web-based system that is used to facilitate the exchange of information between an organization and external partners.

false acceptance rate (FAR) Type II error

A metric used in a biometric system that measures the number of unauthorized individuals given access who should be rejected.

false positive

The generation of an alert by an event that does not represent a true threat.

false rejection rate (FRR) Type I error

A metric used in a biometric system that measures the number of authorized individuals who should be given access but are rejected.

feasibility study

A study that is implemented to identify and quantify the cost savings of a new system and estimate the payback schedule for costs incurred in implementing the system.

File Transfer Protocol (FTP)

A protocol that enables users and systems to transfer files from one computer to another on the Internet.

financial audit

An audit that is used to assess the correctness or accuracy of the organization's financial statements.

firewall

A hardware or software device that restricts access between network segments by implementing rules that identify logical addresses, services, or ports and their level of access.

firmware

A type of "software" that is contained on a chip within the component of the computer hardware (motherboard, video card, modem, and so on).

full backup

A backup of all data files by copying them to a tape or other storage medium.

full duplex

A method of communication in which both the sending and receiving stations can communicate simultaneously.

function point analysis (FPA)

Used to provide an estimate of the size of an information system based on the number and complexity of a system's inputs, outputs, and files (examples of function points), to calculate the resources required to develop the information system.

function/validation testing

Tests the functionality of the system against the detailed requirements.

halon

Used in a type of fire-suppression system in which pressurized halon gas is released. The halon gas interferes with the chemical reaction of a fire. Halon is banned and has been replaced by FM-200, NAF SIII, and NAF PIII.

honey pot

A computer program that is employed to entice and trap intruders. Honey pots are computer systems that are expressly set up to attract and trap individuals who attempt to penetrate other individuals' computer systems.

hot sites

A facility that is a mirror image of the organization's critical processing applications. It can be ready for use immediately or within a short period of time, and will contain the equipment, network, operating systems, and applications that are compatible with the primary facility that is being backed up.

hub

Operates at the physical layer (Layer 1) of the OSI model and can serve as the center of a star topology. A hub can be considered a concentrator because hubs concentrate all network communications for the devices attached to them.

impact

The result of a threat exercising a vulnerability resulting in the compromise of confidentiality, integrity, or availability of an information system.

incremental backup

A procedure that backs up only the files that have been added or changed since the last backup (whether full or differential).

information systems audit

Audit process that evaluates evidence to determine whether information systems and related resources adequately safeguard assets, maintain data and system integrity, provide relevant and reliable information, achieve organizational goals effectively, consume resources efficiently, and have in effect internal controls that provide reasonable assurance that business, operation, and control objectives will be met.

Information Systems Auditing Association (ISACA)

A membership organization that provides the auditing community with guidance in the form of auditing guidelines, standards, and polices specific to information systems (IS) auditing.

inherent risk

The possibility that a material error could occur, assuming that there are no related internal controls to prevent or detect the error.

input/output (I/O) components

Components used to pass instructions or information to the computer and to generate output from the computer. These types of devices include the keyboard, the mouse (input), and monitors/terminal displays.

integrated audit

Audit that combines the testing of controls as well as substantive testing for the completeness, validity, and integrity of the information.

integrity

The assurance of accuracy and reliability of data, and the prevention of unauthorized data modification (intentional or unintentional).

integrity checker

A program that is designed to detect changes to systems,

applications, and data. Integrity checkers compute a binary number for each selected program, called a cyclical redundancy check (CRC). When initially installed, an integrity checker scans the system, places these results in a database file, and then compares subsequent checks against the database to determine whether the files have changed.

interface/integration testing

Tests used for testing modules that pass data between them and are used to validate the interchange of data and the connection among multiple system components.

internal accounting controls

Controls designed to safeguard the assets and reliability of financial data and records.

internal control objectives

Objectives that define the desired purpose or outcome associated with the implementation of the internal controls.

internal controls

The combination of organizational structure, policies and procedures, and best practices that are implemented to reduce risk and ensure that business goals are achieved.

Internet

A large, interconnected network comprised of a series of smaller commercial, academic, and government networks that use the TCP/IP protocol.

Internet Protocol (IP)

A protocol in the TCP/IP suite used in communicating data from one computer to another. The IP protocol uses unique addresses (IP number) to identify networks and hosts, to route packets to destination computers.

interoperability

The capability for hardware and software from different vendors to work together efficiently and effectively.

intranet

A network (usually web based) that is accessible by internal users of an organization and that can contain internal calendaring, web email, and information designed specifically for the authorized internal users.

intrusion-detection system (IDS)

Designed to gather evidence of systems or network attacks. An IDS can be network based (detects network attacks) or host based (detects attacks on a host).

intrusion-prevention system (IPS)

A software or hardware device that is capable of detecting both known and unknown attacks, and preventing them from being successful.

IS auditing standards

Standards that define the mandatory requirements for IS auditing and reporting, as well as provide a minimum level of performance for auditors.

ISACA Code of Professional Ethics

Code created to provide guidance in the professional and personal conduct of members of the association (ISACA) and its certification holders.

IT steering committee

The governance structure responsible for reviewing issues such as new and ongoing projects, major equipment acquisitions, and the review and approval of IT budgets.

job description

Provides levels of authority and tasks that a specific individual should perform.

just-in-time (JIT)

Delivery that reduces the overall cycle time associated with manufacture and inventory by creating products and services based on customer demand.

key performance indicators (KPI)

Quantifiable measurements that are created as long-term measurements of an organization's operational activities against its goals.

local area networks (LAN)

Private or nonpublic packet-based switched networks contained within a limited area, providing services within a particular organization or group.

logical access controls

The policies and electronic access controls that are designed to restrict access to resources such as software and data files.

mainframes

Large general-purpose computers that support large user populations simultaneously. A mainframe environment, as opposed to a client/server environment, is generally more controlled with regard to access and authorization to programs; the entire processing function takes place centrally on the mainframe.

mandatory access control (MAC)

All subjects and objects have security labels, and the decision for access is determined by the operating or security system.

material error

An error that should be considered significant to any party concerned with the item in question.

materiality

The importance of an event, observation, or information with regard to its relevance to the audit objectives.

messaging services

User requests (messages) can be prioritized, queued, and processed on remote servers.

middleware

Application interfaces that provide integration between otherwise distinct applications by allowing access to higher- or lower-level services.

minicomputer

Essentially, a smaller mainframe. Minicomputers provide similar capabilities but support a smaller user population and generally have less processing power than a mainframe.

modem (modulator-demodulator)

A communications device that converts data from digital format to analog format for transmission.

multiprocessing

Links more than one processor (CPU) sharing the same memory, to execute programs simultaneously.

multitasking

Allows computing systems to run two or more applications concurrently by allocating a certain amount of processing power to each application.

multithreading

Enables operating systems to run several processes in rapid sequence within a single program, or to execute (run) different parts, or threads, of a program simultaneously.

nondisclosure agreement

An agreement between two parties that restricts the information that one or both of the parties may disclose about one another.

nonrepudiation

Provides proof of the origin of data and protects the sender against a false denial by the recipient that the data has been received, or to protect the recipient against false denial by the sender that the data has been sent.

normalization

The structuring of data within a database that minimizes redundancy.

off-site storage

A storage facility that is located away from the organization's processing facility, used for off-site tape storage.

Open Systems Interconnect (OSI) model

Developed in the early 1980s as a proof-of-concept model that all vendors could use to ensure that their products could communicate and interact. The OSI model contains seven layers, each with specific functions. Each layer has its own responsibilities with regard to tasks, processes, and services.

operating system

A program that provides an interface for the user, processor, and applications software.

operational audit

Evaluates the internal control structure in a given process or area.

operational controls

Controls used in day-to-day operations to ensure that the operation is meeting business objectives.

outsourcing

A contractual arrangement between the organization and a third party for various services such as development, processing, or hosting.

parallel testing

A process of testing applications in which test data is fed into both the new and old systems, and the results are compared.

password

A character string (usually encrypted) that is used as part of a user or systems credentials to authenticate to the computer system.

penetration test

The application of knowledge, skill, and tools to circumvent the security controls associated with an asset.

personal digital assistants (PDAs)

Handheld portable devices that can be used for an individual organization, including the maintenance of tasks, contact lists, calendars, and expense managers.

physical security controls

Controls that limit access to facilities, computers, and telecommunications equipment and other assets of the organization's infrastructure.

piggybacking

A method used by unauthorized users to gain access to a physical location by closely following an authorized user in.

preventive controls

Controls that are designed to prevent problems before they arise, monitor both operations and inputs, and prevent errors, omissions, or malicious acts from occurring.

problem management

The process of recording, monitoring, and documenting incidents to resolve them.

program evaluation review technique (PERT)

A project-management technique for developing an estimate of development project duration. A PERT chart depicts task, duration, and dependency information.

project management

The application of skills, tools, best practices, and knowledge to meet the requirements of a project.

prototyping

A system-development technique that uses a process to rapidly develop and test code through trial and error. In general, prototyping reduces the time required to deploy applications through iterative development and testing.

public-key infrastructure (PKI)

A system that incorporates public-key cryptography, digital certificates, and standards that enable key maintenance. Key maintenance includes user identification, key distribution, and revocation through the use of digital certificates.

quality assurance (QA)

Ensures that the organization is following prescribed quality standards.

quality control (QC)

The application of tests or reviews to verify that information systems are free from defects and meet the expectation of the organization.

reciprocal agreements

Arrangements between two or more organizations with similar equipment and applications. The organizations agree to provide computer time (and sometimes facility space) to one another in the event of an emergency.

Registration Authority (RA)

Performs registration duties to offload some of the work from the CAs. The RA can confirm individual identities, distribute keys, and perform maintenance functions, but it cannot issue certificates.

regression testing

A program-testing methodology in which portions of test scenarios are rerun to ensure that changes or corrections have not introduced new errors to the existing modules. Regression testing should use data from previous tests to obtain accurate conclusions regarding the effects of changes or corrections to a program, and to ensure that those changes and corrections have not introduced new errors to the existing modules.

remote-access services

Services that provide remote-access capabilities from a user location to where a computing device appears; they emulate a direct connection to the device. Examples include Telnet and remote access through a VPN.

remote procedure calls (RPC)

A function call in client/server computing that enables clients to request that a particular function or set of functions be performed on a remote computer.

Remote Terminal Control Protocol (Telnet)
Terminal-emulation protocol that enables users to log in to remote systems and use resources as if they were connected locally.

residual risk
The risk remaining after controls have been implemented to reduce risk.

risk
The possibility of a threat exercising a vulnerability to cause loss or damage to assets.

risk analysis
The process of identifying risk in the organization, quantifying the impact of potential threats, and providing cost/benefit justification for the implementation of controls.

risk assessment
A process that reviews threats and vulnerabilities to determine the degree of risk they have on organizational assets if they occur.

risk-based audit
An audit technique that prioritizes audit engagements through the identification of high-risk areas within the organization.

risk management
The process of assessing risk, taking steps to reduce risk to an acceptable level (mitigation), and maintaining that acceptable level of risk.

risk mitigation
Reducing risk to an acceptable level by implementing controls.

router
A network device that links two or more physically separate network segments and that works at the network layer (Layer 3) of the OSI model. A router is used to direct or route traffic on a network.

rule-based access control (RBAC)
A type of access control that is generally used between networks or applications and that involves a set of rules from which incoming requests can be matched and either accepted or rejected.

run-to-run totals
A report verifying that all transmitted data has been read and processed.

SAS 70 Type I
An audit that describes the use of controls within a service provider's organization.

SAS 70 Type II
A SAS 70 Type II includes an opinion on the items in Type I and whether the controls that were tested were operating effectively to provide reasonable assurance that the control objectives were achieved.

SAS 94
An integrated audit in which the auditor must evaluate controls around a client's information system and the entries that are processed through that system.

Secure Sockets Layer (SSL)

A protocol that provides confidentiality through symmetric encryption such as the Data Encryption Standard (DES). This is an application-/session-layer protocol often used for secure communication between web browsers and servers.

security risk

The risk that unauthorized access to data will adversely affect the integrity, confidentiality, and availability of that data.

segregation of duties

The separation of tasks between individuals to reduce the likelihood of fraudulent or malicious acts.

service-level agreement (SLA)

Outlines a guaranteed level of service for information systems or business processes.

Simple Mail Transfer Protocol (SMTP)

A protocol within the TCP/IP suite that provides standard electronic (email) transfer services.

sniffing

A type of network attack in which an intruder uses automated tools to collect packets on the network. These packets can be reassembled into messages and can include email, names and passwords, and system information.

software business risk

The likelihood that software will not meet the application user's business needs, requirements, or expectations.

storage area networks (SAN)

A special-purpose network in which different types of data storage are associated with servers and users.

strategic plan

Plan outlining the goals and objectives of the organization.

substantive testing

Type of test that is used to substantiate the integrity of actual processing through transaction verification, recalculation, and verification.

supercomputer

Computer that has a large capacity of processing speed and power. Supercomputers generally perform a small number of very specific functions that require extensive processing power (decryption, modeling, and so on).

supply chain management (SCM)

The improvement of an organization's product and service design, purchasing, invoicing and distribution. Supply chain management generally serves the common goals of reducing costs and improving customer service.

system-development life cycle (SDLC)

A framework or methodology that is used in the acquisition, implementation, maintenance, and disposition of information systems. The SDLC uses a structured approach to minimize risk and maximize return on investment, and ensure that the new system meets the application user's business requirements and expectations.

terminal-emulation software (TES)

Software that provides remote-access capabilities with a user interface as if that user were sitting on the console of the device being accessed. As an example, Microsoft Terminal Services connects to the remote device and displays the desktop of the remote device as if the user were sitting at the console.

threat

A potential danger (hazard) to information systems; the hazard is something that increases the likelihood of loss.

topology (physical arrangement)

The connectivity of the network cabling and devices. Network topologies commonly fall into the categories of bus, star, ring, and mesh.

trade secret agreement

Agreement that protects the trade secrets of an organization from disclosure.

traffic analysis

An intruder uses tools capable of monitoring network traffic to determine traffic volume, patterns, and start and end points. This analysis gives intruders a better understanding of the communication points and potential vulnerabilities.

transaction-processing (TP) monitors

Applications or programs that monitor and process database transactions.

Transmission Control Protocol (TCP)

Transport-layer protocol that establishes a reliable, full-duplex data-delivery service that many TCP/IP applications use. TCP is a connection-oriented protocol, which means that it guarantees both the delivery of data and the order of the packets: They will be delivered in the same order as they were sent.

trojan horse

A malicious program that masquerades as another program or that is even embedded within a program. Trojan horse programs or code can delete files, shut down the systems, or send system and network information to an email or Internet address.

two-factor authentication

A type of authentication that requires authentication by two of the following three methods: something the user knows, something the user possesses, or something the user is. A smart card requiring a user's PIN is an example of two-factor authentication.

uninterruptible power supply (UPS)

Can provide enough short-term power to either shut down systems gracefully in the event of a power

failure or keep mission-critical systems operating until power returns.
A UPS contains batteries that continue to charge as the system has
power and provides battery backup
power in case of a failure.

unit testing
A testing technique that is used for
testing individual modules (program logic) that tests the control
structure and design of the module.

User Datagram Protocol (UDP)
Transport-layer protocol (TCP/IP)
that provides connectionless delivery of data on the network. UDP
does not provide error-recovery
services and is primarily used for
broadcasting data on the network.

variable sampling
A sampling technique used to identify the average or total value of a
population based on a sample.

virtual private networking (VPN)
Creates encrypted links over
untrusted networks and enables
remote users to access the organization's network securely using
encrypted packets sent via virtual
connections.

virus
A malicious program that infects
computer systems. The virus can
damage computer systems through
reconfiguration and file deletion. A
virus requires a carrier program,
such as email, for replication and
further propagation.

vulnerability
A weakness in internal controls
that can be exploited by a threat to
gain unauthorized access to information or disrupt systems.

warm site
Used for recovery in the event of
an emergency. A warm site usually
contains a portion of the equipment and applications required for
recovery. In a warm site recovery, it
is assumed that computer equipment and operating software can
be procured quickly.

whitebox testing
Process of testing logical paths
through the software using test
cases that exercise specific sets of
conditions and loops.

wide area network (WAN)
A network that provides connectivity for LANs that are geographically dispersed by providing network
connectivity and services across
large distances.

X.25
A data-communications interface
specification developed to describe
how data passes into and out of
switched packet networks.

Index

How can we make this index more useful? Email us at indexes@quepublishing.com

How can we make this index more useful? Email us at indexes@quepublishing.com

How can we make this index more useful? Email us at indexes@quepublishing.com

SLAs (service-level agreements), 71, 288
SMEs (subject matter experts), 81
smoke detectors, 196
SMTP (Simple Mail Transfer Protocol), 146
social engineering, 168
software. *See* applications systems
Software Capability Maturity Model (CMM), 82-83, 257
Software Development Life Cycle. *See* SDLC
software teams, 246
spamming, 202
spikes (voltage), 195
SSL (Secure Sockets Layer), 191
SSO (single sign-on) systems, 193
standards
  ISACA IS Auditing Standards, 2
  codification, 3-4
  table of, 4-6
  SAS (Statement on Auditing Standards)
  SAS 70, 26
  SAS 94, 26-27
star topology, 141
stateful packet-inspection firewalls, 150
Statement on Auditing Standards. *See* SAS
steering committees, 57-58
steering committees (IT), 13-14
storage, 232
  evaluating, 241-242
  SANs (storage area networks), 235
  tape storage, 233-235
storage area networks (SANs), 235
strategic planning, 14-15, 56-57
strategies, 56. *See also* BCPs (business continuity plans); DRPs (disaster recovery plans); policies
  contract management, 95-96
    confidentiality agreements, 96
    contract audit objectives, 97-98
    discovery agreements, 97
    employee contracts, 96
    noncompete agreements, 97
    trade secret agreements, 96
  IS steering committees, 57-58
  problem- and change management, 80-82
  project management, 74-79
    project life cycle, 75-76
    risk indicators, 76-77
    system upgrade risks, 77-79
  quality management, 82-86
    accreditation, 85
    certification, 85
    ISO 9001, 84
    ISO 9126, 84-85
    QA (quality assurance), 82
    QC (quality control), 82
    Software Capability Maturity Model (CMM), 82-83
  risk-mitigation strategies, 71-73
  security management, 86-93
    CIA triad, 87
    data integrity risks, 90-92
    logical controls, 87-89
    physical controls, 87-88
  strategic planning, 56-57
strong authentication, 175
structure (IS)
  evaluating, 67-70

outsourcing
  evaluating, 70-73
  risk-mitigation strategies, 71-73
  SLAs (service-level agreements), 71
  when to use, 71
  segregation of duties, 69-70
subject matter experts (SMEs), 81
subjects, 171
substantive testing, 29
supercomputers, 110
supplies teams, 247
supply chain management (SCM), 287
surges (voltage), 195
switches, 156
symmetric encryption, 182
symmetric keys, 182
system development life cycle (SDLC), 62, 119
system performance and monitoring processes, 160-161
system testing, 277
system upgrades, 77-79
systems administrators, 108
systems development, 69
systems software, 121
  change control, 126-127
  configuration management, 126-127
  DBMS (database management systems), 123-126
  firmware, 122
  middleware, 123
  operating systems, 122
  risks and controls, 126

T

table look-ups, 294
tape storage, 233-235
task-based access, 172
TCP (Transmission Control Protocol), 146
TCP/IP (Transmission Control Protocol/Internet Protocol), 146-147
technical infrastructure, 107
  exam prep questions, 162-165
  hardware
    change control, 119-121
    configuration management, 119-121
    CPUs (central processing units), 110
    I/O components, 110
    mainframes, 110
    microcomputers, 111
    minicomputers, 111
    multiprocessing, 112
    multitasking, 112
    multithreading, 112
    notebooks/laptops, 111
    PDAs (personal digital assistants), 111
    risks and controls, 112-119
    supercomputers, 110
  IS operational practices, 159-160
  IT organizational structure, 108-110
  networks, 127-129
    bridges, 155
    bus topology, 140
    collisions, 139-140
    data encapsulation, 129-130
    Ethernet, 139-140
    extranets, 156-157

How can we make this index more useful? Email us at indexes@quepublishing.com